MARKET SQUARE HEROES

MARKET SQUARE HEROES

THE AUTHORIZED STORY OF MARILLION

MICK WALL

Foreword by Fish

SIDGWICK & JACKSON
LONDON

This book is very respectfully dedicated to the memory of
Evelyn Wall

First published in Great Britain in November 1987 by
Sidgwick and Jackson Limited

First reprint January 1988
Second reprint May 1988

ISBN 0–283–99426–6

Typeset by Columns of Reading
Printed and bound by
Adlard and Son Limited
Dorking, Surrey, and Letchworth, Herts

for Sidgwick & Jackson Limited
1 Tavistock Chambers
Bloomsbury Way
London WC1A 2SG

CONTENTS

FOREWORD by Fish

The main reason the band and I wanted this book to be written was because there's never really been anything published that truly got to grips with the real story of Marillion. Speaking as the member of the band most used to having a microphone shoved in his face in the dead of night and asked all the sorts of weird questions people like to pose, I have, over the years, read some tremendous articles about us that have appeared in the press in every different part of the world we've ever visited. But none that ever said enough of what needs to be said to make me sit back and think, well, that's good, that's right, I may not like or agree with absolutely all of it, but yeah, that pretty much sums up the story of Marillion . . . so far.

Usually, it's been the story of me glued to the late-hours bar in some hotel, telling tales like an old soldier just back from the frontline . . . Verbal snap-shots composed in the dark and not always meant for daylight reading hours . . . In short, nothing that ever attempted to really tell the full, uninterrupted story of this band. Right from the thorny beginnings and up to where I, and the rest of the band, are now – as I write, a month into the *Clutching At Straws* world tour, on the fast road to Germany.

We wanted to read a version of events that was as accurate as possible to the way we truthfully remember them. And there are five people in Marillion, all with their own perspective on the tide of events that have carried us from the backroom dreams of our early days in Aylesbury, to where we stand today. Each one of us sees things in his own way. So the only reasonable way we could think of to get our stories told, but made into something like one voice, was to find someone willing to sit down and listen to us, one by one, telling it the way each of us thinks it really happened, then write it all down later and see what we had to look at.

The result is this book you now hold in your hands.

We asked Mick Wall to take on the job of writing it not just because he's one of our favourite rock writers, but because he's also one of the few music journalists to have actually penetrated the circle of the band to the extent where the journo-interviewing-muso rap is left far behind and he's actually got to know us all as the people we really are. He started turning up at our gigs on the *Fugazi* tour in 1984, writing frenzied stories about us and helping himself to the drinks-table backstage. We hit it off straight away. And we've never been able to get rid of him since . . .

Over the years, Mick has had his pick of the drinks-tables in all our houses; he's sat in our best chairs, slept on our cleanest floors in the days before we could afford chairs, chatted up our wives and girlfriends when he thought we weren't looking, and then had the gall to sit us all down in front of his home-made tape-recorder every now and then, and ask us: 'Well, boys . . . What's it all about then? Tell me *everything*!'

Most of the interviews that took place for the purposes of this book were taped by Mick during our January/February 1986 UK tour. One by one, whenever any of us had some time to kill, we would troop off to an empty room with him somewhere – the tuning room, the bus, the corner of the bar, the corner of the street, 'anywhere – and Mick would hit the red light on his machine and we would go off at the mouth . . . At times it felt like a mini-version of the Watergate hearings – 'So let me take you back to May 1978 – what were you doing exactly? Oh yeah? Why?'

We talked and he listened until we'd all finally run out of things to say. It was intense sometimes, but mostly it was just a lot of fun.

We left it up to Mick to make what he could of the results: we wanted the story told from all our sides, but we wanted the way he might have seen it in there as well to help fasten an outside perspective onto an otherwise very insular story.

Well, we certainly got that.

Is this the true story of Marillion, though? This is the true story of Marillion as heard through the ears of Mick Wall. It tells no lies. Read it when you feel good and ready.

ACKNOWLEDGEMENTS

The author wishes to express his extra-special thanks to the following: Linda La Ban (personal rabbit); Joe and Dicky B. (vital supplies); Geoff Barton ('ead 'itter of *Kerrang!*), Gale Claydon (my pie in the Sky), and Susan Hill and Jane MacAndrew (Sidgwick & Jackson), for your patience and goodwill beyond the call of Kafka; Anne Lawler, Brian Munns, Keith Goodwin, Patsy Smith and John Tobler (for answering *all* those weird questions); Steve 'Krush Def' Joule and Malcom 'Dudesickle' Dome (for their bitchin', their bullshit, and their love); Ray Palmer (for the trips and the tips); John Arnison, Paul Lewis, Privet Hedge, Andy Fields, and all the Marillion crew that served on the same tours I did, and who let me get away with Murder on the Drinks-Table Express; Eileen Fitches (for the transcription prescription); Rymans in Ealing (for always calling me 'sir'); the Olympia Traveller de Luxe; Tipp-Ex; and last, but hardly least, I would like to say thank you to Fish, Steve, Mark, Pete and Ian for the wine, the turn-ons, and for sharing the passing times . . . .

1

Tequila Sunsets

Two long black limousines sit purring in the rain outside L.A.X. The sky is gun-metal grey this afternoon in Los Angeles and the glistening sheets of warm March rain hit the ground hard and dissolve into running gutter streams.

Marillion's tour manager, Paul Lewis, is first through the glass swing doors, the rain trickling down the lenses of his mirror shades, his hair and his clothes a picture of lost sleep, bad appetites, the Filofax blues, and next month's tour news; in control of everything, even now nine months into this thing, Paul is *ready* and *up for it*. Or at least doing his edgy best to try and look the part.

The two limousine chauffeurs snap to attention when they spot Paul skidding down the wet steps towards them, and within moments the band's personal baggage and carry-round gear is being loaded into the yawning dark boots of the two parked cars.

Then, one by one, Marillion troop down from the Domestic Flights exit into the waiting limos, nobody bothering to swivel their heads around long enough for a good look out over the potted airport palms, into the pulsing neon ooze of the sprawling Los Angeles freeways. It's just another airport, after all, and nothing much to look at on a hungover and stormy Saturday afternoon.

'Wouldn't you believe it?' cries John Arnison, Marillion's manager, as he settles himself in the back seat. 'The band's first ever visit to LA to play some gigs and it's bloody raining! The least you would have expected was that they could lay a bit of that good Californian sunshine on for us. It's probably better bloody weather in London,' he chuckles.

Fish settles his giant frame down next to John, lights another

Benson & Hedges, and gazes slant-eyed out of the nearside window. He's got used to all kinds of weather in the five years it's taken him and the rest of Marillion to get as far as playing their first major shows in Los Angeles, home of the American record industry Big Wheels, where the milk-and-dollar music biz heart lies, or so they say. Now he's as ready as he's ever going to be for whatever comes next, rain or shine.

Limo doors slam shut and the chauffeur switches on the local FM radio station, K.M.E.T. They're playing Elton John's 'Don't Let The Sun Go Down On Me'. Just in time for the chorus the first limousine slowly takes off, gliding on a cloud of purple exhaust fumes, melting and hissing in the rain, merging into the early afternoon traffic that crowds the winding Los Angeles freeway.

Billboard City, comin' atcha!

The Sunset Marquis, situated half-way down North Alta Loma, just off Sunset Boulevard in North Hollywood, will be home for Marillion over the next five days. In the 1970s, hotels like the Continental Hyatt House and the Chateau Marmont were the 'in' places to stay for a travelling rock and roll band laid up in LA for a few days' rest in the middle of another American tour. The Continental Hyatt House in particular – dubbed the Continental Riot House in the days not so long ago when the notorious Led Zeppelin entourage converged regularly on the hotel – was the *only* place to stay if a band was to enjoy the high profile usually associated with a successful American visit.

In the 1980s, however, the Sunset Marquis has taken over as *the* rock-and-roll watering-hole. Staying there at the same time as Marillion are the various members of Big Audio Dynamite, over from London on their first promotional trip to LA; Little Steven, Bruce Springsteen's former lead guitarist, who's in town on business; Robbin Crosby, lead guitarist with mega-platinum selling US outfit, Ratt, here hanging-out in the rain by the pool, under cover of cloud, sipping a fat Bloody Mary; and a certain gentleman by the name of Phil Collins, a fact which will put some edge into Fish's afternoon as he looks forward to Marillion's first all-important show in LA at the Roxy, later that night.

With a voice he himself admits is 'only about seventy-five per cent there' and with all the attendant pressures of future American stardom weighing evenly on his broad Scottish

shoulders, what Fish doesn't want to be told is that Phil Collins –
Mr Genesis himself, ancient teenhood idol and widely recognised
as one of the two or three major influences in the early, early
Marillion scheme-of-things – just might put in a brief appearance
at the Roxy for his first glimpse of the band the British media
have been accusing for years of ripping-off Genesis.

That no request for Marillion guest tickets has yet arrived
from the Collins camp is not going to be enough to settle Fish's
nerves. The fact that Phil Collins is even here is just something
else for him to worry about as the countdown to showtime
begins.

The band all check into the hotel under aliases. On this tour
they're using the names of the main characters in 'Thunderbirds',
the old TV puppet show. The Sunset Marquis guest register has
rooms booked for Marillion under the names of: Scott Tracey –
Fish; Virgil Tracey – Steve Rothery; Alan Tracey – Pete
Trewavas; Gordon Tracey – Ian Mosley; and Brains – Mark
Kelly.

Paul makes a slow circle of the Marquis reception area
repeating over and over in his sternest tour-manager-on-the-case
voice: 'Sound check is at *five*, and we will be *leaving* the hotel on
the *tour bus*, which will be parked *right outside* the hotel, at a
quarter to five . . . OK? Sound check is at *five* . . .'

After he's dumped his gear in his room, Fish throws on his
faded brown sheepskin flying jacket and heads on out of the hotel
for a quick jog in the rain over to the Roxy. A right into North
Alta Loma and a left onto Sunset Boulevard, and the Roxy is just
a couple of blocks up the street. This is all still new territory for
Fish, for the whole Marillion set-up, and besides, he can't wait to
plant his big size eleven feet firmly on that tiny but illustrious
Roxy stage. The rest of the band retire for a couple of hours' rest
and some snatched sleep before the soundcheck.`

Outside the Roxy there is already a long line of kids queue-
jumping for Marillion tickets they have already been told they
have no chance of getting. Marillion are playing two nights at
the Roxy, Saturday and Sunday – the band's first time ever in
LA, and tickets for both shows sold out within thirty minutes of
going on sale three weeks before.

'Standing room, man! Hey! You got *standing* room, right?' a
gang of blond teenage hairies beseech the implacable bouncers
standing shoulder-to-shoulder guarding the Roxy front doors.

'Hey man, Fish is, like, a *personal* friend of mine . . . If he knew I was stuck out here in the goddamn rain I *know* he'd wanna see me,' one of them, a girl with honey-pot eyes, is saying as Fish goes jogging past her, at speed, through the rain and around the corner of the club into a side entrance.

Nobody at the front of the queue notices until it's too late and the bouncers have turned their backs on the street and disappeared into the warm dry dark of the Roxy, closing the doors behind them . . .

For Marillion, the fuss all started in earnest with the release of their album *Misplaced Childhood* and the accompanying single from the album, 'Kayleigh'.

That both records should have proved to be such massive hits for them in Britain ('Kayleigh' reached number two in the UK charts, and *Misplaced Childhood* hit the hallowed number one spot) was a pleasant enough surprise for the band, although hardly beyond the realms of the imagination, as Marillion had always enjoyed major chart status in their homeland. Indeed, both their previous studio albums – *Script for a Jester's Tear*, which reached number seven in the UK in March 1983, and *Fugazi*, which made it to number four a year later – had earned Marillion gold and silver records in Britain and, latterly, Europe. And they had had no less than four entries in the UK Top Forty singles chart in the two years prior to the success, in June 1985, of 'Kayleigh'.

But finally making it to their first platinum record in Britain for the *Misplaced Childhood* album was only the start.

Across Europe, both 'Kayleigh' and *Misplaced Childhood* had repeated the giant commercial steps Marillion were now making in the UK, and by the end of 1985 the band had sold over 500,000 copies of the album in West Germany alone. The latter half of that year had seen Marillion taking on a massive fifty-date headlining tour of Europe, culminating in the band being officially named as the biggest ticket-selling touring act in West Germany in 1985, where they regularly performed for 12,000 people in every sports hall and indoor arena they could cram into their increasingly hectic schedule.

They followed that with seven special Christmas gigs in Britain, including their first headline appearance at the giant N.E.C. building in Birmingham, where over 11,000 grinning, screaming Marillion-heads turned up to watch. And then they really brought the old hammer down with their first full-stretch

UK tour since all the *Misplaced Childhood* madness began, over January and February of the New Year. Twenty-three big dates, this time including eight sold-out nights at the Hammersmith Odeon in London.

By the time Marillion arrived in Upstate New York for their first date on this latest and most serious American tour, they could look back with a kind of muted pride on almost eight solid months of sold-out headline concerts in thirteen different countries, picking up a veritable host of gold, silver and platinum singles and albums along the way. Now they were brimming over with new self-confidence boosted by their formidable international success on the other side of the Atlantic. Not even the thought of grappling perilously once again with big, bad-assed, Young America could shake the belief Marillion now held in their own dazzling future.

Three times the band had played in America before March 1986, and three times they had courted disaster. The first time, in June 1983, the band never made it further than a smattering of club dates on the East Coast. Former drummer, Andy Ward, put paid to whatever chance Marillion may have had of making any impact when it became clear that he was heading for a nervous breakdown.

Marillion's second US visit, less than two months later, with temporary session drummer John Martyr filling in for them, proved to be an even more spectacular failure, when the band accepted an engagement to open the show for the Canadian band Rush, over five miserable nights at the Radio City Music Hall in New York.

'Some of the most *awful* support gigs we've ever done!' is how guitarist Steve Rothery later described those lamentable concerts.

One of the toughest audiences in the world for a support band to work, the late-nite New York crowds that poured into the Radio City to see Rush sat impatiently through Marillion's opening spot, gobbling down their Quaaludes and red wine, and heaping loud and vulgar abuse on the band. Try as they might, the only reaction the band could whip up to their forty-five-minute sets was one of pure contempt. They returned home to England dragging their tails, burned by the experience.

However, less than a year later, in the summer of 1984, the band were persuaded back to America for another short-burst tour of the clubs. This time they had Ian Mosley already nicely installed as the new drummer and permanent full-time member, and confidence was high. But again the tour never went beyond a clutch of club and college appearances, again out on the East Coast, wholly unsupported, and largely unfrequented, by key staff figures from the band's American record company, Capitol Records.

As a result, the combined sales·in America for the *Script for a Jester's Tear* and *Fugazi* albums amounted to considerably less than either album had achieved individually in Britain and Europe. The third official Marillion album release – a budget-priced live recording the band looked upon more as an extended-length 12-inch EP, called *Real to Reel*, which went on sale in the UK, Europe, and Canada in November 1984 – was never to see an official US release. So far, so-so . . .

Now, in March 1986, Marillion's status in America had subtly altered. *Misplaced Childhood* and 'Kayleigh' had made sure of that. That one Marillion album alone outstripped all their previous US sales by a ratio of five to one, cruising into the Billboard Top 50 in the late summer of 1985, and staying hinged to the Hot 100 for the rest of the year. And 'Kayleigh' picked up the band's first serious radio airplay in America, jumping into the Billboard Top 75 and earning Marillion their first appearances on the heavily influential MTV cable channel with the accompanying video.

Where just twelve months before the American Capitol Records execs held that Marillion's music – no matter how popular in Britain and Europe, where the markets are more eclectic and less conservative than in the Mid-West of America – was uncommercial and too esoteric for mass American tastes, now, a quarter of a million American album sales later, corporate opinion of Marillion's chances of success in the US had made a dramatic U-turn.

The hype was on, and good, as of this tour.

Twenty-three American dates had been booked: eleven shows out on their own, headlining at clubs and colleges, playing before anticipated crowds of between 1,000 and 2,000 a night; and for the remaining twelve dates the band would again be opening the show for Rush at giant 20,000 seater stadiums – only this time at the express request of Rush mainman, Geddy Lee, who assured Marillion he felt confident, following the success in the States of *Misplaced Childhood*, that there would be no repeat of the Radio City Music Hall debacle.

Timed to coincide with the tour, Capitol Records rush-released a budget-priced Marillion compilation album called *Brief Encoun-*

ter. Intended for release originally in America only, *Brief Encounter* contains five tracks: two recorded in the studio, 'Lady Nina' and 'Freaks', both of which were written and recorded originally as B sides for the UK and European releases of the 'Kayleigh' and 'Lavender' hit singles, but never before included on any of their US releases; and live recordings of 'Kayleigh', 'Fugazi' and the eponymous 'Script For a Jester's Tear'.

According to the American sleeve-notes to *Brief Encounter*, the three live recordings date back only as far as Marillion's January/February 1986 U.K. tour. In truth, both 'Fugazi' and 'Script . . .' are much older recordings than the sleeve-notes admit, dating back to the band's performance at Leicester De Montfort Hall two years before, the concert, in fact, from which Side Two of the *Real to Real* album was culled. 'Kayleigh' is the only legitimate live recording taken from Marillion's 1986 British tour.

Quibbling details aside, *Brief Encounter* is still an impressive and satisfying addition to the Marillion canon. Apart from 'Kayleigh', which closes Side One and is too note-perfectly faithful to the studio original, the remaining four tracks, seen as a celebratory eye-opener for a new American audience not yet intimately acquainted with the quintessential Marillion sound, work wonderfully well together, particularly Side Two which is taken up by stunning live performances of 'Fugazi' and 'Script for a Jester's Tear'. Both numbers represent the apex of Marillion's creative achievement: more than 'Kayleigh', with her teeth-bared swirling romanticism, more even than classical Marillion moon-stompers like 'Garden Party' or 'Market Square Heroes'; beyond all the myths and legends, Marillion's career rests on magnificent corner-stones like the title tracks to the band's first two studio albums.

Both the live 'Fugazi' and 'Script . . .', as evinced on *Brief Encounter*, eclipse their recorded progenitors. These are darker, more rounded performances, the build-up of tension black and palpable as Fish wrestles his own poetic visions to the ground on 'Fugazi', the band growing wings for the grotesque finale, Fish on his knees at the end, self-immolation on any dirty street corner, singing in a voice like broken glass: '*Decriminalised genocide, providing door-to-door Belsens/Pandora's Box of holocausts, gracefully cruising satellite infested heavens . . .*'

And 'Script . . .' summons forth the same schizophrenic demons amidst the same loose whiskey-talk of '*another emotional suicide*'.

Capitol Records had also talked the band into allowing them to release 'Lady Nina' as an American-only single.

Originally recorded in Berlin in April 1985, as producer Chris Kimsey was beginning his final mix of the *Misplaced Childhood* album, 'Lady Nina' started life out as a nifty electronic drum pattern Ian Mosley had pieced together late one night in the studio after an evening of heavy drinking with the rest of the band. Half-heartedly, in search of something to attach to the B side of the first intended single from the album, 'Kayleigh', the rest of the band eventually threw some casual embellishments together and laid them over Ian Mosley's abandoned synthetic rhythm, and by the time Fish had added a completed lead vocal, with lyrics as loaded with wounds as anything on the album, Kimsey was there to add all the champagne touches in the mix, and at the end of it all, Marillion suddenly discovered, as would Capitol Records in America later on, that they had themselves a B side to end all others. Nevertheless, 'Lady Nina' was very *un*-Marillion. Ian Mosley, despite being the author of the original drum pattern, never actually plays drums himself anywhere on the track: this is metal-machine music, rarefied by computers and shedding digital tears.

Ultimately, 'Lady Nina' gave good rides, but she wasn't studied, contemplated, and evolved like the material the band had spent so long fashioning for the *Misplaced Childhood* album. Yet Capitol Records in America immediately fell in love with her. For a time they even went as far as trying to *insist* that 'Lady Nina' be included as an extra track on the *Misplaced Childhood* album. Of course, the band refused, threatening to take their album to another record company if Capitol tried to interfere with the band's choice of running order. In response, Capitol deliberately withdrew 'Lady Nina' from the B side of the US edition 'Kayleigh' single, replacing it with another track from the album, 'Heart of Lothian'.

Right from the beginning, Capitol had always wanted to release 'Lady Nina' as a single in America, convinced that it had all the potential for large-scale commercial airplay that so many previous American Marillion singles so patently lacked – at least, in the 'specialised' view of the Capitol higher-ups.

However, the fact that the American record company people liked the number so much precisely because 'Lady Nina' was so emphatically different from the bulk and core of the Marillion catalogue was not lost on the band. In the context of the semi-introductory *Brief Encounter* package, allowing also for the fact that 'Lady Nina' had not, as yet, appeared anywhere on the US market, and given that Capitol obviously fancied its chances strongly with radio and TV exposure, Marillion agreed to let 'Lady Nina' go out as their new single in America, in time for the dates with Rush. But they would not bow down to inside pressure and agree to perform the number live at any of their shows. They did shoot a video to go out with it, in London before the tour started, but 'Lady Nina' had never been a part of the Marillion live set and, as the band were now telling it, never would be.

And so the scene was set, in March 1986, for what was considered to be Marillion's first really serious US tour. By the time the band machine had moved into its Los Angeles stint, it was already clear that 'Lady Nina' was, as the band had felt all along, not really the single to break for them in America that Capitol had always insisted it was, barely scraping the underbelly of the Billboard Hot 100, and then only for a couple of weeks. But singles come and go very quickly in the vast hinterlands of American radio-programming, and Marillion's tour rolled swiftly on, picking up a dizzy momentum as the band skillfully wheeled through gigs in Utica, Buffalo, Waterloo Ontario, Seattle, Portland, San Francisco . . . This was to be Lights! Action! & Keep Those Goddamned Cameras Rolling! as Capitol Records threw their giant corporate shoulder into promoting the band properly for the first time in America, and Marillion set out in earnest on their journey to the heart of the American Rock Dream, right to the bitter end of that peculiar rainbow every successful British band in history has tried to chase.

And why not?

Indeed.

It's another Saturday night at the Roxy in Los Angeles. Outside, it's still raining cats and dogs. Inside, it's raining people . . .

Capitol Records' LA office is here in force tonight, crowding the front three rows of tables on the opposite side of the miniature dance-floor that separates them from the stage. Tonight's 'jest list' also includes David Coverdale, the singer in Whitesnake; Jimmy Bain, bassist with Dio; Robbin Crosby from Ratt; singer, Bob Seger, and . . .

Well, Phil Collins couldn't make it. He was asked, but

9

declined. Phil would be busy all weekend, he said, working in the studio. 'Thank God,' said Fish, then changed his mind.

But judging by the crowd assembled at the Roxy tonight, he's about the only rock celebrity in town this week that did miss it. The media blitz is on, and that means there are press wizards, radio sharks, cable TV goons, all kinds of whizzo-bizzo LA types represented here tonight, and the time left before the show begins is spent in a frenzy of back-slapping an' yaw-hawing, everybody trying to wind everybody else up about this whole nervous, first-time-in-town, Marillion deal. Here and there, in knotty colourful little groups, you can see the gangs of real fans, leafing through the tour programme, or just limbering up with their girlfriends and boyfriends, impatient just to get into it.

Marillion are huddled in the safety of their dressing rooms, upstairs above the stage, locked into all their last-minute chit-chat with John Arnison, with Paul Lewis, with Andy Field, the band's invaluable crew manager . . . cha-cha-ing back and forth about broken guitar strings, about missing foot-pedals, about the rogue on-stage monitors . . . all the whispered gaffa-tape conversations that every band in the world has five minutes before they're due to go on stage.

When the lights in the club finally die, an enormous, whooping American cheer goes up as the five shifting silhouettes jostle silently for position in the unnatural darkness of the stage. Somewhere, just out of range of normal hearing, Ian Mosley counts in the beat and the band kick-start their way, amidst a dazzling flash of sudden blue light, into the intro of 'Emerald Lies'. Fish, dancing around with his long, ornately patterned, blue and silver cape splayed-out behind him, both arms out-stretched in mock-crucifixion pose, the band segueing neatly into the set's big opening gambit, 'Script for a Jester's Tear'.

Eyes closed, Fish begins the first line alone, save for Mark Kelly's one theatrical piano chord: '*So here I am once more . . .*' But as he starts the second line, 400 Roxy voices go right with him '*. . . in the playground of the bro-ken hearts!*'

It's a magical, very typically Marillion moment, and every-body shudders. Fish opens his eyes and hands down a long, hard, piercing stare from the stage. The band make their move and the number starts to take off. The dance-floor is shaking like a worn-out trampoline and even the tables by the rear wall, opposite the stage, stop drinking long enough to lose the next ninety minutes eyeballing the band.

It's a very stripped-down live show compared to the production Marillion were carrying around Britain and Europe for the last eight months. The lights, save for a few choicely-placed spots, are club-minimal, monochromatic and stark, and on stage there isn't enough room to swing a cat, let alone a mike-stand, but Fish still gives an opening performance full of jagged elbows and high scissor-kicks, cupping his hand and spitting a kiss over the vocal monitors, his eyes elsewhere for a moment, the band crunching down hard at the climax of 'Script . . .'

Then, silence. For almost a full second, followed by mad, hysterical applause, the Roxy comes alight at the startling spectacle of Marillion letting it all come down. Steve Rothery almost breaks into a smile; meanwhile, Fish, his back to the audience, is screaming at his on-stage vocal-monitor roadie, bitterly complaining that he cannot hear himself sing. Suddenly, far too close to the beginning of a long and important show, there is a tension on-stage you can see reflected in the quick looks Mark Kelly and Pete Trewavas throw each other's way.

Ian maps out the beat to 'Incubus', Mark Kelly's keyboards take a backward somersault into the melody, and Fish grips the microphone and leans heavy into the first line: '*When footlights dim in reverence to prescient passion/Forewarned my audience leaves the stage . . .*' The band play with a powerful, practised ease, the rhythm pounding like a heart as Steve Rothery's guitar rips into the guts of the song, and Fish turns his cold camera-eye on this strange and new Los Angeles gathering. And again, at the death, the applause is heavy, people starting to call out for the numbers they want to hear next.

'Jigsaw', which follows, Fish dedicates to 'all the romantics seated at the tables'. Word-perfect already, the dance-floor crowd all come in on the chanted chorus . . . '*Stand straight!/Look me in the eye and say goodbye!*' Second time around even the tables are mouthing the words. The number flames then winks out, like a dead star.

'The Web' is dedicated to 'all the people that waited four years to see us play here in Los Angeles!' and the band burst into the riff, Mark Kelly's keyboards weaving through a tightly-drawn backdrop of bludgeoning guitars and drums; Fish at his most pained and theatrical, sweeping his personal dramas up past the footlights, past the tables and guests, and out the door to haunt the streets.

11

As Pete Trewavas and Steve Rothery start zig-zagging like toy trains about the stage for the jigging high-finale of 'The Web', Fish disappears side-stage where Paul Lewis is waiting with the kimono and tartan trousers Fish always changes into in time for the intro to *Misplaced Childhood*, which is next in the set. John Arnison is also standing by. Fish is not going to be happy with the fact that he still can't hear himself singing on stage, and John and Paul both know it.

'I bet he's going to be *steaming* when he comes off stage for the costume change,' says John. They're waiting for it all right. It arrives.

'Get fucking rid of that cunt on the monitors or I'm going to KILL HIM!' Fish screams at them as he clambers into the side-stage corridor. Out front, oblivious of Fish's problems, the Roxy are clapping and cheering like mad things as 'The Web' rolls towards its frenzied, chanting climax; feet stamping and glasses being pounded on tables, Ian Mosley topping up the pace a notch, Mark Kelly giving it plenty of 'widdly-widdly' as he likes to call it.

Back in the corridor Fish has got his breath back.

'I start screaming at the cunt to do something and he stands there shrugging his shoulders, as if to say, "What can *I* do?" WHAT CAN HE FUCKING DO?' Fish cries in a voice like thunder. 'He can get on the first plane home tomorrow because as far as I'm concerned that bastard is *fired*!'

'All right, Fish, all right, calm down, I'll sort it out,' John says hopefully, wondering how best to deflate the situation, his mind racing.

Then the singer figures out the way for himself. Fish, the on-stage adrenalin still pounding through his body, spins in an angry, blind circle to face the plastic wall-mirror that stands by the entrance to the stage. Bunching his right hand into a football-sized fist he pulls his arm way back past his shoulders then lets fly with a heavyweight right hook straight to the jaw of the mirror. It lands with an almighty *thwack!* and the last three knuckles in his right hand collapse into a bloodied mess of white bone and red skin.

'Fuck me, what have you done to your hand?' asks Paul Lewis, the kimono still draped apologetically over one arm. Tight-lipped, Fish does the quick change routine into his Scottish 'trews' and blue silk kimono, and Paul leaves to hunt down the delinquent on-stage monitor roadie with the singer's last words on the subject, 'Fire the bastard!', still burning holes in his ears.

Fish ties the belt tight on his kimono, lights another cigarette, and allows John Arnison to hand him back the microphone. Then he walks to the edge of the stage and from the wings begins his spoken introduction-cum-dedication to *Misplaced Childhood*. Though they still can't see anything of him yet, the crowd start to howl and whistle at the sound of his gruff voice, and he ends his small speech with the words, 'This is a song about perimeter walkers . . . and this is very respectfully dedicated to John Belushi.'

Surprised and thrilled by the dedication to one of Hollywood's most notorious prodigal sons, the Roxy cognoscenti howl and slap their hands together with even more fury. (Belushi, before his untimely death from an accidental drug over-dose, was a patron of the exclusive upstairs club at the Roxy, frequented in the past by filmland luminaries such as Steve McQueen and Robert Mitchum – the bad boy crowd – and he used it as one of his regular hang-outs whenever he was in town, which was often. The local spook-pedlars will tell you his spectre still haunts the parking lot behind the club, where Belushi is alleged to have made many of his more infamous drug deals. Fish's on-stage identification with the Belushi cult will cap his own notoriety in LA circles this week and confirm his reputation as something of a 'bad boy' himself).

Then there is a deep sigh as the first, ghostly refrains of Mark Kelly's deep-throated keyboard seep like a grey mist from the darkened rear of the stage and Fish, cigarette still glowing in his left hand, the damaged right cradling the mike, strolls into a lone blue spotlight and begins his starry invocation. '*Huddled in the safety of a pseudo-silk kimono/Wearing bracelets of smoke/Naked of understanding . . .*'

The mist deepens, and by the time Steve Rothery is stroking out the cartwheeling guitar intro to 'Kayleigh' Marillion have seized this Roxy crowd by the hair. By now everybody's along for the ride and, as form demands, that means everybody gets to sing along on the chorus – Capitol Records execs, Bob Seger, David Coverdale, *everybody altogether now* . . . 'KAYLEE!' they cry, '*is it too late to say I'm sorry/KAY-LEE! could we get it to-gether again . . .?*'

There's a lot of grinning, singing idiots walking around here tonight, and two well-known local stringers for the American rockzines *Creem* and *Faces* ease back in their chairs and one leans over and yells into the other's ear so hard you can hear him three tables away: 'I haven't seen this place looking so *happening* for a new English band since Dire Straits played here and, Christ, that's got to be *five years* ago!'

Steve Rothery's last, back-arching guitar lines to 'Lavender' spin to their conclusion, and Ian Mosley begins his tremendous percussion-break intro to the 'Bitter Suite' section of *Misplaced Childhood*, Mark Kelly's synthesisers belching and hissing by his side, Rothery's guitar searing across the landscape, Pete Trewavas' bass moving with a low growl into the beginnings of a distant riff. Fish picks up his pint glass of Jack Daniels and Coke, takes a good long pull on it, then strides purposefully up to the mike and points with his eyes . . . '*A spider wanders aimlessly through the warmth of a shadow . . .*' With an eerie tread, the piece begins.

Deciding to perform the *Misplaced Childhood* album in its entirety was a brave move. Planning this American tour a month before at home in England, the band would have been forgiven for changing around the set somewhat in their efforts to breach the gap between their firmly-established British and European audiences and their suddenly burgeoning American following. Instead, Marillion opted for a forty-five minute set on the dates with Rush, comprising the whole of the *Misplaced Childhood* set-piece, only ending on 'Childhood's End?' and adapting the last 'White Feather' segment as the encore whenever they picked one up. For their own shows they reverted to the same set as they had been touting around the rest of the world for the last eight months. This was still very much the American leg of the *Misplaced Childhood* World Tour, no matter how belated. That was the view the band were taking, and through headline appearances in Seattle, Portland, and San Francisco, Marillion proved they didn't need to pretty-up their act one iota to drive large sections of this new American audience right out of their MTV-satiated minds.

'*Well, I hit the streets back in '81/I found a heart in the gutter and a poet's crown . . .*' The band bubbles contagiously over the intro to 'White Feather', playing with a light in their eyes as Ian Mosley rattles those curling off-beats home, over half the Roxy tables abandoned as the house gets to its feet and cheers the band. The music dies and Marillion exit, stage-left, the noise of deafening, beautiful applause chasing them down the backstage corridor. Encores are a cert. The question now is how many do they want? John Arnison walks into the dressing room and smiles and someone mentions champagne.

'This time, we came across to America with a frontman that knew at last what an American audience is about, you know, and we weren't staring at every Chevy that passed us in the street. This time we weren't fucking *begging*.' Fish and I are sitting at a booth at the Rainbow Bar & Grill, next door to the Roxy, late the following afternoon. He's finished his sound-check for the show and now he's draining a couple of tall, spicy Bloody Marys, killing time until he starts to get ready for the gig in a couple of hours.

Two young fans wander over and ask him to sign a dog-eared copy of Tolkien's novel *The Silmarillion*.

'Was this book an influence on your writing?' one of them, a teenage boy with long thin wisps of yellow beard drooping from his chin, asks. 'Naw,' Fish shakes his head and coughs, 'I couldn't say any of his stuff was really an influence.'

'What do you think of this book, though? You took the name of the band from its title, right?' the other, almost a twin of the first, persists.

'I've never actually read that book,' Fish tells them.

'But you took your name from it, right?'

'Well, the original band did, I didn't.'

'So they must have read it, right?'

'Uh . . . I don't know, yeah, I suppose so, one of them might. You'll have to ask the rest of the band when they arrive. Look! There they are now. Go on, ask them.'

Fish points his enquirers in the direction of Pete Trewavas and Mark Kelly, who have just entered the club. 'Will they be able to help us?' asks yellow wisps. 'Oh, definitely,' Fish assures them and they leave, taking their signed copy of *The Silmarillion* with them, bearing it like a magic staff as they glide over to where Pete and Mark have just sat down and taken a table.

'Two headcase hobbits on a mission from God, obviously,' Fish smiles. He and the rest of the band are a lot more relaxed about the prospect of their second show at the Roxy tonight. Last night's gig, despite the hassles and hoo-hah surrounding the sacking of Fish's vocal-monitor roadie, inspired a lot of the Capitol Records chiefs to wander around at the party they'd thrown for the band after the show waving their arms excitedly and predicting in extravagant tones to anyone who would listen that Marillion would and could be 'the new Moody Blues', 'the next Jethro Tull', and one day even 'as big as Pink Floyd'.

This tour is going good and everybody knows it. Even Fish.

'It's not just these few gigs we've been doing on our own either, playing to the people who have come along specifically to see us,' he says. 'Even on the Rush shows the reactions we've been getting in some places have been so outrageous, so totally mental it's shocked us. Honestly, we've had the Rush merchandising people coming backstage some nights complaining that Marillion are selling more T-shirts and sweat-shirts than Rush! It's because suddenly we're *hip* in America; we're *new*. So new you still can't hear any of our records being played on any of the FM radio stations yet. But the underground college radio networks are plugging us like mad. They've been finding out all about us since *Misplaced Childhood* was released, and now that we're here and playing for them they can't wait to come down and check us out live. Which is where this group really scores, because Marillion are nothing if not a fucking *great* live band. They may not *all* love us the first time they see us, but they'll never forget about us, not after they've seen us play live. I, as the frontman, guarantee it!'

'Also,' he goes on, 'I think the essential difference between this American tour and all our previous tours is that in the past we were always treated as the underdogs nobody gave a fuck about; this time we're the underdogs everybody suddenly wants to win!'

At this half-way stage of the tour though, Fish knows that a lot of the real slog still lies ahead.

'After tonight's show, I think we've got one, or maybe two more shows left to do on our own, then for the rest of the time we're going to be supporting Rush. If we can crack most of those audiences straight, with no props, no backdrops, no real lights, we really will have made a lasting impression here in America. The kids will know we've got the potential to deliver a stunning stage-show and, if they like us, they're going to come back and see us when we return and start to headline at our own gigs in some of these places.'

He also points out that so far on the Rush dates there has been no repeat of the squalid animosity that wrecked the Radio City Hall shows in 1983.

'Rush have been all for us, and the kids know that this time Geddy Lee *asked* us to do this tour with them, which has helped us a lot, I expect,' says Fish. 'And we didn't come to America as prima donnas. We just came across and said, "Hi! Want a Marillion T-shirt?" We won them over completely by being . . . well, by just being *us*.'

Outside the Roxy the touts on the street have been passing Marillion tickets out at 150 dollars a head; there have been plenty of last-minute takers, too. Word is out on the band, and Sunday night's show is the hottest ticket in town draw in all LA.

For 'White Feather' about half the Roxy crowd hold white feathers or white flags aloft, Fish really getting into the Scottish voodoo for the marching, triumphant crescendo: '. . . *And the LA chil-dren! And the Moscow chil-dren! And the London chil-dren!'*

The first encore is 'Fugazi'. Fish introduces the number with a long monologue explaining how 'Fugazi' began as 'an anxiety attack I had once, on the London Underground', growing eventually to embrace, in theme, not just the war in Vietnam (the word 'fugazi' was popular slang amongst the enlisted American G.I.s; to be fugazi means to be 'all fucked up') but all wars everywhere, the wars that are 'fought both without and within'.

The band roar menacingly through the number and dizzy bodies start to fly at the front of the stage. The Capitol Records execs, again out in force, sit at their tables smiling and banging ash-trays, their eyes full of green billy dolls. 'Fugazi' thunders to its climax with the ageless LA chil-dren singing: '*Where are the PROPHETS?/Where are the VISIONARIES?* At the end Marillion bow and wave and laugh their way off stage only to be yanked back again for another encore.

'You're one of the best audiences we've ever played to in America!' cries Fish as he bounces up to the mike. 'You've really kept up your reputation here tonight, Los Angeles!' Then Mark Kelly trots out the intro to 'Garden Party' and the band start to romp and roll. This is Marillion putting on the swing in their most decadent English dance-band mode. The Roxy eats it up.

The band segue into 'Market Square Heroes', Ian Mosley doubling up the beat in lusty, flamboyant flourishes, Rothery slashing out the chords, Kelly's keyboard 'widdly-widdly' pulsing like a hot strobe, Fish's voice cracked and raw at the edges now.

With Mosley still pounding out the beat like a thirty-pound jack-hammer, Steve Rothery lets his guitar go, taking off into the night, exploding like a gun under the choked indoor sky, and then he returns suddenly and begins punching out the riff to 'Let's Twist Again (Like We Did Last Summer)', the old Chubby Checker hit.

It makes for a quite surreal scene: Fish turns his back on the audience and, still twisting, starts to wriggle his bottom like a schoolgirl in the footlights, everybody else in the band grinning like happy hyenas, the Roxy getting her own bottom twisted good and proper.

Then, with an invisible signal, Mark Kelly and Steve Rothery lead the band back into the last few choruses of 'Market Square Heroes', and then out. With a commanding ba-boom! finish, Marillion make their last exit to the upstairs dressing rooms, wreathed in sweat and smothered in the glory of having finally kicked LA's ass, and good.

In the dressing room there are no recriminations, no bad vibes about the on-stage monitors, no doubts expressed about anything save for whose turn it is to buy the first round of drinks next door at the Rainbow.

It's 5.30 a.m., Monday. At 10 a.m. Fish and Mark Kelly are scheduled to begin a day-long round of local press and radio interviews. Mark is asleep in his room at the Sunset Marquis. Fish is not.

He and Pete Trewavas are sitting at a big oak table, stripped to their underpants, drinking from a bottle of Tequila Gold and smoking, listening to Pink Floyd's 'Dark Side of the Moon', of all things, blaring out of a portable compact disc player, and watching, entranced, as an orange Los Angeles sun rises slowly to the top of the window in the room where they sit, overlooking a kidney-shaped pool. Then the spell breaks and they glance at each other and break down into helpless fits of laughter, giggling like naughty schoolboys.

They've both spent half the night throwing people, themselves included, into the pool – Paul Lewis was one of the first to go, naturally, then Mark Kelly, and then some people they'd only just been introduced to from Capitol. It had been some party all right: a real post-gig, post-Rainbow, crash-course for the ravers. Now, with the last party guests long gone, here they sit, still dripping in their sodden, baggy underpants, waiting for their clothes to dry, and then that last taxi home . . . or at least as far as the hotel.

18

Sitting with them, though not, of course, in just his underpants, is Rod Smallwood, avuncular manager of the British rock band Iron Maiden, themselves a mega-platinum selling, arena-headlining act in America. Rod's been working with Marillion on this tour as their officially appointed US consultant. This is his house. It is huge, with enough rooms to get lost in, a regular millionaire's Hollywood mansion, set in the side of the steep brown hills that run to the north of Sunset Boulevard.

Originally, the house was owned by James Cagney. Then Peter Sellers bought the property from him in the 1970s. After Sellers' death, his widow, Lyn Frederick, eventually decided she didn't want to keep the place on and put the house on the market.

And that's when Rod bought it. A Yorkshireman who always likes to be generous with his house-guests, Smallwood is happy to share his sunrise, his Tequila Gold and his swimming pool with the two young Marillion men.

Fish starts to croon softly along with the record . . . 'and after all we're only or-di-nary men . . .' and then he stops and smiles impishly. Earlier, Rod had told them that on the strength of the reaction the band had got from just those two small Roxy shows, he was now able to book the band into a couple of larger, more prestigious theatre dates, which he advised them to tack on to the end of the tour. There would be three extra shows in all: the first at the California Theatre in San Diego, capacity 1,700, and an expected sell-out, according to Rod; and two final shows planned to end the tour on a high and fine note at the Beverly Theatre in downtown LA, where Marillion could now expect to play to 3,000 new fans over both nights.

It stopped raining in LA about four hours ago, while the band were still flitting like happy ghosts from one crowded booth to another over at the Rainbow, sipping iced Long Island Teas, and slurping from expensive bottles of champagne, the room swinging to its own flip yackety-yak beat . . . Now the slow, red dawn threatens to give way to the first clear, sun-full day since the band arrived in town.

Rod's still making plans for the rest of Marillion's stay in Los Angeles when the taxi Fish and Pete have ordered finally pulls into the drive and honks.

'Tonight I'll take you all down to the Cat & Fiddle for a real slap-up bangers-and-mash English dinner, they've got real ale

19

and everything! And then, on Tuesday we'll hire a couple of limos and take a trip out to Disney Land. Nobody in the band has been to Disney Land yet, have they?'

Not yet.

2

The Dark Star
(*Profile – Steve Rothery*)

Steve Rothery is the Dark Star in the Marillion firmament; the quiet, unperturbable knight in hidden armour. The longest-serving member of the band, his origins dating back to the times when they were still called the Silmarillion, Rothery has a very quiet, studied presence. Not for him the crooked jester's smile Fish will often present before the public. Instead, both on stage and off, Rothery appears a far more self-contained, introspective, almost untouchable personage.

A Yorkshireman by birth and by temperament, Steve Rothery is very much his own man, staunchly determined to get things done in his own way and in his own time. Not stubborn exactly, but with an innate confidence in his own ability to deliver the goods no matter what the setbacks anybody else in the group might experience.

No, he doesn't talk much, but you can almost always hear his mind working overtime, his thoughts revolving like an endlessly turning wheel. Sometimes it's just a faint hum, or echo, in the dressing room you can catch if you stop what you're doing and just stand still and listen hard for a moment. You might glance across to the other side of the room and spot Steve Rothery hunched over his guitar in the corner, and it may strike you that his face and his eyes haven't *stopped* talking since he walked in, unnoticed, and sat down fifteen minutes ago . . .

Of the five members that make up the present Marillion line-up, Steve Rothery is one of the two dominant creative personalities. Though the other – Fish – has always successfully presided over the domain of Marillion's heady public image as a new British rock band ready and willing to be taken seriously, providing complex and poetical lyrics that have invested the band's direction with a thrust it certainly would never have enjoyed otherwise, it is Steve Rothery's unique guitar-artistry that lies smouldering at the heart of everything important this strange and often quirky group have ever recorded.

Together, as the dual spearhead of a more lasting five-strong musical partnership, Steve Rothery and Fish have developed an intense, sometimes temperamental, working relationship over the last six years. Inside the rehearsal studio, the cerebral songwriting partnership between the moody guitarist and the flamboyant singer is more often than not the catalyst that sets the rest of the band-machine in motion, elaborating on the framework they create. Individually, however, Steve Rothery and Fish couldn't be more different. He of the tartan eyes and the appetites of an alligator, striding up and down lonely hotel corridors at four in the morning, Bourbon glass in hand, is not often accompanied by the forthright and increasingly sensible Mr Rothery. No, these two, they choose to walk alone.

And if Fish is sometimes too easily seduced into the role of verbal assassin, swaying like a pendulum between the twin masks of comedy and tragedy, then Steve Rothery prefers to stand apart, a little to one side, the accusing silence, perhaps, behind the jokes. Certainly, Steve will enjoy razzling with you for a while, but not every night; Fish is just the opposite, he *always* wants to party, *never* wants to quit it and go to sleep, then calls you a 'lightweight' when you complain you can't keep up.

Even on stage some nights, during the latter half of 'Incubus' perhaps, at the very moment his beautifully controlled guitar lines start to tumble and fall like fast running water over Fish's dirt and stone words, you can sense Rothery's *separateness*. He is a musician whose only prop is his own silence, happy to exist without the social graces of a full-blown media-persona. Unlike Fish, Rothery is utterly unburdened by such considerations, leaving himself free to nurture the 'separateness' he seems to desire.

Rothery's relationships with the rest of the band always appear relaxed and friendly. Mostly, they will tell you, he is a very easy person to get along with. And so far, the subtle tensions that exist between Steve Rothery and Fish have always resulted in a healthy creative *frisson* that, somehow, at their best, Marillion have managed to capture, contain, and capitalise on to extravagant effect.

And aside from anything else, he is, of course, a quite brilliant lead guitarist whose unique textures will guide the band through the most delicate shifts in romantic pace, and then ascend into a fire of shattering notes. A very dark star indeed.

Steve Rothery was born in South Yorkshire, in a small town called Brampton, on 25 November 1959.

He came from a small family whose background was working-class. His father, Peter, worked in a local bank and his mother, Marian, worked as a cook. Steve's sister Julie had been born two and a half years before.

'My parents separated when I was five though,' says Steve. 'And they were divorced by the time I was seven. Me and my sister stayed with my mum. We all moved to a place just outside of Whitby, in North Yorkshire, another small place called Newholme. That was where I lived until I was eleven years old, and then we moved into Whitby itself.'

Attending a local comprehensive school, Steve's academic interests extended to 'quite liking' art and maths, but by the time he'd reached his early teens school lessons were already taking a back seat to his fast-growing fascination with music. 'My mother says that when we were still living in South Yorkshire, when I was still a small child, the place we lived in used to belong to an undertaker and there were a lot of these wire frames he used to use to make wreaths with lying around the place. Well, one of them I found was in the shape of a guitar, and I used to sit around pretending to strum it like a guitar. Weird, you know? And then after that I got into all the usual posing around with a tennis racquet, pretending to play that like a guitar. By this time I must have been about seven or eight years old.

'I started listening to rock music seriously when I was about fourteen. Funnily enough, before that the sort of music I was most interested in was mainly film scores – the James Bond films and a lot of war movies always had theme tunes and incidental music that I really liked, Ron Goodwin and the *Battle of Britain*, all that kind of stuff.

'The first rock album I ever bought was *Saucerful of Secrets* by Pink Floyd. And I first heard that because a lot of my friends had started getting heavily into Pink Floyd, Camel, Yes, Rick Wakeman . . . you know the sort of thing.'

23

And Genesis? From day one in Marillion's recording career, the pundits have never wasted an opportunity to point out the obvious similarities between the earliest works of Marillion and the neo-classical, Peter Gabriel-era, Genesis sound of the early 1970s. In reality, how big an influence were Genesis on Steve Rothery the fledgling musician?

'Oh, I was a big fan, all right,' he smiles. 'Of all the people in Marillion, I would say that Fish and I were the biggest fans of early Genesis. I first got into them by listening to the Alan Freeman Rock Show, which used to go out on Radio One on Saturday afternoons when I was a teenager. Me and some mates used to get together every Saturday afternoon and play snooker on this miniature-sized table, and we'd have Alan Freeman's show on the whole time. The first thing I actually heard by them that Alan Freeman played was the second half of 'The Knife', and I remember thinking, "Wow, what an amazing piece of music!" It just went through all these different changes. After that, I went out and bought my first Genesis album, which was a live recording they released back in 1972, and that was *it*! I was totally hooked, on their strange intensity, on their weird imagery . . . on the whole thing that they were starting to get into in the early 70s.

'I didn't come from a particularly musical background,' he says. 'Although my grandfather, who was a miner, used to play the banjo and the piano-accordion. He was pretty good, apparently. He almost got signed to a record company as well, so I'm told. But apart from that, no-one in my family could really play anything.'

At the age of fourteen, Steve bought his first acoustic guitar for £5 from a neighbour in Whitby.

'It was hardly a real guitar,' he remembers, 'More like a piece of hard wood with strings on it. The action was like a cheese-grater, but that's what I started with. After that, an electric guitar seemed like the easiest thing in the world to play . . .'

Steve bought his first 'real' guitar, an electric Stratocaster Copy, when he was sixteen, using the money he was given to spend on a holiday in Italy which his uncle had treated him to.

'From that point on, I started to take the whole business of learning to play the guitar a lot more seriously. I got a couple of self-teachers, books like "Improvising Rock Guitar", that sort of thing,' he says. 'I never actually managed to work my way through entire books, but I would just pick out the best aspects of each one and work the rest out for myself. As for sitting around trying to play along to records, well, I did that once or twice but analysing a piece of music too thoroughly always seemed to destroy the magic of the piece for me – you know, is that all there is to it, *three chords*?

'And anyway, once I got my hands on my first Strat Copy, there was no restraint on my technique any more, from the physical point of view, and I started to learn things really quite easily. Six months or so of that and I felt confident enough to go out and buy my first Yamaha S.G. 2000, this is when I was seventeen. I still use a version of that guitar now, the 3000, although I occasionally revert back to the old 2000 some nights on stage.'

By his mid-teens, Steve was also starting to experiment with the idea of playing in his own band.

'It was the usual scenario,' he recalls. 'I started playing in different bands with old school friends, but of course it never really amounted to much. The first gig I ever did was at a lunchtime disco at my old school in Whitby. I'd left at sixteen but I still had some friends left there who'd stayed on to take their A Levels, and they arranged the gig for us. We played a lot of old Beatles' songs and loads of old rock and roll numbers, it was all very funny, really. We even got reviewed in the school magazine: it said something like, "Edwin Hart is a really good singer and Steve Rothery is a really good guitar player", you know? I read that and I thought, "Wow! Fame at last!" ' he laughs.

'From there we went on to playing in village halls, the odd local pubs, and Scarborough Football Supporters' Club, which was one room above a shoe shop. Great fun.'

For the first year, after leaving school with three O Levels, Steve held down the occasional job as van driver, but, as he says, 'My idea was never to go out looking for a good job, instead all I wanted to do was concentrate full-time on playing the guitar. I used to sit at home and practise for six or seven hours every day, just trying to get to grips with developing some sort of distinctive style.'

Eventually, with just those handful of gigs behind them, Steve and his band's singer, Edwin Hart, progressed from rehearsing cover versions of other people's better-known material to writing down their own sketchy, first-time goes at some original material of their own. Using that most primitive of multi-tracking devices, the Two Cassette Players Method, Rothery and

Hart actually got as far as producing a demo-tape which the hopeful pair lost no time in sending around to all the major record companies they could think of in London.

'Yeah,' he smiles, 'and we got a list of rejection slips as long as my arm. Mind you,' he goes on, 'the stuff me and Edwin were writing *was* a bit of a strange mixture. He was a bit of a Beatles fanatic, so everything he was writing tended to sound a lot like that, and with me at that time, I was getting into a sort of cross between Dire Straits and Santana – if you can imagine what that sounded like! I've still got a tape somewhere of the things we were doing then, very weird stuff . . . In fact, that was the tape I took down with me when I first auditioned for Marillion. And they were *not* impressed!'

Increasingly disillusioned with the less than sparkling prospects of making any real headway with his band in Whitby – 'As far as "making it" in Whitby goes, if you didn't play Country & Western or old-style rock and roll you could forget it, really!' – Steve started to think seriously about leaving town and joining up with a brand new outfit somewhat closer, in terms of musical ability as well as geography, to the bright lights of the London-based music business. Tentatively, he began scouring the classified ads section of the *Melody Maker*. And then, in 1979, he ran across an advertisement in the *MM* which began: 'Silmarillion requires lead guitarist' . . . Steve replied to the ad and was immediately invited down to audition.

'The address they gave me was in Long Marston, which is about eight miles outside of Aylesbury, but it was still, like, 200 miles closer to London than bloody Whitby, so off I went.'

At that time, Silmarillion was actually just two people: drummer Mick Pointer and bass player Doug Irving. 'There was a third guy originally, when I first played them my tape,' Steve remembers, 'He was a keyboard player, but I never got to know him at all. He left about a week after I joined, God knows what his name was, I really can't remember.'

As Steve has already suggested, neither Mick Pointer nor Doug Irving was exactly bowled over by the Dire Beatles-cum-Santana tape Steve handed over for them to play.

'I could tell just by the way they kept sneaking glances at each other that they were ready to tell me to piss off back to Whitby,' he says. 'Fortunately, though, I'd brought down my guitar and some equipment in the back of the car, so I managed to persuade them to let me set up my gear and have a little jam, just to give them some idea of the sort of stuff I was interested in playing now. It was just me and the bass player, Doug, no drums. But I was already writing the kind of stuff I do now and I started showing them a couple of little things I'd been working on and they were both knocked out! I think they auditioned one more guitarist after me and then they offered me the gig.'

Irving and Pointer shared a small cottage together, along with a larger circle of friends, including a certain Mr Christopher 'Privet' Hedge, a long-time (Sil)Marillion stalwart who was to later graduate to being the band's permanent live sound engineer, a job he still holds today. Back then, however, Privet's duties with the band were confined more to his touch-and-go abilities as the resident in-house pyrotechnician. But we'll get to that later . . .

Joining Silmarillion meant Steve Rothery moving into the cottage in Long Marston, too.

'I gave up the life I'd been leading in Whitby, left my mother's house for the first time, and moved in with Mick, Doug and Privet. At one stage there must have been six people all living in that cottage. I was sleeping on a sofa in the living room. It was a dingy little place really, damp on the walls, no hot running water, and hundreds of cats all over the place. I used to try and go to sleep at night with all these cats crawling all over my face. Eventually I graduated from sleeping on the sofa to sleeping in a little corridor between two bedrooms. Talk about moving up in the world!'

Unlike Steve, who was still unemployed, Doug Irving and Mick Pointer both had well-paid, steady jobs: Doug worked servicing photocopying machines, and Mick had a job fitting luxury kitchens.

'They were both earning good money,' Steve recalls, 'Which is how they were able to afford to buy all this amazing equipment that they had already amassed by the time I joined the band. The only thing we didn't have, at that stage, was a keyboard player. And until we found one we couldn't really do any gigs. So in the meantime I started looking for some sort of job as well, only I didn't have much luck.'

Adding to his list of useless, one-off jobs, Steve took a one-day job with a local bakery as a van driver and another working in a factory that manufactured caravans. He only stuck at it for a short time.

'It was a production line I was on, turning out aluminium

panels for the caravans they were assembling. Huge factory, huge machinery, churning out all these bits and pieces. I was stacking these huge sheets of metal, you know, and I thought "I don't need this". Then one of the women I was working with accidentally chopped one of her fingers off and I thought "I *definitely* don't need this!' And so I left that job as well.'

Finally, the band found a new keyboard player. His name was Brian Jelliman.

'Brian was a pretty good player,' says Steve. 'He had a lot of imagination, but . . . well, he was a bit of a strange character to get on with, a bit of an aggravating personality to have in a band. One of those respectable types who was very intense and pigheaded and arrogant, in his own way. But very talented, too, and we all wrote together and, eventually, started doing a few gigs.'

After Jelliman joined the band, who by now had dropped the 'Sil' from their name, and with Doug Irving handling the lead vocals after a fashion – 'Oh, Doug had a really *nasal* voice, really quite awful if you want to know the truth, but he did try hard and anyway, Doug had always fancied himself as a bit of a singer' – they rehearsed for several weeks at a studio in Buckinghamshire owned by Wild Willy Barrett, formerly the guitar-playing half of a zany partnership with another local Aylesbury boy, John Otway, which spawned one hit single in the mid-70s, 'Cor Baby, That's Really Free'.

And then, at long last, came the very first spate of Marillion gigs.

'The first gig we ever played, and this was months after I'd first agreed to move down to Long Marston and joined the band, was at the Berkhamstead Civic Centre. We played to about a hundred people and we ended up getting about six encores! Mind you, that could have been because they were all stoned out of their heads!' he laughs.

'And Privet really came into his own that night!' he chortles. 'He was really into getting the pyrotechnics together and he had all these explosions and God knows what else organised. So all through the set we had these little flashes going off, then one of them didn't go off and Privet being Privet he takes the one that hasn't gone off and straps it to another and makes that one go off! So, like, you get this huge great double explosion! I'm in the middle of a guitar solo and this thing goes off behind me, big jets of flame shooting past my ears, and I thought my back was on fire!'

Musically, the band tended to concentrate on instrumentals, with Doug occasionally stepping up to the microphone to take the lead vocal wherever they had one written.

'We were already working on bits and pieces of the material that, with later versions of the band, we turned into some of the songs we were eventually to record. The beginnings of "The Web" go back to those days. And part of "Grendel" was originally in a song we had called "The Tower". But there was a lot of weird stuff, too. There was one number we'd written called "The Haunting of Your House" which, when we used to play it live, would have hundreds of explosions all the way through, real Hammer House of Horror stuff. And there was one called "Hare and the Hunter", which was our go at a sort of *folk legend* . . !

'Actually,' he smiles, 'some of that stuff wasn't as bad as I'm probably making it sound. I mean, obviously the people in the band then were all quite Lord of the Rings; not so much out and out hippies, but very into that sort of literature and music. But when it worked, which it did now and again, some of that stuff was really quite good.'

The Doug Irving/Mick Pointer/Steve Rothery/Brian Jelliman line-up of Marillion staggered through 1980 on a round of small-time gigs, performing at a street carnival in Watford once, another time supporting a magician at St Albans Mental Hospital.

'That was a real last-minute gig,' Steve remembers. 'The band that had originally been booked pulled out suddenly so we said we'd do it, but when we got there we discovered that they had been expecting a *cabaret* band. To compromise we ended up playing a half-hour version of "Johnny B. Good", but it was quite a sad sight watching these poor mental patients fox-trotting to that . . . That was one of the weirdest early gigs we ever did.'

And then, as suddenly as the band had started to turn up gigs, everything came to a temporary halt when Doug Irving, to everyone's surprise, announced his imminent retirement from the band.

'Doug was the oldest member of the band and he seemed to expect things to happen for us too easily. He'd always said that if the band hadn't made it by the time he was twenty-five he'd quit. Then twenty-five came along and he did it – he quit! He said he wanted to settle down and forget all about rock and roll, which came as a bit of a blow, especially to me as Doug and I had always been good friends.

'But Mick, Brian and I decided that *we* didn't want to call it a day so we stuck another ad in one of the music papers. (The ad in question actually appeared in *Musicians Only* dated 6 December 1980 and began: Competent bassist/vocalist required for established progressive rock group with own material, in Aylesbury area.) And we got quite a few replies.'

Indeed. Including one tape from two characters called Diz Minnitt and Fish: one was a bass player, and one was a . . . .

'We got this tape through the post on one side of which there was Fish singing along to a Yes number, though I can't remember which one, followed by him singing along to a Genesis track – "More Fool Me", a song that Phil Collins, *not* Peter Gabriel, sang on the *Selling England by the Pound* album. Well, we sat there and listened to this tape and we all thought his voice was *brilliant*. He had the amazing ability to mimic Jon Anderson *perfectly* one moment, then Phil Collins, again *perfectly*, the next! We thought, this guy has got to be *it*!

'And there was a track on the tape of just him and the bass player doing something together. We thought the bass player was a bit iffy but the singer was brilliant, but we invited them both down for an audition.'

Considering now the significance of that first meeting between Fish and Marillion, how auspicious a moment does Steve Rothery recall that original introduction being?

'Oh, very! I remember thinking when I met him, "Oh, a big, loud, tall, arrogant Scotsman, just what I needed!" ' he laughs. 'We were living in another small cottage by then – just me, Privet and another bloke who helped with the band called Guy. This was in a little place just outside of Aylesbury called Aston Clinton. Fish and Diz turned up and had a meal with us and a few beers at the cottage. It was all a bit strange, really. And then the next night Privet took Fish down to the local pub, which was about two miles away, and they both got completely rat-arsed! It was in the middle of winter, towards the end of 1980, and on their way back from the pub they both stripped naked, they were so pissed, and fell in a ditch. It was a very typical Fish beginning, actually.'

Disguising their reservations about Diz Minnitt's bass playing in their eagerness to secure the services of this fascinating new singer, Mick Pointer and Steve offered the pair the gig and Marillion assumed its first incarnation of the classic five-piece format that was to prove so successful in the years to come.

'Diz was a very nice guy, I thought. He came from somewhere near Nottingham and he and Fish had obviously been hanging around together for some time. They had played together in a band called the Stone Dome Band, which was based in the Nottinghamshire area. And for a time they'd moved down to Cambridge together and tried to form a band there. That was because Fish's girlfriend at that time was going to Cambridge. When they found they couldn't get a band together there they'd both moved back to the Border area of Scotland where I think Fish had some friends and a place for them to stay.

'The thing is, Diz hadn't been playing for very long and his technique was a bit limited for the sort of music we wanted to play. But the truth is we got the impression that Diz was very much a part of the deal if we wanted Fish in the band. And so . . . .'

The new Pointer/Rothery/Jelliman/Fish/Minnitt Marillion line-up went into the rehearsal studios in January 1981 and began working at once on new material with which to baptise the new band. The first piece Fish ever put lyrics to was a number the band had already written called 'Close', which, after the singer's poetically crafted lyrics had been added, evolved into a version of 'The Web' they would keep and eventually record for their first album nearly two years later. And if Mick and Steve had been impressed by the versatility and pitch of Fish's lead vocals, now they were astounded at his talent for writing lyrics.

'I loved his lyrics straight away,' says Steve. 'I admit, I thought he could be a bit *too* wordy for its own sake, occasionally. But he was just a million times better than anyone we had ever come across before. Basically, we just thought he was amazing . . . .'

After lengthy rehearsals the new Marillion played their first live gig at a pub called the Red Lion, in nearby Bicester, on 14 March 1981. It was a nervous occasion for everybody, particularly Fish who was greatly aware of the high expectations everybody now held for his anticipated role as the new frontman.

'As it turned out I remember it as a pretty good gig,' says Steve. 'But there were only about thirty people there and at first

Fish was wetting himself he was so nervous. But when we got on stage he started to loosen up and do well. There were a couple of hecklers in the audience which he managed to put down straight away, despite his nerves. And he was just starting to experiment with the face make-up, too. Nothing very elaborate for that first gig, though. Just these two fish-eyes. And he was starting to introduce bits of mime that he wanted to incorporate into his performance. In lots of ways it was a good gig, and a bit of an eye-opener for us all. We were starting to believe in ourselves.'

For the next few months of 1981 Marillion continued to rehearse as often as time and money allowed, picking up gigs here and there around the country while still refining their act into a musical and visual showcase they would soon feel confident enough to unveil before the hard-nosed London club audiences.

'We did our first-ever support at the Marquee in London with that line-up,' Steve remembers. 'I can't properly remember who was headlining that night, it was either Girl or Spider, someone like that. Anyway, it was supposed to be a big gig for us back then, but that was also the night we all decided Brian Jelliman had to go.'

Never purely a case of 'musical differences', Jelliman's sacking from the group was prompted more by personal differences between the keyboard player and the rest of the people in Marillion. According to Steve Rothery, Brian Jelliman's biggest problem was that 'we all found him difficult to get on with. Though he was pretty limited as a keyboard player, in terms of pure technique, he was also very creative at times. But as a character nobody even really *liked* Brian to begin with, and as time went on things just got worse with him. The last straw was that everybody in the band was now totally committed to turning completely professional – everybody, that is, except Brian. He wanted to keep the band on more as a hobby. And that just wasn't good enough for us any more. So Brian got the chop!'

Some weeks prior to that first Marquee date, with the question of Jelliman's future involvement in the band already an issue on everybody's mind, Marillion had played a gig in Chadwell Heath, in Romford, supporting a local band called Chemical Alice.

'After we'd finished playing we all decided to stay and watch

32

the headlining band,' says Steve. 'They were a bit too Hawkwind for me to like too much, I think they even did a version of "Silver Machine", and it was all weird noises and long freak-outs. But, I remember, we were all quite impressed with the keyboard player.'

Fish, in particular, was keen to find out more about the keyboard player in Chemical Alice. Trying not to appear too interested, Fish got talking to various members of the Chemical Alice band later that night after the show. He came away with a telephone number that would put him in touch with the guitarist, and the keyboard player's name: Mark Kelly.

'For the next few days Fish kept ringing up this guitarist from Chemical Alice and trying to wheedle Mark's phone number out of him without making him suspicious as to why Fish wanted it in the first place.'

Finally, Fish managed to cajole the number out of the innocent guitarist and rang Mark, inviting him down to the next Marillion gig, which was at the Civic Centre in Chesham a couple of weeks later.

'I don't know if it puzzled Brian, you know, what the keyboard player in Chemical Alice was doing coming all the way to Chesham to see us play,' says Steve, 'But Mark came down anyway, this very young man with very long hair. He watched us play, said he liked it afterwards, and we got on really well with him, he seemed like a really nice guy, very easy to get along with. And that's when we decided we were definitely going to sack Brian. We asked Mark if he wanted to join the band first; he said yes straight away, and that was it for us as far as Brian goes.'

With Jelliman out and Mark Kelly in, Marillion saw in 1982 by continuing their pursuit of every gig they could net.

'Fish used to book most of our gigs back then. He was great at it, too. He'd scour the gig-guides listed in *Sounds* and *Melody Maker*, taking out all the telephone numbers and ringing these people up every day. Our phone bills were outrageous; I don't think there was a club, pub or college in Britain that he didn't try and get us gigs in!' Steve recalls.

'And it paid off. It really did; every time we went back and played somewhere we'd played before there would be more and more people coming to the shows, and our confidence was really building. The music we were writing was getting better as well; we were starting to write things that had a real *ring* to them – stuff like "Garden Party" dates back to that time.

'The only trouble now was that we were progressing so rapidly musically that whatever weak links we still had left in the band were really starting to show themselves. Diz was our most obvious weak link at that point: he wasn't nearly proficient enough technically and he didn't work at improving his style enough. Which is a shame because he *could* have been quite good – he plays in a local Aylesbury outfit these days and he's really not that bad at all.

'But at that time, Diz just wasn't really up to it any more. As a band, we were getting better and better all the time, and Diz was starting to hold us back. So Diz got the chop, too.'

Axing Diz Minnitt from the band was a tough decision for Fish to come to terms with at first – the two had been through a great many good (and bad) times together and, ironically, it was Diz who had first spotted the ad and persuaded Fish that they should both apply for the gig in Marillion. But it was a move he quickly learned to live with. Diz *was* holding back the music; he was breaking the unwritten rule of the road – he wasn't cutting it with the rest of the band any more. He had to go. Auditions to find a new bass were held immediately.

'A few people came down but nobody that particularly impressed us. And then this guy from another local Aylesbury band, the Metros, came down to see us about an audition. It was Pete Trewavas, of course. But none of us really knew him or anything. I think Fish might have spoken to him once or twice, it was probably Fish who invited him down, I can't remember. But anyway, Pete came down to this garage at the back of the house we were all living in, which we were using to audition bass players in.

'I think I was a bit sceptical about Pete at first, because the Metros were such a different band from Marillion. They were a sort of pop band who had gone through about half a dozen "image changes" in the search for success. The Metros were about cute make-up and long blond wigs, you know?' he laughs.

'I suppose I just didn't know why someone like that might want to play with us. But Pete came down, probably knowing that some of us would feel like that, didn't say much at first, just got down to the bass playing. We jammed around with "Garden Party" for a while. And I was stunned! I thought to myself, "Well, at least this bloke can play!" I mean, we'd never played with a real bass player like that before. His playing just brought

34

everything that much more alive. Everybody in the band just looked at each other and we all knew instantly that we had to have him in the band.'

It was early spring 1982 and Marillion finally had themselves a fixed line-up they were ready to tell the rest of the world about: Fish (vocals), Steve Rothery (guitar), Pete Trewavas (bass), Mark Kelly (keyboards) and Mick Pointer (drums); the same group in fact that was now just a year away, though they didn't know it then, from their first Top 10 album.

Gig followed gig in the time-honoured Marillion fashion. In fact, Fish had arranged a quite staggering twenty-five date tour of Scotland, which the band embarked on within days of Pete Trewavas joining them.

'I don't know quite how he did it but Fish had somehow managed to book about twenty-five or thirty gigs for us in Scotland. I didn't even know twenty-five places *existed* where we could play in Scotland, but somehow he'd arranged it all! Odd places, some of them – hotels, pubs, the odd club, the odd backroom dive. And it was really great. It was the first time we'd ever been truly on the road for whole weeks at a time.

'I think it must have been a strange indoctrination for Pete, though. Because like all groups, Marillion has its own twisted sense of humour, and sometimes outsiders must feel completely shut out by it. I mean, Privet, who by then was mixing our live sound for us, his piss-taking could be *merciless*, and so could Mick's, although Mick's sense of humour was always a bit *too* sour. But between those two and the rest of us I think Pete must have wondered what exactly he'd let himself in for when we first started out on that tour. Which was very unfair of us, looking back on it now, because Pete did try so hard himself to fit in with all of us.

'Pete still had fairly short hair – you know, it was like *all* the Metros had short hair – and we were all a long-haired scruffy bunch of bastards. But he still did his best to fit in: I remember he grew a beard for that first tour and tried to make himself look a bit more untidy than he really was!' Steve laughs.

'By about half-way through those Scottish dates, though, I think we calmed down a bit on all the leg-pulling. It just wasn't funny any more. And besides, Pete had proved himself to us, both off-stage and on, a hundred times over by then. And we all realised that the band was just so much better off for having Pete in it. We didn't want to lose him. Not when things were just starting to look like they were going to happen for us.' The secret Rothery smile creeps across his face.

Fish and Diz Minnitt officially joined Marillion on 2 January 1981. The transition the band underwent over the next twelve months, from small-time Aylesbury pub crawlers to their first headlining spots at the Marquee Club in London, was swift and all-encompassing.

By the start of 1982, when Pete Trewavas joined the band, Marillion were regularly being listed as the pundits' choice for major success in the coming year. And that was without any hype at all being mustered on their behalf; this surging popularity was won the hard way, the only way a band like Marillion knows how: by constantly working the clubs, pubs, outdoors, indoors, day, night, any time, any place Fish thought he could locate an audience, Marillion played it for all they were worth.

On stage, commencing with their live debut at the Red Lion in Bicester in March 1981, the band were undergoing a musical renaissance. As 1981 itself deepened in age, so did Marillion, writing a great many of the songs they were already beginning to suspect might one day make them famous: 'Garden Party', 'Margaret', 'Three Boats Down From the Candy', 'Grendel', 'Forgotten Sons', 'The Web', and 'He Knows You Know', were all performed for the first time by Marillion at some point in 1981.

And as the band's music took on startling new shapes, assuming the cloak of fiction cast off by early 70s giants like Yes, Pink Floyd, and Genesis, so too did Fish's increasingly theatrical performances. As early on as Marillion's third ever gig, at a local Aylesbury boozer called The Britannia, on 5 May, Fish had expanded his painted fish-eyes into a full-blown red, white and blue Union Jack mask. And by the time the band were offered their first gig at the biggest local Aylesbury venue, Friars, situated in a corner of the proverbial Market Square, Fish had purchased five costumes for £15 from the House of Hammer warehouse in London, and persuaded everybody to wear them on stage. Made up of what looked like old sack-cloth, hooded, with great flared sleeves and wide, gaping eyes painted on the backs, fronts and sides of them, the absurdity of their garb

matched the effortless eccentricity of their early performances . . .
Marillion coming on, some nights, like a bad-minded sect of
costumed monks hammering out their prayers from behind a
smoke-screen of guitars, keyboards and drums. What they were
after, of course, and what they succeeded so well in getting with
Fish's bizarre, shoe-string theatricalities, was *impact*.

Marillion's first Friars date – actually in the Aston Hall, which
is a smaller room adjoining the official Friars concert hall – won
them the lasting attention of a new gaggle of local followers. The
local weekly newspaper, the *Bucks Herald*, also gave the band the
first of a series of encouraging press notices. And Marillion won
a new and important friend: Dave Stopps, the promoter of all the
Friars shows in those days, and a man who would, in his own
small way, help shape their future over the coming year. For the
Aston Hall gig, Stopps paid the band the princely sum of £50,
less all PA and/or lighting costs, that is – a fairly standard fee for
Marillion in those early summer evenings of 1981. But with the
promise that if he liked what he saw, Stopps would book the
band back, this time for a proper go on the larger, more
prestigious Friars stage itself.

Impressed by what he discovered at the Aston Hall show, and
as good as his word, Dave Stopps booked Marillion back to open
the bill, beneath a now-obscure outfit called Legion, and
headliners, Spirit, at Aylesbury's beloved Friars on Saturday 1
August. In the brief weeks since he had last seen the band play
they had significantly increased their live following, and Stopps
was amazed to find that many of the local kids who turned up
that night did so on the strength of Marillion's name alone.

It was an auspicious occasion and the band went down a
storm, thundering bravely through their set, reaching for
unattainable heights even they were still too young to properly
comprehend. If they weren't careful people were going to start
reading all sorts of weird and wonderful things into Marillion:
every time they played more and more people wanted to peek
between the lines Fish and the boys handed them. 'Factor X' is
what Fish liked to call it at the time – the ability to make the fans
want to see *more*. And the more they looked into what Marillion
had to offer, the more they were trapped by what they saw.

After that second Friars date, the band continued with their
ever-widening circle of regular pub and club gigs around the
country. On 14 September they supported Budgie at the St

37

Albans Civic Centre, and in October the band got invited by Dave Stopps back to Friars, this time billed as special guests of the headliner, John Martyn.

For the first nine months of 1981 Marillion had planned and plotted their rise to local popularity without the aid of a manager, a regular booking agent, or a professional publicity agent. They were getting by on the sheer attraction of a muscle-flexing array of live performances and the off-stage confrontational tactics of Fish in his day-to-day role as Marillion's self-appointed spokesman: gig-getter, singer, PR, and costumier, in every respect Fish was the man to contact in all matters related to the well-being and furtherment of Marillion. From his cramped tiny headquarters in 13 Winchester House, Bishop's Walk, Aylesbury, where various band members and affiliates lived throughout the latter half of 1981, working by day as a clerk at the local DHSS office, Fish spent every available moment he wasn't actually on stage running up impossible bills on the telephone, lambasting everyone he spoke to in his urgent hunt for more Marillion gigs, more Marillion publicity, above all more Marillion *exposure*.

However, by September 1981, with all the basic groundwork under way, Fish understood that what the band badly needed now was media exposure on a national scale. First he put together a promotional package, including black-and-white pix of the group, a self-penned recent history, some press cuttings (mostly from the good and faithful *Bucks Herald*), and, in some cases, a cassette of demos of some of the new songs. This little package he would mail out to local newspapers and radio stations, and then, eventually, as confidence in the band grew, to the major record companies and radio stations down in London.

Like so many ambitious but little-known bands before them, Marillion experienced at first nothing but rejection from the various sources they touched upon for approval in the London-based music business. By September 1981 Fish had received letters of rejection from both Radio One, the UK's only national radio pop station, and Capital Radio, London's biggest commercial pop station. He had tried to obtain a session for Marillion on both stations' Rock Shows, but without success. And by November the band had a whole stack of further thanks-but-no-thanks correspondence filed from major record companies like CBS, WEA, RSO, Arista, Island, Bronze, and A&M. As always, the world seemed able to move backwards as well as forwards.

It was also in September 1981 that Marillion struck up their first lasting friendship with a genuine London contact. His name was Keith Goodwin, he ran his own independent publicity company called Kaygee Publicity, had run the press office of both Black Sabbath and Yes during the most popular and innovative phases of their respective careers, and one Friday night in the late summer of 1981 he happened to be drinking in a pub in Aylesbury, where a thoroughly popular local band – Marillion – also happened to be playing.

'I didn't stay very long and, to be perfectly honest, I didn't even really pay much attention to what the band were up to. I'd had bands breathing down my neck all day and I was out for a quiet drink, you know?' he says now.

'Anyway, somebody must have told Fish that I'd been there and, never being one to miss an opportunity in those days, the next thing I know he's got hold of my office address in London and I'm sitting there nice and quiet one afternoon when this huge, tall Scotsman comes bounding through the door. "You're Keith Goodwin!" he cried. "You get press for bands – well I want you to get some press for us, Marillion! My name's Fish, I'm the singer." He just stood there and basically *told* me that I was going to get press for the band, you know, whether I liked it or not!' Keith laughs at the memory.

'He gave me a tape to play of some of their songs and I asked him to leave it with me and said I would listen to it in private and then let him know what I thought, but he wasn't having *any* of that: "No, no, no! You've got to play it *now*!" he told me. What could I do? I wasn't about to argue with a strange six-foot-five Scotsman, was I? So I played the tape. And, thank God, I was really impressed! I mean, really very impressed! It didn't sound strikingly original, not to me, not then, but of course I'd lived in the music business all through the late 60s and early 70s and so none of this stuff was unfamiliar to me. But the thing I really liked was the fact that there was really nobody left around who was still playing music like this, not in 1981. I suppose you'd have to call it Progressive Rock, and obviously very influenced by all those bands like Yes and Pink Floyd and Genesis, but the thing was this was all emanating from a *new* band, and I hadn't heard a new band sound like *that* for nearly ten years . . . I admit, I was quite bowled over. I thought, I'll have to look into this tall Scotsman a bit more carefully. So I asked him to sit down and we started talking . . .'

And didn't stop until he and Fish had struck up an equitable deal between Kaygee Publicity and Marillion, and a solid bond of friendship between Keith Goodwin and Fish that survives to this day. Realising that, as yet, Marillion hadn't earned more than £100 for a single gig, Keith offered Fish a cut-rate cover charge for his services of £35 a week, approximately a third of the going rate for a good independent PR in London in those days. From this point onwards, Marillion's name and photograph started appearing regularly in the news pages and nationwide gig guides of every important and influential music paper in Britain.

It was also Keith Goodwin, via his numerous long-standing connections with the management and clientele of the vitally prestigious Marquee Club in Soho, who got the band their first support slot at the Marquee in October 1981.

Dressed in their by now customary brown sack-cloth smocks – the ones with the hoods and the flared sleeves and the big staring eyes painted across their backs – Marillion's first Marquee performance stood in stark contrast to the on-stage apparel of the headlining act that night, Girl, a band, now defunct, who were deeply into the cheap flash and satin frills of the glam-rock aesthetic. If anything, the obvious differences between the support and the headliners only drew more attention to the left-field muse Marillion were now bent on taking.

It was also the first Marillion gig ever to be reviewed by a national weekly UK rock magazine: in the 21 November 1981 issue of *Sounds*, under the distinctly tongue-in-cheek headline banner – 'A return to kaftans and loonpants' – Xavier Russell, after making suitably Xavier-like hearty and encouraging noises, summed up his first review thus: 'The sooner Marillion get signed the better. Now if someone could tell me what the big eye on the back of those potato sacks means, I'll join the sect.' Right on, Mr X.

As 1981 dwindled to its conclusion, with the live work beginning to gobble up most of their free time and some press attention at last starting to pick up, Fish quit his day-job at the DHSS in Aylesbury and redoubled his efforts to keep Marillion working. It was around this time that Fish first got involved with some of the various high-profile booking agencies that exist in London. He wanted to put together a tour to capitalise on their small successes at Friars, at the Marquee, and now in the legit music press.

However, Fish never felt that any of the agents he worked

with at that time could do the job half as well as he had been doing it on his own; they weren't earning their ten per cent, he said, and Marillion flitted from agency to agency throughout the tail end of 1981 and much of 1982. Terry King Associates, The Agency, P.M.I., and Nems Artistes all had Marillion on their books for varying lengths of time throughout this period. None lasted long.

Little by little, though, Fish and Marillion pieced together a twenty-date tour of England, christened the 'Saliva Tears Tour', that opened at the Red Lion in Gravesend on 1 November, and culminated on Christmas Eve at the Starting Gate in Milton Keynes, a popular Marillion stronghold in those early days, taking in little nightspots like The Electric Stadium in Chadwell Heath, which burned down three days after they appeared there; the 101 Club in South London, who paid them nothing for their support spot and even had the gall to demand money from the band towards the cost of hiring the PA – Fish's big, bad-mouthed Scotsman routine came in handy on that one; and strangely named hide-outs like the Badger Bars in Bournemouth, and the Caribbean Club in Oxford.

And all the while Marillion were adding to their stature as a live band, the word-of-mouth following they had been attracting all year was multiplying from hundreds into thousands. With Keith Goodwin now assuring them that major features and interviews in all the weekly music papers, and a major record deal, were all in the offing for Marillion in 1982, all looked well in the band's world. However . . . .

The first letter the band received in January 1982 was a dry-eyed 'Dear John . . .' from Virgin Records. Thanks *but*. On Sunday, 3 January, Marillion opened their most important year yet with their second gig at the Marquee, again as the support act, this time to a band called Spider, a straightforward no-nonsense denim-and-badges outfit that performed a straight-laced heavy-rock boogie; very Slade in places, very Status Quo in others. Hardly the most appropriate billing, everyone agreed, but beggars can't be choosers, not always, and Marillion were still the beggars on the all-important London club circuit in January 1982.

From a professional point of view, the gig was a success for Marillion inasmuch as they thrilled Spider's usually bawdy crowd enough for the headliners to accuse Marillion of somehow 'sabotaging' the gig. And Jack Barry, the Marquee's ebullient manager, was impressed enough to offer the band their own headlining show at the club, which he hurriedly scheduled for the 25th of the month. It was their first top-of-the-bill booking at London's most famous little sweat-box, over 400 new and not-so-new fans there to see it, and, according to the *Bucks Herald* at the time, they had a guest-list crowded with the names of A&R men from the offices of record companies like Chrysalis, Polydor, and Phonogram.

Suddenly, in February 1982, as the band continued on their never-ending round of club appearances around the country, the UK rock press was alight with rave reviews of this startling new enigma called Marillion: *Melody Maker*, *Sounds* (again), *NME*, *Kerrang!*, even dismally contrived glossy poppets like *Record Mirror*, all had terribly *interesting* things to say about the live Marillion in February 1982.

On 20 February Dave Stopps again offered the second-on-the-bill slot at Friars to Marillion, this time supporting the only other local Aylesbury act more popular than Marillion themselves in those days – John Otway and Wild Willy Barrett! And though nobody could have known it then, this was to be the last time the band would play second-fiddle on the bill to anybody on that cramped Friars stage.

Then, on the 26th, DJ Tommy Vance, on his Friday night Rock Show on Radio One, broadcast the band's first in-house BBC session, the low growl of 'The Web', 'Forgotten Sons', and 'Three Boats Down From the Candy' trilling over the nation's late-nite airways.

The same week in February they also picked up their first two-page spread in *Sounds* with a glowing feature penned by the dab hand of Philip Bell. Interestingly, the piece is accompanied by a pic of Fish sporting the full transcendental face-paint regalia, dark and heavy around the eyes, edged by a strong thick beard on the verge of bushy, leering wide-mouthed into the face of the camera, already hinting at every future song and dance he and the rest of the band had in mind to write one day. Indeed, Philip Bell's article was the first to speak in terms of 'greatness' and 'stardom' in relation to Marillion. Though, of course, it would not be the last. *Melody Maker* also ran their first feature on the band in February 1982, and by March so too did *Record Mirror* and that strong right arm of the heavy-rock lore, *Kerrang!*

February 1982 also saw the launch of issue one of Marillion's official fan club news-sheet, *The Web*. These days, *The Web* is run by the ubiquitous Angie – no surname has she ever given, just Angie, from PO Box 533, Richmond, Surrey. But the original issue of *The Web* that got mailed out to enquiring fans or sold at gigs was put together, at the urging of the band, by another local Aylesbury character called Tim – again, Tim never supplied a surname and not even the band can now remember ever having known it!

The band had wanted Stef, Mick Pointer's girlfriend, to put together a news-sheet, with all the relevant info on current and past Marillion affairs, since the end of 1981. But Stef could never find the time at first to get down to all the fiddly details attached to getting a halfway decent fact-sheet for the fans organised. In the event, she turned the task over to . . . Tim.

Issue one of *The Web* comprised three hand-written and drawn sheets of photocopy stapled together on varying sized sheets of xeroxed paper. It contained the lyrics to 'Garden Party'; a brief potted history of the band with a to-be-continued appendange; and, most importantly, 'The Good Gig Guide', which gave a list of the band's current date-sheet through February and March: the Canterbury College of Technology, the Starlight, West Hampstead, the 'Buy More Beer' night at the Wheatsheaf, Dunstable, Bedford College . . . all those small-time brief encounters Marillion had been thriving on over the months were meticulously listed.

In March there was a second issue of *The Web*, again signed just Tim, this time featuring the lyrics to 'Forgotten Sons', more from 'The Good Gig Guide', and more chronological profiles of the band. And this time it stretched to four sheets of paper. By the time Marillion returned from their protracted stint on the road in Scotland, issue three of *The Web* was already on the streets – now stretched to five pages and jointly signed at the end by Tim *and* Stef. Tim's days as the name at the bottom of the last page of *The Web* were definitely numbered . . . Stef was taking the reins from here on in.

One of the very last gigs Diz did with Marillion was at the Marquee on 7 March 1982, where the band headlined to their first sold-out London audience. And then – the chop! – as Steve Rothery says.

With Pete Trewavas fully blooded by the band's Scottish tour, Marillion returned to their Aylesbury homes in May 1982 faced with the golden promise of their first headlining date at Dave

43

Stopps' ever-accommodating Friars hall, on 19 June, and the mouth-watering prospect of two consecutive guaranteed sell-out nights at the Marquee on 1 and 2 July.

'We came back from Scotland and we had a couple of what we considered at the time to be these really amazing dates coming up – at Friars and in London – and we decided that the thing we desperately needed now was good management,' says Steve Rothery. 'We had been on at Dave Stopps to have a go at managing us for ages,' he recalls, 'but up until then he'd always refused.

'So we went around town and spoke to a few people – I remember Fish even asked Keith Goodwin if he would manage us, but Keith flat-out refused. He was quite honest about it, he just didn't think he would be as good a manager for the band as he was our PR, simple as that, really. We carried on looking, sort of half-heartedly, and all the time Fish kept on at Dave Stopps, trying to talk him into having a crack at managing us. And eventually, Fish being Fish, he succeeded, and for about six weeks in the summer of 1982 Dave Stopps became our first manager.'

With no previous experience of managing a speedily up-and-coming band, Dave Stopps nevertheless ploughed gamely into the task Marillion had set him. What he had going for him, and what attracted the band to him, was his obvious talent to succeed at whatever he was doing.

'He had all the potential to be a great manager,' says Steve. 'He proved that later on when he became Howard Jones' manager. But at that time in our career things were starting to happen really fast for us, we needed somebody who could get on and sort things out for us *now*. And in that department, Dave's lack of experience was what held him back.

'We had record companies seriously interested in us for the first time, and we had a good momentum going in the press, and above all else we wanted a manager who could tie that all together *right away*. Otherwise we all felt we might permanently miss out on what might be our only opportunity of getting anywhere . . . And so, very regretfully, because Dave had always been a very good friend to the band, we parted company with him after about a month and a half.'

Before Dave Stopps' temporary stint as Marillion manager was terminated, he had made one important contact the band would find useful over the coming months: Tony Stratton-Smith, long-time boss of Charisma Records and, as chance would have it, the very person who had steered Genesis' career through the vitally important years when they were making the jump from their cultish and eclectic origins into the hugely famous class international act they are today.

'Dave got Strat down to see us one night at the Marquee, in about May 1982, and he seemed to really like us. But I remember that the funniest thing about Tony Stratton-Smith coming down to see us was Dave Stopps asking to borrow a fiver from John Arnison, so Dave could buy Strat a drink! I mean, of all the people to ask! And I think that was probably the first time John had ever seen us play, too.'

In May 1982, John Arnison had recently set up his own management company, taking care of business for John Cooper-Clarke, Pauline Murray, and a little-known Liverpool-based rock band called Rage. For four years before that he had worked for a promotions company in London called Quarry, caretaker managing acts like Status Quo and Rory Gallagher, with whom, in conjunction with Rory's brother/manager, Donnell Gallagher, Arnison was also still involved on a consultancy basis in May 1982.

Like so many locally-placed music business entrepreneurs, John Arnison would often work late in his Soho Square office and more often than not conclude the day's work by popping into the Marquee for a drink before heading home.

That night at the Marquee, when Dave Stopps had asked to borrow £5, *was* John Arnison's first glimpse of Marillion.

'It was the first time, in fact, that I'd bothered to watch a band do their set the whole of the way through in months,' he was to say later. 'And I was captivated! I'd never even heard of them but the minute they came off the stage I ran over and asked Keith Goodwin if they had a manager. He said, "Yes, Dave Stopps . . ." I thought, "Oh no! I'm too late . . ." '

'From that night on we knew that John was interested in managing us,' Steve Rothery takes up the story. 'So when we parted company with Dave Stopps we basically got in touch with two people – one of whom was John Arnison.'

The other likely candidate Marillion had short-listed was Peter Mensch. Mensch had learned his craft in the latter half of the 1970s working for Leiber Krebbs, a big and influential American management organisation, where he put in time as a backroom boy aiding the causes of acts like Ted Nugent and Aerosmith, before getting up-graded to manager and looking after AC/DC.

By May 1982, however, Peter Mensch had struck out on his own, with much the same intentions as John Arnison, and was already managing a young and infinitely promising UK outfit called Def Leppard, who would one day, under his managerial wing, go on to sell over six million copies of their album *Pyromania*.

'After Dave Stopps was gone we decided it was down to either John Arnison or Peter Mensch to manage us,' says Steve. 'So we made an appointment to see them both. Peter Mensch took us to his house in London – very posh, gold albums all over the walls, you know. So we sat down and talked to him and he had a lot of ideas. But the thing that really struck us, I think, is that he was far more interested in getting hold of Fish's name on a management contract than he was in getting the rest of us to sign.

'Then we went to see John, who we met in a pub in Earls Court, around the corner from a small flat Fish was spending most of his time in. He came across as a bit of a local rogue but ultimately somebody you could trust. John impressed us after Peter Mensch because he was so down-to-earth by comparison.

'He was interested in making the *band* happen and, like us, he saw it all in terms of albums; we definitely didn't want to be a band that relied on a constant stream of hit singles, and he said he totally agreed with us on all that. And then, one by one, we all sort of "went to the toilet", and we all huddled together in a bog in this pub in Earls Court and asked each other what we thought of him.'

Steve Rothery and Marillion thought enough of John Arnison to offer him the job.

'We didn't offer him the job on the spot,' Steve recalls. 'We said we would phone him in two or three days. Then we went back to Aylesbury, thought about it some more, and decided John was our man. Fish phoned him up early one morning and said, "Congratulations, John! You're the new manager of Marillion!" And then he paused and said, "That is, if you still want to be . . .?" John just laughed down the phone at him and said yes immediately.'

John Arnison suggested to the band that they hand over all authority to act on their behalf to him for a three-month period. If at the end of that time either party was not happy with the present state of affairs they could honourably withdraw, no strings attached. It was an unwritten, amicable arrangement that would remain unchanged for the next two years.

John Arnison's highest priority as the new Marillion manager was to strike a deal – a good, strong deal, and fast – for the band with a major record company. Everything in June 1982 hinged on making that particular dream come true.

'We already knew that Tony Stratton-Smith desperately wanted to sign us,' says Steve. 'And John's first job was to set up negotiations with Charisma, and also EMI, who had invited us to demo for them in their studios in London. The proposed Charisma deal fell apart though when the company's business manager offered us a ridiculously small deal – it was, like, for two singles and £5,000 with an option on the rest of our lives, that sort of thing,' he sneers.

'And Strat was *so* eager to sign us, apparently he'd told this guy to sign us at any cost! But Strat's business manager came to see us, decided he didn't like what he saw and offered us the crummiest deal he could think of. We were really down about the whole thing and told Charisma to forget it.'

The American independent giants, Geffen Records, also expressed a keen interest, at this time, in sitting down and talking preliminary terms with the band.

'That fell apart when we realised they were talking about cutting all the songs down to three minutes long! We dispensed with the idea of signing to them *very* quickly when we found that out,' Steve grimaces.

Though the band had been invited to make an in-house demo at EMI's Manchester Square headquarters in London, the man who had extended that invitation, Ashley Goodall, had subsequently left the company, and his job in the A & R department had taken over by a new face, Hugh Stanley Clarke. John Arnison was convinced that the only proper place for Hugh to judge the frenetic potential of the band was not walled-in in a strange studio with engineers they did not know and a clock screaming down at them from the wall, but at one of their gigs, preferably one hot and smoky night at the Marquee. And so that's what he did, dragging Hugh Stanley Clarke down to the Marquee on just such a night in July 1982.

'When he saw what was going on down there, Hugh told John he definitely wanted to sign us,' says Steve. 'He saw that the Marillion audience wasn't a load of old 70s rock fans there for a nostalgic night out. It was young kids coming to see us. I mean,

47

obviously our music is rooted in the 70s, that's when we were all teenagers, but this is an *80s* band, using 80s technology and with all the knowledge of the 80s. And our audience's average age was from between about fifteen and eighteen. Seeing us at the Marquee really swung it for us with Hugh, I think.'

John Arnison decided that the clincher would be to fly all the various heads of department at EMI up to a club in Glasgow called The Mayflower where Marillion had a gig scheduled early in August.

'There were only about 200 people there for that gig,' Steve recalls. 'But we went out and played as though we had a couple of thousand there. We had to, it was our only chance. And I think Hugh and all the others who had come up were really knocked out! The Scottish fans have always been really wild anyway and that night they really went over the top.

'At that time though, John was still doing his managerial bit and he made it known to EMI that he'd kept all our options open with Charisma and Tony Stratton-Smith. Strat had sacked his business manager over messing the deal up with us and he was still very interested in getting us on Charisma. So suddenly, we were bargaining, or at least John was, from a position of strength.'

The real clincher came on that famous Sunday afternoon of 29 August, on-stage at the Reading Festival, where Marillion, making their first-ever appearance at one of Britain and Europe's most prestigious outdoor summer festivals, wooed a crowd of 35,000 people into their arms then rocked them off their feet. It was a dazzling performance, as most of the reviews that followed joyously pointed out, and from the pulpit of the stage, Fish announced to the audience that Marillion had that day agreed terms on a major, world-wide record deal with EMI Records! The cheer that rose from the crowd, sweet as it was, was deafening.

It was the 22nd National Jazz, Blues and Rock Festival, Reading 1982. Marillion were sixth on the bill below the Jackie Lynton Band, Bernie Marsden's SOS, Wilko Johnson, Dave Edmunds, and the headliners, the Michael Schenker Group. They arrived on stage early in the afternoon and left it forty-five minutes later having set the pace for every subsequent act.

'Reading really sort of set the seal on our fate,' says Steve. 'Fish announced that we had done a deal with EMI and we went down a storm. And the publicity we got from that gig was unbelievable. I mean, you just don't get noticed like that when you're only sixth on the bill, not usually. That gig definitely put our career up a couple more notches. Actually, although Reading was very much the Big One for us, I probably have more memories about the gig we played the day *before* Reading.'

The afternoon before the Reading Festival concert Marillion opened the show at another outdoor summer rock festival: Theakston's Music Festival, in Nostel Priory, on a bill that also featured Wang Chung, the Blues Band, and Lindisfarne, with Jethro Tull headlining.

'We went on stage at Theakston's, with Ian Anderson, the singer in Jethro Tull, standing at the side of the stage watching us from the wings, which was enough to make most of us completely nervous. But what made it worse was that one of Mark's keyboards refused to work, he couldn't get a sound out of it! And then it turned out that one of our roadies had miked-up the wrong guitar cabinet, so there I was merrily playing away and no-one could hear a thing from me either – absolute *silence* from the stage! Our first gig to a crowd of, like, 15 or 20,000 people, Ian Anderson, one of our old heroes, standing there watching us from the side of the stage, and us making a complete disaster of it!' Steve laughs.

'After that, Reading wasn't exactly easy, but a lot less nerve-racking. And as far as we were concerned, with the EMI deal now firmed-up, and a great Reading behind us, we were definitely on our way up in everything we did from now on.'

Up and over. For Steve Rothery and Marillion 1982 had only just begun.

3

Manchester Square Heroes

It was Wednesday morning, 8 September 1982: the day the deal finally went down for Marillion. Everybody looked like fat Cheshire cats with cream on their whiskers, all round smiles and stupid jokes as they climbed one by one into the back of Mick Pointer's big red Vauxhall Estate car, stretching out in the shared good humour of the day as they got ready to make the drive from Aylesbury down to London.

The band had a noon appointment at EMI Records, in Manchester Square, W1. Or, more precisely, in the offices of Terry Slater, then director-in-chief of EMI's A & R department, where he and Hugh Stanley Clarke and John Arnison were waiting for Steve, Mick, Fish, Mark and Pete to arrive and set their signatures down on the five-album, worldwide recording contract that EMI were now prepared to offer them.

Over at the offices of Charisma Records, elsewhere in the West End sprawl, Tony Stratton-Smith had been tearing out his hair since Fish had announced from the stage of the Reading Festival that Marillion had agreed final terms with EMI. Within days Strat had called John Arnison's office to tell him Charisma, under Strat's personal authority, were ready to make the band an offer that, financially, would match anything EMI had got to offer them.

But each time John related Tony Stratton-Smith's latest offer to the band they turned it down.

'It wasn't that we didn't like Strat, or trust him, because we did, we had a hell of a lot of respect for him and what he'd done in the past,' says Mark Kelly. 'But as far as the rest of Charisma was concerned, they were so involved in making everything so

50

political amongst themselves that we could never get any straight talking out of them. Whereas EMI and Hugh Stanley Clarke had been straight with us right down the line.'

'As far as we were all concerned in Marillion, EMI had come up with a decent offer and some decent proposals, whereas Charisma had done nothing but play stupid games with us,' says Fish. 'It wasn't anything we had against Strat personally, just his idiot business manager. So for us the decision was simple – we were signing with EMI.'

In the event, Tony Stratton-Smith didn't walk away from Marillion empty-handed. As a conciliatory gesture to Strat's obviously sincere belief in the band, Marillion signed the publishing of their original material over to Charisma's own in-house publishing company, a bond which also served to strengthen the already tenuous links which existed between new-style Marillion and old-style Genesis.

At any rate, the gap between success and failure was closing.

Total advances on the deal with EMI, assuming of course that EMI were to pick up each album-by-album option at their disposal under the agreed terms of the contract, were worth in the region of £500,000.

'Add up all the money that EMI might give us in advances over a possible five-album period, and then write that figure down on a piece of paper and it begins to look like a lot of money,' John Arnison points out in his characteristically pragmatic fashion. 'But in reality all it meant the day that we signed the deal was that I'd got enough money out of EMI to buy all the equipment and things the band needed to see them through three or four big tours the first year, and some money to put the boys in the band on some reasonable wages. Until they signed to EMI the band had never earned enough money from the gigs to pay anybody a wage before.'

'As far as I was concerned that meant we were *big*, you know? Actually having someone prepared to pay us *wages* for being in the band! I thought we *must* have made it for that to happen,' Mark Kelly laughs. 'Suddenly, we were all getting £200 a month; Dave Stopps was paid back some money we still owed him; Fish was able to pay back all the money the Bank of Scotland had loaned him – which, by now, was thousands of pounds! And we had enough money to go out and buy some new equipment. It was like . . . At last, at last, at last!'

51

A little after midday, Marillion presented themselves in EMI's lobby and were quickly escorted up to the second floor, where Terry Slater's office was located.

The actual signing was, as Fish describes it, 'an extraordinary little event. We got ushered into Terry Slater's office, totally big-time, signed all these bits of paper, had our picture taken with Terry, Hugh and John, all sort of pen to paper stuff, then everybody shook hands and we had a glass of champagne. It was all terribly civilised up to that point. But then we started celebrating, started drinking, and we all ended up getting pissed out of our heads!'

Marillion's little signing party carried right on through the languorous EMI lunchtime. Apart from Terry Slater, Hugh Stanley Clarke and John Arnison, the band were also joined by a gaggle of pretty secretaries from the various departments within shouting distance of the second-floor A&R offices, and by Nick Beggs, the bass player in another, as yet under-wraps, EMI signing in 1982 called Kajagoogoo, as well as at least one member of the legitimate rock press, Geoff Banks, who in those days was still a regular contributor to *Kerrang!*, there to lend his bellicose presence to the proceedings and to extract a story of the band's much-touted 'mega-deal', as the rest of the press were already calling it, replete with shots of Marillion signing their various bits of paper all wearing the *Kerrang!* T-shirts Geoff had provided for the occasion . . .

'I remember we all sat down on this couch together, drinking EMI beer and eating EMI sandwiches, and all wearing these *Kerrang!* T-shirts Geoff Banks had given us,' smiles Pete Trewavas. 'We sat there feeling really proud of ourselves, having just done the deal and all that, and we thought we were well in with *Kerrang!*, asking us to wear their T-shirts. Although, looking back now, I think it was probably just Geoff Banks' excuse to get invited to the party,' Pete laughs. 'I mean, Geoff *does* like a drink . . . And so he stayed and had a few with us. And the more and more drunk we were getting, well, Geoff was going at twice our speed by that time anyway and he started trying to rip down the blinds from the office windows and tearing down posters they had stuck up on the walls . . . We had to give him another drink just to calm him down!'

'Banks was out of his mind all right, but so was I, so was *everybody* that afternoon,' sighs Fish. 'I think maybe I'd even started drinking *before* we got to EMI. Either way, I was totally pissed after the first two hours of all this, by which time Hugh was trying to round everybody up for a bloody band meeting he'd suddenly decided we ought to be having!

'As soon as I heard that I got up and went to the toilet and threw up, the whole lot, everything! I was all right after that, though . . . At least I could see straight again . . .'

Draped inelegantly across every available chair in Hugh's office, the band sat, bored and drunk, at most only half-listening to Hugh Stanley Clarke prattle on about all the good things EMI were going to do for Marillion. 'It was like The World According to Hugh!' says Pete Trewavas. 'Terrifically boring!'

Never a man to be over-impressed by anything short of a verified Act of God, Steve Rothery found this latest development in his day all rather too taxing and chose just that moment in Hugh's long-winded and needlessly officious opening preamble to fall fast asleep!

'And not just *quietly* asleep,' Fish laughs. 'Steve was loud, snoring, mouth-wide-open *asleep*! Hugh was *so* pissed off, you could see it in his face . . . Served him right for being such a wally and trying to get five very drunken young men to sit down and talk sensibly about the rest of their lives!

'One thing that really got my goat, though,' says Fish, 'was that Hugh Stanley Clarke had this big box full of tapes and stuff that unknown, unsigned bands had sent in for him to listen to. When Mick asked him if any of them were any good – I think we wanted some music on in the background – Hugh turned around and said, "I don't know, I've only played a few of them. Most of them are so boring, and we get sent so many." I tell you, I sat there thinking back to the days not so long before when I'd bought all the stamps and spent hours putting packages together to send off to people like Hugh. And then to sit there, the day we finally got signed, looking at this big box of useless, forgotten tapes lying there, it really pissed me off!'

The upshot of the meeting was that Hugh wanted the band to go straight into a recording studio and start work on what would be their first release under the new deal with EMI: a single, to be promoted by a British tour, with massive fly-posting around the country of some brand new Marillion posters, a bit of muscle from the marketing division in the form of some spot ads in the trade and the consumer magazines, and plenty of promised front from all corners of the promotions department. After that, said Hugh, back into the recording studio by December and the band could begin work on their first album, having consolidated their hardcore following of fans, now estimated to be about 25,000, thus paving the way for the release in the New Year of that all-important debut LP.

It was a neat plan, and one Marillion put to work immediately. On 25 September the band had a date booked at the Marquee; a Saturday night and their first appearance live since putting their names under contract with EMI. Over a thousand fans were expected to turn up. Until then, the band were locked away in a small studio in a small town called Battle, near Hastings.

They travelled down in the green Coma van they had christened Margaret, the same battered old jalopy that had carried them everywhere over the last eighteen months, from the Red Lion in Bicester to the fields of Reading Festival. Waiting for them when they arrived was producer David Hitchcock.

In the early 1970s Hitchcock had made a name for himself as the producer of several key early recordings by groups like Caravan and Genesis, to name just two. But in more recent years his name had all but disappeared from the credits of any, save the most obscure, contemporary releases.

'We knew David's work from "Foxtrot", of course,' says Fish. 'And some of the Caravan stuff he'd worked on. But the point wasn't to get David in to help us sound even more like Genesis, as some of the music press so *playfully* suggested at the time,' he growls. 'We were given a choice of producers who were available to us immediately and his name stuck out because we knew it from all those years ago, but we also felt – and here we were playing a bit of a head-game – that the last thing David would want now was to make us sound like early Genesis. We thought he would be as determined as us to make sure that didn't happen. Only, as it turned out, we were wrong, and we got a terrible sound on "Market Square Heroes"! Awful!'

The band had already decided that their first single would consist of tracks not intended for inclusion on the debut album that would follow: the A side would be 'Market Square Heroes', a more recent composition, with 'Three Boats Down From the Candy' moulded as the B side, plus a seventeen minutes, forty seconds-long recorded version of 'Grendel', to be included on the twelve-inch edition of the record.

'I thought David Hitchcock was an extremely nice bloke,' says Steve Rothery. 'But he had the odds against him from the word go, really. The studio – Park Gate – was fairly decrepit, Mick's drumming, which at the best of times needed as much coaching as you could give it, was pretty naff, and worst of all, David seemed to get completely hung up on "Grendel".'

Pete Trewavas takes up the story: 'In his infinite wisdom, David Hitchcock decided we should work on "Grendel" first. Whether that was because it was the longest and most difficult number we had planned to record, or whether it was because he really wanted to get his teeth into it, I don't know. But it turned out to be a big mistake.'

Marillion had been allowed two weeks to record and finish mixing three tracks for a single, but 'Grendel' alone was as long as one side of a more conventional rock band's album. And the kid gloves Hitchcock insisted on wearing throughout those prolonged and painful 'Grendel' sessions meant that by the end of their 'fortnight' in Hastings – which by now EMI had, at the band's urgent request, extended to three weeks – everybody, the band, the producer, and engineer, were all working around the clock in an attempt to get the recordings finished in time for EMI's projected October release schedule.

Before the budget finally ran out, though, Marillion took time off from recording their first single to keep that Saturday night date they'd promised themselves at the Marquee, where on 25 September they headlined to an estimated weekend crowd of over 800 people (this, of course, was in the days before the introduction of more strict GLC fire regulations which, by 1983, would limit the club's legal capacity to a mere 450). It was a triumphant night in many ways: the hardcore fans congratulated themselves as much as the band on the good fortune of finally landing a long-term deal with a record company; brand new copies of *The Web* were on sale and being snapped up in the main bar by the entrance to the club; while on stage Marillion ripped into the spoils of their latest victory. The band, pouring the sweat on, dived into their set with an intense satisfaction, pulling the songs from out of back-pockets, combing the hair of the night, pleased to be back amongst their tribe, Fish pleased to be able to announce the imminent release of the first Marillion single.

The next day the band returned to Park Gate studios where they worked non-stop through the next seven days with David Hitchcock. At the end of that they had most of the job completed; only the final mix and some vocal treatments Fish had still to tag on to 'Grendel' remained to be done.

'I remember the last few hours of those sessions in Battle really well,' says Mark Kelly. 'Our last day there was a Sunday, they were kicking us out of the studio because they had someone else booked in for the Monday morning, and so we had to work right through the night. And the thing is I was getting *married* the next morning! So not only is everybody working like crazy to get things finished, but I'm panicking about getting to the wedding and trying to get all my bits and pieces done so that I can catch the milk-train up to Aylesbury.

'It got to, like, three a.m. and I was still nowhere near finished, and by then we were all at the stage where our heads were exploding inside from complete lack of sleep for days on end. We were like walking zombies wandering around in the middle of the night somehow trying to get this bloody music recorded. Eventually, I got finished by about five a.m. I just walked out of the studio and went straight down to the railway station and bought a ticket to Aylesbury.'

A bit bleary-eyed, still walking around with the occasional 'explosion' going off inside his head, Mark Kelly made it to the wedding on time, marrying his girlfriend Susie at the Aylesbury Register Office on 4 October 1982.

In the meantime, David Hitchcock had retreated into Wessex Sound Studios, in Highbury, North London, to complete his unfinished work on the final mix.

With the single now just days away from the pressing plant, John Arnison came through with the band's most co-ordinated UK tour yet: twenty-five dates that began with two consecutive nights at the Marquee – where else? – on 27 and 28 October, taking in a stream of engagements at a host of famous and not-so-famous little rock clubs dotted around the country that Marillion, whether the fans sensed it or not, were destined never to play in again: the Gallery, Manchester; the Warehouse, Liverpool; Night Moves, Glasgow; the Night Club, Edinburgh; the Granary, Bristol; and the Limit Club, Sheffield. There were those and many more, all known Marillion strongholds by the end of 1982, all sold on the twisted hootch of the first single, all about to be bid adieu to in the hectic weeks that followed.

However, John Arnison was still keeping his best trick up his long managerial sleeve. On 26 November, on the penultimate night of the tour, John had booked the band into their first headline appearance at the Venue, in London. In 1982, before Richard Branson who owned the Venue sold the property to developers and the club closed down, it was generally regarded as the rung on the career-ladder that lay between packing out a club like the Marquee and selling out a concert hall like the Hammersmith Odeon: the Venue, though not so prestigious as the Hammy O, could hold a couple of thousand people, if need be. To make any kind of lasting impression there at all, Marillion would have to pull in over half that many people just to stop the place from looking empty. It seemed like a fairly bold move John was making, gambling with the band's profile on one of the most prestigious stages in London, but he argued that the time was right.

'What else could we do by then except stick our toes in the water and see if it was OK for us to jump in or not?' he says. 'There was nowhere else for the band to go, at the time. I mean, how many nights do you sell out on the trot at the Marquee before you try your hand at something a bit bigger?'

'John was the man-with-the-plan,' says Pete Trewavas. 'And I admit some of us thought perhaps we might be going into somewhere like the Venue a bit too early. But that's where John's always really scored – in his sense of timing! He's always prodded us into the next stage of our career at just the right moment.'

Ah, plans, plans, plans. In October 1982 everybody was making plans for Marillion.

EMI called the band in to discuss the artwork for the single. The band pointed out that it had never been their idea to release a record with a picture of themselves adorning the sleeve. Rather, they were looking for a striking visual image, something with a strong theme, but open to interpretation.

'We were up at EMI in the production office going through ideas for artwork for "Market Square Heroes",' says Fish. 'And we looked at a lot of different artists' portfolios. Then we came across one by a guy called Mark Wilkinson. It was very sort of *painterly*, he had this sort of acid touch, semi-psychedelic almost, and a real eye for all the hideous details. We thought he was great. And so we met up with him and talked.

'The thing is, although we loved his work, I wanted to be able to suggest ideas and themes and references that we wanted in there. It all had to be relevant to the band in terms of what all our songs are about. And on that basis we sent Mark off to work on a sleeve for the first single. I'd suggested the jester image as a theme for him to develop, and a few other things just to explain

57

the sort of idea we had in mind. He took it from there.'

The sleeve for 'Market Square Heroes' Mark Wilkinson came up with was exactly what Fish and the rest of the band seemed to be looking for. The Jester was there, all right, only this was no grinning, idiot thing in a pixie's tunic and three-corner hat. Mark Wilkinson's jester was a head and shoulders illustration that looked like it was gripped with torment, half the face concealed behind a blank, hand-held mask, one corner of the mouth contorted into the beginnings of a scream, just the right eye exposed, red and insane, glaring out at the world with the same mixture of fear and fascination as the eyes that once decorated the band's old stage-clothes. In the background a luminous flux of greens, blues and more reds suggest a gaseous landscape, bloated clouds on the horizon, and in the distance the merest traces of the foot of a rainbow glides into view.

Marillion gave Mark Wilkinson the thumbs up unhesitatingly, and from that day to this he has provided the band with original illustrations to every single, album, poster, T-shirt and tour programme produced under the official Marillion banner.

David Hitchcock's finished tapes were rushed to the pressing plant and EMI set a firm release date for the record, 25 October. But on the very night Hitchcock left Wessex Studio for the last time, the completed master-tapes in a box under his arm, tragedy struck. Exhausted by the three-week endurance course he had set himself, working through every night towards the end, with no sleep and no time left to play with, he got into his car for the long drive home. But before he'd got more than a few miles from the studio he passed out over the wheel and his car left the road at 60 m.p.h. and suffered a terrifying collision with a wall. The fire-brigade had to cut his broken body out of the twisted hunk of metal that was once a car. And, so the story goes, his first words when he recovered consciousness, while firemen still worked furiously to free him from the mangled shards of metal under which he was trapped, were to instruct them to retrieve the tapes which were still lying safe in their box somewhere underneath where the back seat used to be.

'To this day I don't think anybody in the band knows the full extent of what happened that night,' says Pete Trewavas. 'But we know it was a very bad crash, and David ended up in hospital for a couple of months. We all felt terrible for him.'

'And to be honest, what made matters worse was that before he had that crash we had already decided in our hearts that he wasn't the person we wanted to produce the first album,' says Fish. 'We thought he'd done a fair job on "Grendel", although considering the amount of time he spent on it I didn't think what we ended up with sounded *that* great. I liked what he did with "Three Boats Down. . ." But I wasn't at all pleased with the sound on "Market Square Heroes", and that was supposed to be the A side, ferchrissakes!'

'But you can imagine how we felt when the time came to tell him,' says Mark Kelly, pulling a face. 'I mean, I think he was probably still in hospital when he first heard.'

In more ways than one, Marillion looked forward to the release of their first single with mixed feelings.

'It was a funny old time, all right,' says Pete. 'On the one hand we were all pretty excited about getting a record out, but then what with what happened to David Hitchcock. . . . And then we weren't even a hundred per cent sure if we should even be releasing a single so quickly; we were supposed to be an albums band, after all. In a way it was just a relief when it finally came out.'

'Market Square Heroes' was released by EMI on 25 October 1982 – the same week the tour started with those two nights at the Marquee. Eight days later it entered the UK singles chart at 102. That night the band celebrated with an inspired performance at the Gallery, in Manchester. And afterwards out came the cheap champagne as the band toasted their luck long into the night.

One week later it had jumped up to 68. It was time to celebrate all over again. By now they were in Scotland, playing at the Ayr Pavillion. Another outpost demolished in a fit of singing and drinking. Though not necessarily in that order.

'We got some good reviews and the day-time radio played it about three times, and for the first time ever we actually started to sell out a lot of dates on the tour. Everywhere we went it seemed the place was having a party on our behalf,' smiles Fish. 'We all kept looking at each other and going, "Oh, this is good! This is very, very good!" And then the following week it went down, and actually we were all a bit surprised. I think we dreamed it would just keep getting higher and higher.'

On Friday, 26 November, the band drove from their last gig at the Limit Club in Sheffield down to London late in the afternoon for their show at the Venue. This was to be a showcase gig in every sense: the press were all coming, several heads of department from EMI would be there, and the guest-list was growing faster than Jack's beanstalk. This was billed as the hottest night in town this week, and anyone at all connected with the rock business who fancied a Friday night out was either on the list or still trying to get on the list.

Solstice, who had done an admirable job of supporting the band on tour, would open the show, and everybody had high hopes for the occasion.

John Arnison most of all was convinced this was going to be a great night. But the band were still worried about ticket sales. They hadn't sold out on advance sales, hadn't even come close. But John assured them that the important thing to take into consideration about the Venue was that it always attracted a large 'walk-up' crowd off the streets every night anyway.

And then, as the van that was carrying them swung around the corner of Buckingham Palace Road and into Victoria Street, they saw it: people, a massive, squirming throng of people queuing in an ungainly line that stretched from the unopened front doors of the Venue right down the street and around the corner, and then all the way down that street and around the next corner. All waiting in the gathering darkness for seven o'clock when the doors would open and they could get inside . . . to see Marillion.

'I honestly couldn't believe it!' Mark Kelly cries. 'I thought someone must have made a huge mistake and we'd turned up on the wrong night or something – all those people couldn't possibly be queuing there to see us! Could they?'

'It was definitely a bit of a shock,' agrees Steve Rothery. 'I mean, we were thrilled! We'd actually sold out at the Venue! We couldn't get over it.'

When the evening at last began, Solstice took to the stage, but they made few waves with their tastefully brief set, drawing polite but reserved applause. The Venue Friday night crowd was too hungry for the main attraction, and business between the tables, the restaurant and the bar was brisk and to the point during the hours they waited for the band to appear.

Marillion arrived on stage for their biggest London date so far and at once people started squeezing out from behind the tables and on to the dance floor. The floor started bouncing and the walls shook; two waitresses were spotted dancing through the aisles, while serving drinks – a thing rarely, if ever, seen at the Venue in those days; and at least one very drunk A & R man, who shall remain nameless, was actually seen wobbling his belly in an obscene manner in the general direction of the stage during 'Market Square Heroes'.

Face and arms daubed in vivid greens and blues, with slashes of black and, of course, red, Fish strode and prowled the stage, dancing slowly in the soft footlights. The band swung like a pendulum into the maudlin after-hours drama of 'He Knows You Know', destined to be their next single, and they glistened and swayed under rainbow-tinted stage lights through the sweeping, mellifluous terrains of the ghostly 'Grendel' . . .

The Venue ate it up and then spewed it back at the band in a slavish round of rave reviews in the rock weeklies, and a further clutch of 'in-depth' features. 'Prog Rock': 'the Progressive Rock Revival'; suddenly it was all in the papers and magazines and they all had different names for it. Bands like Pallas, Solstice, Pendragon, IQ, and the Dagaband, all were new in 1982 and beginning to fill clubs around the country, and all were unashamedly into (sshhh! say it quietly.) the Floyd, early Genesis, some Yes, maybe even the very early Roxy Music, or before that perhaps King Crimson. They were all *out there*, and they were all doing it *now*: and, above all, the press argued, they were all spearheaded by the only band so far of their strange and shadowy ilk to have actually been signed by a major record company – Marillion.

Of course, within the eclectic pages of the British rock weeklies, talk of 'revivals' may come and go on a monthly basis. But whatever the outcome of the supposed Prog Rock Revival the received wisdom of the press still held that Marillion had something going for them which would out-live the vacillating whims of the passing times.

A quote from a feature in *Sounds*, 27 November 1982, written by former Genesis biographer Hugh Fielder, pretty much summed up the more cautious party line of the time: 'And while the rhythm end of the group is sometimes a bit pedestrian, the guitar and keyboards throw out a never-ending stream of party pieces around Fish's passionate vocals. And if I can still find the resemblance to Genesis circa 1972 quite uncanny you can put that down to Fish's voice . . . Mark Kelly's keyboards, and my age.'

A surface reading, of course, but an honest appraisal. Either way, love them or loath them, suddenly everybody had an opinion on this enigmatic new group of cult-stars.

And besides, nineteen-seventy-*when*? Most of Marillion's fans were still learning the alphabet back in the days of you-know-when. The past was dead to them, and their fascination with the music of Marillion grew from more honest instincts: they just liked the songs and couldn't wait to buy the album.

On Monday 6 December, Marillion took up temporary residence at the Marquee recording studio in Wardour Street, above the club they had already sold out no less than seven times in the course of their journey to making this, their first album.

Producing the sessions for them this time would be Nick Tauber, a young man of maverick production talents whose gift for fashioning countless hits for Toyah impressed Marillion enough to hire him.

'Hugh Stanley Clarke was mad keen for us to try and get hold of Martin Birch for the album,' says Fish. 'Martin was producing all the Iron Maiden albums for EMI and by 1982 Iron Maiden were a huge band, and I think Hugh sort of saw the same formula working for us. But we could never see it. Martin Birch might be a great rock producer, but as a band we're not really anything like Iron Maiden. We might share some of the same fans, we might not, but we wanted to find our own way and with our own producer to help us do it.

'And then John Crawley, our publisher at Charisma, suggested Nick; he was good, not too stereotyped yet, and he was, like, the sort of in-house Marquee producer at the time as well! Which suited us just *fine*.'

With a producer and a studio everybody felt comfortable with now secured, work began on the album the band had secretly christened *Script for a Jester's Tear*.

Only one small cloud hung over the start of the recording: EMI had expressed doubts about Mick Pointer's ability to sustain the high level of performance required for modern recording standards – meaning, Hugh Stanley Clarke made it thoroughly known to the band that he didn't think Mick could cut it as a drummer; not at this level, he said.

'It actually started brewing a long time before that,' says Mark Kelly. 'Before the first single had even come out, Hugh had told both John Arnison and Fish that we should get rid of Mick *and* Steve! I think we told him to fuck off about Steve; Hugh just didn't like Steve because he'd fallen asleep that time in his office. But with Mick, in our hearts, we could at least see his point.'

Mick Pointer's prowess as a drummer had never quite made the leap from a sort of inspired, bullish amateurism, to the more polished, increasingly diverse levels of proficiency the rest of the band were now busy attaining. But so far, he'd always bluffed it quite admirably. However, on album, in the cold light of day, buried beneath no matter how much studio technology, Hugh argued that it would be a major headache concealing Mick's more obvious limitations.

'Hugh even told Nick Tauber that if he thought Mick wasn't up to it he would get him replaced with a sessionman,' says Mark. 'Which was really unfair, we weren't even consulted.'

Eventually Hugh was taken to one side while the band explained to him that they certainly were not going to sack one of the founding members of the band on the eve of making the album they had all spent the last two years dreaming of and working for.

'We knew we had a problem with Mick's playing,' says Fish. 'But now was not the time for sorting all that out. We had an album to record, and maybe Mick would pull through and surprise us all.'

Mick Pointer was reassured that for the time being his place in the band remained firm. But he would have to work hard on his playing, and this he agreed to do.

The first number the band worked on was the title track: 'Script for a Jester's Tear'.

'We hadn't even really begun writing it until we got to the Marquee Studio,' says Pete Trewavas. 'But we had the title and we knew we wanted it to be the title track of the album, and so we were quite nervous putting it together, to begin with. And the studios were charging £1,000 a day, or something. But in the end we got it together quite quickly. It took two days, at the most three, and it was written.'

The first number they actually recorded was 'Charting the Single', which was to be the B side of their second single, and not included on the album. 'He Knows You Know' was next, the track from the album selected as the single. And from there they moved steadily through 'The Web', 'Forgotten Sons', 'Garden Party', 'Chelsea Monday', and 'Script for a Jester's Tear' itself.

They had twelve weeks to do it in, with Christmas smack in the middle of everything as well, and work proceeded slowly at first, only beginning to gain its frantic momentum as the project sped towards its late February deadline.

The week between Christmas and New Year the Marquee

studio was closed. But the club itself remained open for most of that week, so Marillion immediately decided to check themselves into three consecutive nights at the Marquee – 28, 29, and 30 December – where they would celebrate the festivities and kick out the year in traditional Marillion style: balloons, streamers, crazy foam, custard pies, a couple of 'borrowed' bottles of John Arnison's secret supply of champagne. These gigs were going to be *parties*! And no, you couldn't bring your grandmother.

True to the spirit of the times, Marillion invited Pendragon to open the show the first night; Solstice the second; and the Dagaband the third.

January found them back in the studios working on the album. Meanwhile, EMI's hit-making machines were about to set to work on the band's second single, 'He Knows You Know', which they released on 31 January 1983.

Again, under the band's careful direction, Mark Wilkinson concocted a startlingly visual facsimile of the disintegrating personality Fish introduces us to on 'He Knows . . .' It's the anguished face of the Jester again, his crimson eyes flashing in disbelief as he tears apart with his hands the grotesque, compassionless mask he has been hiding behind.

' "He Knows You Know" is the song I always call our anti-drug song,' says Fish. 'And it's about that, all right, but it's also about the splitting of a personality that has been driven underground in his search for some understanding of his own problems. The trouble is the further he goes, the more he's hooked. By the time we reach him in the song, he's at the end. We're witnessing his breakdown.'

Hardly the most toe-tapping theme for your second stab at a life in the Top Of The Pops fruity forty, but then Marillion didn't care – they wanted to make statements! They wanted to fry the tubes and shellshock the airwaves!

'He Knows You Know' ploughed into the UK singles chart at number 35 a week later! Marillion were still ensconced in the Marquee studio piecing together the last of the album when they were told they had broken the back of the Top 40 for the first time.

'We had a lot of help from a lot of guys in radio who had been fighting for the band for a long time,' says Fish. 'There was Tom Russell up on Radio Clyde, he really pushed for our stuff to be played; Andy Fox on Radio West; Dave Steward on Radio Forth; and Tommy Vance, of course, who played us a lot on his Radio

One Rock Show. It all helped and added up and suddenly we had a small hit single!

'We all started celebrating and got wrecked in the Marquee bar, and then of course the usual thing happened – it went down the next week! About ten bloody places.'

To cheer them up, though, the 19 February 1983 issue of *Sounds* ran their first front-cover story on the band: under the headline 'THIS YEAR'S CATCH: Sounds Readers Vote Marillion Best New Act', there was a head-and-shoulders shot of Fish, wearing the grease-paint mask of the Jester and biting into what looks to be something like an eight-pound salmon. Inside, amidst more inane and tacky shots of Fish eating a fish, Edwin Pouncey did his best to explain the case for Marillion, confessing an initial bafflement at their music, but warming to their muse enough to scoff at the Genesis comparisons other rock hacks had resorted to in connection with the question of *musical influences*. Never mind all that, said Edwin, the *Sounds* readers have voted Marillion Best New Act of 1982 in the latest polls! And that mattered a hell of a lot more than the thin-haired debates being conducted by a lot of ageing, lukewarm hacks elsewhere. And Edwin made no apologies when he ended his article by concluding that 'Marillion are indeed going to be HUGE.'

Five days later the new issue of *Kerrang!* flooded the newsstands, dated 24 February 1983, with *their* first front cover story on the band! The *Kerrang!* cover also featured a stunning full-colour shot, or rather, *two* full-colour shots re-made into a quite superb collage – two figures seemingly shoulder-to-shoulder on the same dimly-lit stage, singing but away from each other; on the left, the gaunt, costumed figure of Peter Gabriel, w/Genesis, circa 1973, his face made up in glowing greens and yellows, absorbed by a pale light; on the right, Fish, tall and broad-shouldered, his face and arms daubed in the familiar layers of thick grease-paint.

The headline read: 'PROGRESSIVE ROCK: 1973–1983'. *Kerrang!* were taking the serious approach for a change and began a two-part study of the whole origins and off-shots of the much-maligned 'prog-rock' genre. Predictably – and why not? – Marillion came out of the piece again quite properly cited as The Ones To Watch on all fronts.

All the world needed and asked for now to round this whole nervous deal off was the release of the new album.

★ ★ ★

Even as 'He Knows You Know' dug its nails into the Top 40, albeit just for one short week, EMI were already beginnng to breathe down the band's neck about the album, which was seriously over-budget and certain to overrun the deadline. EMI's chief execs wanted to know what was going on at the Marquee studio, and Hugh Stanley Clarke was instructed to go down there and report back on the progress being made. The only trouble was, Hugh hadn't been allowed in to hear any of the semi-finished recordings yet. Nick Tauber was stubbornly refusing to play Hugh, or anyone else outside the band, anything from the unfinished album.

'Nick utterly refused to play anyone from EMI anything until we were all finished,' says Pete Trewavas. 'So towards the end, although the pressure was taken off us initially by 'He Knows You Know' doing so well, we knew we had to come up with something really good for the album. Towards the end it got very tense, a bit heads-down and no letting up.'

Bad tensions and last-minute nerves notwithstanding, Marillion delivered the six finished tracks nominated for inclusion on their first album to EMI in the last week of February, 1983. *Script for a Jester's Tear*, their first little masterpiece, had taken twelve weeks to make, and at the end of it all, and in spite of all the trapped thunder the latter half of the recording had been fraught with, Mark Kelly saw the album as 'a little piece of magic'.

'It had been quite nerve-wracking to make,' he says. 'But when it was finished we were all so excited by what we'd done we forgot about how difficult some of it had been.' The only problem in the studio, said the band, was Nick Tauber's *laissez-faire* attitude to the work at hand.

'On the one hand Nick was great because he really took us in hand right from the word go. Don't forget that none of the rest of us had ever been in an expensive recording studio making an album before,' says Fish. 'And he was willing to listen to all our ideas about different sound-effects we wanted between some of the tracks, and that sort of thing. But Nick liked to hop from one thing to the next a bit too much. It took us a while to notice, but we didn't know any different, at least not at first.'

'Nick Tauber worked really hard with Mick, though,' says Mark Kelly. 'It took ages to get the backing tracks done, but Nick persisted and persisted until he got something out of Mick he thought would be all right to use. And although he would leave things half-done for days on end, his obsession with small details meant that we ended up with an album of songs that sounded like they all *belonged* together; in that way he really helped define all the best elements of our early sound. Like I say, I found the end result quite . . . magical! It's the only way I can think of to describe what it felt like to have finally recorded our first album! We'll never sound so *innocent* again,' he laughs.

Script for a Jester's Tear was released on 14 March 1983. It was to be Mick Pointer's one and only album with the band, and, indeed, I doubt if they could ever sound quite the same again. Unlike later Marillion recordings the sound on *Script* . . . has an almost frail, egg-shell quality. The percussion never rains down from the heavens as it will on the albums to come, instead it gasps and collapses in front of the beat, always trailing the pulse of the rhythm with its feet shackled.

And the guitars are muted, less cutting and deliberately raunchy than Steve Rothery might have played them live. But, as Mark Kelly points out, this is very much an idealised version of the quintessential, Mick Pointer era, early Marillion sound. The songs are everything and where the production really scores is the way in which it does manage to invest the entire collection with an identity as coherent and enflamed as the passions which spawned it. These are Art School Dance home-movies from a misplaced generation of 70s kids grown up on dreams of piercing the hymen of the 80s with all the twisted logic of their times. And this was no revival, this was just the first bitter despatch from the frontline. And yes, there was a magic about it all. It was very much Marillion's statement. Made with their own magic words.

The title track, which opens the album, is still one of the finest numbers the band have ever written. It begins with the faint sound of Fish's voice approaching from the distance, the words, '*So here I am once more . . .*' echo off the walls, and Mark Kelly sounds the first bell with his deep piano chord. The original 'Script for a Jester's Tear' is less sinewy than it would later come to be performed live but it is just as sensuous and emotional.

'It *is* about trying to write that love song,' says Fish. 'The one you know you have to write. The *hard* one.'

After the halting, Germanic intro abates, Fish puts his pen back to his lips and bites as Mark Kelly makes the room sway to a new drunken rhythm.

'Actually, that bit just before Fish starts singing, "*I'm losing on the swings, I'm losing on the roundabouts.*", that sort of lah-de-dah-de-dah tune I'm playing is pretty heavily influenced by "Lazy

Sunday Afternoon" by the Small Faces!' Mark laughs. 'You know, the bit that goes, "*Wouldn't it be nice/To get on with me neighbours . . !*" I sort of slowed the tempo down and changed the mood entirely.'

And from there Marillion unveiled their latest number in a show of dynamics that added size and meaning to every drop of blood Fish squeezed from his lines. The voice, in those days, still a little mannered, but full of song, a penetrating falsetto razor-edged and charged with emotion.

'He Knows You Know', which follows, fades in gently then explodes into its intense rhythm, Fish spitting out the words: '*Fast feed, crystal fever, screaming through a fractured mind/Chilling needles freeze emotion, the blind shall lead the blind/You've got venom in your stomach, you've got poison in your head/When your conscience whispered, the vein lines stiffened, you were walking with the dead.*'

And it was a Top 40 single!

'The Web', the first number Fish ever wrote the words for, closes side one. It's a wonderful version, though, again, like 'Script . . .', nowhere near as fleshy and bold as it would grow to be in time played live. It's a transitional song, dealing with dreams and ambitions and the knowledge of foul weather ahead, and the band play it with a feather-light, airy restraint that makes its message even more ethereal.

With the three tracks clocking in at 7 mins 40 secs, 5 mins 5 secs, and 8 mins 39 secs respectively, Marillion had what was for them a well-rounded opening side to their album.

'Originally, though,' Fish confides, 'I had written some lines which I wanted to use right at the start of the album as a sort of spoken introduction. But when the time came for me to record them the rest of the band turned around and said they didn't want me to do it! I was really pissed off at first, but then I calmed down and listened to what they had to say, and then Mark, I think, said why don't you keep them and try and make them into a new number entirely? And, as it turns out, that's exactly what happened. They ended up as the lyrics to "Incubus" on the next album.'

Side Two begins with the sound of twittering birds and the muffled hum of polite conversation on some polite, green English summer lawn, the barely audible words, 'Hello Vicar, grab a glass of fizz!' uttered just as Mark Kelly's swirling keyboard takes over and spins out the dizzy intro to 'Garden Party', Pointer's oddball timing adding a jazzy slow beat to the rhythm, Fish breathlessly reciting his ritzy rhymes, all the convoluted irony twisting off his tongue: '*Garden Party held today/ Invites call the debs to play/Social climbers polish ladders/Wayward sons again have fathers.*'

'Chelsea Monday', which follows, is one of my all-time favourite Marillion things from those early days. In many respects one of the more straightforward pieces on an album loaded with intricacies and bold, unequivocal statements, 'Chelsea Monday' makes its presence felt through the pulsing, hypnotic pace the band set and the stark, tremulous longings the words express, the guitars kept slinky and low, their bellies scraping the ground: '*Catalogue princess, apprentice seductress/Living in her cellophane world in glitter town.*' The sour taste of the words slipping back down the singer's throat, Steve's guitar solo at the end quite chilling.

Then there is some radio static, an unknown hand turning the dials, chasing the channels . . . A snatch of 'Market Square Heroes' pumping out of somebody's window . . . And then *blam!* Into 'Forgotten Sons'; the Big One, as Fish calls it.

'Every single track on that first album is alive in its own right,' he says. 'They're all special, and sum up everything good about the band up to that stage. But 'Forgotten Sons' was the one that I fretted over the most. We used a few effects and things on it and they were all taking time to achieve. The section towards the end where you can hear, like, a choir all raving in the background, that's like forty voices over-dubbed. I remember freaking out when I came to sing the lead vocal over that bit, all the voices had a ten-second delay on them and I kept getting these incredible sounds roaring into my ears from out of nowhere, I was frozen on the spot.'

'And the verse that begins, "*Your mother sits at the edge of the world as the cameras start to roll*", where you have Fish singing the words and another voice reading them, originally we asked Trevor MacDonald, the TV newscaster, to do it,' says Mark Kelly. 'But he wanted to charge us too much money for what would have amounted to about five minutes' work! So we said, sod that, and we got this guy called Peter Coven in and he did it for us.'

'Forgotten Sons' was Marillion's most overtly political statement, played as a symbol of protest against the wilful cruelty of the British army's occupation of Northern Ireland. The second longest number on the album, clocking in at eight minutes dead, 'Forgotten Sons' moves through three main sections, musically, beginning with a jagged guitar riff and the sound of the drums stamping their feet, the words delivered unexpectedly harsh, like death in the shadows.

'*Armalite, street-lights, night-sights/Searching the roofs for a sniper, viper, fighter/Death in the shadows he'll maim you, wound you, kill you/For a long forgotten cause, on not so foreign shores/Boys baptised in wars.*'

This was Fish at his most eloquent, a moment of poetic realism that tugged at the barbed wire to find its voice and ended in the grave of modern disillusion. The band are anthemic, Steve Rothery's guitar curled like a snake over everything, shaking its poisonous tail . . .

Script for a Jester's Tear was a marvellously potent debut. The material is all first class, beautifully written and blessed with the practised performance that two years of walking in the wilderness of the clubs and backroom bars had taught them. And as a first album it far outstripped the expectations of even their most ardent fans over at EMI. The machines were getting ready to roll.

The cherry on the cake was to be a gatefold sleeve the band had talked Hugh Stanley Clarke into wangling for them. Popular of course in the middle 70s with all self-respecting album-oriented acts, the gatefold sleeve had fallen from grace with record company production budgets at about the same time as the World Recession hit in 1979. But somehow (and Keith Goodwin's remark about not wanting to argue with a strange-looking six-and-a-half-foot-tall Scotsman comes back to me here,) Marillion managed to squeeze a gatefold sleeve out of EMI for their first album.

The original Mark Wilkinson artwork for *Script for a Jester's Tear* was his most stunning and inspired Jester creation to date, and is still considered by several members of the Marillion die-hards to be the finest illustration of all his album sleeves and posters, etc.

Again acting on the information the band had told him they wanted spotlighted, Mark came up with a visual landscape dominated by the arch figure of the Jester, a violin cradled against his shoulder and a quill poised in his right hand. He stands at a desk beside the only window in a small and dingy one-room bedsit, a mattress, unsheeted, lies across the middle of the floor, and if you hunt with your eyes you can find all sorts of clues as to the Jester's past and, in some cases, his future.

On the torn and stained mattress sit discarded copies of the *Daily Mirror*, *Kerrang!*, and *Sounds*. On the left-hand side wall the two posters distributed for 'Market Square Heroes' and 'He Knows You Know' hang side by side. In the same dark corner of the room an old black and white TV set flickers with the frozen image of the Punch puppet – blank eyes, maniacal leering smile.

'That was obviously an oblique reference to a song we didn't record until the next album called "Punch and Judy", which Fish had already written the lyrics for,' says Steve Rothery.

A fireplace next to the TV lies dormant, just the thick, tangled web of the spider that hangs in the grate there to give it meaning, and above the fireplace is a painting of a young woman with a mane of red wavy hair that falls with an elegant, voluptuous curve to her waist – an Ophelia in burnt dark red.

'We wanted the original Ophelia painting in there first of all,' says Fish. 'But we couldn't get permission to reproduce it. She's a real girl, she was the model for the original Ophelia painting. And funnily enough, that was actually the cover of that John Fowles' book, *The Ebony Tower*, which of course provided Toyah's little hook-up with Sir Laurence Olivier in the play they made of it.'

In front of the TV is a dinky little mono record player, vintage 1973 by the looks of it, and scattered in and out of their sleeves across the floor lie several records – 'He Knows You Know', 'Market Square Heroes', Bill Nelson's, 'Do You Dream in Colour?', and Pink Floyd's 'Saucerful of Secrets'.

'They were all Mark Wilkinson's idea, those records, but they sort of fitted in quite well,' says Fish.

Balanced precariously on all fours across the back of a chair beside the pitiful figure of the Jester is an ugly green lizard creature, squat features and orbital eyes. It is, Fish says, a symbol of the chameleon whose nature was to be revealed in another as yet unrecorded song Fish had already begun working on and that would not surface until the time of the second album, called 'She Chameleon'. And lying open upon the chair is the violin case, inside a crumpled sheet of paper with the words, '*Yesterday, all my troubles seemed so far away . . . Now it looks as though they're here to stay,*' hand-written on it. The words to the old Beatles song, of course. Another coy Mark Wilkinson idea for the pot.

At the jester's bare feet there are more crumpled sheets of music; an empty Coke can with a Marillion logo embossed across its side; and another squeezed and empty bottle. On the

71

desk, just the ink for his quill, an ashtray, the violin bow, a cup, a jar of coffee, some sugar cubes and a dirty spoon.

The scene is cloaked in hapless shadows and the expression on the Jester's painted face is pained and back-broken. The imagery is clear: this is the mouth of the road that has no end, and this is how it all starts. And the clues littered everywhere like so much garbage swept out from under the carpet will lead only to more clues. Foul weather ahead, all right, but still trying to write that love song . . . .

On 15 March Marillion kicked off their most ambitious and important UK tour to date with a show at Norwich University. *Script for a Jester's Tear* had been released the day before and now there was nothing for it but to keep their toes crossed, say their prayers every night, and get their act out on the road. John Arnison had excelled himself this time by booking the band into their first headlining tour of some of the biggest, most prestigious concert halls in the country, twenty-eight dates at venues that ranged from a riotous return appearance at Friars in Aylesbury, on 18 March, to Marillion's first-ever appearance at the Hammersmith Odeon in London, on the last night of the tour a month later, taking in a variety of halls Marillion had never dared play in before: Guildford Civic Hall, Reading Top Rank, Malvern Winter Gardens, Newcastle Mayfair, Bournemouth Winter Gardens, Birmingham Odeon, Ipswich Gaumont, Edinburgh Playhouse, a special occasion Fish's mother and father attended, and on through first nights at Liverpool's Royal Court and Manchester's Apollo Theatre. With this tour Marillion and John Arnison were *daring* success to show its face and let the band have a shot at it.

On 22 March 1983, the band were getting ready for that night's show at the Cardiff Top Rank when they got the news: *Script for a Jester's Tear* had rocketed straight into the national UK Top 40 album charts at number 7! Bang! First week of release! The band were delighted and thrilled, surprised as much as anyone else that the album had gone in so high.

'What we expected to happen, or rather what we *hoped* would happen,' says Mark Kelly, 'was that all the fans we had would go out and buy the album the moment it came out, and with any luck that would get us into the Top 40 and then, hopefully, we'd get a bit more attention from radio and the press. When it went straight in at 7 it was unbelievable! We had no idea it was going to be so popular.'

'Oh, it was brilliant when the album went straight in the Top 10,' says Pete Trewavas. 'I mean, what more could we ask for? Not that it changed anything financially for us,' he adds, laughing. 'Honestly, it didn't make a blind bit of difference to us in the short term. The success was very, very important, but there was no money. I remember we were all on about £75 a week in the band, and our roadies, our crew which we had working for us for the first time, were all on at least twice that amount *and* that was taking a dip in what good roadies can earn with other more successful bands.

'So there was no real difference in our personal lives by the album going in the Top 10, but as a band suddenly we were on this big tour headlining in places we'd only ever seen other bands play in. I tell you, it was great, we loved every minute of it. Still travelling everywhere in the back of a van, of course, but staying in a few proper hotels, eating the occasional cooked meal,' he smiles. 'This is the life, we thought.'

In the finest Marillion tradition, the following week *Script . . .* moved down five notches in the charts, landing at twelve, where it would stay again for only one week. Eight weeks after its release, and just prior to the release of the third single and the second track to be edited down and lifted from the album as a potential hit 45 by EMI, 'Garden Party', the album could still be found sniffing around like a stray dog at the legs of the Top 40.

Meantime, Marillion were still out on their first major UK tour, learning about a life on the road with the ephemeral luxuries offered by the occasional stop-over at a secluded Holiday Inn and the stolen keys to John Arnison's mini-bar placed in the wrong hands (usually John's).

'It started out as a great tour,' says Fish. 'Apart from the trouble we were seriously starting to have with Mick, which ended that tour on a rather sour note, everything else that happened for us then was almost too perfect!

'The album came out one day, the next it's gone straight in at 7 in the charts! Then John tells us we've already sold out the Hammersmith Odeon! It had sold out before the album had even had a chance to come out. Christ! It was unreal. So then John tells us he wants to book us into a *second* night at the Hammy Odeon, and we're going, whoah, hang on a minute, you know, *what*? But John kept saying, "Let's go for the big gamble! Let's go for the big gamble!" Another fucking Arnison gamble. But it worked! He was right! Two nights at the Hammersmith Odeon.

Both sold-out! It was like – what next? What do we do *next*, John? Here, drink this! It was a bit like that at times, when it was good. Very blissful . . .'

In many respects the March–April 1983 UK tour was like one long continuous Coming of Age party for Marillion. Afterwards, when it was over, the sight of sold-out concert halls begging for one more number, the hotel mini-bars that would never cease to please and plaster, the press, the radio, the album charts and the growing adulation of the fans would all intensify and double, then triple in size, but none of it would ever again be seen, by the band, through the same innocent, half-believing eyes.

Supporting Marillion on the tour and shedding some of his own peculiar credibility on the occasion was Peter Hammill.

'I was dead pleased with getting Hammill on the bill,' says Fish. 'People were still spending so much time comparing us to Genesis and not one of them had the gumption to spot other more seminal influences like the music of Peter Hammill. We knew that most of the younger fans would probably never have even heard of any of his albums, but for the band, and me especially, Hammill was a massive influence in lots of ways; his solo stuff and the stuff he recorded with Van Der Graaf Generator. The very same thing in fact that not only influenced the whole punk thing to begin with, but precluded it in many ways.'

The only dark spot growing ever larger on Marillion's horizon as the tour rolled on towards those two final Hammersmiths, was *the problem with Mick* . . .

'The problem with Mick,' says Steve Rothery, who of all the current band was the closest to the errant drummer, 'was that we weren't going to impress anybody with a drummer as bad as that. Mick simply wasn't very good. That tour really brought it home to us – he wasn't going to improve, he was starting to hold us back. We got so many private and public criticisms of his playing – from the record company, the press, other musicians . . . And, in the end, that much weight of criticism is almost impossible to defend. It was getting to the point of stupidity. Something had to be done.'

'The problem with Mick,' says Fish, 'was that his playing just wasn't up to it any more and he couldn't see it because he was always letting his ego get in the way. He was too busy walking around telling people how well *his* band were doing. He thought he was the leader of the band, it was always *his* band as far as he was concerned, and he thought he was untouchable. He couldn't

74

see that this band leads itself, and as each special requirement has to be met it will be met, and that means whoever doesn't hold his end up will always end up slung out.'

The final night of the tour, at the Hammersmith Odeon in London, was the last time Marillion would appear on stage with Mick Pointer. It had been more or less agreed over the days just prior to those two Hammersmith shows amongst the rest of the band and John Arnison that Mick's time was up.

The occasion itself saw the Odeon crowd swooning to the surging, mystical tempo of the band's aggressive new set. Fabulous lights wreathed the stage in dark, swirling colours, the round-shouldered silhouette of the Jester inclined over his fearful violin flashing intermittently on backdrops that lined the horizon of the stage. Drums on a riser to the left, Mark's new bank of keyboards to the right. Between them, firmly fixed at the back of the stage, huddled beneath a cold spotlight, stood Steve Rothery, an almost motionless figure in those days, a serious face on the wall, his guitar striking like a whip on 'Forgotten Sons', then stroking like an expensive fur against the naked skin of the girl in 'Chelsea Monday'.

Fish, his face a handsome mask of carefully applied lines, displayed a charismatic strength and assertion in his performance that had reviewers groping for adjectives to describe. Though he was a big man, he could move about the stage with a familiar, animal grace, his eyes wide and sending out signals on 'He Knows You Know', his hands cupping the words to his lips in 'The Web' . . . For 'Grendel', Fish appeared on stage in a medieval helmet, made of plastic, but a fearful-looking thing when worn, and halfway through the number he reached down into the front-row audience jammed up against the catwalks and plucked out the first fan whose hand he touched. Then the kid was up and dancing on the stage with the tall, helmeted singer towering by his side. It was a mind-boggling sight.

'Some nights Fish would pull someone out of the audience during "Grendel" and it would be brilliant,' says Pete Trewavas. 'I remember one guy getting up somewhere, it might have been in Bath, and he started to match all of Fish's gestures on-stage, imitating his mime and really going for it! It was great watching the two of them go at it. And then other times people who had been begging for him to grab their hands would completely freak when he dragged them up on stage.'

'It was all about having that *contact* with people,' says Fish,

75

enigmatically. 'In order to cross that small division between you The Performer and yourself The Fan; to try and communicate with an audience on an eye-to-eye level, you have to be prepared to go out on a limb now and again, just to see what happens.'

During the latter stages of 'Forgotten Sons', he appeared from the side-shadows, this time with an army-issue helmet on his immaculately painted head, the mike-stand held like a rifle, firing invisible rounds into the stalls and balconies.

When it was over, the strains of 'Market Square Heroes' still echoing in the foyer, Marillion had established themselves as full-time concert hall headliners in the UK. EMI were preparing to fire their latest salvo on behalf of the band in the form of releasing the third Marillion single, 'Garden Party', and John was already talking about some open-air festivals in Europe to start the summer off nicely, followed by a prolonged eight-week stretch in America. Never having played abroad before, Marillion looked forward expectantly to the weeks ahead. First though, Mick Pointer had to be told that he was out of the group.

A few days after the tour ended, John, Fish, Steve, Mark and Pete turned up on Mick's doorstep at eleven one morning.

'It must have looked pretty ominous everybody turning up out of the blue like that, on his doorstep first thing in the morning,' says Pete.

Whether Mick guessed the purpose of the visit or not, he welcomed the band in and everybody sat down. Fish and John came straight to the point. Mick could resign gracefully and the band would issue a press release saying that he had left of his own choosing, citing 'musical differences', that great catch-all phrase, as the official reason for his departure; or he could be sacked and let the whole world know about it.

'But Mick just wouldn't accept the situation as it stood at all,' says Fish. 'He actually said something like, "You'll never find a drummer to replace me, I'm the only drummer for this band!" Which just summed up the guy's attitude.

'Mick was a weekend rock star who got lucky. But now the ride was over. We just couldn't afford to carry him any further.'

Pointer was bitterly upset over his dismissal from Marillion. Refusing utterly to accept that his playing was anything but tailor-made for the band's music, his departure from their ranks was fuelled with acrimony on both sides. None of Marillion have

76

spoken to Mick since the day they fired him. And, significantly, Mick Pointer never touched his drums from that day to this, at least, not in any professional sense.

'He just wasn't a natural musician,' says Pete Trewavas. 'And I think time has proved that. I mean, he never worked, nor as far as I know even tried to work, with any other full-time band. I think he works in computers now. And probably happier for it.'

Mick had been an integral personality in Marillion from day one. His girlfriend, Stef, still ran *The Web* and was setting up the band's first official fan club. But his drums-by-numbers style of playing betrayed a weak and halting talent. With his departure officially announced in the music press the following week, Mick Pointer settled down to a life of obscurity and Marillion went looking for a new drummer.

Time was booked at Nomis Rehearsal Studios in London where auditions would be held. First, though, the band had to shoot a video. EMI had just released 'He Knows You Know' in Europe and now, with word received that the New York office were hot for it, they wanted to release it as a single in America. There had never been time to put a video-shoot production together when the record first raced into the UK charts – it had raced out again so fast its chances of prime-time TV exposure were virtually nil. But with the wide spread of cable and satellite channels that smothered most of Europe and America, and with the enforced break in their live schedule conveniently coinciding, EMI asked the band to come up with a video for 'He Knows You Know'.

There had been a video to go out with 'Market Place Heroes', which the band shot at Guildford University under the direction of Derek Burbidge. It was a fairly straightforward performance piece, strung together on a mini-budget and released quickly in November 1982 when the single was still hovering around the deep end of the charts.

'He Knows You Know' would be a much more expensive and artful affair, directed by Simon Milne. The band recorded it as a four-piece, though at no time are they depicted as a band playing on a stage. Instead, Fish is first seen cross-legged on the floor of a padded cell, a strait-jacket done up tight over his bent torso. Mark, Steve and Pete are doctors, ministering to the patient's final deliverance. The walls split and crack, as do the pavements, tables, and people's faces. Our friend the Jester is glimpsed weaving through trees, and at different moments Fish shares his hell, his cage, with a lizard, the jester, and a small baby.

'The baby was my daughter Freya', smiles Mark Kelly. 'She'd just been born about three weeks before while we were still out on the road.'

It was an accomplished and gripping video, full of haphazard visual imagery and crooked impact, and it was also the first time Fish had ever been seen performing a Marillion song without his make-up!

'It would have looked completely out of place wearing it in the video,' he says. 'And I didn't need to try and enhance my performance visually the way I would do on stage. Why bother? It was all happening *around* me.'

The band returned to Nomis Studios and began the long, shuffling line of auditions to find a replacement for Mick. It wasn't easy going. No-one quite fitted. The band wanted experience and expertise, but they were still looking for a new soul-mate as much as a drummer.

'And then this guy stuck his head around the door one day and said, "Hi, I'm Andy Ward, I used to be in Camel!" sort of thing, and we started chatting, and, of course, within about ten minutes we'd persuaded Andy to sit in on the drums and have a blow. And then about ten minutes after that we all started giving each other the secret nods of the head routine,' Pete Trewavas smiles, 'and the next thing you know Andy's being offered the gig as our new drummer! It happened that fast.'

EMI had delayed releasing 'Garden Party' until the band had found themselves a new drummer. In the meantime, at the end of May 1983, Marillion, with Andy Ward installed on the drums, took off for their first taste of playing live before festival crowds in Scandinavia and Germany; always low on the bill, but making constant ripples every time they stepped on a stage. With a drummer who could not only play to their satisfaction, but who had already been once down the road they now saw themselves embarking on, things were starting to look rosy again.

'At least, at *first*,' says Fish. 'It wasn't until we got out on those European festivals that we discovered that Andy liked his drink just a bit too much.'

'I don't think you could call him anything worse than that though,' says Pete Trewavas. 'Because when he wasn't drinking he was a great musician and a friendly bloke to be with.'

Some members of the London-based International Department of EMI had flown across for some of the dates in Germany, by way of introducing the band to the locally-based reps and heads of department on the continent. In the evening the band were taken out to dinner by the visiting EMI execs. Andy had been drinking since the band had gone on stage early in the afternoon. By the time dinner arrived he was tanked-up.

'It was awful!' says Steve Rothery. 'There we were, surrounded by local EMI people, and the people from the London office, and Andy starts throwing his food around . . . And none of this is funny, *no-one* is laughing, everybody is just sitting there looking embarrassed! I mean, we've all gotten into stuff like that at band parties, where at least we're paying for the food and the drinks. But not on our first trip to Europe to meet the people who want to help us break the band over there.'

When Marillion returned to their Aylesbury homes at the start of June, Andy's appointment had already been made official in stories to the press, and EMI capitalised on the free publicity to announce the release of the band's third single, 'Garden Party'. A new video, again with Simon Milne directing, and this time featuring Andy Ward, was shot immediately – if this one had even a sniff of the Top 30 John Arnison wanted the band ready to promote it properly. And early.

Andy had been warned by the rest of the band in no uncertain terms that they had not come this far only to have him blow things royally for them: he must get his act together and promise not to let the band down again in public. He agreed, and Marillion settled back to rehearse for their forthcoming series of first-time dates in America, set to begin at the end of June.

Much to everyone's delight, 'Garden Party', like its predecessor, punched a hole in the UK Top 40 in its first week of release. It hopped gracefully into the number 28 spot and, according to the EMI sales force, was in grave danger of even going higher next week! Seven days later, with the day-time radio now forced into adding it to their prime-time play-lists, 'Garden Party' had leapt another twelve places up the charts, hitting sixteen, their highest placing yet in the singles chart. The same afternoon, Marillion were offered their first appearance on that week's Top Of the Pops – BBC 1's weekly TV chart show, which attracts the biggest viewing audience of any pop show in Britain.

'Aha! I thought!' cries Fish. 'The wicked lure of fame at last and the temptation to do something naughty before the cameras!' he laughs. 'I mean, what fun! Crusty old Top Of the Pops, and us on it! At first, there was some talk that perhaps we shouldn't do a show like Top Of the Pops, you know, get very high-minded and snub them. But in the end, the urge to run out and ring up our mums and dads and tell them to look out for us on the telly proved too much. So we did it!'

The one bone of contention about the band's first appearance on the ratings-conscious show was the line, *'I'm fucking!'* which Fish croons at the end of the song. The BBC said the band had to change it or pass up their chance to appear.

'It was very funny though,' says Mark Kelly. 'We had to re-record that one line just for Top Of the Pops. When we came to do it for the cameras Fish sang the line as, *'I'm miming!'* only he didn't move his mouth, he just *glared* into the camera . . .'

Running true to form at last, the single dropped the following week, and a fortnight later was lost forever from the Top 40. But by then Marillion had arrived in America for their first, brief tour of the East Coast.

The band were opening the show some nights for Todd Rungren's Utopia at theatres designed to hold around 5,000. Some nights were OK, when the house was full and people bothered to listen. Other nights it was much less than OK. Utopia weren't quite the big attraction in 1983 Marillion had been led to believe they were, and in some halls they were drawing as little as a third of the possible capacity crowds.

When they weren't being kept busy warming up Utopia's dwindling audience every night, the band spent the rest of the time touring tiny 'B' market clubs and poker-faced dives that ranged from the sublime at a gig in Upstate New York where the crowd howled long into the night for encores, to the truly ridiculous when the band turned up for a gig in Boston only to discover that their American agent had booked them as the opening act on a bill headed by a Wet T-shirt Competition!

There was an underground buzz about the album from the just emerging college radio networks, but the majority of the FM and AM radio stations said they found the single 'He Knows You Know' far too left-field to make it safely onto their prime-timed network play-lists. Nationally, the album sold relatively poorly by established mega-buck American standards, but just enough to break the name for the first time.

The major problems the band were having revolved around Andy Ward's increasingly unpredictable behaviour. Andy was drinking again, and the band feared he wasn't going to make it through the tour.

'He was a walking nervous breakdown,' says Fish. 'One minute he'd be laughing hysterically about something and the next he'd have his head in his hands and he'd be sobbing his heart out!'

'And the drinking only made everything worse,' says Mark Kelly. 'Andy would get into the van in the morning for the 500-mile drive to the next gig and he'd have a can of Coke in his hand, he'd just be taking little sips at it. Then you'd look around two hours later and he'd still have this same can of Coke in his hand, still taking little sips from it. By the time we arrived at the next place, ten hours later, Andy would *still* have this bloody can of Coke in his hand! Of course, he'd been topping it up all day with *brandy*! And by the time we arrived anywhere he'd be completely *gone*. And then the dramatics would start, getting into fights with people, refusing to pay for drinks he'd ordered. Breaking down and crying and begging the band to forgive him and to give him one more chance. It was always one more chance with Andy.'

The situation came to a head in the lobby of the Holiday Inn in New York.

'For some God-forsaken reason the clerks at the reception desk wouldn't accept any of our credit cards, and we'd just driven 600 miles to get there. We didn't have enough cash to cover the charge of all the rooms we had booked, and Paul our tour manager and John Arnison are arguing till they're blue in the face with these jerks at reception,' Fish recalls.

'And then Andy starts wandering off. He goes to a cigarette machine to buy a pack, puts the money in and half the machine empties into his lap! You know, it could only happen to Andy.

'Then he starts handing out free packets of cigarettes to anybody that happens to be passing in the lobby of this big New York hotel. Then he decides to open his suitcase and empty it all over the floor! Then he wanders into the bar and orders half a dozen brandies for himself, drinks them, then gets up and leaves the bar without paying the tab and comes back to the reception desk where John and Paul are still arguing about getting us some rooms. The people in the bar start chasing Andy out the door, Andy starts picking a fight with them. And suddenly everything is just total and utter fucking chaos and aggravation. You know, *thanks Andy*, this really puts me in the mood for conquering New York this does!'

Something, as the band would say, would have to be done.

'We finally got Andy up to his room and in bed asleep,' says Pete Trewavas. 'By this time I think he was just blubbering and feeling sorry for himself. And then we all sort of met in John's room to decide what the best thing was to do.'

'The thing is it was a tough enough tour already, with next to no support from the record company, and having Andy constantly cracking up on us was slowly starting to drive the rest of us mad,' says Mark Kelly.

Andy had to go, it was decided. He wasn't a fit enough replacement, neither mentally nor physically, for Mick Pointer. He was out.

John cancelled what remained of the American tour, and booked Andy on the first available flight to London the next morning. Later that evening, when Andy awoke from his tearful black-out, John and the rest of the band broke the news to him.

On the whole he took the news well and with all good grace. 'There was a horrible moment when I thought he was going to start pleading,' says Fish. 'But, thank God, it never came to that.'

There had been no question about Andy Ward's playing; at times, although only when he was sober, he could regain some of the old fire and elemental funk from his best days with Camel. But as an individual he had a lot of personal problems the band weren't qualified to pass judgement on. But the bottom line was this: Andy had become an expensive liability Marillion would never be rich enough to afford.

At the start of August, with just a few short weeks left until that year's Reading Festival where Marillion would again be playing, only this time as second on the bill special guests of the Saturday night headliners, Black Sabbath, the band returned home to England already decided on a temporary course of action. John would hire a session drummer to fulfil whatever live commitments they still had left, and then, when the time came to write and record the next album, they would see about a permanent replacement.

John Martyr, a sessionman of many years', was offered the gig on the strength of his ability to pick everything up quickly and easily.

'It was like a three-month, no strings attached, offer of live work with maybe the odd bit of recording. He accepted and we got ready for Reading,' says Fish. 'Second on the bill where we'd been *sixth* just the year before. I couldn't wait!'

On Saturday, 27 August 1983, as the sun began its slow descent from the centre of the sky down the hill of clouds to the west, almost a year to the day since Fish had announced the band's signing with EMI, Marillion took to the stage at Reading amidst a huge, marvellous roar of approval from the giant blue-denimed sea of fans.

'I remember standing in the backstage toilets taking a slash just before the band came on stage,' says John Arnison. 'And there were these two blokes talking to each other in there. One was saying to the other, "Either Marillion are going to steal the day and go on to greater things, or Black Sabbath are going to do it and begin another successful comeback!" That was the year that Black Sabbath got back together with Ian Gillan singing for them, and of course this was a tremendously important gig for them. For us, too, because making it to second on the bill at Reading before 35,000 odd people in just our first year together was really quite something. We desperately wanted to prove that we deserved to be so high on the bill, that we were here to stay. So it was like do or die for both bands that day.'

Everybody had expected Marillion to arrive on stage with as big a bang as possible in their opening attempt at stealing some of that precious thunder Sabbath were praying was reserved exclusively for them. Instead, the band walked on stage shrouded in silent mysterious expressions, the cheers and applause raining down on them, and Steve Rothery very quietly began picking out the first gentle chords to 'Grendel'.

'It was such a quiet opening that the BBC, who were broadcasting the concert on the radio, missed the beginning of the number because they hadn't turned on the mikes yet – they hadn't realised we'd started playing,' says Steve.

'We thought now this will *really* zap them!' says Fish. 'We were expected to go for it like our lives depended on it, but instead we opened the show by giving them twenty minutes of "Grendel". It was *brilliant*! The crowd went absolutely *apeshit* they were so surprised! No-one else could have got away with it, but we did.'

The mammoth and all-consuming passions of the 'Grendel' finally put to rest in a gleeful fit of exploding guitar crescendos, Fish paused breathlessly at the mike to say, 'Good evening Reading! (*loud cheers from the crowd*) This is a special gig . . . Some of you were here with us last year. (*more loud cheers*) A year ago exactly on this very stage we announced the deal with

EMI. This is our anniversary celebration. And this is called . . . the "Garden Party".' (*deafening applause*)

And so it was. Marillion's fantasy garden party, there in the wide green fields of Reading Festival, under a hot gloating sun.

The band ploughed through dynamic versions of 'Script . . .', 'Chelsea Monday', 'Charting the Single', and a new number, called 'Assassing', which Fish said was about, 'the sacking of various members . . . . and the elegant strategies of the business world.'

The band clawed through the new number, led by dark guitars that chopped malevolently at the ground beneath your feet and a pulsing rhythm that scorched the twilight, squeezed by the neck for words which Fish hurled like stones, more 'rock and roll' than anything they had ever attempted before. The Reading crowd lapped 'Assassing' up and screamed for more.

They would get it. Marillion promised them at least that much.

'It was definitely our day,' smiles Fish. 'We were just about arrogant enough now, and confident that we would do it. And then we did.' He licks his lips.

The performance of the 'new' Ian Gillan-sized Black Sabbath was spoiled by the uninspired and drained mood of the après-Marillion crowd.

Marillion had swept the show right out from under the big bad headliners' pointy-toed boots. After the debacle of the American dates it was good to be back in Britain on the winning side again.

American success remained an enigma Marillion would not penetrate with any depth for another two and a half years.

Not that they didn't try, though.

4

And the Giant Sleeps
With One Eye Open

(Profile – Fish/Derek W. Dick)

Garrulous, independent, uncompromising, fiery-tempered, and
generous to a fault, Fish is Old School rock and roll. For him,
the whole sordid business of making rock music could never be
undertaken as just another branch of populist entertainment. His
lyrics have to *mean* something, or he gets no kick out of singing
them. And like every other Old School rocker that ever walked
this road, Fish is into getting his kicks.

The songs he writes are about sex and death, drugs and
madness, the games people play to lose deliberately, and the
politics of control and manipulation. However, his lyrics are
never merely didactic; they are impressionistic, surreal, haunted
by awful ambiguities and the reek of blood turned cold. 'I have
never been what you could call an optimistic writer of songs,' he
once told me. 'It's very rare that I look around at the world and
decide there's something loving and beautiful about it . . . The
world is fucked, the planet's dying, and we've known it for years
and years. But do we do anything about it? Are we even capable
of doing anything about it? Is there any magic left that isn't
second-hand? I've written about all these things.'

On stage most nights, Fish is a shaman, hurling spells into the
footlights, eyes slitted as he gallops up to the mike-stand like a
centaur. Between songs, delving into character as the irrepressible
Celt with another funny story to tell, the kiss of a bottle still
smudging his lips, grinning like an alligator, and when the music
strikes and the band start to pulse and weave, dancing like a

dervish, a long brutal figure wrestling with the red and the green of the spotlight, chest-high leg-kicks and arms thrown out in mock-crucifixion pose, a grease-paint leer masking the jester's uncertain frown.

Acknowledged as an anachronistic product of the 80s, Fish has little, if anything, in common with the received idea of what a living, breathing, sad-eyed pop star should look and talk like in the late 80s. He's not glib enough, pert-bottomed enough, kissy enough, straight enough, or boy enough to be considered in the same acrylic light as a Simon Le Bon, a George Michael, or a George O'Dowd.

No, Fish's lineage as a stray-footed frontman stretches back to grittier, far more artful times. Long before the cry-babies on the British music press got their hands on the first Marillion recordings and had him tied and branded as a Peter Gabriel clone, Fish had already aligned himself with a brooding tradition of avant-garde rock performers and stylists. Long before Marillion even, Fish was already deeply smitten by the dark graces of a host of teenage idols – people like Jim Morrison, Roger Waters, Peter Hammill, and Peter Gabriel, all of whom represented some unspoken ideal to the young, aspiring singer.

'Would you consider yourself a hedonist by nature?' I once asked him.

'Yes, definitely,' he replied. 'But I take my pleasure very seriously. People that think of themselves as hedonistic by inclination but don't take what they do seriously are the ones you have to watch, though. They're the ones that end up burned-out and wasted. I don't tinker about with things and then leave them to fester. If I decide to get into something I always try and push myself the whole way into it, because once I do get involved in something, or somebody, I won't short-change my emotions, and I won't yield until the finish comes of its own accord.

'But I *insist* on surviving. The trick is not to be too judgemental about anything, but to involve myself completely in whatever new context my life suddenly finds itself in. And then, later, to write it all down as honestly and accurately as possible, warts and all, everything.'

When he's not working with the band, Fish has always been an avid party-goer. At heart he's an incredibly social animal. He likes talking to people, and he likes drinking with them too. The night is only ever as young as Fish wants it to be. But that's not a rock star's gimmick, the black circles around the faded eyes routine. Fish has been giving up his night's sleep in favour of more fascinating party games for most of his adult life.

In person, he can be every bit as charismatic as he appears in concert or on TV, but he doesn't act or put people on. Money and fame is just another set he's built for himself. It's changed nothing about him. What arrogance he possesses needed no material props to flourish. His art and his killing way with words aren't bought or acquired, they are merely contained. And the twin faces of comedy and tragedy he expounds in all his work are merely the remote reflections of his own continually shifting, contradictory nature.

'I have the magpie's roving eye, especially for objects or people that glitter or throw off their own special light,' he says. 'And I collect things and keep them stored away; the pieces of my life that mean something still to me, the pieces of others' lives I've found lying around. And just when I think I've got all the pieces sorted out into some kind of readable pattern, I see something else I must have, something new I've never experienced, which throws the whole thing into disarray again.'

When exactly 'Fish' was born has never been recorded. The name goes back to his late teens, when Fish was still plain old Derek William Dick, an itinerant youth of extraordinary build matched only by his extraordinarily sized dreams and ambitions. He used to like to take long, uninterrupted baths: cans of beer, cigarettes, a full ash-tray, and the radio all vying with the rubber duck and the back-scrubber for his attention over the space of a couple of long hot hours rolling around in the tub.

'A friend called round to see me one day, while I was having one of my extra-long baths,' he smiles, 'and he ended up waiting an hour and half for me to finish. When I finally came out of the bathroom he was completely disgusted with me. He said, "Christ! What's your bloody name? Fish?" And I thought . . . hmm. *Maybe* . . .

'The thing is, by then I was already sort of looking around for a new name, a new way of people getting to know me. I mean, I just didn't see myself making any kind of mark in the world as the famous Derek Dick,' he laughs. 'So I took Fish as my nickname and after a while that's how I was known by everybody except my family . . . . And *no*, it has nothing to do with my fondness for a drink! Although if you ask the rest of the guys in the band they'll probably tell you something different.'

87

The 'Fish' persona as perceived on-stage with Marillion – bawdy, passionate, wanton, comic, tragic, morosely introspective, then plumed and gesticulating, the crooked jester's smile unreadable, unbluffable, warm and at the same time cold – has its origins buried deep beneath a quagmire of childhood experiences that left the adolescent Derek William Dick with a fiercely introspective nature.

'I was terribly self-conscious about my body because I was a very late developer, physically. And that manifested itself in a shyness I had with people. I wasn't in the least bit outgoing. I had too many hang-ups about myself to do anything but sit around *thinking*. Everything that came later – the extroverted personality of Fish and the big mouth and the drinking and the fighting and the joking – all of that began as a reaction to the way my adolescence was always cloistered in doubts and fears and not wanting to join in with anything, just wanting to be invisible.'

However, where Derek William Dick ends and Fish begins is a point still open to debate. Of course, they are one and the same person, after all, but there are things Fish would do, or indeed has done, that Derek would never dream of doing. And vice-versa.

'Derek would like nothing better than to settle down and get married and have loads of kids running about the place,' he smiles. 'But Fish doesn't have a lot of time for those ideas. Fish is an extremist. Fish wants to be out there with his neck on the chopping block, taking life to the limit and no turning back! Somewhere in between the two points of view is where you'll locate me.'

Derek William Dick was born on 25 April 1958 in Edinburgh, Scotland. He was brought up in a small town called Dalkeith, just east of Edinburgh, the eldest, by three years, of two children.

'I have one younger sister, Laura,' he says, 'but because of the differences in our age and sex, I always felt more like an only child. I was always a big brother to Laura, but we didn't really hang out together or anything. I made my own way.'

Derek's father, Robert, owned and ran a small garage, and his mother, Isabella, had worked as a sales assistant in a gentlemen's outfitters before giving up work to become a full-time mother. Derek says that the family was 'resoundingly middle-class in its

Derek Dick, aged five, with his family

Pete Trewavas getting in some early
practice

Steve Rothery, with feathered friend

Pete and Steve, early 1981

One of the early publicity shots, 1981

'Come and join our band . . .', Christmas 1980

[partial handwritten text along the edge of the first page:]
(songlist) was recorded at the be... Davy (old bass?) or ... has the ... Som ... scraw... it to ...

'Waddesdon 8104'
...ber we do. It Eric's place upsr.

53 Quainton Road
Waddesdon
Bucks

10 December 1980

Dear Derek & Diz (I think !?)

I'm writing this because nobody in the band can write — at least that's their excuse.
When you hear this you'll understand why they've placed so much emphasis on the vocals!

We're hoping to lay down a tape with the present set on it to get to you before you come down but this may not be possible as the old bassist has now refused to play through it with them and the tape made at the last gig did not come out (Basically because someone who shall remain nameless forgot to press the 'record' button)

Anyway I hope this gives you a rough idea of the sort of thing we do and doesn't

Issue 1 of *The Web*, February 1982

ISSUE ONE
FEB 1982

GRENDAL

THE WEB

Hi,
This newsletter is designed as a means of expression for both the band and more importantly, yes, the people who've supported Marillion in the past and we hope, the future. Planned to come out at regular intervals, the Web will provide news of the bands events, review gigs etc. We would like you to write to the Web, what do you think of the band, the songs, the gigs, infact anything at all. (You could even write and complain about the weather if you like, just let us know there is someone out there!)

'LYRICAL NONSENSE', said Alice!

GARDEN PARTY

Garden Party held today, invites call the debs to play
Social climbers polish ladders, wayward sons again have fathers

Edgy eggs and curing-cumbers, ruddy waltered from their slumbers
Time has come again for slaughter, on the lawn by still cool water

Champagne corks are firing at the sun, sweeping swallows chased by violins
Straussed by Strauss, they sulk in crumbling eaves again

Aperitifs consumed en masse, displaying their owners on the grass
Couples loiter in the cloisters, social leeches quoting Chaucer
Doctors sons, a parsons daughter, where why not and should they ought to
Please don't lie upon the grass, unless accompanied by a fellow

Perhaps Othello!

Punting on the Cam is jolly fun they say, Beagling on the downs oh
please do come they say, Rugger is the tops, a game for men they say
I'm punting, I'm beagling, I'm winning, reclining, I'm rucking, I'm fucking

So welcome to Garden Party.

Angie chalks another blue, Mother smiles she did it too.
chatters chat and gossips lash, posers pose, pressmen flash
Smiles polluted with false charm, locking onto Royal arms
Society columns now ensued, return to mingle with the crowds.
Oh punting on the Cam is jolly fun they say, Beagling on the downs oh
please do come they say, Rugger is the tops, a game for men they say

(Forgotten Sons next time -)

Scourge of the Chiltern Seas ✝

First review of a gig in a national music paper, November 1981

A return to kaftans and loonpants

Marillion
Marquee

MARILLION (NOW there's an original name) hail from Aylesbury and have been regularly playing SRO (sold right out) showcase gigs at the legendary Friars boozer, which believe it or not is in Aylesbury.

Marillion recently took London by storm, and gave Aerosmith rip-off merchants Girl a bit of a scare. It's not often a support act gets an encore at the Marquee, although to be fair to Girl Marillion had brought down rather a large contingent of ageing hippy 'eadbangers. No denim and leather here mate, more like kaftans and loonpants.

A trip back to the mid seventies maybe, but at least Marillion aren't jumping on the NWOBHM bandwagon. Instead they're more at home borrowing licks from the old school of Genesis, Styx, Yes, Canuck rockers Zon, and wait for it Trillion, just a few names that spring to mind.

Onstage Marillion come across very bizarre, not dissimilar to Agony Bag. Whatever happened to them? Lead singer Fish, a rather tall and mysterious Scot, stalks around the stage in jerky movements and at times reminded me of Gene Simmons, although Fish's make-up coulda been more outrageous.

The rest of the band look like some weird religious sect, wearing what looked like old potato sacks, each one with a bright coloured eye painted on the back, giving that mythical look. Perhaps the Band have been reading too many Stephen King novels.

Marillion have a very tight sound. Songs like 'He Knows You Know', 'Garden Party' and 'Charting The Single' are all long workouts, well crafted, not too much guitar, and synthesizer drifting in and out. Fronting this rather complicated sound is Fish, who does have a good voice, and sings pretty off the wall lyrics. So what a surprise when they encored with an old Scottish jig classic, 'Loch Lomond', a real show stopper.

The sooner Marillion get signed the better. Now if someone could tell me what the big eye on the back of those potato sacks means, I'll join the sect.
XAVIER RUSSELL.

The big announcement, from *Aylesbury Plus*, September 1982

Group signs for EMI

MELODIC rock group Marillion has signed a major five-year recording contract with EMI.

The Aylesbury-based band, which has a large following in the town, signed the recording deal earlier this month in Scotland while on a tour of the country. A sum of £500,000 has been mentioned.

The group's first single with EMI is due to be released in the next few weeks.

It is entitled Market Square Heroes and has been written about Aylesbury's Market Square.

AYLESBURY PLUS

Marillion — major recording contract

The Marillion line-up includes Peter Trewaves on bass, Steven Rothery, lead guitar, Mark Kelly, keyboards, Mick Pointer, drums, and vocalist Fish.

Fish, October 1982 (EMI)

Marillion sign with EMI. *Left to right:* John Arnison, Mick Pointer, Steve Rothery, Mark Kelly, Pete Trewavas, Fish (seated), Terry Slater, Hugh Stanley-Clarke (EMI)

Publicity shot, February 1983 (Simon Fowler)

Pete, Mark and baby Freya, form the 'He Knows You Know' video, April 1983

Fish by Brian Aris, 1984

(a) Pete Trewavas

(b) Ian Mosley

Brian Aris's portraits

(c) Mark Kelly

(d) Steve Rothery

attitudes', though he adds, 'they had no money though, not when I was born. None at all. They were broke.'

The garage which Robert Dick ran was a business that had been in the family for over a century, beginning life as a blacksmith's in the 1850s. It was a modest business, consistently lucrative enough, though, to support three succeeding generations of his family. But by the mid-1950s, when Derek's father inherited ownership on the property from his grandmother, the profit margin had all but been sacrificed to pay for death duties.

'My father had been hit by two lots of death duties – my grandmother's and my grandfather's; like a lot of old married couples they'd both died within a short time of each other – so he was totally broke and up to his neck in debt until I was already started in school and Laura was growing up,' says Derek. 'As long as they still owned their own house though, and knew that they weren't always going to be poor, my parents made sure I was kept blissfully unaware, as a child, of all the difficulties they were having keeping the money coming in.'

As a child, Derek attended a small Dalkeith primary school: King's Park. He says he remembers his early years there as quiet and comfortable.

'I was very much the small-town boy,' says Derek. 'Although you could get on a bus and be in Edinburgh in twenty-five minutes, if you drove twenty-five minutes in the other direction you'd be heading down into the borders and out into open country. Dalkeith, which is a sort of half-mining, half-market town, was caught in the middle somewhere, not really one thing or the other.

'The chief forms of entertainment that I remember from those days are occasional things like the miner's galas, or when a travelling carnival hit the town about twice a year. By the age of ten I had my routine fairly well worked out – I used to go to school; come home again; watch 'Blue Peter' on the TV while I was having my tea; do my homework; then get straight up to the park to play football.'

His blossoming passion for football aside, Derek was not naturally born athletic. At school he shunned sports by and large in favour of more academic pursuits. History, English, and Geography; they were the subjects that fired his imagination. As a result, he was always in the top three or four of his class.

'As a youngster I was very tall for my age, and a bit overweight, and I was starting to become very shy, and I couldn't get into team sports or contact sports at all. I was OK at football, but I never enjoyed it more than when it was just me kicking a ball against a wall on my own. I was good at lessons, where I was left to get on with things on my own, but outside of class I wouldn't go near the sports field. I was much more into reading books and collecting comics. While all the other kids in my school were always outside running around the playground playing games, I was always inside in the warm reading my Biggles books. Biggles was *it*, as far as I was concerned. And my two comics were always *The Eagle* and *The Victor*. I was never a *Beano* man, or a *Dandy* man. I wasn't into laughs, I was into war and conflict!' he laughs.

Young Derek's first experience of pop music began with a passion for the Beatles.

'I was on holiday with my mum and dad at a caravan site near Dunbar,' he says, 'and I used to sit around all day listening to the radio. That was the first time I ever heard the Beatles. I was about five years old at the time and they were *the* big thing, everyone was talking about them, and I just fell in love with them. I immediately wanted to learn how to play an instrument! But the closest I ever got to that was miming with a tennis racquet in front of the mirror.

'I was never into buying singles, though. I used to buy those crappy Top of the Pops albums they used to have, with ten tracks on each side, sort of cheap recorded copies of the hits of the day. I used to really like them though, because they always came in these glossy covers with pictures of scantily-clad girls posing around on them! That's what I was into when I was little!' he grins.

'The first single I ever bought was actually 'Lola' by the Kinks. But by then I was nearly thirteen and starting to take rock music a lot more seriously.'

When Derek was eight years old, his father had successfully reactivated the family's business fortunes and was now in a position financially to offer his son a private education. Wisely, he left the final choice of which schools Derek should attend for the remainder of his school-years entirely up to his son, who vetoed the idea at once.

'My father offered me the chance of going to the equivalent of what would be called a public school in England; an expensive, private education at an upper-crust school somewhere in

Scotland,' says Derek. 'Or he told me I could stay where I was in Dalkeith and eventually go to one of the local comprehensives – the High Schools, as they call them in Scotland. And although a lot of my friends from the street where my family lived went away to private schools, I really didn't fancy the idea at all. I was happy right where I was, amongst my mates. And anyway, the thought of being tucked away somewhere in a boys' school, with no chance of ever seeing any girls, was enough to put me right off the idea straight away! A life without women, even at that age, was unthinkable to me. So when I was twelve and had left my primary school, I ended up going to Dalkeith High School, a place that turned out to be so heavy I was scared to open my mouth for the first two years I was there!'

Dalkeith High was, says Derek, 'a total catharsis of violent adolescent charms.' A large sprawling building, the school housed over a thousand pupils filling eight separate classes per year. Mostly, the teenagers at Dalkeith weren't encouraged to excel at anything, they were told to learn how to get by. Going there, for the gentle-mannered, increasingly shy and introspective twelve-year-old Derek was, he says, traumatic.

'Going to Dalkeith High for the first time was a total culture shock for me!' he cries. 'Where my mother and father lived was in one of the posh parts of Dalkeith, and King's Park was the nice, posh little primary school. But Dalkeith High took kids from all the council estates and places like Woodburn Primary, which had a bad reputation for being a very hard place, despite only being an infant school

'Dalkeith High was full of miners' sons and they were very rough and tumble. My first day there I had people talking to me about so-and-so getting chibbed (stabbed) at a disco. And "Have you heard about young Woody getting arrested?" I'd never heard people talk like that before, except on telly, and it nearly scared me out of my wits!'

The class Derek was placed in at Dalkeith High had two chief distinctions: it was the only class out of the eight in his year that took German as a subject; and it was soon to be renowned as one of the toughest, most difficult classes to manage in the entire year.

'Every boy in my class got the belt at least twice a term,' Derek chuckles. 'But with about two weeks to go 'til the end of my first year I'd never actually been belted by a teacher myself. And the rest of the guys in the class got on at me and told me I *had* to do something so that I'd end up getting the belt at least once before the end of the year. Every boy in the class had been punished with the belt except me, and it became a big macho thing for them – I had to have the belt too, then we could all boast that we were the hardest, baddest class in our year! Honestly, it was *pathetic* . . .

'But even some of the girls were getting the belt from the teachers in my class, and it became a big thing that everyone was really, like, *proud of*! So that was it, I had no choice. I spent the last two weeks of my first year at Dalkeith High rolling around in class and collapsing over desks and chairs, causing complete fucking havoc wherever I went, until one of the teachers at last gave in and punished me with the belt! I thought, thank fuck *that's* over! I hope I don't have to do this every year.'

Interestingly, the one subject at school, even more than sports, that Derek says he truly loathed was music!

'I couldn't stand it!' he cries. 'Not the kind they taught in school. It was always old hymns and ancient classical stuff that totally bored the pants off me. They tried to teach me how to play the recorder. I was hopeless at it! I couldn't even get it together to learn "Three Blind Mice"! I found it easier trying to get the belt than I did to play the bloody recorder!'

Of course, that didn't stop Derek, now approaching his early teens, from nurturing a growing fascination for the more modern forms of music he was starting to encounter as 1970 turned slowly into 1971.

'Genesis and Emerson Lake & Palmer were the first big ones, for me,' says Derek. 'I remember hearing the first ELP album when I was about thirteen and thinking stuff like "Lucky Man" was brilliant! The first Genesis album I got into was *Trespass*; stuff like "Looking for Someone" and "Visions of Angels" were compulsive listening round my house when I got in from school every night.

'And that's when I started buying the music papers and going out and buying albums every Saturday with my pocket money . . . After Genesis and ELP I got into Pink Floyd; *Medal* and *Dark Side of the Moon* were the first two Floyd albums I bought. Then I was into Marc Bolan and T. Rex. I still love Marc Bolan, and when I was thirteen and heard his *Electric Warrior* album for the first time I just thought it was the coolest thing I'd ever heard. It was just so new, what he was doing. He had this incredibly sexy let-it-all-hang-out sound.

'But I never really got into Bowie, not in those days. Which is funny I suppose, being such a T. Rex fan. I was put off by the glitter and the haircuts, and the camp Roxy Music connotations. He wasn't as rock and roll as Bolan, and that's what put me off back then. These days, of course, I think he's a genius! But don't forget, in 1971 and 1972 when Bowie was riding that whole Ziggy Stardust thing, I was still living in a tiny little town up in the wilds of Scotland. It took a long time for that whole glitter thing to gain any real credibility with the young kids up in places like Dalkeith.

'By the time it had reached us it was pretty much all over down in London. It wasn't until years later that I discovered the significance of that whole period, in terms of the history of pop music. I was too busy getting deep and meaningful with my Genesis, my Floyd, and my Van Der Graaf Generator albums,' he smiles.

At the age of fourteen, Derek was already beginning to think in terms of perhaps getting his own band together. The only problem was he couldn't actually play anything.

'I'd had a bit of a bash around on a friend's guitar, and I'd plink-plonked around on a piano, but I couldn't make any sense of it at all. I just didn't have the mental discipline to sit down and learn how to play them,' he shrugs his shoulders.

'I thought perhaps I might make a good drummer, at one time. I thought, "Well, I know how to *hit* things all right! Maybe I'll be a great drummer!" So, again, I found a friend who had a drum-kit, and I used to go over to his parents' house once a week and knock hell out of his drums. It didn't last, though. I couldn't even keep a decent beat going for longer than about three seconds! But I was really taken with the idea of being the next John Bonham for a while, and I remember I even went as far as asking my dad if he would buy me a drum-kit. Thank God he said no! Two months after I first got interested in playing the drums, I'd forgotten all about it. As usual, it was taking me too long to get the hang of, and I used to get bored so quickly I soon lost all interest in being a drummer.

'But by then I'd found something else that I liked the idea of much more – I was starting to sing. It was a damn sight easier for me to sing than it was to play the bloody drums. So that was it: I decided I might as well give myself a go as a singer.'

Derek began his amateur singing career by setting up a cassette recorder to pick up his voice and then singing over any track he felt he could handle, played in the background on the family stereo.

'One of the first songs I can remember singing into a tape-recorder was a Paul McCartney tune called "Skyline Pigeon" from the Wings album, *Red Rose Speedway*,' he grins. 'I used to get really into recording my voice singing over records by Yes, Genesis, Pink Floyd, Elton John, Deep Purple, anything that moved me enough I would try and sing along to.

'And, of course, I started imitating all these singers like mad, really *studying* every vocal inflection that they made. And Robert Plant from Led Zeppelin, of course, I used to try and pull off some of his best moves too.'

For Derek, laying down copy-cat vocals to some of his favourite songs was all part of his self-education. He was learning the only way he knew how.

'I didn't take any singing lessons, the very idea bored me too much,' he says. 'And I didn't know anything about practising to sing scales – although I had been in my primary school choir for a while, but I got kicked out for always turning up late for rehearsals – I just knew how to sing all these weird rock songs in different voices. Jon Anderson, Robert Plant, Paul McCartney, Peter Gabriel, even Rod Stewart who was a singer I used to love in those days. I could do them all by the time I was about sixteen.'

Naturally enough, his youthful imagination fired by the plethora of vintage early 70s progressive rock albums he was now busily amassing at home, it wasn't long before Derek was persuaded to venture out to his first live rock concert.

'The first proper show I ever saw was Yes, supported by a band called Gryphon, at the Usher Hall in Edinburgh, in 1974,' he says. 'I don't suppose I should resort to cliché and say "that night changed my life!",' he smiles, 'so I'll just say that it came very close. I had never witnessed anything like it in all my born days! This was in the days when Yes had the full over-the-top production: amazing lights, brilliant sound, and all sorts of weird surreal images being flaunted on screens and things. I couldn't believe people had been going to shows like these for years while I was still stuck at home! For days afterwards I drove my mother apeshit lying around in the bath for hours, singing in my best and loudest Jon Anderson voice every Yes song I could remember from the concert.

'But out of all the kids in our year, there were only me and two mates that had gone and seen them play, so immediately I became the school authority on Yes. I went out and bought all their albums and got really into what they were doing . . .'

Aside from his rapidly-maturing taste in rock music, the teenage Derek Dick was also developing an even more mature taste for the contents of his father's drinks cabinet.

'I started drinking when I was about fourteen,' he says thoughtfully. 'I used to go to the cabinet to get myself a glass of lemonade, and when my father wasn't looking I'd sneak in a drop of vodka or gin. I did it for years thinking he hadn't noticed before I realised that he'd been on to me all along. He just wasn't commenting on it. He didn't want to turn it into a crisis and I think he was hoping it was just a phase I was going through. Meantime, I kept right on drinking his booze.

'I mean, I wasn't heavily into alcohol, it wasn't that I used to hit the bottle every night or anything. But by the time I was sixteen I was quite used to the idea of having a few pints and a night out. My mother and father were frankly horrified, though. We had a few terrible rows about my behaviour and my habits outside of the house which I was starting to bring home with me. But I was their eldest child, and it's always the eldest child that takes the most shit from his parents, because it's all as new to them, this game of growing up and being a teenager, as it is to him. It's the old, old story of the son coming up to challenge his father's values, his father's rules, his whole way of living life. And actually, it's very healthy. That's just the way of the world; the young rising to replace the old. As long as things don't get too *bitter*.'

At sixteen, Derek was displaying all the outward signs of the typically hard-eyed and intense teenage rebel he was later to eulogise, as Fish, in songs like 'The Web', 'Market Square Heroes', and 'Heart of Lothian'. Already over six feet tall, long-haired, a chain-smoker, and a regular cheap beer and whisky tippler by sixteen, Derek was learning how to disguise his painful introspection in a show of bullish anti-social graces.

'By my mid-to-late teens I hardly spent any time at all in the company of my own family,' he says. 'My dad had put floorboards in and decorated the loft when I was small and I used to have my trainset and my toy soldiers up there. I used it all the time as a playroom. Then when I got to about sixteen or so I practically lived up there. I wasn't getting on with my parents, and you could pull up the steel stairs to the loft and be completely unbothered by what was going on in the rest of the house. So that's what I used to do. I was completely cut off from the rest of the family.

'I used to get my mates over to my loft and we'd sit up there for days and nights drinking beer, and whisky when we could afford it. It was very seedy, really. I remember when we couldn't afford more beer one afternoon one of my mates resorted to drinking after-shave! He was the same guy that used to try and make up alcoholic drinks in the science lab at school – a total nutter!

'The strange part is it never affected my progress at school at all. Which is why I was probably allowed to get away with it all,' he smiles. 'I did brilliantly in my O levels; I got seven of them in all – five straight A passes; History, English, Maths, Biology and Chemistry; and two Bs, German and English Literature!'

However, the two years that followed, as Derek half-heartedly approached his A level examinations, did eventually put paid to the youngster's chances of successfully furthering his education at school.

'I passed my driving test when I was seventeen and my dad bought me my first car,' Derek smiles. 'So from that point on I really was foot-loose and fancy-free! And that was the downfall of my academic career. I started going out with girls, and I was always hanging out with little gangs of mates that used to like having a good time and going to gigs in Edinburgh. And that was it for me; school was definitely *out* from that point on. The only people I could still relate to there were the headmaster, funnily enough, a totally unshockable guy called Mr Sleater, and the history teacher, Mr James. They were both good guys, both impossible to wind up, the way we would all the other teachers. Mr Sleater used to call me up to his office regularly to discuss 'the future', and all that. We used to sit there smoking cigarettes and discussing the world.

'But by then I really had lost interest in school. I was starting to come out of my shell a lot more, and I was starting to enjoy myself. From about the age of sixteen to eighteen I may have blown my chances at school, but the changes that were going on in my personality and my whole outlook were occurring so rapidly I was becoming self-obsessed. I didn't have time for any-thing outside of myself. The world was moving too fast.

'It was the first time in my life that I'd been able to

communicate with other kids my age. I realised that they liked the more flamboyant side of my nature, and I realised that I could hold their attention and respect by being able to make up stories and make them laugh. So overnight I became this dramatic, unpredictable character to all my friends, and I really played everything up. I came to school one day dressed in the full Clint Eastwood regalia: cowboy hat, unlit cigar, a poncho a mate had lent to me, straight black jeans, and cowboy boots. I just walked into class and put my feet up on the desk. My mates *loved* it! But the teachers didn't know how to handle it at all. They thought there was something seriously wrong with me.

'But it was just me playing different characters. I came in another time like a character out of Charlie Brown; I wouldn't go anywhere without this big tartan blanket over my shoulders. The little kids at school liked that one.'

When Derek left Dalkeith High at eighteen, he considered accepting a place at Edinburgh University for a time. 'I wanted to be an archaeologist for about a month!' he says. Through a combination of his enthusiasm for history and a childhood fascination for hand-painted toy armies, Derek decided next that he might rather be a military historian.

'I actually got quite serious about that idea for a while,' he admits. 'I even got as far as having two interviews at Sandhurst in Edinburgh! I passed the first one, easy. The second I completely blew. But it was a deliberate move on my part. I walked in the interview room and decided I hated the guy on the other side of the desk. One look at his pompous supercilious face and I knew right away he was going to be a prick. And as it turned out my first impression was the correct one. He was a completely obnoxious upper-class twat!

'He started asking me some questions that he said were designed to determine whether I had the qualities to lead men, and I just couldn't relate to what he was talking about at all. I ended up telling him he was full of shit and got up and walked out! "I can't join your bloody army! The whole idea sickens me after talking to you!" I told him. So that was that.

'I went home and said "I'm not going there mum, I don't bloody like what they're about." My mum and dad just sat there on the couch. "Well, what are you going to do now, son?" they asked. "I don't know," I said. "But I've made up my mind that it has to be something better than that".'

★　　★　　★

Finally deciding against embarking on a full-time course of studies at University, Derek Dick took a job as a genetics research worker for the Forestry Commission at the Northern Research Station, in the nearby Bow Hill Estate. Derek says the job entailed 'watering plants, mostly'.

'I came about the job in an oblique way,' he says. 'Not knowing what to do with myself after leaving school, I took a temporary summer job in the local Parks Department. I did that for three weeks, they saw that I was a bright boy who knew how to water a few plants, and offered me the job as "genetic research worker". It was pretty boring, I have to admit, and I used to sit around a lot of the time reading *Sounds* and *Melody Maker* and wondering why *I* wasn't out there in the big wide world doing something with my life. But at eighteen, the future still seemed endless to me, and I was in no hurry to make my move just yet. I just kept drifting with whatever turned up next.'

Next came the opportunity, via several loose connections at the Forestry Commission, for Derek to take an O.N.D. course in Forestry at a private college called Newtonrigg, in Cumbria. The course would mean spending the next three years alternating between full-time studies in Cumbria, for the first and third year, and practical on-site work on the Bow Hill Estate the second.

'I thought, why not?' he says. 'It was a decent enough job, I liked the company of the other guys in the Forestry Commission, everything had a real gang feel to it, and because doing the course meant taking two years of practical apprenticeship first, that meant I could still carry on working out-of-doors and living a fairly easy, uncomplicated work life. Which suited me fine. It gave me enough money to keep going to gigs and buying new albums and having enough to drink. As long as I had that, for the time being I was happy.'

Derek's first year at Newtonrigg College was to begin in September 1978. In the meantime, he spent the summer months leading up to his departure for Cumbria working in a place called Speymouth Forest, near Elgin in the North East of Scotland.

'I used to cut down trees, build fences, dig ditches, and drive things around,' he says. 'To be honest, I was never very good at the work, though. The other guys used to rib me that all I was was a jumped-up van driver, which wasn't far from the truth, actually.

'One thing it did for me, though: I got incredibly fit up there.

I lost all my excess weight and became lean and muscly. I knew I wouldn't stay that way forever, of course,' he laughs. 'But it was good while it lasted!'

Derek says his days up in Speymouth Forest were a time of great change for him.

'The months I'd spent up in Speymouth Forest had shown me how to look after myself. Apart from the last couple of years I spent at school, when I adopted the guise of the clown for a lot of the time, most of the time I was there I was a real wimp! I let other kids push me around and I was scared of everybody.

'Well, that all changed while I was up at Speymouth. I'd learned not to back away from every fight, and I discovered how to handle myself at last. And then I lost my virginity when I came back to Dalkeith one weekend, to a girl I'd been dating for about two years beforehand. And of course, it was while I was away in Speymouth that I really developed what you might call a 'habit' for the drink!' he smiles. 'There was just nothing else to do in the evenings except get drunk. And that's when I finally found out what they meant when people used to talk about the power of positive drinking.

'The whole business probably boiled down to nothing more than the fact that I had never lived away from home before, and so I really made the most of it and set out to discover new and hidden depths to the levels of depravity I was capable of. I was in a hurry to grow up and learn things, suddenly, and although a few of my lessons left me feeling once bitten twice shy, I was unstoppable!'

The nine months that he spent from September 1978 'til June 1979, at Newtonrigg, Derek says he remembers as 'swift and largely uneventful'.

'When I got back to Dalkeith, I heard about this two-week trust-funded study course in Forestry that was going on out in Germany. So I decided to go for it and take off to Germany for a couple of weeks. Apart from anything else I thought it might give me a bit more time to decide what I really wanted to do. I was nearly twenty-one by then, and the prospects for the immediate future of Derek William Dick weren't looking nearly as exciting as I wanted them to.

'It was when I got home from Germany that I decided to take the name Fish for the first time, really. I came back to Dalkeith determined to give myself enough breathing space to get up the courage to eventually have a crack at being a singer in a band.

The first step was changing the name. I thought if I could get enough people to think of me in a totally new way, to the point where they even called me by a new name, then I had a chance of re-inventing my whole personality. Instead of waiting for things to happen, I would make things start happening around me. So, after thinking about it for ages, I decided to call myself Fish.'

Fish, says Fish, suited him because of the nickname the friend had bestowed after waiting nearly two hours for him to finish having a bath, and because it was also the off-stage nickname of Chris Squire, the bass player in Yes, who Fish says he greatly admired, and not least because it was the name of the leader of a gang of romantic street-smarts in a TV show from Derek's teenage years.

'It was for all those reasons. I identified with all those characters in my head, the partying musician, the leader of the outlaws, and the lazy slob lying in the bath for hours keeping his bottom warm.'

By the end of Summer 1979, however, Fish – as he was now becoming known to friends and foes alike – was back working on the Bow Hill Estate, growing increasingly disillusioned with the idea of having what his parents liked to call a 'proper job'.

'I was still going to loads and loads of gigs, reading all the music papers voraciously, and dreaming of becoming a singer. I'd already decided that my best bet was to get myself down to London somehow, because I didn't really have the first idea of how you became a singer, but I knew that however it was done, it didn't happen by staying at home in Dalkeith and learning the Latin names of trees!

'My mother and father were very insistent though that I should at least have some sort of job training behind me before I went traipsing off to London in search of fame and fortune. I was stuck, and I couldn't see any way out of the predicament. I was still lacking that last tiny spur I still needed to sever all ties with the known world of my family and really go for it on my own as anything I damn well pleased.'

Ironically enough, the last small push from inside that Fish still needed came, of all places, at a Peter Gabriel concert at the Usher Hall, in Edinburgh on 1 March 1980.

'Obviously, I had been a big fan of Gabriel's since his early, early days with Genesis. I'd seem him with them on the "Lamb Lies Down on Broadway" tour five years before and thought then that he was a brilliant live performer, totally innovative, and over the years, of course, I'd built a really big thing up about him in my mind,' says Fish.

'Well, it turned out to be a pretty rotten gig for him. The PA broke down, he didn't sing well, and he didn't look very happy. I remember that really put things into perspective for me. He looked so fragile up there on the stage, so helpless, all his mystique fell away and I realised I was just looking at another man, the same as me, and that anybody could get up on a stage and do this singing thing. It just required a bit of guts and an inflated view of your own talents,' he laughs. 'And I had plenty of both!'

As if to reinforce his new point of view, Fish managed to blag his way backstage after the show by posing as a German rock journalist there to review the show. He desperately wanted to see his hero in close-up.

'I put on this big heavy fake German accent,' he laughs, 'and it managed to fool the bouncers on the backstage doors. The next thing I know I'm on my way up the stairs to see Peter Gabriel! Anyway, as I was walking in, there he was suddenly, standing in the corridor talking to two fans. The first thing I thought was how *tiny* he looked. I realise that's probably as much to do with my own height as his, but all the same, I got exactly the same feeling when I watched him on stage that night. He looked, well, *fragile*, distant, almost two-dimensional.

'I said something to him like, "It's really great to see somebody doing something original these days," and he said "Thanks very much". Then I just sort of stood there looking at him for a moment, watching him chatting to these fans, and all the time I just couldn't stop thinking how *tiny* he looked!

'I left thinking, "If that wee guy in there can do it, then so can I."

'And then the weirdest part of all is as I was walking away from the gig I bumped into an old mate of mine that I hadn't seen in years. It was the same guy that first introduced me to bands like ELP and Van Der Graaf Generator when I was about thirteen years old. Anyway, it turned out that he had his own band now, he said. They were called Not Quite Red Fox, and they were looking for a new frontman who could sing. He said a couple of guys were handling the singing for the time being, but what they were looking for was someone who could come in and really front the band on stage. And then he asked me if I was still interested in having a go at singing myself? Well, I didn't need to be asked twice, and so we organised a meeting for me to come down and audition for the band . . . I was over the moon! Then two minutes later we said cheerio and I was left standing there thinking, "Oh hell! I've gone and done it now! I'm not a singer! I can't sing!" And then I thought, "Hang on, of course I can sing. Other people can do it, I can do it! Or can I?" It just went round and round in my head like that every day leading up to my first audition," he says, cringing a bit at the memory. 'When the day of the audition finally arrived, outwardly I was quite cool and calm, I think, but inwardly I was a seething mass of bad nerves.'

The audition was held in Edinburgh, at a place called the Netherbow Theatre, situated in the Royal Mile. It was the first time either Fish or Derek had ever stepped on a stage, let alone sung into a microphone, and at first his total lack of experience was all too obvious. As he himself puts it, 'I wasn't really getting that good bathroom sound to my voice'. As a result, the boys in Not Quite Red Fox hesitated over offering the gig full-time to so patently inexperienced a young performer.

'They told me to come up to their next gig, which was at the University in Aberdeen,' says Fish. 'My job that night was to hand the guitarist his acoustic guitar half-way through one number!

'Then, after the gig, they sat me down and asked me if I would be prepared to give up my course at the Forestry Commission college if they were to offer me a full-time gig as the singer in the band. Of course, I was like, yes, yes, yes, *anything you say!* I thought this was my first big opportunity to get involved in the music business and really prove myself!

'When I got back to Dalkeith they still hadn't really made up their minds about me, but I was convinced that they would at least give me a trial run. And then about a week after that they met me and told me that although my voice was OK they were really looking for a singer that could show off a bit and be very visual on stage! They suggested that because I had absolutely no experience in that role perhaps I should go off and join somebody else's band for six months or so, gain the experience, then come back to them and see about the job. I couldn't believe it! They told me I didn't have enough presence on stage and that I lacked charisma! I was really pissed off!

'The first thing I did was drive down to see some girl friends of mine who shared a flat together that I used to hang out in a lot. I told them what had happened, they'd both been sort of encouraging me to have a crack at being a singer, and I asked them if they knew someone, anyone, that might have a band that needed a singer. I was fucking determined to prove I could do it.

'They said, "Well, there is this one guy we know . . . his name's Dotol".'

Dotol – real name Donald K. Little – was indeed looking for a singer. His band, Blewitt, were a loose boogie outfit that liked to specialise in Little Feat and Average White Band covers. After taking part in the most perfunctory of 'auditions' in a room at the cottage where Dotol lived, Fish was thrown in at the deep end and asked if he would come along and sing at the band's next gig.

'At the so-called audition at Dotol's place, the guys in the band asked me what numbers I knew well enough to sing for them. I said, "Do you know how to play any Genesis numbers? Or anything by Yes?",' Fish smiles, 'and they all just looked at me as though I'd suddenly grown two heads . . . They said "You must be joking! We don't play any of that crap!" So I thought about if for a moment, and then I suggested doing something by Free. Of course, they were all into a bit of that and so we banged out a really rough and ready version of "All Right Now" by Free that went on for about ten minutes. And afterwards they said "OK, you've got the gig". It was as simple as that.

'My first ever actual gig with them was a nightmare, though! I was utterly shit scared. It was at a pub in Galashiels called the Golden Lion. I got there about two hours before the rest of the band turned up, and I just sat there getting drunker and drunker on my own at the bar. By the time the band had arrived and I was helping them set their gear up, I was completely pissed out of my head! By the time we went on I could barely walk straight, and I sang about five or six numbers in this big horrible WAARRGGHH-I'M-DRUNNKK sort of voice. We were doing numbers like "Walk On By" by Dionne Warwick, "Atlantic Avenue" by the Average White Band, and Eric Clapton's version of Bob Marley's "I Shot the Sheriff", real sort of middle-of-the-road funk-rock, mostly. And although the band proved they could definitely play a bit, I was *awful*!

'When we'd finished the set I ran off-stage straight into the toilets and threw up! When I'd recovered a bit I went into the dressing room to apologise to the rest of the band for being so drunk and they all said "No, don't apologise, it was a great gig, man!" It wasn't until months later I discovered that they thought I had been terrible that first night. But none of them had been that fussed about it. They thought that they might as well keep me on for the time being until either somebody better came along, or I drastically improved.

'In the meantime, I was going around town like Jack the Lad, I thought I was well and truly *in*! It was like, "Hey ma, look at me now, I'm going to be a bloody rock star!",' he chortles.

Blewitt, with Fish, played the Golden Lion in Galashiels every Thursday night and the Cross Keys Hotel in Kelso every other Sunday. Slowly, the newly-begun singer did start to show signs of improvement. He got more used to relaxing before an audience, and he remembered not to get too drunk during the set. But the biggest aid and confidence booster he says he found was the close friendship he struck up with Blewitt's lead guitarist, Frank Usher.

'The first thing Frank ever told me was to *never* apologise to an audience. If you fuck up, don't stand there saying sorry, just get on with it and entertain them. People didn't come to rock and roll shows to hear the singer standing there saying sorry! It was good advice,' says Fish, 'Frank was a real professional. In the past, he'd played with people like Alan Hull from Lindisfarne, and Mike Heron from the Incredible String Band. I used to go back to his place after the gig sometimes and we'd have a drink together and talk. I remember searching through his record collection and pulling out albums with his name on them, and thinking "Wow! This is really big time!"

'But the main thing about my friendship with Frank was that it was him that used to sit there telling me that if I really wanted to make it as a singer then I could! He told me he thought I had the makings of a really good voice and that I shouldn't fuck around wasting more time working for the Forestry Commission, I should just get myself out of Dalkeith and down to London, maybe, or one of the other big cities in England, where the chances of me finding a band I could really throw my lot into were much greater.

'Frank was the first person that had ever said anything like that to me, and it really got me thinking. I was supposed to go back down to Newtonrigg College at the beginning of September 1980, for the start of my last year of study there, but that would have meant quitting the band for nine months, and I just couldn't bear the thought of waiting around that long. I felt that if I didn't get out of the Forestry Commission soon I might never have the courage to completely uproot myself and try my hand at something a bit more adventurous. I got so uptight about the whole situation I went into a terrible depression. I ended up going home to my parents and saying, "Look, if I don't leave this fucking job soon and have a crack at what I really want to do, I'm going to have a nervous breakdown!"

'My parents and I ended up having another terrible row. My father threatened to completely disown me if I quit the Forestry Commission, and my mother told me I was being stupid and selfish not wanting to stay on and take my last year at Newtonrigg. But I didn't care, by then wild horses wouldn't have been able to drag me back to Cumbria!'

Not wanting to hurt his parents' feelings any more than was necessary, Fish eventually wrote a letter to the Principal of Newtonrigg informing him that due to ill-health, he would like to take an indefinite break from his course at the college.

'I tried to leave it as open-ended with my bosses there as possible,' he says. 'Which helped calm my mother and father down a lot.

'Finally I struck a deal with my dad whereby he gave me his full blessing to go off and try and do something as a singer if, in return, I would agree to knock the whole idea of becoming a rock singer on the head if I hadn't got anywhere after three years. Which I thought was *very* fair, at the time. I mean, I thought three years was *ages*. By then I could have conquered half the world!' he laughs out loud.

Summer 1980 found Fish scouring the Musicians Wanted ads in all the weekly music papers. Blewitt had by now metamorphosed into a larger, more rambling musical outfit, and though Fish kept up his weekly appearances as their singer, he had already let them know that he was only staying until the opportunity to join up with a band as career-oriented as himself came along.

'Having made the break from full-time employment in Scotland, I knew my days left there were numbered,' says Fish. 'So while I was waiting to make my jump down to England, I just threw in my lot with the guys from Blewitt. We had some interesting times together in the end.'

In September 1980, Fish answered one of the ads for a band looking for a new singer that he found in *Sounds*, and landed himself an audition in Kettering with an unknown but promising local outfit called Stranger.

'I paid for myself to go all the way down there and audition for the gig,' says Fish. 'They seemed like a fairly happening young band. They owned their own PA, and had a lot of other nice new gear.

'Anyway, we ran through a few songs, and afterwards we sat down and chatted. I seemed to get on all right with everybody except the guitarist. He and I took an instant dislike to each other. I don't know why, it was just one of those things. He didn't like me and I definitely didn't like him, it was decided the moment I walked through the door. All the same, I still had high hopes of joining the band.'

However, a fortnight later Fish was told, by the guitarist of Stranger, that he hadn't got the job.

'He said my voice was too quiet!' cries Fish, in a very *unquiet* voice. 'That was the first and last time anybody's ever said *that* to me!'

To save himself the further expense of travelling down to every single audition he might turn up in the classified pages of the music press, Fish put together a little package to send out to any bands that might be interested, before committing either party to a full-scale meeting of minds at another dreaded audition.

'I had a tape of Blewitt playing some numbers live, followed by a couple of numbers me and Frank Usher had put together on our own, on a little four-track we'd set up at Frank's place. And I had some photos taken – like, *here I am folks!*' Fish laughs.

'And anybody that was looking for a singer that I thought might be interesting, I would send off this package to them that I'd made.'

Fish says that most of the replies he got were from aspiring young heavy metal bands.

'I think it was just around that time that the heavy metal thing in Britain started to make a huge comeback,' he says, 'and suddenly there were just tons of these new young heavy metal bands being formed. And, of course, they were all looking for singers that could really sing, or bellow out the blues, which so many new wave singers obviously couldn't do, wouldn't even be interested in doing. So I think they all picked on me. Honestly, I got so many replies from these unknown heavy metal bands I started giving the idea of getting into a touch of the old Robert Plant's some serious thought!

'There was one band from Manchester – called Kamikazi, or something like that – that I went as far as exchanging tapes with, and that was a big mistake. I listened to their tape and it was awful! This awful, trite sounding half-arsed sub-heavy metal shit! But they got in contact with me and told me they loved my tape! They couldn't wait to meet me, and when could I come down for an audition? Suddenly it was my turn to make stupid excuses why I wouldn't fit into the band.'

The next ad Fish replied to he found in the pages of *Musicians Only*. Somebody called the Stone Dome Band, from Retford in Nottinghamshire, was looking for a 'vocalist/lyricist'.

'It was worded really oddly,' says Fish. 'Real Hawkwind-type cosmic words. So I phoned up the number they gave and I got through to this guy called Diz Minnit. Anyway, we got on great on the phone, so I ended up jumping on the next train down to Retford to meet him and the rest of the band.'

Musically, the Stone Dome Band were some removes closer to the kind of music Fish was interested in than were the hapless Blewitt. However, they were still very amateurish with more enthusiasm than talent to speak of.

'They didn't really have much going for them,' Fish admits. 'But Diz, who was the bass player, seemed like a good guy, as up for having a crack at the big time as I was. After I passed the audition I moved into Diz's parents' house with him and we became great friends.

'I knew the band wasn't really going anywhere, but I was getting impatient to make my move out of Scotland, and Blewitt. So instead of waiting for the "perfect" band to come along, I jumped in and took my chances with Diz and the guys in Retford.'

Fish's time with the Stone Dome Band was not long.

'We only lasted a few weeks together, really,' he says. 'The music was terrible, really kitsch sub-Hawkwind overtures, and one truly awful number Diz had written the lyrics to called "Astral Shore". And apart from Diz, who I was getting very close to, and the drummer, who was a drinker, I really didn't like the rest of the guys very much.

'Eventually I said to Diz, "Look, I can't stay here with this lot. What about coming down to Cambridge with me, and we'll see if we can't get a new band of our own together there?' I was going out with a girl who went to the University at Cambridge at the time, and so at least we would have somewhere to stay for a while. So that's what we did.'

Fish and Diz spent a fortnight in Cambridge at the end of 1980, sleeping on floors and being snuck through windows and back doors at the students' halls of residence after dark. They never did get that band together, not in Cambridge. Instead, they went punting on the Cam and wangling dinner invitations whenever possible.

'It was while we were bumming around in Cambridge, pretending to be students whenever it suited us, that I first came up with some of the lines for "Garden Party",' says Fish. 'We had a fun two weeks there. But it was a dead loss as far as getting a band, or a place to live together went.'

At the end of their fortnight in Cambridge, Fish and Diz decided to call it a day and return home. Diz made his way back to Retford, while Fish scraped together his last few pennies for the trip back to Dalkeith.

'My parents were *not* pleased to see me,' Fish smiles. 'It was like, "Is that it then, son? Are you home for good?" But I was like no, no, no!

'This was in November 1980. After a couple of weeks home I managed to persuade Diz to come up and join me in Dalkeith. We rented this sort of holiday cottage near the Bow Hill Estate, where I still used to work sometimes for the Duke of Buccleuch who owned the place. It was very secluded and quite tiny, but the rent was only about £6 a week so it suited us fine.'

Armed with just one Shure SM80 microphone, and one bass guitar and an amp, with precious little else besides their own boundless enthusiasm to offer any prospective new musical partners, the unlikely pair again set about trying to form their own band.

'It was useless though,' sighs Fish. 'As soon as I'd got back to Scotland, I'd started singing with Blewitt again whenever they had a gig. But that was more to do with me wanting to keep my hand in working with a gigging band, until me and Diz could get something better together. We weren't having much luck though. We'd find a guitarist or a drummer we thought we could work with and ask them to join the "band". But they would always ask us how many gigs we had lined up, or did we have own our PA, or how many songs had we written? And our answers were always the same – no gigs, yet, no PA, yet, and no real songs, yet, no nothing, in fact . . . *yet*, but what about it, anyway? And that's when the guitarist, or the drummer or whoever, would usually walk out the door.'

By the end of 1980, with the exception of the one or two verses to the song he had got the idea for while he and Diz were in Cambridge, 'Garden Party', Fish still hadn't yet explored the possibilities of writing his own original lyrics.

'When I was about fourteen or fifteen I had written a lot of poetry. Mostly, I was inspired to write rock lyrics, but as I was useless at playing an instrument I never had any music to work with. So instead I wrote verses of poetry,' says Fish. 'But they were all *awful*! When I discovered them lying in a drawer somewhere when I was about seventeen years old, I wanted to burn them! I wanted to tear them into little pieces and bury them in someone else's garden! I was so embarrassed! Ugh!' he pulls a face.

'The closest I ever came to writing a lyric after that was once when I experimented with cut-ups, using the titles to different movies and TV programmes. I just jumbled them all together and pulled them out of a hat one at a time. I was quite pleased with that one. I was still in school and it was more interesting than anything I could have come up with on my own at that time, that's for sure.

'Living at the cottage with Diz that winter I had already started scribbling little things down here and there. But without any music to guide me, it was fairly hopeless trying to write a whole song, just my voice and Diz's bass together. It wasn't until I joined Marillion that I ever really took the idea of writing my own lyrics seriously. And then suddenly I came out with *hundreds* of sets of lyrics, a veritable bloody flood of them! I think I must have been bottling up a lot of feelings, and storing up a lot of insane imagery in all those years I wasn't actually writing, because suddenly I had lyrics to about fifteen different songs in the space of about three months.'

Before that, though, Fish and Diz were left to scrape by as best they could, bandless, penniless, and jobless, at their small cottage out in the frozen wilds of Galashiels.

'Christmas was getting closer and closer and we were getting broker, the weather was getting colder, the nights were getting longer, and we were nowhere nearer getting a band together,' says Fish.

'Finally, I told Diz I didn't think it was working and that we should split up and go our own way. I was back to thinking about being a heavy metal singer, I was so desperate for work. Diz said OK, and we were going to give up the cottage by Christmas. Then a couple of nights later I was sitting in the pub when Diz came in and showed me this ad, in *Musicians Only*. It said something like "bassist/vocalist required" with an Aylesbury telephone number. Diz said why don't we try for it, and I said "Go on then, phone them up!" So he raced outside to the phone-box outside the pub and rang the number. Five minutes later he came back in and said, "Right, the name of the band is Marillion, they do lots of gigs, they've even got their own T-shirts, and they've agreed to see both of us". I said, what? Give me that phone number here.'

Several phone calls and a mutual exchange of tapes later, Fish and Diz were invited down to Aylesbury for an audition.

'I ended up talking to Mick Pointer on the phone a lot, and we both started off by bullshitting each other,' smiles Fish. 'He told me that the band were gigging full-time to 250, 300 people a night, and gave me all this guff about them having their own T-shirts and a high-class demo tape that they'd recorded at The Enid's studio. I was like, "All right, all right, I'm impressed!" But by the same token I was bullshitting him about how many gigs me and Diz had done, and who with.

'That went on for a couple of weeks and then Diz and I arranged to meet them down in Aylesbury sometime in the first week of the New Year, 1981. In the meantime, Diz took off for Xmas at home with his folks in Retford and I went home to my mother and father's house in Dalkeith.

'I'll never forget the day we actually left the cottage for the last time, though. It was the same day John Lennon was killed! I remember driving away from the cottage in Diz's van, and we had the radio on and they were playing a whole string of old Beatles and John Lennon records. I said to Diz, "Something's wrong here. Why are they playing all these Beatles records? Something's happened."

'And I remember, the first little town we pulled into I stopped someone I knew and asked them what was going on, and they said, "John Lennon's dead. He was shot and killed".

'I couldn't believe it! I just started crying. It seemed like an insane idea that John Lennon was dead, had been killed! It was just too much. I'd fucking grown up with John Lennon and the

Beatles. Losing him like that was like suddenly losing a part of my life I'd never see again. I was really broken up about his death. I think a lot of people all over the world probably felt the same way.'

Fish spent a quiet Christmas at home with his family in Dalkeith. His last ever live performance as the singer with Blewitt was on Saturday 13 December 1980, at the Waverly Castle in Melrose, where he and the band supported the famous blues-man, Alexis Korner. Then, on the 2 January 1981, with a righteous Hogmanay hangover still clouding his vision, and with his father's last words on the subject – 'well son, at least you're geting to see a bit of the world, eh? Retford, Cambridge, and now Aylesbury! Where-ever next will you go?' – still ringing in his ears, Fish took the train from Edinburgh to Retford, where he met up with Diz and his Comma van for the long drive the rest of the way down to Aylesbury.

'It was a freezing cold day,' Fish remembers. 'And we had a blow out on one of the van's tyres somewhere in Luton, and then it took us ages to find this address they'd given us.

'When we finally got there, it was a little cottage just outside Aston Clinton, I walked into the dining room and saw all these public-schoolboy lookalikes. There was this real saccharin-looking keyboard player with glasses called Brian, and Privet, of course, grinning horribly from ear to ear, and another dull-looking person called Guy, who was kind of a spare part. And then there was Mick Pointer and Steve Rothery, but I didn't know which was which. Walking into a crowded room like that full of complete strangers was a bit odd. None of us quite knew where to begin.'

Fish and Diz broke the ice by suggesting everyone beat a speedy retreat to the nearest pub, there to imbibe an ale or three. Everybody needed to relax and get acquainted, the pub seemed like a good place to do it in.

Later, back at the cottage, drunk and well on the way to getting properly acquainted, somebody put on 'Supper's Ready', the classic early Peter Gabriel-era Genesis track, on the stereo, and Fish started to sing.

'We were all absolutely *steaming* drunk by this time anyway, and all singing along to everything . . . Then it got to about two a.m. and somebody put "Supper's Ready" on and I really let loose on it. I was very drunk and suddenly *very* intense,' Fish laughs. 'But when I finished they all looked at me, amazed. they

111

said, "You can sing! You can sing! You've got a voice that sounds just like Peter Gabriel's!" Of course, I revelled in that. I loved it!

'It's funny, though,' he reflects, 'as time wore on I quickly grew to hate it when people kept on saying I sounded like Peter Gabriel. It became a real burden I had to carry around with me for a long, long time.

'But back then, that first night with Marillion, them saying that was like getting the final seal of approval. I could sing! I was as good as Peter Gabriel! *All right!*'

Work on redefining the new Marillion sound, along with some new sets of original lyrics Fish had been working on from the tapes he had already received of the band's music from Mick Pointer, began the following day. The first number the band completed together was an older instrumental piece Steve Rothery had written called 'Close', which, when given new life and meaning with a curiously wordy, profane set of verses that began *'The rain auditions at my window, its symphony echoes in my womb.'* which Fish had written, metamorphosed into a new, panoramic piece called 'The Web'.

Another older pre-Fish number the band still had hopes for was called 'Lady Fantasy'. After Fish had added some more of his casually surreal word-images, the song involved into a far more adventurous, if a little pretentious, number retitled 'The Madcap's Embrace'. It was, says Fish, his 'Ode to Syd Barrett' – the original singer and guitarist with Pink Floyd.

'Apart from "The Web", though, which we were all very pleased with, the very earliest things we worked on together were fairly naff,' says Fish, matter-of-factly. 'But that wasn't a problem, we were coming up with new material all the time. Mostly, though, it was Steve and me that actually wrote the bulk of the songs back then, when I first joined the band. Brian Jelliman just did what Steve told him to, he never really came up with anything on his own; Diz just wasn't in it at all, he'd never had any major ambitions as a song-writer anyway, Diz just wanted to play the bass in a rock and roll band; as for Mick, well, he definitely saw Marillion as *his* band, that much was made clear to me from the word go, but as a drummer with a very limited talent for his chosen craft, he couldn't really be expected to come up with too many new ideas for songs.

'So most of the writing was really left to me and Steve. And very quickly, I think we both realised we had something going together. Musically, when any decisions were being made about the arrangements of the new material, me and Steve always tended to side together against the others if ever there was any argument. We pretty much led the way to begin with.'

Apart from Mick Pointer, who lived with his girlfriend Stef, in their own flat in Aylesbury, and Brian Jelliman, who lived in digs elsewhere in the town, when they weren't rehearsing, the rest of Marillion spent the first few months of 1981 living together in the small cottage in Aston Clinton. Guy and Privet shared one bedroom, while Steve Rothery had the only other bedroom, about the size of a large closet, to himself. Being less senior in the ranks than the others in those days, Fish and Diz were relegated to sleeping downstairs on the dining room floor.

Money was tight, meals could never be counted on, but that was nothing new to Fish. The important thing, as he saw it, was that he had finally been given a shot with a band he actually believed in. Against the odds, not only had he teamed up with an act bent on the same esoteric musical aspirations as his own, but in Steve Rothery Fish had found his perfect creative foil. Steve made the same kind of music with his guitar that Fish could always hear inside his own head but never hope to express.

As people, they were very different: Steve was quiet and thoughtful, Fish was loud and extravagant in his wishes. But when paired together on the rehearsal room floor, undercover of the low studio lights, something happened between them that always sparked ideas.

'Steve and I seem to have an almost yin-yang relationship when we work together,' says Fish. 'I don't mean that to sound hopelessly pretentious, but that's what it feels like sometimes. We may be very different as people, but right from the start we always worked incredibly well together. Maybe it's because we're so different that we manage to spark off each other so well, I don't know. But right from the beginning it was there between us – the ability to make magic out of bits and pieces of words and music.'

In March 1981, just prior to his first live gig with Marillion, Fish took a job at a company called Hoe Lock Ltd as a quality inspector. He lasted just over a week before getting fired.

'I was back to the business of watering plants,' he smiles. 'Only this time I was the bloke who tested garden water-sprinklers. I used to stand at the end of the production line, and one out of every hundred of these sprinklers would have to be pulled out by me and taken off and tested. I was supposed to check the spray to make sure it was even, and I had to make sure there were no marks on the casing.

'A more boring job would have been hard to find, but I hadn't had a steady wage for nearly nine months at this point, and I was getting desperate for cash. We all were. There was absolutely no money whatsoever coming in yet from the band, and everybody was always permanently skint. After about a week and a half though, my work reference from the Bow Hill Estate came through and that was the end of my career as a water-sprinkler tester! The reference said something like "Unable to keep a grip on reality, a dreamer." I remember the best part described me as a "disruptive influence amongst the work-force".

'Well, I was quite proud of such a glowing description of my character,' he chuckles, 'but needless to say, Hoe Lock saw things differently and sacked me on the spot. It was like, never darken our doorstep again! But by then the band had started gigging, and I was really getting into that in a big way, so shit on their water-sprinklers.'

A week later, however, Fish was working full-time behind a desk at the local Department of Health and Social Security offices in Aylesbury.

'Brian Jelliman got me an interview there through some friends of his that worked there,' says Fish. 'I'd been paid over £100 for the week and a half's work I'd done at Hoe Lock, and I'd already put most of the money down as a deposit on a room in a flat – by then I'd had all I could stand of sleeping on the floor in the cottage in Aston Clinton. So when I got offered this job out of the blue, in the Unemployment Benefit offices of the DHSS, I thought, why not? It's only money, and right then I needed all I could get my hands on.'

Fish's first gig with Marillion, at the Red Lion pub in Bicester, on 15 March 1981, was, he says, both a terrifying and exhilarating experience.

'It was so unlike any other live gig I had ever done before. It was the first time I'd ever gone on stage with a band and sung a set of songs with lyrics that *I* had written, and it was the first time I had ever experimented with face make-up on stage – nothing too elaborate for that first gig, just some lines and some extra colour around the eyes . . . the Fish eyes . . . And I started

114

off really nervous. By about the third or fourth number though, I was starting to relax and take control of the situation. By the end of the set I thought we'd all played a real blinder! I mean, there had been loads of mistakes, of course, but it was still the most exciting thing I'd ever experienced. To play all our own original material and have people stand there and applaud at the end was something that was still totally new to me! It felt amazing! I was hooked on it straight away.'

The weeks that followed found Fish gradually taking over most of the responsibility for finding and arranging the band's gigs.

'Before I came along, Guy was the person who was supposed to sort out the band's gigs. He did OK, but once I'd watched him working for a while and caught on to how it was done, I found I was much better at blagging gigs for the band than he was. I'd long ago learned how to be quick with my mouth and how to make my voice so much louder than anybody else's in the room, so getting on the phone and persuading all these pub owners and club promoters and college student union reps to book us in for some gigs came very naturally to me.'

By summer 1981, Marillion were playing two or three times a week regularly, building up a workable and impressive live set, and gaining a solid following of about 200 people in the Aylesbury area. The new material was starting to gel, and Fish's scope as a live performer was beginning to grab the attention of the pundits.

'By then we had "Grendel", "Garden Party", and "The Web" all in the set, and all sorts of other stuff we eventually dropped like "Skyline Drifter" and "The Madcap's Embrace". And I was starting to explore and experiment more and more with the theatrical possibilities presented by some of the songs.

'I got into the make-up in a big way and painted different designs on my face each time we played. And I got everybody to dress up in these ridiculous-looking monk's robes, with hoods and big flared sleeves and a big eye painted on the sides and back. Then the first time Dave Stopps ever booked us for a gig at Friar's, I arranged to have all these cardboard grave-stones dotted around the stage, and Privet got into making what stage-lighting we had quite stark and dramatic.

'The band were getting tight enough to ensure the songs came across with plenty of impact, and I was getting into mime, and acting out every little drama I'd written about in the songs.

'It was a very creative period for us all. We were starting to take what we were doing very seriously.'

Most of Marillion's earliest fans did like to compare their music to that of early Genesis. But in those days that was still a point of view Fish took very much as a compliment.

'People used to come up to me after we'd just done a gig and say, "You really sound like Genesis in places, but there's still something about your music that's different enough to make it interesting",' Fish smiles. 'Which in 1981 was still music to our ears. I mean, never at any time, contradictory to what anyone else might think, did this band sit down and try and write a "Genesis song" together. They were a big influence on a lot of us, there was no denying that. But they were really only one of hundreds of different influences we had, and not even the biggest. For me, that might be Pink Floyd. For somebody else in the band, it would be somebody different.'

However, with the first signs that the 'complimentary' Genesis comparisons they were continually picking up might soon translate into wicked taunts in the press, Fish arranged to have a demo-tape of some Marillion songs sent to Peter Gabriel for *his* opinion on the matter.

'Dave Stopps had Gabriel's home address, and he agreed to mail him a tape,' says Fish. 'I wanted to see what, if anything, he might have to say about Marillion. To be honest, I never really expected a reply, but I thought what the hell, it's only a tape. If he hates it that much he can always throw it in the bin and forget about it.'

To Fish's surprise and amazement, a week or so after Dave Stopps had mailed him the Marillion tape, Peter Gabriel rang Fish up to congratulate him and the rest of the band on the songs.

'I must admit, I freaked out,' laughs Fish. 'I mean, totally! Here was one of my big boyhood heroes ringing me to tell me what he thought of our songs! I couldn't believe it!

'The thing is, I wasn't in when he rang, but he left his number and I rang him back the next night. I was a bundle of nerves; I didn't even know what I wanted to say to him except maybe "What do you think then, Peter? Are we copying you, or what?"

'But his wife answered the phone and said "Peter's eating his dinner, can you call back later?" Of course, I was like "Yes, yes, *no problem!*" Then I finally got through to him later that night and he was really nice, very quiet, and he said some very nice things about the tape. He said he didn't think we sounded like Genesis particularly, here and there maybe, he said, but nothing we wouldn't lose with time and more practice at writing our own material.

'And he suggested that I should try pushing my singing voice to the limit a bit more than I was doing; he told me not to be afraid of making mistakes and going out on a limb occasionally, it would help stop too many repetitious mannerisms from creeping in. It was a good sort of pep-talk he gave me.

'Afterwards, as soon as I put the phone down everyone in the band was like "What did he say? What did he say?" I said "I don't know. I think he said he thought we were all right." Then for the rest of the night I was walking around with this I-know-something-you-don't-know smile on my face. For about the next three weeks, it didn't matter what anybody might say about us. Peter Gabriel had rung to tell us we were all right. So we were,' he smiles.

By September 1981, with two scrap-books already filled with cuttings accumulated in the local press, Fish sensed the time was right for Marillion to widen the scope of their publicity and start getting their names and faces into the national music press. In short, the band needed a press agent. Someone not too expensive, of course, and preferably with some previous experience promoting a band like themselves, who were staunchly anti-fashion, unbudgingly album-oriented in their musical ambitions, and intent on being taken very seriously indeed. And someone, ideally, who could combine all those services with the kind of glazed good humour Fish and the band thrived on. Someone, in fact, like Keith Goodwin.

'We had already agreed amongst ourselves that the band desperately needed someone professional to start handling our publicity. We were getting more and more enquiries from different local media people, now we just needed someone good to come in and focus it all for us and get us into the national press,' says Fish.

'So I started making a few enquiries amongst one or two people I had got to know slightly down in London. One was a freelance journalist called Pippa Laing, who suggested we try this guy, Keith Goodwin. She said he used to work for Yes and Black Sabbath, and all sorts of other people back in the 70s, but that these days he often offered cut-rate deals to new and unsigned bands if he felt they were promising enough for him to work on.'

Understandably, Keith Goodwin's Yes connection struck just the right note of intrigue and credibility with Fish and the rest of Marillion. The singer immediately put together another of his impressively bumptious little packages, containing a demo-tape, some of the more prominent cuttings from the *Bucks Herald*, and a brief, self-penned Marillion biography, and hot-footed it onto the next train down to London and the offices of Kaygee Publicity.

'I was a bit nervous just bursting into Keith's office unannounced,' says Fish. 'But I knew I'd stand a much better chance of grabbing his attention if I turned up in person and just took the bull by the horns and told him straight out that I wanted him to work for us. So, to hide my nerves more than anything else, when I got there I suddenly switched to Mr Super Confident mode, ready to take over the place. I stormed in there and turned on all the charm, wouldn't give anybody a moment's peace, all trying to impress Keith.

'I told him Marillion were going to be huge, that we were already the darlings of the local press, that we were regularly packing out gigs, and that he'd be a fool not to get involved with us!' he laughs. 'And, bless his grimy heart, the old bugger went for it!'

As documented elsewhere in these pages, the veteran music biz PR and the young, up-and-coming unknown hit it off together famously. Keith was impressed by the younger man's casual aplomb, his sense of humour, and his seemingly unshakeable belief that his band, Marillithingy, were indeed something special. Moreover, Keith liked the tape of some of the band's songs that Fish had brought along for him to listen to (but not to keep).

At the end of their afternoon together, Keith Goodwin was enamoured enough of the rough ideas and proposals put forward by the motor-mouthed young singer to offer him a bargain-priced, band earnings-related deal to take Marillion on; and Fish returned home to Aylesbury that night having secured for the band not only the services of a professional press agent, but their first real and important contact with the legitimate music business down in London.

It was a contact that was to prove invaluable over the next twelve months.

'Not only did Keith and I become great mates over the next

year or so,' says Fish, 'but he was the first person outside of myself and the band who actually stepped in and helped shape where our career was going. It was Keith that first got us written about in the music press; it was Keith that got us our first couple of gigs supporting at the Marquee; and it was Keith that knew all the people that were to play a big part in the band's future: Tony Stratton-Smith, John Arnison, Jack Barry, all the guys at the Marquee, Keith knew all those people, and a lot more besides, years before me and Marillion arrived on the scene. So all through the months leading up to the deal with EMI, Keith was always a good guy to consult with occasionally. He was always full of information – he'd tell me about such-and-such a person's experience, or such-and-such a record company's reputation. He was nothing but a help to the band in the days when we knew no-one. Keith was great.'

The six months that followed Keith Goodwin's appointment as the band's PR was, on the surface, an exciting and busy time for Fish and Marillion. Late in 1981, with some push from Keith, they picked up their first live reviews in the UK music press. By the New Year, they were looking forward to their first spate of headliners at the Marquee; both *Sounds* and *Melody Maker* were ready to run their first features on the band; national Radio One was already planning to air a special in-house session Marillion had recorded for the Tommy Vance show; and, suddenly, Fish and the band were riding the crest of a wave that would guide their fortunes all the way to their first six-figure deal; which was, by March 1982, just another half-year away.

However, away from the stage, not all the under-currents were running so smoothly. As Marillion's home-spun successes began to repeat themselves elsewhere around the country, and several eyes in London started to point in their direction, Fish grew increasingly unhappy about the role of certain members of the band.

'As I saw it,' says Fish, 'it was time to make the most of ourselves and give the idea of getting the band signed our best shot. The fact alone that more and more new people – not just fans, but press people, record company people, agents, managers, even other bands – were coming to see us every time we played, meant that we all started to examine the band a lot closer ourselves. We were keen to rid ourselves of any obvious weaknesses before the really big boys from the record companies

119

started coming down to make up their minds whether we were worth signing or not. Well, for me, first off that meant getting rid of Brian Jelliman.'

Fish had never been able to understand Jelliman's role in the band.

'He played keyboards fairly well, but so what? So did lots of guys. But Brian never got involved with the writing, he never had anything but snidey little remarks to make whenever anyone suggested a new idea, and as far as I was concerned he was just lagging miles behind the rest of us.

'Over the months, Steve and I had already confided in each other who we thought the weak links were in the band,' Fish goes on, 'and we'd both agreed that Brian's days were numbered. I'd tried to suggest to Steve that Mick Pointer wasn't really good enough for the job either, but Steve always hesitated over that one. The trouble was, Steve was still very close to Mick in those days, and he didn't want to appear ungenerous or disloyal.'

In the meantime, however, Steve Rothery was beginning to voice his own doubts to Fish, as was Mick Pointer, over the wavering abilities of Diz as a bass player.

'That's where things started getting complicated,' sighs Fish. 'Ideally, I wanted rid of Brian *and* Mick. Steve knew it, and so did Diz. But I think Steve genuinely felt that Mick would improve with time, enough at least not to let us down when our chance came. Also, he argued that with a better bass player in the band it could only help tighten up Mick's playing.

'I was very dubious, though, at first. I thought it must be just a power play by Mick to reassert his will over the band. But, without Steve on my side, there was nothing I could really do about it, except warn Diz to pull his socks up. But all my words fell on deaf ears in the end, and first we sacked Brian Jelliman, at the end of 1981, and then, in the beginning of the New Year '82 we sacked Diz.'

Their replacements in Marillion, however, were both more or less hand-picked by Fish personally.

'Mark Kelly appealed to me right away because not only was he a good keyboard player, he wasn't a drip like Brian. He could talk to people and get on with them, and was very open and good-humoured. He also made it clear that he wanted to write as well, which was very important to us. The first time I saw him play with his band, Chemical Alice, I made up my mind there and then to try and persuade the others that Mark should be Brian's replacement in the band. Once the others had met him, though, and heard him play, it was easy.'

Not so easy was introducing the band to the idea of auditioning an ex-member of the Metros for the vacant job as bass player.

'Everybody in the band, including me, used to think of the Metros as the big joke local Aylesbury band,' Fish admits. 'But I'd heard that they were supposed to be playing a farewell gig and then splitting up, so I went along, more out of curiosity than anything else.

'Always having one eye open for an opportunity, though, I couldn't help but focus in on the bass player. We had this massive tour of Scotland that I'd arranged about to start soon, and we were still desperately looking around for someone to fill Diz's shoes.

'Then when I saw what the bass player in the Metros could do on stage, I knew I had to get him down for the others to have a listen to.'

Fish admits he didn't know how Mick, Steve, and Mark would take to the fresh-faced young bassist with the cute brown curls in his hair and the dinky white shoes he liked to wear sometimes on stage with the Metros.

'They were dead against the idea of even seeing him, at first,' says Fish. 'But once Pete (Trewavas) came down and plugged in his bass and started to show Mick Pointer a few things about rhythm and pace and melody, everybody suddenly changed their mind and we couldn't get Pete in the band fast enough.'

Marillion's Fish-inspired Scottish sojourn of the spring of '82 was a good testing ground for the new and, as long as Mick Pointer had things his way, finalised band line-up.

'Apart from all the fun we had travelling about from place to place through the wilds of Scotland for six weeks, we actually played a couple of really stunning gigs. In Edinburgh, of course, we went down well, but mostly we played our best when our backs were up against the wall, playing to about twenty-five people in some God-forsaken hotel out in the middle of nowhere on a cold Tuesday night.

'Also, because it was the first time we'd ever been properly out on the road together for weeks at a time, we started to get a real team spirit going. Somebody else in the band described it as an us-against-the-world feeling, and that says it perfectly. That attitude is so essential in keeping a band's dreams and ambitions really burning. And there were plenty of cold dawn sunrises watched through the windscreen of the van, on our way back from some gig the night before, wasted from too much alcohol and too many cigarettes and not enough sleep, when me and Steve, or me and Mark, or whoever, would have these quiet 5 a.m. conversations like, "Do you think we'll ever make it any further than this?" and "I know just what numbers I'd like on the first album", all that dreamy band stuff that made me realise what a responsibility we all now had to each other. The personal responsibility of not wanting to blow it for anybody else in the band, no matter what personal problems might arise in the future for any of us. Unlike the days when Jelliman and Diz were still in the band, we weren't weekend rock stars anymore. We weren't fucking around anymore. As of that Scottish tour, the band would always come first in all our lives; everything else would just have to come second.

'And although that was quite a scary feeling, even to have committed ourselves that much, at the same time it felt like a great comfort and security, in that, whatever happened next for us as a band, we would all be in there fighting for our chances together.'

The summer of 1982 was a hectic and adventurous time for Marillion in general, and Fish in particular. In June, the band headlined for the first time at Friar's in Aylesbury. In July, they set a new attendance record for themselves in London by headlining two consecutive sold-out nights at the Marquee. And by August, they had made their first legendary appearance at the Reading Rock Festival, still in 1982 the biggest, most prestigious date on the live rock and roll calendar in Britain.

On a personal level, Fish was also enjoying something of a new high. Not long after he first joined Marillion, Fish had met and started dating the girl he would one day write that unfinished love song to called 'Kayleigh'. Kay was blond-haired, beautiful, and, he says, the first major, ill-fated, *grande-passion* of Fish's young life. By the summer of 1982, she was living in a small flat in Earl's Court, London, to which Fish was a frequent visitor.

Aside from his relationship with Kay, though, spending so much of his free time down in London meant that Fish was always in the thick of things as they were taking place daily for Marillion.

'Although I still had somewhere up in Aylesbury to stay, I was spending most of my spare time away from the band down at Kay's flat in those days,' says Fish. 'Which, of course, meant that I used to spend an awful lot of time acquiring all sorts of bad habits at places like the bar in the Marquee, or across the road at the St Moritz club.

'By day, though, I was always running around to Keith Goodwin's office, or meeting somebody from the music press for a drink, or sizing up yet another new agent for the band. Or, as was the case by about June and July, meeting people like Peter Mensch and John Arnison.

Before that, though, Fish had spent a considerable amount of his time persuading Dave Stopps to try his hand at managing the band, only to have Dave finally accept, and then be sacked less than six weeks later.

'That whole business with Dave was a bummer all right,' says Fish, frowning. 'Right from the earliest days of our first little gig in the Aston Hall at Friar's, Dave had always been a brilliant mate to the band. I'd been trying to persuade him for *months* to have a go at managing us, but he'd always said he didn't really think he had it in him. But I was always urging him to do it.

'When he finally accepted, we'd just come back from Scotland, and we were all totally flat broke. None of us had been able to keep down a regular day-job for months and we didn't have a penny. But Dave Stopps bailed us out when we were at our most desperate.

'When he finally told me he'd do it, I was really pleased, I thought he was *perfect* for the job. And then, I don't know exactly for what specific reason, it was just a jumble of little things, we all suddenly lost a bit of faith in him. Dave was energetic and thorough, but because he lacked hard experience of managing a band and having to deal with sorting out a deal with a major record company, or talking to the music press, or other promoters, it just seemed sometimes like he was taking the long way around things.

'Whatever it was that made us decide that maybe Dave had been right all along and he really *wasn't* good enough to manage us at that point, we all decided it was best to make a clean breast of things and tell him that we didn't think it was working out. It was a drag having to do it. None of us relished the idea of telling him, but it was something we had to do, or we thought we'd see the whole build-up we'd been making go down the toilet. And I wasn't going to let *that* happen.'

Marillion's meetings with John Arnison and Peter Mensch Fish remembers for what he describes delicately as their 'contrasting atmospheres'.

'Peter Mensch was very urbane, very American, very obviously big-time, and I think, still being so sort of parochial in our tastes in those days, we were offended by all that,' says Fish. 'On a professional level, Mensch was very honest with us and offered some sound advice. And he told us to look around at some other managers and then decide for ourselves if we wanted to come back and have another talk with him.

'But the rest of the guys felt distanced by the whispers that he might only really be after me as a *solo* singer. And while the band still had doubts as basic as that, I couldn't see that going with him as our new manager would be the wisest thing for us to do. I mean, there was no way I was going to kiss the band goodbye for a crock of gold, and although Peter never once really said anything along those lines, if the band felt restless about him, it wouldn't have been right to carry things on any further.

'Meeting John Arnison was completely different,' he goes on. 'We met in this seedy little pub that me and Kay used to go into sometimes near the flat in Earl's Court. The thing is, John had plenty of big-time experience too – John was out there organising huge world tours for Status Quo when he was still in his early twenties – but he talked to us more as equals. He was very down to earth, very straightforward, knew how to crack a good joke, and we all got on at the meeting really well together.

'Afterwards, when we went away and discussed which of the two we thought would be the best manager for us, on balance we thought that John was our best bet.'

The short weeks that lay between John Arnison's appointment as Marillion's manager and the band's first appearance at Reading, almost saw Fish and the band sign with a handful of different companies before finally setting their signatures down on a contract with EMI.

First in line, and the company originally widely tipped as the

124

one most likely to land a contract with the band, was Tony Stratton-Smith's Charisma Records.

'Tony had been into Marillion since he first saw us playing at the Marquee one night in early '82,' says Fish. 'Naturally, since he was the man who had managed Genesis, we were all really flattered that he, of all people, should be into what we were doing.

'Originally, Dave Stopps had been dealing with Charisma, trying to talk terms for a deal with them. But between when Dave faded from the picture and we took John on, I was more or less dealing with Strat and the other people at his office on my own. Strat made it clear to me from the start that he was *very* into having us on his label. I think, Genesis comparisons aside, he really understood the long-term potential of the band.

'On a more personal level, though, me and Strat really hit it off from the word go. He was a very nice man, and though I came to realise that he didn't have much of a business head, he really had all the instinct and personal insight to know what made a band great. He and I would spend hours talking together in the Marquee or the St Moritz, and it was clear he had tremendous faith in us as a band to go on and really do something special with our career.

'Eventually, though, it all fell through between us and Tony when he sent his business manager along to sort out the details of a recording contract between us and Charisma. Like I said, Tony didn't actually involve himself in working out the nitty-gritty of contracts and things, he left that all to the people he employed. Anyway, he'd told his business manager to sign us up at any cost and to offer us a long-term major deal. But this faceless accountant turned up at one of our gigs, decided we were a load of crap and not worth wasting the company's money and resources on, and offered us the lowest deal he could cobble together on the spur of the moment! The deal he offered was for something like two lousy singles, with options on what we had for breakfast for the next five years . . . you know, *really* impressive.

'I remember me and Mick Pointer had this meeting with the business manager and another guy from Charisma. And they kept telling us that we'd never get offered a better deal than the one he was offering us, how all the major record companies were now offering their new signings exactly the same kind of deals because nobody liked to throw money around any more, how the recession had changed everything and anyway we were bound to be successful enough with our first two singles for Charisma to then sit down and talk about a more long-term deal with the band . . . and on and on with all this utter *bullshit*.

'In the end, I was talking to someone else I met from Charisma, Mike Allen, who was a really nice guy. I remember turning to Mike and saying, "Listen, this deal is a load of shit, isn't it?" And he just looked at me and nodded. There was no going back after that. The next day we told Strat's business manager what he could do with his two-bit shitty deal.'

Fish says he found the whole sordid business of retreating from the Charisma deal that Tony Stratton-Smith had been promising him so earnestly very disillusioning.

'It was a real shame, that whole Charisma thing. But it wasn't Strat's fault. He was furious when he found out what had happened. By the time Tony tried to patch things up between us we'd already been approached by EMI, discussed the ins and outs of a major deal, and shaken hands on it. Which was the end of Charisma's chances of getting the band on their label. Although we hadn't actually signed anything yet, when Strat came back to us with a proper offer we'd already shaken hands on a deal with EMI. And that's always been a Marillion thing – to shake on a deal or agreement is to give our word, our bond. And we wouldn't break that. Not even when Tony came to us and told us he'd better anything EMI had offered us. Not even for Tony.'

Reading Festival 1982, Fish says he remembers as possibly 'one of the greatest days of my life!'

The show itself, Fish remembers as a performance fittingly climactic enough to be the pinnacle of Marillion's grand achievements in 1982.

'We had as good as signed the deal we had been dreaming of all these years, with a record company I had nothing but respect for in those days, and now here we were stealiing everybody else's thunder at the biggest outdoor rock event of the year! It was an *ecstatic* moment for all of us. Even as we stood there on stage playing, I think we all knew we were living the first big landmark of our career. We were something like sixth on the bill that day, but we were the first band everybody remembered to mention in the weeks that followed.

'Suddenly we were *happening*! We couldn't put a foot wrong! Next would come the hard part, though. Actually making records, and that's when the men really did get sorted out from the boys.'

5

Foo–Gah–Zey!

September 1983 was another busy month for Marillion. Having grabbed all the best headlines that followed their triumphant appearance at the Reading Festival, the band felt bold enough to accept an offer from Canadian mega-stars Rush to open the show for them over five consecutive nights at the Radio City Music Hall, in New York, later that month.

Despite the bitter disappointment of their first visit to America just two months before, John Arnison and the band both felt that the prospect of five big nights in the Bad Apple playing to guaranteed sell-out houses of over 6,000 people a night was simply too good to refuse. These dates in New York, they decided, might provide the perfect short, sharp shock Marillion still needed to help launch their name in America.

And after all, what could they lose from just five shows and no travelling in between? And what they stood to gain in terms of credibility might be significant. Or so the arguments went as John prepared to book their flights and hotels.

First, though, EMI wanted Marillion back in the studio, again with producer Nick Tauber and his engineer, Simon Hanhart, this time to re-record versions of 'Market Square Heroes' and 'Three Boats Down From the Candy'. At the time, EMI were considering offering the revamped tracks to their American counterparts, Capitol, as the next possible US single.

The band completed the sessions with sessionman, John Martyr, filling in on the drums and percussion. The end result is two much beefier, better played and better produced versions of the original David Hitchcock recordings. The sound is distinctly heavier, and 'Market Square Heroes' in particular is a big improvement, if just for the drums which now start to run where before it seemed they could barely walk straight.

The sessions were brief and to the point. After a week or so at the Marquee Studios with Nick and Simon, the band delivered the finished tapes to EMI, who proceeded to sit on them and not turn them over to Capital, or anyone else for that matter, after all. The band were mystified, but for the time being there was nothing to be done about it. Rush, and five nights of swinging New York-Noo Yawk boogaloo under the skyscraper lights of Sixth Avenue awaited them.

Most big cities on the rock and roll road map will throw up a tough audience for support bands. In London, they don't so much openly insult the support act, most of the audience simply vanishes to the bar/hot-dog stand/T-shirt kiosk while the unfortunate band run vacantly through their set. In San Francisco, they just might prefer to sit in on the whole show and studiously take into account the support band's role, bristling with polite whistles and applause in a hearty show of contrived good manners. In Madrid, they simply tear the support band apart in a hail of bottles and catcalls and loud, vulgar threats.

In New York City, it can go either one of two ways: they either already know and love the support band, or they give them the finger, Spanish style!

Marillion, it seemed, were neither known nor loved by enough of the 30,000 kids that crammed into the Radio City Hall for those ill-fated shows with Rush to save themselves from suffering the worst forms of bad-tempered abuse from the fanatically partisan New York fans.

'The day we arrived in New York we really thought we were in for a great week ahead of us with Rush,' says Steve Rothery. 'All of their people – their crew, engineers, and managers – seemed to be as up for it as we were, and everybody was looking forward quite confidently to some good shows.'

'But then when we turned up for our sound check, the night of the first gig, we started having horrendous problems almost immediately.' Pete Trewavas takes up the story. 'For a start we had to deal with the Rush crew, which with one or two exceptions was quite kind to us, but then we also had to work with the in-house Radio City crew, which was a complete nightmare!

'They've got about four separate unions, all with 101 different rules designed for no apparent purpose other than to drive the support band round the bend,' Pete goes on. 'You couldn't have people up on stage when the fire-curtain was lowered, it was against the rules, and of course the fire-curtain always went down as soon as Rush had finished their sound check, so we'd have to sit around and wait for it to come up again. Half an hour later up it came and we'd start getting some of our equipment on stage. Half an hour of that and the crew had to have their coffee-break – I mean, *had* to, it was union rules, they said.

'By the time we actually got to have anything like a real sound check we would have exactly five minutes to ourselves before the crew would tell us our time was up and we'd have to leave the stage! You know, thanks a lot! And it was like that *every* night. We just had to learn to put up with it.'

To add that extra Kafkaesque edge to their mounting frustrations, at the same time every night, five minutes or so before the band went on stage, one of the Radio City technicians would arrive in the Marillion dressing room with the news that the on-stage monitors were 'inexplicably' refusing to work properly: two-thirds of their on-stage sound would be lost to them, and what remained would be buried in an ear-piercing whine that screamed from one of the recalcitrant monitors.

'It would get sorted out eventually, about halfway through the set, by which time we'd lost it anyway,' says Steve Rothery. 'But the fact that the same thing kept happening at exactly the same time every night really pissed us off! It was obvious that things were going on behind our backs to ensure that we didn't get an easy ride of it. I don't mean the Rush guys, particularly, mostly they were fine. I mean the in-house Radio City guys: they seemed to assume that wrecking the support band's plans was all part of their job. For instance, whoever was responsible for putting on the tape they used to play before we came on every night must have been a real joker – every bloody night he always managed to make the last song but one before we went on either a Genesis track or a Peter Gabriel track!

'Every single night,' he smiles and grits his teeth, 'it was so predictable you could almost set your watch by it – like, five minutes to go and . . . Cue on-stage monitor break-down! Cue Genesis track! Cue Marillion, and then, cue large amounts of booing and objects being thrown at the stage! I couldn't believe it! It was *horrendous*.'

The first night it happened, the booing, the cat-calls, the fuck you fingers, and the cries of 'Go home to England, man!', hit Marillion like a ton of bricks. They hadn't experienced anything quite as intense as this on the shows with Utopia, and they were visibly stunned by how unwelcome they were made to feel.

'If we'd bored them to tears and they fell asleep, or just ignored us, somehow that I could understand,' says Mark Kelly. 'But such a display of out-and-out hatred really shocked us. Even Fish kept his mouth shut and his head down as we went through the set. It was frightening.'

'The thing is I'd been told by lots of people who are supposed to know about these things that the best thing for me to do, if the crowd started off being openly hostile to us, was to ignore it and just get down to throwing the music at them,' says Fish. 'Which, as everybody knows, is completely out of character for me. On stage, I'm usually anything but silent. And when these fuckers started chucking things at us and booing and screaming at us to fuck off back to England, I wanted to give them *hell*! But I remembered what I'd been told and stuck to the advice, thinking it's got to quieten down a bit once we get into the set and a few people start listening to us.

'But, of course, the exact reverse happened and they booed us off the fucking stage for four nights straight, me not saying a word to any of these bastards from the stage,' he says with disgust. 'The final night I cracked and I really let them have it; classic Scotsman losing the head style!' he laughs. 'You know, come up here and I'll take on every single one of you! And I just screamed at them all to shut up . . . And the amazing thing is it worked! Against all the so-called professional advice from the Americans. And, as it turned out, the last night we played was easily the best, the only one in fact where the crowd finally settled down and gave us a chance.'

Dispirited by the awful response they were getting, and with the odds against a recovery stacked as high as the resident Radio City Hall crew could make them, the band passed the week in New York together in a slow, dizzy fit of drinking and partying. The nightly shows with Rush were a bad joke, as far as Marillion were concerned, and the situation was out of their control. They would just have to ride it out to the bitter end. In the meantime, stranded thousands of miles away from home and friends and staying in a hotel they couldn't possibly afford to eat *and* drink in, there was nothing for it but to keep themselves entertained by

131

making regular visits to any one of the hundreds of small-hours bars and clubs that line the open twenty-four-hour streets of downtown New York.

'We would have gone off our heads if we'd sat around brooding about what a mess the shows with Rush were,' says Fish. 'So we decided to take the bull by the horns and really *do* New York in classic after-midnight style! Don't forget that our only previous time in America we'd been travelling hundreds of miles most days with a mad-hatter drummer to watch out for, so we'd never really had a chance to investigate the place before. If anything, we were still suffering from culture-shock, and that week in New York was a mixture of turning up for the gig every night, *knowing* we were going to get yelled at and abused, and then spending the rest of the night getting totally wasted in some typically seedy New York hang-out.

'I remember though that we weren't exactly rich at the time,' he smiles. 'We were still only getting something like £70 a week wages and about £10 per day on-the-road living expenses, which when converted into dollars equalled not very much at all. So we used to put all our expenses money together into the pot and spend it on keeping ourselves suitably distracted between these horrendous shows we had to do every night with Rush. When the pot money ran out we used to sell our complimentary guest tickets for the show outside the hall! We couldn't take the shit we were getting at the gigs seriously anymore, so we thought why not?'

Walking down Broadway in the dead of the night, staring at the shuffling sidewalk vision of freaks, most of whom resembled costumed extras from the Bladerunner film-set, Fish in particular found the adrenal rush of the neon-muddied late-nite New York streets a subject worthy of some serious personal study.

'I couldn't stay off the streets,' he says. 'Except for when I went into a bar or a club, I spent the rest of the time pounding the streets, taking it all in, the real New York City street life. I rode the subway, walked around Central Park at two in the morning, just getting into it. Because, you know, really the shows with Rush were going so terribly I didn't know when we might ever come back to New York again. And anyway, like I say, we wanted to *do* the city while we still had the chance.

'New York is supposed to be a very dangerous place to go out and do any of those things, but I just used to brazen it, like I knew all about the place, and nobody bothered me. In fact, I remember going to do this photo-session on my own with an English guy who used to be a drummer with John Otway and who was now working as a photographer for an American art magazine; he wanted to take some shots of me in my stage gear. Anyway, I did the session and I remember walking back from his studio to the hotel, on my own quite late at night, through this really tough part of the city, about twelve blocks of pimps, hustlers, junkies, a lot of young gangs flitting about in twos and threes. But I had no money on me for a taxi, so there was nothing for it but to walk.

'I was walking down this one particularly bombed-out street, God knows where I was exactly, and I had the army helmet I used to wear on "Forgotten Sons" slung over my shoulder, a big combat jacket and trousers on, big Doc Marten boots, and I still had some of last night's make-up smeared over my face, and a big black sweatband pulled back tight across my forehead – six-and-a-half foot of nervous weird-looking Scotsman pounding down the street in the dead of night!' he chuckles. 'And everybody just *scattered* from my path! They couldn't get out of my way fast enough! I must have been the weirdest motherfucker they'd seen on the street that night!'

With the debacle of that long wasted week in New York behind them at last, Marillion returned to London to the more work-conscious surrounds of Nomis Rehearsal Studios, where they began work on some of the new material that would surface six months later on the band's second EMI album, *Fugazi*.

Sessionman John Martyr, who had faithfully seen the band through Reading, the re-recording of the 'Market Square Heroes' sessions, and the snake-pit of the Radio City Hall shows with Rush, originally returned with Marillion to Nomis, but by the end of the first week had been told in no uncertain terms that his services were no longer required. Fish, who never rated John Martyr from the beginning, was the one to give him the news.

'He was quite callous about it,' says Mark Kelly. 'I remember we'd been invited over to do a gig in West Germany by a German radio programme which was going to broadcast the concert live. So we started thinking about rehearsing a set. But most of the band had already decided that the time had come to get someone in a bit better suited to the band's music than John. And we were getting our passports together and stuff, and making arrangements for the trip to Germany, when Fish turned around and said to John Martyr, "You know we've got this gig in Germany coming up? Well, don't worry about making arrangements to go because we won't be needing you for this one. In fact, we won't be needing you at all any more." '

'He struck me as too much of a bullshitter,' says Fish. 'And he wasn't percussive enough for the band. The time had come for him to go.'

In his place, John Arnison contacted a young American drummer he and the band had been introduced to in New York called Jonathan Mover. By now Marillion had retreated to the relative peace and quiet of the Welsh countryside, setting up temporary home at the Old Mill House Rehearsal Studio in Monmouth.

'Jonathan had been put in touch with the band by Nick Tauber when Mick Pointer had first been fired,' says Pete Trewavas. 'But we never actually met him until he came to see us at one of the Radio City Hall shows. And he was very young and terribly enthusiastic, and he seemed to know all our songs and said there and then that he'd love to audition for the band if ever we decided we needed another drummer. And we knew he could play a bit because Nick Tauber had used him to replace Simon Philips on some recording sessions with Toyah when Simon was too busy to make it.'

As a drummer, Jonathan Mover was, in the words of Mark Kelly, 'quite ridiculously talented, very technical, and tremendously dedicated.' His only immediate drawback, as Pete Trewavas describes it, was his 'tendency to throw everything and the kitchen sink into a song. He was young and I think he liked to show off a bit too much. A lot of very technically adept, quite flash rock drummers go through that stage early on in their careers, and Jonathan was obviously no exception.'

Promised nothing more than an audition in Monmouth alongside a dozen other hopefuls up for the gig, Jonathan Mover flew to England from his home town of Boston three days before the band's concert in Germany, in October 1983. The last in line to audition, but the most obviously talented and genuinely enthusiastic of the bunch, Mover was offered the job on the spot as the new drummer in Marillion and the band went into hurried last-minute rehearsals for their most prestigious European concert date yet.

'We offered the gig to Jonathan on the basis that there would

134

be a kind of probationary period,' says Steve Rothery. 'We were obviously having terrible trouble trying to come up with a replacement for Mick, like, six months after we'd sacked him even, and we wanted to be careful, but we had to choose someone quick because of this live radio-show gig in Germany we had coming up.'

Jonathan Mover's appointment to the band was duly announced in the British music press, though of course no-one mentioned that he was still merely a salaried musician the band had hired, and not as yet entitled to a full one-fifth share of the future Marillion estate.

'We did it that way just to be on the safe side,' says Steve. 'I mean, we knew he was good, but we didn't know much else about him, didn't know how he'd fit in. And anyway, by then we'd pretty much given up on the idea of getting a proper full-time/forever new member in the band, someone who really felt a part of it the way we did, so we just more or less hijacked Jonathan for that one gig in Germany.'

'I remember,' says Mark Kelly, 'I was rooming with him – I used to room with all the drummers in those days – and the poor guy didn't even have a proper change of clothes. He'd obviously flown over from America expecting to fly back the next day, but instead we'd said no, you're coming to Germany with us!'

The concert, broadcast live from a small but packed concert hall in Kassel, was, in fact, to be Jonathan Mover's one and only live performance in Marillion. The show itself was only the band's second gig in Germany, and the first time they had been asked to headline, but already they were beginning to witness the origins of a wild and loyal following that would one day out-number even the hardcore British-based fans.

In typically comprehensive and methodical fashion, Mover had learned all the regular Marillion set-pieces inside-out, and he provided a solid, immovable force from which the band launched into a performance that shifted breathlessly from the spine-tingling other-worldly scenes of another 'Chelsea Monday', to the searing power-chords that lashed like fists into the drunken Teutonic rhythms of the dark-eyed 'Assassing'.

At the end of the night, cloaked again in the applause and cries for more they had grown accustomed to at home in England, but could never quite count on in America, the lingering doubts and depressions they came home with from those twisted shows with Rush had at last been exorcised, and the band marked the occasion by celebrating in truly monumental Marillion style with a room-to-room party back at their hotel later that night that would prove so popular even the local police force, fire brigade and ambulance services would eventually feel obliged to gate-crash it!

To this day nobody quite remembers the correct order of events that night, but everybody seems to agree that the party got started in the hotel bar.

'Everybody was feeling good about the band again,' says Pete Trewavas. 'We really weren't used to the kind of bad crowds we had faced in New York, and it was really reassuring to go out and play again after that and do so well.

'So there we were, sort of all slapping each other on the back and knocking back the drinks just as fast as John Arnison could persuade Paul Lewis to buy them,' he chuckles. 'Everybody that is, except Jonathan, who never touched alcohol, a fact which Fish *never* forgave him for!' he laughs. 'And that went on for a couple of hours and then I went up to my room to take a shower.'

'In fact everybody sort of disappeared to their rooms for half an hour,' says Mark Kelly. 'And then the next thing I remember is Steve knocking on my door and asking to borrow my Sony Walkman, and when I got to the door and opened it, it was like WHOOOSSSHHH!! I got hit full-on by this big jet of fire-extinguisher foam, which sort of *exploded* through the door and knocked me into a backwards somersault over the bed! And then Jonathan, who was in the room with me, got hit by it and he collapsed, and the whole room was absolutely smothered!'

'I only did that because someone had just done it to me!' protests Steve Rothery. 'There was a knock on my door and when I opened it – BANG! A room full of shit and me rolling around in it! But whoever it was ran off before I could see them.'

Of course, the oldest fire-extinguisher fetishist in the Marillion camp is John Arnison. He was a seasoned practitioner of the exploding fire-extinguisher under the door routine, and his over-arm lob down the fire-exit stairs of an empty fire-extinguisher cannister was known to have pinpoint accuracy. And of course, it was John, though he's never really admitted it, who first started the ball rolling by attacking Steve's room that night with a loaded cannister under his arm.

The only problem was that instead of containing the more usual foam, which extinguishes fires and leaves people healthy but wet, the German variety the hotel stocked contained an

136

asbestos-based powder so fine it would poison the air at once and make it almost impossible to breathe.

'But what happened was that everything escalated really quickly into a battle and about five or six of these bloody fire-extinguishers went off in the space of about five minutes, with all of us going mad and chasing each other down the corridor,' says Fish, laughing at the memory. 'And then within *seconds* we were all fucking falling over and choking to death! It was like, SOMEBODY OPEN A FUCKING WINDOW *OR I'M GONNA DIE!!*'

When enough windows had been opened and the toxic clouds of asbestos fumes were sucked out into the night air, everybody lay back coughing and laughing, over half the corridor of rooms they were occupying now hidden under grey puffy layers of the all-pervading foam-extinguisher.

'We thought that was the end of it,' says Pete Trewavas. 'And then the next thing I know I open my door and there's all these policemen in the hall, and hotel managers, and people running around with fire helmets on.'

From the ground, other guests arriving at the hotel had reported large clouds of 'smoke' billowing from some of the top-floor windows. The reception staff had immediately assumed that the hotel was on fire and wasted no time in telephoning for the local fire brigade and an ambulance, which in turn meant a routine visit from the police. When they arrived the hotel was already in the throes of evacuating guests and staff from the hotel.

'It was horrendous, of course, but at the same time it *was* very funny,' smiles Mark Kelly. 'We all ran off and hid in our rooms, and when the police knocked on our doors we all sort of pretended to be in the bath or asleep in bed or something, and not really aware of what was going on – you know, what *me*? I'm sorry, I don't speak any German.

'The minute they walked into my room though and saw everything plastered in this dust and foam I knew the game was up! They started demanding to see the band's manager so we took them all off to see John.'

The upshot of Marillion's clash with the police was that the hotel management threatened to press charges and have the whole band and their crew arrested and thrown in gaol unless John coughed up enough money to cover the cost of all likely damages incurred by the hotel and its guests.

137

Marillion returned, somewhat scathed financially from their brief but licentious flying-visit to Germany, but with all their rediscovered high spirits still splendidly intact, and set to work again on writing new material for the next album.

By the beginning of November, tucked away once again in the shielding, countrified seclusion of the Old Mill House in Monmouth, the band had applied a lot of the finishing touches to 'Assassing' and had finished writing the music to Fish's 'Punch and Judy' saga. Work proceeded at a steady rate, but still the spectre of Mick Pointer would not let them alone. In Fish's own words, 'we had never really laid that ghost to rest, and I wasn't happy any more with having a guy in the band, no matter how good he was technically, that wasn't really one of *us*.'

'Fish and Jonathan never really hit it off,' says Steve Rothery, 'and things just continued to degenerate between them over the weeks we spent together in Monmouth.'

'Everybody says that the real reason I didn't like Jonathan was because he was young and good-looking and had lots of hair,' says Fish. 'And of course, it was all true!' he laughs.

'No, seriously, the reason I couldn't get on with Jonathan was simply that he was so boring! He couldn't sit and talk about anything except the drums, and drum pedals, and cymbals, and new designs for snares, and on and on until your head was ready to explode! And of course, he *was* American, *and* he didn't drink – neither of which were exactly *crimes* in my book back then, but they both definitely counted as black marks against him. You have to remember, I was much less a man of the world in those days,' he jokes, showing his teeth in a long crocodile smile. 'The truth is I did harbour a lot of stupid superficial prejudices against him, but underneath all that lay the simple fact that I couldn't relate to the guy on a personal level deep or interesting enough for me to work with, to pledge my life to, and I *hated* not working like that. This next album was our most important step yet and I thought we deserved someone I could at least believe in, even just on a superficial level, even if that's *all* there was to it, I didn't care, but Jonathan and I couldn't even get it together like that. We had *nothing* in common! And as far as I was concerned that just wasn't good enough. There had to be another drummer in the whole wide world I could sit in the same room as for longer than ten minutes without wanting to crawl the walls! There just *had* to be.'

'Fish's concern over Jonathan's involvement with the band was growing more serious by the day,' says Mark Kelly. 'He was rankled by him and didn't think we should be working with him, and to a large extent a lot of us could see his point. Jonathan did tend to stick out like a sore thumb, socially. It wasn't really his fault, he was just a bit too young to have hanging around with us all the time; a bit like having a distant, much younger American cousin over for the summer holidays, and you run out of things to say to each other after about five minutes. It was a bit like that at times. But Fish, in particular, was getting so pissed off by it we knew something would have to be done.'

Finally, a band meeting – minus Jonathan Mover – was called.

'We all agreed to meet downstairs in the kitchen at midnight,' says Pete Trewavas. 'Jonathan was so predictable he *always* went to bed by about 11.30 anyway and so we knew we'd be left alone to have a chat amongst ourselves.'

The band remained sympathetic to Fish's point of view, but argued that with less than a month to go before recording began in earnest on the new album time was running out to find a good replacement.

'Whatever else he was, Jonathan was still an excellent drummer,' says Steve Rothery. 'But in the end Fish really put his foot down and we decided if he felt that strongly about it then we should support his wishes.'

'I didn't want Jonathan to stay on for the album and then get into the same situation we'd found ourselves in with Mick, and have to get rid of him after one tour,' says Fish. 'That wouldn't have been fair to him, to the band, or to the fans.'

John Arnison, who had been snatching a few days' holiday while the band were still supposed to be writing up in Monmouth, returned home to find Jonathan Mover packing his bags and the rest of the band struggling indifferently through rehearsals with the aid of a drum-machine.

'I couldn't believe it!' cried John. 'Mover was the fourth drummer they'd sacked in seven months! I thought next I'd have to start putting the bloody drum-machine on wages!'

'The first time I ever met the band was when I gave some of them a lift up from Aylesbury to Monmouth,' says Ian Mosley, smiling at the memory. 'John Arnison had been in touch and asked me if I'd go up as a sessionman and help the boys put their new material together, and if things worked out I would stay on for the album. Well, as coincidence would have it I only lived five miles or so from Aylesbury and – Steve and Pete I think it was – were planning on going up to Monmouth the same day as I was, so I offered to give them a lift. I thought it might be a good way of sort of casually getting to know each other a bit before we started working.

'I was about twenty-nine years old at the time and Steve had his girlfriend with him, and she looked about fourteen! Pete and Steve were both obviously younger than me and I thought, "Christ, I hope I'm not too old for all this!"

'But then when we got to the house in Monmouth the first person we saw was Fish, who'd only just got up and was still sitting around in his dressing gown. I felt better straight away! He'd obviously been out on a huge binge the night before and he looked about forty! He was in a right state. I looked like a teenager compared to him,' Ian laughs.

Ian Mosley came highly recommended to Marillion with a hard-won reputation as an immensely fluid and imaginative rock drummer. For the last two years he had played all over the world as a member of former Genesis guitarist Steve Hackett's backing band, recording one critically acclaimed album together, *Highly Strung*, released in 1982.

Before that, Mosley had picked up gigs wherever he could find them. A sometime Mahavishnu Orchestra freak with a heavy penchant for the quick-fire percussive abstracts of people like Billy Cobham, Lenny White, and Chick Corea, Ian had paid his way at different times drumming with acts as wilfully diverse as Gordon Giltrap, Darryl Way, an obscure and short-lived jazz-rock outfit called Walrus, and an even more obscure Dutch conglomeration in the early seventies called the Latin Explosion!

In between meals, Ian had also dabbled with several West End theatre orchestras in London, including a hit production of *Hair*, and a musical version of *Billy Liar*. He even stepped in briefly as the drummer in cabaret star Peter Gordino's backing band, headlining at the Talk of the Town in London.

'All my life, though, I'd wanted to get involved in a proper band,' he says. 'Meaning, not just a gig where I got my wages at the end of the week and thank you very much goodbye. I dreamed of getting in a *real* band, where we were all equal partners, and stood to lose or gain as much. But for some reason I'd never once found myself in that situation. I'd played with loads of different people, but I'd never really been in a real "band", not in the true sense of the word.'

In November 1983, Ian Mosley was picking up occasional session work recording radio and TV jingles. When he wasn't doing that he was paying the rent conducting 'drum-clinics' at small exhibitions around the country sponsored by Zildjian Cymbals.

He had already expressed an interest in auditioning for Marillion before Jonathan Mover had arrived on the scene. 'I was gonna call him back but the band got Jonathan in so fast there wasn't any point,' says John Arnison. 'And then when Mover was fired, Ian was the only person I could think of that might still be available that the band hadn't already seen – or seen, hired, and then sacked!' he remarks dryly.

Originally taken on as a sessionman, the experienced new drummer fitted quickly and easily into the fold.

'I kept a very low profile at first,' says Ian. 'I gave off quite a serious vibe, I think. I remember at rehearsals, this is like the second day or something, and Mark suddenly went for it and let off a fire-extinguisher, and then somebody else started trying to rip the door off its hinges! But I didn't bat an eye, I just stayed in the background and let it all go on around me.

'And then when they calmed down a bit and got back down to playing I really tried to give them my best. And it seemed to work like that and I started to open up a bit more and we got on really well together. They were still quite naïve in some of their ways, but very funny and very easy to get along with – one minute it was all heads down and intense doom and gloom, writing this big new serious number, and the next it was let's let off all the fire-extinguishers in John Arnison's bedroom! Barmy, really. And I just sat back on my drum stool and enjoyed it.'

'We all took to Ian straight away,' says Fish. 'Not only was he probably the best all-round drummer and percussionist we'd ever played with, he was also a brilliant guy! His sense of humour was very low-key, but always very crafty, and it always really hit the nerve.'

'I remember sitting chatting with Fish the first time we met,' says Ian Mosley, 'and I asked him what had been wrong with the last drummer they had. And he turned around and said, "He was American."

'And I said, "Oh, my wife's American." And then he just looked at me, thought about it for a moment, and I think he realised he'd said something stupid, and then we both just burst out laughing. We got on well with each other straight away. We shared the same sort of humour.'

'Musically, Ian really pulled the band together,' says Pete Trewavas. 'And in various ways I think we all learned something from Ian about how to play our own music. He was one hundred per cent professional, and I had to really pull my socks up to keep up with a lot of the stuff he was capable of playing.'

'But it wasn't deliberately flash and self-indulgent in the way Jonathan might have done certain things,' Mark Kelly points out. 'Ian was much more subtle, much more cutting.'

The last three weeks Marillion spent in Monmouth, piecing together the threads of their new songs with Ian Mosley, there was a new atmosphere at work. Scorching new numbers like 'Incubus', 'She Chameleon', and the outlandish title track, 'Fugazi', were slowly taking shape, and the band, Fish in particular, relaxed into the task that lay ahead with a fresh confidence Mosley's avuncular presence as the man with the magic rhythm-stick only served to reinforce.

'After Ian started working with us in Monmouth everything seemed to start clicking in the band again,' says Fish. 'We were all in high spirits again and getting ready to knock 'em dead with the next album,' he smiles. 'And we had quite a few memorable nights down in Monmouth in the end: the music was really starting to come together and we started to relax and enjoy ourselves.

'I remember 5 November, Guy Fawkes Night, we'd all gone down to the local pub and got slaughtered on real ale and tequila, a foul concoction guaranteed to send the most sensitive creature *mad*,' he grins, 'and don't ask me how but by the time we'd crawled out of the pub at closing time and staggered back up to the Old Mill House, somehow we had about £40 worth of firecrackers in the house! I think one of the crew might have gone out to get them – I was too pissed to notice who started it – but anyway, of course the next thing is: let's tie six bangers to a giant rocket with two roman candles nailed to its sides, and then let's try and aim that through someone's bedroom window! Oh, you can imagine the scene: sheep scattering all over the Welsh countryside, people in danger of blowing their bits off throwing burning fire-crackers at each other, all mad drunk and howling!'

It was also in Monmouth that Fish made the unexpected acquaintance of one of his former teenhood heroes – Robert Plant, ex-lead singer with the legendary Led Zeppelin, now a successful solo artist in his own right, who was up in Wales at the same time as Marillion, working just a few miles down the road at Rockfield Studios.

'Now that *was* a weird one,' says Fish. 'Me and some of the guys from the band and crew were drinking in the local pub one lunchtime, and I got talking to this guy I'd just been introduced to and it turned out he was a producer and played a bit of keyboards, and he was telling me all about it. And I asked him his name and he said Pat Moran, which rang a few bells but nothing I could place. Then he said, "You should come around to the other side of the bar and meet a mate of mine, I'm sure he'd like to meet you". And I said OK, and we walked around the corner of this bar and this bloke gets up from his seat and says "Good afternoon, I'm Robert Plant. You're Fish aren't you? Yes, I've heard a bit about you. Sit down and have a drink."

'So I did, and he was amazing! Such a nice bloke. I remember telling him what a drag it was always getting compared to other people and not being taken seriously for ourselves, and he was very kind and very sweet and said that Zeppelin had gone through exactly the same sort of shit when they were first coming up. He said that until the band recorded their fourth album and that one track, 'Stairway to Heaven', nobody in the press had ever taken them seriously and had accused them of ripping just about everybody off that had gone before them for the last fifteen years! He said it was just a stage me and the band would have to go through and live with, and that sooner or later people would forget all about the tedious Genesis comparisons. And looking at it now, of course, he was right.

'He was very cool without being the least bit posey, and I was very impressed by him. I remember thinking I'd like to retain that kind of quiet dignity if ever, you know, we really, really made it.'

Ian Mosley's wide experience and his lack of obvious personality defects were qualities Marillion came to admire more and more as their time in Monmouth came to an end, and when the band entered the Manor recording studios in Shipton-on-Cherwell, in the small town of Kidlington, near Oxford, in the last week of November 1983, Ian went with them.

'He was still employed as a sessionman for the album,' says Steve Rothery. 'But we were already hoping he might stay on permanently after that.'

143

Marillion's second album for EMI was to be called *Fugazi*: a slang term invented by American soldiers in Vietnam to describe their predicament all too often in the war – specifically, it translated as, 'all fucked up'.

'A most suitable title in retrospect, considering the fucked-up circumstances that surrounded its conception!' Fish would later remark of the long and painful months that went into the recording of the much-maligned, but truly aptly titled, *Fugazi*.

Script for a Jester's Tear had been allowed a £50,000 production budget: a hefty sum in 1982 for an unproven band to play with on their first album. Even so, Marillion and Nick Tauber had still failed to bring home the bacon for under £70,000. That fact, added to the band's increased stature in the market-place since their first album had been released and plunged into the heart of the UK Top 10 nine months before, allowed Nick Tauber to persuade EMI to enlarge the production budget for *Fugazi* to a cool £75,000. More than enough, Hugh Stanley Clarke argued, to see the band through the recording of their second studio album.

However, after fourteen weeks of intensive around-the-clock operations in over half a dozen different studios in and around London, the album had already cost nearly £150,000, EMI were slowly tearing Hugh Stanley Clarke's hair out, and Marillion were still nowhere near finishing the most expensive and foolhardy album of the band's young career.

'We wasted so much time right at the beginning, it was untrue,' says Pete Trewavas. 'Getting up in the middle of the afternoon, and then working for a few hours on the backing tracks, and then we'd go off down the pub at night and get plastered and start all over again with the same thing the next day.'

As they had begun a year before, the band started off with the track they had already decided would be their first single from the album: 'Punch and Judy'.

'Actually, putting the single together was probably the easiest part of recording *Fugazi*,' says Mark Kelly. ' "Punch and Judy" was one of the first numbers we had finished writing, so recording it was fairly straightforward; it took a long time but at least we all knew what we were doing. And we had decided not to write a special B side like we would have normally done – we still had the new versions of "Market Square Heroes" and "Three Boats Down From the Candy" that hadn't been used for anything yet, and we thought it might be nice to have them as the B side.'

'Besides,' says Fish, 'we didn't like the idea of EMI having unreleased Marillion material in the can. We figured that if we were ever going to be really successful anything we recorded would probably end up getting released one day, whether we liked it or not, so it might as well come out now while we still had control over it.

'Anyway, they *were* much better versions of the original and we thought our fans would like to hear them.'

As November turned into December, with another Christmas looming ever nearer and the days growing shorter and colder, work over at the Manor was starting to pick up at a fearsome pace. Spurred on by the success of their initial collaboration together a year previously, the band proved all too eager to get locked into producer Nick Tauber's self-obsessed dream to now make what he called 'the perfect rock album'.

'In the year between recording *Script . . .* and *Fugazi*, something strange had happened to Nick,' says Pete Trewavas. 'He'd always been very obsessed with detail, almost to the point of forgetting what the overall picture was supposed to be. But the first time we worked with him he was always generally together by the end of things and we were very happy, by and large, with what he'd done for us.

'But by the time he came to work with us on *Fugazi* he'd changed a lot. We didn't notice anything at first, but as we got more and more into recording the album, Nick started to go more and more over the top about details we couldn't even hear ourselves,' he says, frowning.

'And then he brought in all this extra ultra-expensive equipment that kept breaking down so that he could turn the Manor from a regular twenty-four track studio into a much bigger, forty-eight track affair,' says Steve Rothery. 'Nick was working under the idea that time and money were of no object – this was *genius* we were going for here!

'And, at first anyway, we really went along with him. But then as time wore on and we seemed to be getting less and less done, even though we were spending longer and longer hours locked away in the studio, we realised that Nick was becoming completely obsessed, and despite all his hours spent working through the night we weren't actually getting anywhere.'

In fact, according to the band, their most productive moments

145

in the studio were almost always when Tauber's engineer, Simon Hanhart, was left to supervise basic recording for a few hours while the errant producer snatched some rest.

'Simon was our life-saver on that album, most of the time,' says Mark Kelly. 'Nick was always having another of his great ideas from dream-world, but it was Simon Hanhart that really did a lot of the actual work twiddling the knobs helping us to get the right sound. Nick was too busy having visions, and it got more impossible to communicate with him as time went on.'

'By Christmas, we were all getting a bit worried about Nick Tauber,' says John Arnison. 'But the problems with Nick didn't really get severe until the band started work on the album again after the Christmas holidays. In the meantime, we thought a week or so off might calm him down a bit, because he *was* starting to get a bit manic – I remember he even wanted the band to work through Christmas day but we said no way – only of course, things didn't work out quite the way we hoped they would.'

In by now traditional Marillion fashion, the band announced that they would be playing five special Christmas/New Year concerts around the UK, kicking off at the Nottingham Rock City on 27 December, and winding through one-night stands at the Hammersmith Odeon in London on the 28th; Aylesbury Friars (of course!) on the 29th; Birmingham Odeon on the 30th; and an especially momentous Hogmanay Special on the final night of the tour, at the Odeon in Edinburgh, before Fish's home-town fans who welcomed the singer back to the stage like the original long-lost Son of Lothian returned to tell his strange tales.

Recording ceased temporarily at the Manor on Christmas Eve, and all of the band, with the exception of Fish, returned home to Aylesbury for a forty-eight-hour break from the schedule.

'I actually had nowhere to live at the time,' says Fish, 'and we'd spent the best part of the year either on the road or actually in residence at a rehearsal studio, so I hadn't had much time or inclination to get a place properly sorted out for myself. I mean, even for Christmas we were only having two days off, so what was the point in worrying, I thought.'

Deciding against a trek up to his parents home in Edinburgh – he would be there soon enough once the tour started – Fish, along with a member of the band's regular crew also at a loose-end for Christmas, Gary Townsend, drove down to London in the band's van and headed straight for the faithful ambience of the Marquee.

'Only it was closed by the time we got there,' says Fish, 'and so we ended up going across the street to the St Moritz and staying there getting plastered until about three in the morning!'

That night, Fish and Gary Townsend slept off the previous evening's mad excesses at the small converted flat John Arnison had installed for just such 'emergencies' in a spare room attached to his office, which by now had moved from its old Soho Square address to more spacious quarters in Redcliffe Gardens, just off the Old Brompton Road in Kensington. In the morning, the pair intended to drive back up to the Manor where they were expected to arrive in time for a special Christmas lunch the catering staff had arranged for them. They never made it.

'Gary got up before me and decided to go out on his own and get some petrol for the van and one or two things he wanted to pick up quickly while we were in town,' says Fish. 'Only he was gone *hours*! Hours and hours . . . I was sitting there on my own in John's office, Christmas day, nothing to do but smoke cigarettes and wait for Gary to come back . . . brilliant!'

Eventually, more than five hours after he'd first left with the van, Townsend returned to find Fish ready to chew through wood and punch holes in the walls.

'The van had broken down, he said, somewhere near London Bridge, and it had taken him this long to try and get it repaired, fail miserably because no-one was open on Christmas day, and then get a cab back to me in the office. Anyway, he was back, thank God, only now we were both stranded in John's office.'

With no option but to make the best of a bad situation, they made a quick inventory of all vital supplies.

'We had no food whatsoever, but we had about four bottles of John's champagne, a bottle of brandy and a bottle of whiskey,' Fish says. 'And we had about £6 in cash between us. So we went down the Old Brompton Road to the only shop we could find open, a little Indian grocery store, and we bought a skinny rancid chicken, a packet of instant mash-potato, a king-size packet of frozen peas, a couple of cans of rice pudding, and a couple more packets of cigarettes. And then we went back to John's office and got stuck in. We ended up spending the whole night drinking all the booze and ringing all our friends and wishing them a Merry Christmas!'

On the morning of Boxing Day, having passed their second

alcholic night on the portable beds in John Arnison's office, Fish and Gary Townsend were finally rescued by two of the ladies from the catering staff of the Manor, who arrived at their door bright and early with a Christmas hamper laden with all the goodies the pair had missed out on the day before.

'It was great,' Fish remembers. 'Mince pies, cold turkey, roast potatoes, stuffing, and wine. That cheered us up no end. And then the very next day we were out on the road again. It was a short Christmas for me and Gary all right, but a very *long* New Year.'

Ian Mosley's first live gig with Marillion was at the Rock City in Nottingham, an enlarged club venue with enough stand-up room to hold over 2,000 people.

'When I first went up to Monmouth I had no idea whether I would last a week, a month, or a year with this lot,' says Ian. 'But things started going so well between us that I told John Arnison I would stay on for the album, if they wanted me to, and I would even take a drop in salary to do it. I was still getting paid session-rates for the *Fugazi* album, which meant that I was still earning over twice as much as the rest of the boys per week, but I still took a drop in what I could have asked for because I knew they were a real band and not just in it for the money.

'So I struck a deal with John to do the album as cheaply as I could. And then the band said what about these Christmas dates? Would I do them? I said yeah, I'd love to, but we better get some rehearsals in first, and they all turned around and laughed at me! They said no, bollocks to rehearsals, we'll give you the first album and some live tapes and you can work it out from there!

'So there I was, plunged in at the deep end. I was terrified for that first gig! I had all these bits of paper with all the notes I'd made stuck up on bits of the drum-kit . . .

'But I remember thinking what a great vibe it was to play with the band on a live stage. The boys all related to each other like a real *band*, everybody knew everybody else's moves and you could anticipate when somebody wanted to add a bit of spontaneity and leave room for them. It was a band in every sense, who really enjoyed playing together, and it felt great to be there amongst them.

'The other thing that really got me though was the crowd! I'd never played to a crowd like it before; it was wild, people singing all the words to songs I didn't even know the first verse to yet all the way through the set, and they were all going bonkers!

'And then the next night we played the Hammersmith Odeon, and that was the real clincher, for me. I mean, I'd played there before, with Steve Hackett, and the audience were good, but they were nothing compared to this Marillion lot – they spent the whole show jumping up and down and singing all 200 verses to things like 'Script for a Jester's Tear', and going absolutely barmy – not just down the front, either, all over the bloody building it seemed.'

Marillion spun through their five UK dates, laying down back-to-back performances that hinted at something far greater than any previous Marillion line-up had yet yielded. Previewing sparkling new material each night like 'Punch and Judy' and 'Assassing', punctuated by fleshier, more percussive arrangements to existing show-stoppers like 'Forgotten Sons', 'Garden Party', and 'Chelsea Monday', the new Rothery/Fish/Kelly/Trewavas/Mosley Marillion line-up set out to prove that this was to be the one built to last. In Ian Mosley's own words, the band might still need 'another couple of tours before we really started to function the way a real band should', but there's no doubt that the potential was on full ragged display over the short space of the band's December 1983 UK tour.

Back in the studio the first week of January 1984, the band arrived to find Nick Tauber in the same confused frenzy they had left him to recover from over the holidays. If anything, he was worse and as the days and weeks passed, Marillion ran out of time at first the Manor, then Sarm East, Eel Pie, and finally, the Maison Rouge studios in London, Tauber would often desert the studio for hours at a time, leaving the band alone to get on with it with engineer Simon Hanhart.

'He'd just disappear,' says Pete Trewavas. ' "Oh, I've got to make a few quick phone calls," you know, and he'd be off for the next four hours! And then we'd come back to the studio the next day and find more of this impossible and mega-expensive equipment waiting for us that Nick had hired. It was getting ridiculous.'

By the middle of February, with the album still unfinished and already £50,000 over-budget, EMI were all for firing Tauber as producer and getting someone else in to supervise the final stages of recording. Contractually, it worked out a lot cheaper for the company if Tauber agreed to resign from the project on the grounds that he had effectively failed to bring in the album as soon (and as cheaply) as he had promised.

149

'But Nick wouldn't resign,' says Mark Kelly. 'If they wanted to get rid of him they were going to have to fire him and pay him what he was owed, and all sorts of things they didn't have a hope of sorting out in time to get rid of him *and* find a new producer. So Nick stayed.'

For the band, time had already run out. Nobody had really anticipated *Fugazi* taking so long to make, and originaly EMI and John Arnison had agreed that the album should be released by the end of February, would be preceded by a single, and accompanied, throughout February and the first half of March, by a twenty-one date UK tour already arranged and kicking off at the Victoria Halls, in Hanley, on 9 February, and culminating in three consecutive nights at the Hammersmith Odeon, in London, on 9, 10 and 11 March.

'Punch and Judy', the fourth Marillion single, was released on 30 January 1984, nine days before the band's second big headlining tour of the UK began. The week that followed its release passed by in a blur of sudden TV engagements squeezed between frantic sleepless nights of last-minute recording and mixing in the studios with their increasingly bamboozled producer.

Four days after its release, the new UK Top 40 Singles Chart was broadcast on Radio One – and pow! – 'Punch and Judy' had shot straight into the charts at twenty-seven! The band were well pleased, only this time nobody was in a hurry to reach for the champagne; they didn't have time, says Fish.

' "Punch and Judy" hit the Top 30 just as we were in the middle of an insane seventy-two-hour no-sleep cycle in the recording studio,' he grimaces. 'And we got offered spots on three different TV shows all in one week: we did Top of the Pops the day after the single went into the charts, then we drove straight back to Nick in the studio; two days later we were on a plane going up to Manchester for the Oxford Road Show; and then the following Monday we had to go up to Newcastle for a kids' show on Tyne Tees Television called Razzamatazz. And while all this was going on we were trying to get the album finished *and* get ready for our most important tour yet! Honestly, we looked like walking disaster areas when we finally climbed into the van and set off for the first gig in Hanley.'

Leaving Nick Tauber to stew in his own juices in the studio as he feverishly attempted to claw back some of his lost credibility and complete the final mix in time for a projected March release schedule, Marillion were forced in the meantime to embark on their latest British tour with no new album in the shops for the fans to buy, and a single that, despite all the TV and radio exposure, had still managed to drop a crucial notch in the UK charts only a week after it had first made its mark.

'We couldn't believe that,' says Fish. 'It had happened to us before with "He Knows You Know" and with "Script . . .", but we assumed that with the single just out and already in the charts, and having done *three* TV shows in one week, and then starting the tour, well, we just assumed the single couldn't possibly go down. But it did. And I was *so* pissed off!

'I'd never really been that concerned before when a single of ours didn't exactly race into the number one position. I always had my greatest expectations reserved for how well our albums did, but when "Punch . . ." went straight in at twenty-seven and then went down to twenty-eight the very next week, I admit I felt slighted. I was inclined to take it as a bad omen for the album.'

'Actually, looking back on it now,' Mark Kelly observes, 'I think we should be glad "Punch and Judy" did as well as it did. The truth is, it wasn't really the right choice as the first single from the album. It was a good song, and a great number to play live sometimes, just not a terribly commercial choice as a single.'

Unaware of the disguised tensions that still delayed the release of *Fugazi*, the loyal Marillion fans still flocked to the shows in their thousands, making every other night a genuine sell-out performance. Album or no album, live, Marillion were still one of Britain's fastest growing, hottest-ticket-in-town draws on the major concert-hall circuit, and with the dearth of new material on sale a lot of the newer fans were starting to buy the first album, unexpectedly hoisting *Script . . .* back into the UK Top 40 as a result.

'Every cloud has its silver lining, I suppose,' Pete Trewavas smiles. 'I mean, obviously we didn't plan it to happen that way, we hadn't even considered what might happen if we went out on the road without a new album in the shops to promote. And then the first album started selling really well again and the most ironical part of all was that it looked like it might go gold as a result! We'd all got silver discs for *Script . . .* originally, which was for over 60,000 sales in the UK, but by the end of the *Fugazi* tour the new album hadn't come out yet and we were about to top 100,000 sales for *Script . . .* We didn't know whether to laugh or cry, really.'

The backroom contradictions and mounting frustrations that surrounded the UK tour of February and March 1983 were ritually pushed aside every night as Marillion unveiled their most outstanding and extravagant stage-show yet. Though the album never did see the light of day while the tour was still in progress, nevertheless Marillion were intent on ramming the new material home as best they could, usually performing six out of the seven new numbers included on *Fugazi*.

The show opened each night to the slow malevolent strains of 'Assassing' echoing from somewhere beneath the glowing footlights; Ian Mosley signalling the arrival of the band on-stage with a fearful run through his percussion weaponry; Mark Kelly's synthesisers purring beneath the avalanche of fiercely beating drums; Steve Rothery's arch guitar lines cutting dirty fat chunks out of Mosley's pulsing rhythms and transforming them into a raunchy, free-wheeling guitar riff.

Under the unblinking eye of a white spotlight, Fish stalked the stage with a new, brooding self-confidence. The whimsical poet-minstrel with the sad, mocking eyes and the fleeting grease-paint smile, that would surface often enough on the UK tours of 1982 and 1983, was now just a memory of earlier, more tenuous times.

For 'Assassing', Fish appeared clutching a tall, vicious-looking Gurkha Blade, which he wielded like a dagger, a long black cloak dripping from his broad shoulders, his face and arms daubed in smoky layers of new, specially-applied, ultra-violet body-paint that smouldered and shone under the hot white lights of the stage. For 'Punch and Judy', which followed, the cloak and sword were discarded, and in their place Fish sported a king-sized red boxing glove which he used for sparring with the audience on the choruses. On 'Jigsaw', another new and bitter-sweet number from the unreleased album Fish dedicated most nights to 'all the romantics in the audience', a giant mirrored piece of a jigsaw puzzle suspended by invisible wires from the upper-stage rigging was brought into play, Fish aiming its reflected yellow light into the gawping, hungry eyes of the stalls and balconies, then swinging it like an absurdly shaped pendulum.

'Incubus', one of the most powerful of the new numbers, had the Hammersmith Odeon memorising the words and coming back the third night to sing them for the band; and the haunting, magical refrains of the most spectacular new number the band previewed live, and the song so aptly chosen as the title track of their new album, would end the show each night in a whirlwind of tunnelled lights swirling like radioactive hurricanes about the stage . . . the world turned totally foo-gah-zey.

Marillion's much-touted second album for EMI, *Fugazi*, was finally released on 12 March 1984, the day after their latest UK tour ended with the band's third consecutive sold-out night at the Hammersmith Odeon.

While they had been out on the road, the UK music press had again been kind to Marillion, the band picking up successive front cover stories in *Sounds, Melody Maker, Kerrang!*, and *Musicians Only*. The lingering accusations of being second-rate Genesis clones, and the suggestion that Marillion might, after all, turn out to be a one-album-only sensation, were still big shadows hanging drearily over most of the stories, but even their sternest critics had to admit that the basis of the band's growing appeal lay in their ability to fulfill a palpable need among a generation of teenagers oblivious to the doomed echo of the seventies that still permeated much of the band's new music. And anyway, on the evidence of the startling new shows they had been putting on all over Britain, the sharper rock-crits were quick to note that these days Marillion's 'influences' were getting much tougher to detect, the band's essential oeuvre taking on a remarkable identity unmistakably of their own device.

Pleased and encouraged, now they anxiously awaited the outcome of the harder-to-predict reviews for the new album.

Script for a Jester's Tear had, for the most part, despite the charmed life it had led in the UK charts, picked up only fair-to-average reviews, the general consensus at the time being that, though a capable enough achievement, the first album lacked enough maturity for most hard-nosed critics to commit themselves fully to the long-term Marillion cause.

Fugazi fared considerably better in the reviews that heralded its ill-timed, post-tour release. Both *Sounds* and *Melody Maker* blew the trumpets. But it was the respected *Kerrang!* writer, Chris Welch, who put forward the most convincing and emphatic case for *Fugazi*, predicting that it would be the '*Dark Side of the Moon* of the '80s!' And concluding his glowing review with the more sober observation that what *Fugazi* had going for it most was, 'dynamics, light and shade and sensitive interpretation (that) turn these songs from confusions of noise into things of beauty. What

153

the world needs now is a Lady Fish to answer all these charges of infidelity.' Indeed.

'On the whole, I was really pleased with the press we got for that album and that tour,' says Fish. 'It seemed with *Script . . .* that so many of the critics were attacking us for standing for something they had decided was wholly undesirable in the 1980s. But it all came as news to us; we didn't even know ourselves what we were supposed to "stand for". And then with *Fugazi* we started getting the big turn around in our favour.'

'The irony for me,' says Steve Rothery, 'is that though *Fugazi* picked up a lot better reviews than *Script . . .*, I was a lot less pleased with the way *Fugazi* finally came out. There was so much left undone that we had planned to do. My thought was, well, if they liked this version of the album, what would they have said if they had heard what we'd originally had planned.'

Fugazi, for reasons both good and bad, is still probably the hardest Marillion album for first-time buyers to grapple with. The material is not to blame, the seven numbers contained on *Fugazi* represented the band's most elevated and determined work to date; nor can the playing be faulted. The fault all too clearly lies in the production, which is constantly busy and colourfully ambitious, but curiously soulless and tainted by the whiff of a strange introspection that often obscures the album's best moments. Where Tauber's work on the first Marillion album had highlighted the band's vulnerable, early sound, throwing a careful light over fragile backwards waltzes like 'The Web' and 'Chelsea Monday', dressing the rest up with a coat-of-arms stamp that gave meaning to every scattered pause in the music, every sigh, every swing, given twice the money and twice the time and with twice the expertise at his disposal, what Tauber had effectively managed to do to tracks like 'Incubus', 'She Chameleon', and 'Fugazi' was to produce a sound which the band found unacceptable.

Ian Mosley had added a stronger, more vibrant, percussive backdrop to Marillion's imagined underground cityscapes, and the rest of the band sound accordingly more genuinely powerful on record than ever before. The overall sound, though, is condensed to the point of choking claustrophobia, not haunting but desperate, the dynamics inherent in volatile material like the title track, or 'Incubus', too easily stifled beneath a flat, heavy-handed production that, at times, sounds like the work of madmen grinding diamonds into dust.

'Assassing' and 'Punch And Judy' open side one in breath-taking up-tempo fashion, both as deceitfully 'rock and roll' as Marillion could get in 1984 ('There's no doubt that "Assassing", in particular, started out as our ridiculous attempt to write something an American audience might sort of halfway relate to,' admits Fish. 'By the time we'd come to put it on the album though, we'd Marillionised it so much that we forgot all about who was meant to like it and turned it into something quite nasty'), Fish touching collars and naming no names on the former – '*I am the assassin . . . with tongue forged from eloquence/I am the assassin . . . providing your nemesis!*' – cynically reciting the verbal misdeeds of the man with his finger on the trigger; on the latter, recounting the plight of two lovers' emotional defection in the middle years of a confused and desolate marital entrapment, the shrill, piercing voice of Mr Punch blowing hard in Judy's ear. '*Whatever happened to pillow fights, Friday nights and jeans so tight/Lover's Lane, passion's games, Sunday walks in the pouring rain.?*'

What indeed? According to Punch, now doomed to a world of '*curling tongs, mogadons, "I got a headache baby don't take so long"* ', that's the question he can never quite find the answer to.

'Jigsaw', which follows, begins with a gentle, child-like melody that weaves a deceptively coy spell, Kelly's soft, innocent keyboard touches belying the terse, jealous, accusatory tone of the words Fish reaches into the sky for with his lilting falsetto. It's a song about the victims of thinly-disguised emotional deceptions and the guilt-traps people everywhere fall into at least once in their adult lives. The unpleasant smell of a love gone bad . . . '*Drowning in tequila sunsets, stowaways on midnight ships/Refugees of romance plead asylum from the real/Scrambling distress signals on random frequencies/Forever repatriated on guilt laden morning planes.*'

'Emerald Lies', which closes the side, is a fiercely enigmatic piece constructed primarily around a fraught guitar-line Rothery gradually tightens like a noose in the shadow of the percussion, which rains down from the stereo-heavens in big, stomach-churning waves as the blistering climax reaches its destination. Along with 'She Chameleon', which follows immediately afterwards on side two, 'Emerald Lies' is Fish and Marillion at their most ethereal, their most abstract, in a song that speaks of love as the indecipherable message received at dawn alone, helplessly avoiding the '*questions within questions*' that greet its arrival, the cold camera eye of the singer *'Looking in shades of green through shades of blue/I trust you trust in me to mistrust you.'*

'She Chameleon' has the look and feel of another voyeuristic 'Chelsea Monday'; indeed, they could be blood-sisters. Ostensibly, a funereal oration in memory of the girl with a thousand faces, though none known by name, be she groupie, lover, or friend, and the low price of the would-be rock star's self-esteem under cover of the chameleon's clammy repetitive embrace: *'So was it just a fuck, was it just a fuck, just another fuck I said/Loving just for laughs, carnal autograph, lying on the lizard's bed.'*

Mark Kelly gets into a full-tilt Rick-Wakeman-we-salute-you keyboard passage that drifts like grains of sand in an hourglass, making dark sweeping gestures that are suddenly cut short when Steve Rothery leans into another of his aching guitar breaks, silencing the room and piercing the tension.

The production is sparing and a little blank and too quickly to the point perhaps, but by now Marillion are ready to unveil one of the most enduring new numbers of the entire set: 'Incubus' — by definition, a devil who visits and seduces sleeping, luckless virgins in the dead of night. In this context, used as metaphor for the cynical director of human passions who demands that his subject's desire be *'. . . exposed in voyeuristic colour, the public act . . . Let you model your shame on the mannequin catwalk . . . let the cats walk . . .'* The band at their most positively inventive, ticking over in the relentless drive through the built-up terrain of their own elemental funk; Fish's disembodied voice forking like lightning into the silently whispering tongues of the fire that would invade the sex and steal the soul of another being, callously eulogising the act of involuntary spiritual penetration, mental rape:

'Darkroom unleashes imagination in pornographic images in which you will always be the star, untouchable, unapproachable/Constant in the dark, nursing an erection, a misplaced reaction . . . And the walls become enticingly newspaper thin . . .'

'Fugazi', the title track, is saved for last. A long, wordy, rambling song of morbid disillusion delivered from within the eye of the hurricane, 'Fugazi' was Marillion's most transcendental statement since something as righteously epic and wilfully wrong-headed as 'Grendel'. Beginning slowly, hesitantly, with a lone piano repeating its quiet, doomy phrases, by the end of the first verse the rest of the band have arrived; drums and guitars bossing the sound, shunting like an engine as Fish pours on the poison . . . '*A son of the swastika of '45, parading a peroxide standard/Graffitti disciples conjure testaments of hatred/Aerosol wands whisper where the searchlights trim the barbed wire hedges/This is Brixton chess . . .*'

This is the '*bleeding-heart poet*' cracking up on London's underground Piccadilly line, withdrawing into a manic foetal crouch, the voice that cries behind the locked door, beyond the verbal bricks and mortar of a twisted reality without options.

If Marillion began this opus with the hollow, spiteful voice of the hired assassin boasting of his special talents '*on the sacrificial altar to success*', then Fish ends it for them with his head thrown back, mouth begging the questions his eyes say he already knows the answers to . . . the band, led by Rothery's strident, curling guitar, roam by his side, Mosley bringing the hammer down, the marching, chanting, Godless, finale like a dead spirit exhumed . . . '*Where are the prophets, where are the visionaries, where are the poets/To breach the dawn of the sentimental mercenary . . . ?*'

'None of us are ever able to look back on *Fugazi* without picking out all its faults,' says Fish. 'It was really only half the album we wanted to make, in lots of ways it would be churlish of me to worry about now. But at bottom, the songs and the playing were still something we felt justifiably proud of. We still weren't the band we were starting to be some nights on the British tour, but put into perspective it definitely augured well for the future.'

'It wasn't mixed to my satisfaction, and it wasn't produced to anybody's satisfaction,' says Steve Rothery. 'And it took me a long time to forget that I still wasn't happy with some of it, but *Fugazi* was definitely some kind of turning point for the band, I think. We all grew up very fast over the months it took to make that one.'

Despite the reservations Marillion were having about the finished album, the good reviews continued to collect in their bulging press-cuttings file over at Manchester Square, and a week after its release, in March 1984, *Fugazi* leapt into the national UK Top 40 albums chart at number four, and this time it stayed around long enough to kick its heels into the UK Top 5 for three straight weeks! Well up on their scoring-average in the charts, *Fugazi* earned the band another silver disc for over 60,000 sales in the UK within a month of release, and by the end of 1984 went on to win for them their second round of gold records to match the set they already possessed for *Script for a Jester's Tear*.

157

As Steve Rothery astutely points out, *Fugazi*, for all its self-confessed sins, *was* a major turning point for the band. This is a band not yet at the full height of its powers, but more musically adept and swifter in at the kill, than at any time before.

The sleeve, another colourful and original Mark Wilkinson creation, says it all. Once again, the inner, gatefold, world of the Jester is on view. Only this time the circumstances of his situation are dramatically altered. The gloomy bedsit chambers of the cell he occupied on *Script . . .* have been exchanged for the glitzy isolation of an anonymous hotel room located in some nameless city whose murky precincts the Jester has now abandoned for the security-guarded, paranoiac interiors of a new and monied padded-walls world.

Where the sleeve for *Script . . .* was veiled in shadows and dark sharp-angled corners, the artwork for *Fugazi* is alive with bright, pale colours: fuschia pinks and bleached greens merging into shades of Disney blue. In the foreground, the wasted, semi-naked figure of the Jester reclines upon his bed slack-jawed with tranquilised eyes, the ripped tatters of the Harlequin costume at his feet, next to discarded copies of *Billboard* and *Music Week*.

This Jester doesn't look like he would read *Sounds* or *Kerrang!* if they had a photo of his face on every single page. A Walkman covers his ears; in one hand he clutches a blood-red poppy, and the grip of the other loosens on a tumbler of red wine which spills to the carpeted floor.

Propped up against the bed is a portrait of a sad-eyed, white-faced Pierrot, mascara running down his cheeks, his nose and mouth exaggerated in crude daubs of red. On the wall behind the Jester's bed hangs a long mirror, which reflects his prone forlorn figure, only the reflection is fully clothed, a dim visual echo of past allusions. On a couch opposite the bed stands the same lizard that shared the Jester's cramped quarters on *Script . . .* his eyes slitted, he thrusts a forked tongue into the air, aimed at a magpie – a pervading symbol of human fallability in Marillion mythology – clutching a stolen wedding ring in his long pointed beak.

The old black and white TV set has been replaced as well: the set on *Fugazi* is a full, psychedelically-coloured 3D rig, replete with rainbow-coloured lightning and the green, three-fingered hand of the incubus clawing its way out of the screen. Beneath it sits a state-of-the-art VCR and one lone discarded stiletto-heeled shoe.

On the left of the picture, in the far corner of the Jester's tastefully designed private hell, are more relics from his past littered amongst the codified detritus of an unavoidable future: a toy train, a jack-in-the-box, the memoirs of an as yet unrecognised misplaced childhood; a jigsaw puzzle drawn in the image of the *Script for a Jester's Tear* sleeve, with one piece missing over the younger jester's heart; and another scattering of albums across the bedroom floor – this time he's been listening to Pink Floyd's *The Wall*, and two Peter Hammill albums: *Over* and *Fool's Mate*.

'Real music to slash your wrists to,' Mark Kelly chortles. 'Anyone who knows any of those albums will tell you that. But then you see, some of us *did* spend a *lot* of time listening to those very same records. Fish and I in particular spent weeks and weeks listening to those Hammill albums together. I admit it *was* pretty bleak at times, but then life is, for a lot of the time, isn't it?'

Three original paintings, reproduced in cartoon microcosm, line the bedroom walls; figurative glimpses into an impression-istic world . . . And through an open bay window a crumbling cityscape, dominated by a central disfigured monument, dis-solves into pale heavy clouds that hide the sun.

'The paintings on the walls are all originals done by Mark Wilkinson's wife, Julie Hazelwood,' says Fish, 'and I'm not absolutely sure, but I think the city outline you can see out the window is actually Lincoln . . . or somewhere typically bleak and real, anyway.'

The puzzled, innocent figure dreaming of a better future and still trying to write that love song that adorned the *Script for a Jester's Tear* sleeve has undergone a ghastly transformation by the time we catch up with him again on *Fugazi*. Here he is assassin, incubus, amoral rock star, and victim of his own now paralysed emotions; his eyes dry of tears he no longer knows how to shed . . . This is the Jester brought to the edge of a catharsis we would have to wait until the next Marillion album for him to experience . . .

With *Fugazi* still stubbornly riding the UK Top 20, EMI decided to release a second single from the album: this time they opted for a heavily edited-down version of 'Assassing' – the most musically up-tempo number of a determinedly down-beat collection, the company reasoned. The full seven-minutes-plus album-length version would be released as a twelve-inch edition of the single. And the band were asked to shoot a new video to go out with it (no video was ever made for 'Punch And Judy' – suffering the same fate as 'He Knows You Know' did initially, both singles were in and out of the UK Top 40 so fast, there was never any time to prepare an advance shoot).

Insisting on recording a special one-off B side to go with the new single, Marillion returned to the studio for a few days at the end of March, this time with Nick Tauber's former engineer, Simon Hanhart, promoted to the producer's chair.

'As far as we were concerned, Nick Tauber would never work with this band again,' says Fish. 'After the nightmare of those last few weeks we spent with Nick running from one studio to another trying to finish the album, we had decided enough was enough.

'So we asked Simon, who'd been great and worked with us all through the trials and tribulations of making *Fugazi*, to come in and co-produce this new song we had with us. Which he did, and though I don't suppose we ended up with the world's greatest sounding B side or anything, the sessions went well and we had lots of fun doing them.'

'Cinderella Search', recorded and mixed in a matter of days, is a number that wouldn't have fitted comfortably on *Fugazi* – it's far too airy, too fanciful and romantic for those dark waters. A gorgeous lilting melody that trips you up at the knees and leaves you floating on thin colourless clouds. Love on the rebound, the thorn within the proffered rose. The band galvanised and jumping with a spontaneity usually reserved for their live shows.

The video for 'Assassing', directed once again by Simon Milne, who had added a touch of class and humour to the 'Garden Party' and 'He Knows You Know' videos, is a flash, neon-scarred, split-screen extravaganza. 'Assassing' is all action shots of cloistered scenes that hint at a mystery that never really seems to unravel any further than that. It's more like an expensive trailer than a full feature, but containing enough trash-aesthetic erotica to make it appear as though the band are exploding off the screen.

'It's probably my least favourite video,' says Steve Rothery. 'But I'm not even sure why. I think perhaps it just looked a bit too much like Marillion playing at being James Bond,' he smiles.

'Either way, although it's very flash and eye-catching, I think it just came out looking a bit . . . corny.'

Released at the end of April 1984, 'Assassing' became Marillion's fourth Top 40 success in the UK singles charts, landing at number twenty-one the first week of release, climbing to nineteen the following week – thereby earning the video a brief airing on Top of the Pops, still the nation's favourite choice of TV pop prog.

However, in economical and practised Marillion fashion, 'Assassing' peaked at nineteen and dropped to twenty-nine seven days later. By now the band were used to the wavering, unpredictable fortunes of their singles and failed to respond to 'Assassing's decline any other way than positively.

'We were becoming very professional and detached from the whole sordid business of worrying about hit singles,' says Fish, 'they had never been what we were really about, and we just tended to view their limited success as an amusing distraction. And anyway, we weren't kidding ourselves – none of our songs sounded like number one hit singles to me. If they went Top 20, that was just seen as a bonus coming off the back of a hit album.'

The rest of April and for much of May, while *Fugazi* still slogged it out to the last in the UK Top 20, the band took off for another round of European dates.

Marillion had never managed more than a handful of European shows before April 1984, and though John Arnison still thought it unwise and too expensive to tour there on their own terms for any great length of time, the band kept up a steady round of return appearances at small select dates in Germany, Holland, and France, zipping back and forth from their Aylesbury homes to the continent on long weekends and five-day field trips.

Slowly but surely the tide was starting to turn for the band outside of Britain. *Fugazi* doubled the sales of *Script . . .* in key European territories, and except for an occasional outdoor festival date, Marillion continued headlining and putting on the same show that had dazzled the UK just two months before. Applying the same uncompromising strategies that had earned them a slow-building but fanatical following back home in Britain, Marillion carried their foo-gah-zeyed act over to Europe as often as time and finances would sensibly allow throughout April and May of 1984, inspiring ripples of fandom that would start a wave rolling right across the Western hemisphere over the next twenty-four months.

Returning from their latest bout of appearances in Germany, in June 1984, Marillion announced that they would again be taking part in this year's Reading Festival – only this time they would be headlining!

'In two years we'd gone from virtually the bottom of the bill right to the very top,' says Fish. 'From now on our job would be to prove we really belonged there, and then see if we had the balls to stay there.'

6

When Ivory Eyes Are Smiling
(*Profile – Mark Kelly*)

Mark Kelly has Irish eyes. The kind that never stop smiling. Which makes him a very easy person to be around. He's the type of person you feel would fit easily into any new situation; charming, friendly, warm and down-to-earth in a way rock stars don't always make a habit of being. Like Pete Trewavas and Ian Mosley, he is Mr Easy-Going personified.

However, beneath the calm, bucolic exterior lies a darker and more mysterious streak to his good nature. The vein he taps for his musical inspiration is set somewhere deep inside, but it flows like a river through all of his best work with Marillion. The sound of his keyboards permeates everything: those are *his* swamps the singer has to wade through at the start of 'Fugazi', and that's *his* sky that turns black at the very start of *Misplaced Childhood*, on 'Pseudo Silk Kimono'. All his. Mark Kelly's.

The second eldest of seven children, all boys, Mark was born in the city of Dublin, in Southern Ireland, on 9 April 1961. His father, Michael, was a diesel-fitter and worked on the railroads in Ireland. 'He met my mum, Patricia, when he was doing his apprenticeship in Liverpool,' says Mark. 'She's English, but he ended up taking her back to Ireland with him and marrying her.'

Mark Kelly spent the first seven years of his life in a Dublin still untouched and unaffected by the cultural upheavals inflicted by the sudden advent of the Swinging Sixties occurring in London and other big cities in England.

'My only memories of Dublin are of it being a bit of a pit,' he says. 'I mean, we only lived there until I was seven years old, but I still remember the area we lived in – everybody was a thug,

163

you know. And I remember skipping school a lot, from a really early age. Everybody did it so I did it too.

'It was a very poor area in Dublin, where my family lived in those days, and things like school just didn't seem to matter much to me then.'

For a time the Kelly family lived in a large house in Crumlin, a Dublin suburb, owned and still lived in by Mark's grandparents.

'You can imagine what it was like,' he laughs. 'This huge Anglo-Irish family sprawled about in every corner of the house! You had to learn how to get on with the things *you* wanted to do and just block everything else out sometimes. But it was a very close family because of that. There were always lots of aunties and uncles and cousins and God knows who else hanging around. It was all right.'

Eventually, in 1969, Mark's father and mother moved to England and found a house of their own in Hornchurch, Essex, where Mark attended primary school. His days of skipping school had left him with an educational standard far below that of the rest of the children in his new class. He was a good learner, said his teachers, but with an awful lot of missed lessons to catch up on.

By the time he was eleven years old and about to sit his final primary school exams the family had moved again, though not far, this time to a small suburb of a larger Essex town called Romford.

'I sat my eleven-plus exams and failed them miserably, and so I ended up getting sent to this horrible Catholic Comprehensive School for boys,' he says, shuddering at the memory.

'It was a grim, rough place. We were made to go to Confession at least once a week and attend church a couple of times a day, and had to say hundreds of prayers before doing anything. I really didn't go for it at all, I thought it was a horribly oppressive place! I'd stopped going to their Confession by the time I was in the second year. I stopped when the priests started asking me if I was playing with myself at night! I mean, those people *terrified* me. So I never told anybody anything about it, but I just stopped going.'

Declaring a hatred for sports, the young, teenage Mark Kelly was much more interested in the arts classes, excelling at drawing and painting and discovering a sudden, new thrill of pleasure from listening to music.

'By the time I was fifteen I used to work part-time in a local

Co-op supermarket, stacking shelves and that sort of thing. I went from having next to no money of my own – pocket-money was never exactly forthcoming from my parents, not with seven kids to feed and look after – to getting £12.60 a week, and I thought I was rich! That's when I started to buy records and get into music.'

The very first records he heard on the radio that he liked enough to remember the names of were singles by groups like Slade, Sweet, T. Rex. But the first album he ever actually went out and bought was *Journey to the Centre of the Earth* by Rick Wakeman.

'When I used to groove along to records by people like T. Rex or Slade, I used to do it very innocently, I never took pop music that seriously. But then an uncle of mine lent me that Rick Wakeman album and I played it and immediately thought what a pile of old shit this is! But then I kept playing more and more bits of it and suddenly I was really into it. I remember I bought the album at the start of the summer holidays from school in 1976, and I used to play it every morning as soon as I woke up. It was funny though, because I remember a year before that my older brother had been given a copy of *Yessongs* by Yes as a Christmas present, and I can remember listening to it and thinking how awful it was. I had no idea Rick Wakeman was the keyboard player on both albums!

'I think I drove everybody in the house mad with that album, *Journey to the Centre of the Earth*, I just couldn't stop playing it. It was right after that that I talked my mum into lending me the money to buy my first organ.'

By promising faithfully to repay his mother the money over an indefinite period of time, Mark persuaded her into taking out a hire purchase agreement on a small Hammond Everett organ for £185. He still remembers it.

'It was a second-hand model of the first organ that Hammond made that was transistorised,' he says. 'Very small and compact, with a three-octave keyboard, and a lot of these little chord buttons down one end which were a complete waste of time. But it was a great thing to have, just to get me started off and learning something about how to play.'

One of Mark's older brothers, Mike, already owned a guitar and it was he who taught Mark his first tune – 'Greensleeves'.

'I learnt how to play that with one finger,' he laughs. 'And from there I started to struggle my way through learning to read music. I got the music book for *Journey to the Centre of the Earth* and worked my way through that, probably learning about ten bars of it a week – it was that slow.'

It wasn't long before Mark worked out that his new discovery, Rick Wakeman, had also worked on a number of the most innovative and popular Yes albums throughout the early half of the 70s, and from there he started to work his way through a collection of new albums by similarly serious-minded mid-70s acts like Pink Floyd and Camel, though not, strangely, Genesis.

'I hated Genesis in those days,' he says. 'Don't forget, this was 1976, Peter Gabriel had left the band about two years before, and I listened to some of their recent albums and thought they were a *pop* band . . . and I hated them! I was much more into the heavier end of things. I mean, for a while, Pink Floyd and Yes were as light as I would go! I was more into things like Black Sabbath, to begin with, very *doomy* stuff.'

One of the first rock concerts the teenage Mark Kelly was taken by friends to see was Pink Floyd at the Wembley Arena in London during their 1976 *Animals'* world tour. It was a visit that only reinforced his deepening passion for music as spectacle; he loved the extravagances of the stage production, and he admired the limitless indulgence of the music which continued uninterrupted for over two hours.

'I'd never seen anything like it in my life!' he cries. 'I thought they were great, truly great, really impressive, I was absolutely *amazed*! The only thing I couldn't figure out was what the funny smell was in the hall – it was the smell of thousands of people smoking joints, of course, but I was completely innocent at the time and I couldn't understand what all these people were doing that was making such a pong.'

His fascination for live music well and truly fired by his experience of the Floyd Wembley show, Mark started to drift into London more and more, spending his Saturday-job money on tickets for the Marquee, the Hammersmith Odeon, the Rainbow, wherever he thought he could smell the music he liked being played.

'That went on for a couple of years, until I left school,' he says. 'But through that whole period the big one for me was always Rick Wakeman; I was really quite obsessed with laying my hands on everything he'd ever released. I went right through the collection of Yes albums he'd played on, then worked my way through all his solo stuff like *Six Wives of Henry VIII*,

Journey to the Centre of the Earth, and *King Arthur*; in the end I had most of everything he'd ever played on, back to the Strawbs and beyond.'

In September 1979, after leaving school at eighteen with three A level passes, in Art, Technical Drawing, and History of Art, Mark left his parents' home in Romford for the first time and moved down to the West Country, where he began a four-year degree course in Fine Art at the Bath Academy of Art.

Obviously talented at the drawing board, but supremely lacking in ambition, by the time he was eighteen Mark's head was too full of music to contemplate a life as a budding art student, and his hands more used to the touch of an electric keyboard than the grip of an artist's brush or palette-knife. He lasted just a year in Bath before quitting.

'I wasn't thinking about art at all when I first went down there,' he said. 'The only big idea I had in my head was that art college would be a great place to form a band! I wasn't really concerned with anything else.'

During his last year at school, Mark had joined a part-time garage band put together by some friends.

'We never did any gigs or anything, we just used to practise in this bloke's garage,' he says. 'The guitarist was sort of the leader of the band and he was a Rory Gallagher freak, he used to wear the jeans and the check shirt and everything. But he was a really good guitarist and so we used to play a few passable versions of different Rory Gallagher numbers.

'But, like I say, we never used to play for people, we didn't even have a name, I just used to go along for the practice – you can learn things about three times faster by playing in some kind of band, any kind of band really, and playing with those guys really improved my technique and my scope. After that, I started thinking seriously about getting into some kind of semi-professional group, somewhere. That's why I thought art college might be the place.'

However, much to his chagrin, on arrival at the Bath Academy Mark discovered that nobody enrolled on his course, nor any of the other students he was meeting, could play an instrument. His dreams of forming the perfect Art School band started to evaporate.

'Honestly, there was *nobody* around who could play, not a soul!' he cries. 'I took all my gear down to Bath with me expecting to form the next Pink Floyd, and nobody had the remotest idea how to play anything! That year I spent at Bath was the first time I actually sat down and started writing my own bits and pieces of music. I had to, there was nothing else for it. I had an open-reel tape-recorder and I used to bounce tracks back and forth and turn them into finished pieces of music. It was good in that way; it was the first time I really started to experiment with sounds and moods on the synthesiser and keyboard.

'The only trouble was that in the end it all started to sound a bit repetitive, and although it's good fun you can sometimes reach a point where nothing new seems to happen. I wanted to start playing with other people again, getting back into the way a band would do things you could never do on your own.'

After half-heartedly completing his Foundation Year at Bath, in June 1980, Mark decided his re-application to begin the second year was already doomed when he realised that his first-year lecturer in History of Art studies would be amongst the board reviewing his application.

'In all of that first year I never once went to any of her classes,' he laughs. 'And she took one look at me and said, "It's funny how I don't recognise your face as I understand that I'm supposed to have been teaching you for the last nine months!" I knew then I'd blown it. My days in Bath were numbered.'

Returning home to his parents, Mark tried to get in touch with his old garage-band acquaintances, but the band, for what it was worth, had long since split up.

'The only guy I spoke to who was still into the idea of putting a band together was the bass player, called Jack Grigor,' he says. 'He had another mate who played guitar, Dave Weston, and so the three of us got together and started jamming, as they say. The guitarist was very heavily into Hawkwind, though, and his style of playing was *very* Hawkwind. I don't know what it is about the Romford area and lead guitarists, but in those days they all seemed to be obsessed with bloody Hawkwind! Of course, it made my job very easy because I didn't really even have to play chords, I just had to make these weird, freaky noises on the synth. Actually, I hated it – lots of white noise and farting sounds! But I was glad to at least be back playing in a band.'

The band were christened Chemical Alice: 'A sort of cosmic Lewis Carroll rock and roll band, ripping off bits of Pink Floyd and Hawkwind, and making a lot of noise!' And with the addition of another local lad as drummer, they devised a live set built on a solid backbone of obscurantist cover-versions. A twenty-five minute long version of Pink Floyd's 'Echoes'; Hawkwind's perennial anthem, 'Silver Machine'; even the occasional Neil Young ditty!

'We got this odd set together and started off doing some small local gigs, like the Romford Village Hall. And then we got onto the Electric Stadium, which is in Chadwell Heath, a bit nearer to London, and we ended up doing quite a few supports there. It was the big local gig that was on the circuit and a lot of name bands passed through there.'

Chemical Alice had been together and gigging sporadically for about nine months when they got offered their first spate of headlining gigs at the Electric Stadium, over the summer of 1981. Slowly, the band were building a strong local following and starting to fill out more and more of the Stadium hall every time they played there.

'We used to be almost like the in-house local band at the Electric Stadium in those days,' Mark remembers. 'We had a sort of residency set up there: at least twice a month, Chemical Alice headlined at the Electric Stadium in Chadwell Heath. But it was the only gig we ever did that people regularly came to see, and the only time we ever earned any money from playing.'

With Chemical Alice earning next to nothing for much of the time, Mark supported himself by alternately drawing dole-money and taking turns at working in a series of mostly temporary, manual-labour jobs – anything from tiling roofs to lining boilers.

'The thing I did most in those days was make double-glazed windows,' he says. 'It was just something I picked up and learned along the way, doing different jobs here and there for a few weeks at a time. I just used to bluff it and say yeah, *I* can do that, no problem! And it could be quite well paid sometimes. But mostly, throughout 1981, I was just on the dole and practising my playing.'

By the end of the summer of 1981, Mark and the rest of the band were starting to set their sights on the possibility of breaking into a couple of up-market support slots at some of the more famous London rock clubs.

'We desperately wanted to get into somewhere with a bit of clout like the Marquee,' he says. 'But every time we tried we never got anywhere. They kept asking us if we had a demo or a record they could listen to, which we didn't have. So then we

169

decided we ought to record some tracks and get it pressed-up as a single ourselves, just do it as cheaply as we could and order up about a 1,000 copies.'

With three tracks recorded in a 24-track studio called Spaceward in Cambridge, Mark and the band paid £500 to have exactly 1,000 copies made of their first, and only, recording together; an EP, featuring four original Chemical Alice tracks – 'The Judge', 'Goodnight Vienna', 'Lands of Home', and 'Henry the King.' 'I admit, it was all very sixth-form and adolescent, but I *was* responsible for writing the music for one of the tracks, "Henry the King", so it can't have been *all* bad,' he laughs.

The EP sold out of its initial pressing and the band actually stood to make a profit at the end of it. 'I still don't really know who bought all those records,' says Mark. 'But even now I very occasionally see the Chemical Alice EP going for £20 or £30 in the classified ads section of the music press. So I suppose someone somewhere must still be getting their heads down to a bit of the old "Alice"! Good luck to them.'

In the autumn of 1981, Chemical Alice were again booked to appear at the Electric Stadium in Chadwell Heath. It was a Saturday night and they would be headlining of course, but supporting them, and making their first appearance in Chadwell Heath, were a band called Marillion, who came from Aylesbury with a hot word-of-mouth reputation for always trying to walk away with the show no matter who they were supporting or where.

'We'd heard of them, all right,' says Mark Kelly. 'They'd already started breaking into the London gig circuit, which we hadn't, so we knew of them, but none of us except our guitarist had ever seen them play. I remember I made a point of sitting and watching their set before our show. Afterwards, the things I remembered most were, like, the prayer section in "Forgotten Sons", that really stuck in my head for days. And "The Web" was tremendous; I really thought, *yeah*, this is good stuff! I watched the whole of their set and I thought they were seriously good.

'I don't remember paying much attention to Brian Jelliman's keyboard playing, I don't think it struck me one way or the other. To be honest, the only people who really stuck out were Steve and Fish. Steve's playing was particularly good, very imaginative; and Fish looked completely bizarre!

'He apparently used to wear this black priest's costume, with the white collar and everything; but by the time of the Chadwell Heath gig with us it was in complete tatters – the collar had long gone and the front was torn open, it was more like a long black filthy cloak, really. And he stood there in his bare feet, and he's got this weird face make-up on, and he was just so theatrical, I couldn't take my eyes off him. He completely hypnotised me with his performance. I remember they had a terrible live sound though and afterwards they told me that their soundman, Privet, had had a migraine all night, which is why they'd sounded so off. But on the whole, I was really impressed.'

This was the night, of course, that Marillion returned Mark and the rest of Chemical Alice the compliment of staying to watch their set, coming backstage afterwards to congratulate the band on a good show. Fish, in particular, was not slow in expressing his personal appreciation of the headliner's perform-ance, with particular emphasis on the part Mark Kelly played in it.

'In fact,' Mark smiles, 'he came straight up to me after the show and said, "Do you want to join Marillion?", you know? I thought, bloody hell! What do I do now? I think I just mumbled yeah, yeah, I really like your music, or something equally banal, I can't remember, but the next thing I know is I end up going to one of their gigs somewhere else a couple of weeks later. Afterwards, away from Brian Jelliman, they sort of asked me to join them again, properly, and eventually I accepted, though not quite straight away.'

Mark says that it wasn't the easiest of decisions to make; whether to leave Chemical Alice and throw in his lot with this strange new Aylesbury clan, Marillion.

'But at the time, me and Dave, the guitarist in Chemical Alice, just weren't seeing eye to eye at all over the music we were playing. Like I say, he was far too Hawkwind and heavily psychedelic, and in that respect I definitely had more in common with the sort of music I'd heard Marillion playing. But we were all good friends, and I didn't know if I was doing the right thing by leaving them.

'But you know what Fish is like, he kept me up at his place talking all night, and telling me what the band were planning to do next, and had I made my mind up yet about joining them. In the end, I just thought about the music and decided I had to go for Marillion. They already had songs that could send shivers down my spine, and there was nothing we ever did in Chemical

Alice that made me feel like that. So I joined Marillion, which is the smartest move I think I ever made.'

Abandoning a recently begun part-time electronics course at a local Romforrd college, Mark Kelly trekked up to Aylesbury, in November 1981, to begin his life as the new keyboard player in Marillion. He was still only twenty years old and, as Steve Rothery comically and accurately described him at the time, still ' a very young man with very long hair.'

Mark's first gig with Marillion was less than a week later, at a small but sure-to-be-packed venue called the Great Northern, in Cambridge. He had exactly three days (and nights) to learn and rehearse the entire Marillion set before his first show with them, *and* he would have to hold his breath and squeeze into the small brown hooded smock with the large staring eye painted across its front that Brian Jelliman had left behind. He says he was almost paralysed with nerves.

'Nobody had any tapes for some reason and so I had nothing to learn the keyboard parts from,' says Mark. 'It made it practically impossible to learn anything properly. I kept asking them how Brian played a certain line or riff and nobody could show me, or Fish would sort of hum it to me. I thought, oh my God, this first gig is going to be a complete disaster!

'My nerves and the band's nerves, and all the little cock-ups that I was sure I was making, just made things very tense. I remember standing there rehearsing the set with them for the first time, desperately trying to work out what to play next, and thinking to myself, "I didn't really want to join this band in the first place! First thing on Monday I'll go back to Romford." I had notes pinned all over the keyboard with different chords written on them and the notes for "Grendel" were, like, nine sheets long!

'By the time we came to play our first gig together in Cambridge I think I'd just about managed to pick up the gist of most of the songs, but as we were playing it was all going around in my head and I couldn't remember the titles of any of the numbers. I more or less had to wait for the rest of the band to start-up and then I'd make it all up from there, just ad-libbing half the time. Anything I didn't know, or couldn't remember, I just bluffed it! Honestly, I don't know how I ever managed to get through the gig.'

But he did. And he stayed.

By November 1981, numbers like 'He Knows You Know', 'The Web', 'Grendel', 'Garden Party', and 'Forgotten Sons' were already being performed regularly by Marillion. But there was always room for more new material, said the band, and Mark was encouraged to write as much as he liked.

'The first number we wrote together was "Three Boats Down from the Candy", he says. 'But most of the material the band had already written when I joined eventually got changed in some way. Everything except maybe "Garden Party", which stayed more or less exactly the same for the album, had still to be properly arranged. And they had a couple of numbers that got dropped pretty quickly just after I joined – "Skyline Drifter", which I never even bothered to learn, I really didn't like it, and another one called "The Madcap's Embrace", which I only played once or twice. And of course they had a really early, very primitive version of "Charting the Single", which ended up getting completely changed around.

'Strictly speaking though, for all the new input the songs received over that year I was playing with the band before we recorded the first album, the only number on it that I can say I actually had a real hand in writing is the title track, "Script for a Jester's Tear".'

The winter of 1981–82 was one of the longest and coldest spells of bad weather to hit England in the last thirty years. The world was white from top to bottom, and bitterly cold for weeks at a time. Mark Kelly was installed in the small cottage at Aston Clinton where Fish and one of the band's unpaid helpers and friend, Guy, still lived.

'It was the most freezing house I'd ever lived in,' Mark recalls. 'One of the coldest winters since the last world war and all we've got to heat the place is one paraffin heater which used to sit in the middle of the front room. It was useless in that kind of weather! We were all freezing to death.

'The toilet was permanently frozen over, so there was nowhere in the house except the garden to relieve yourself. Even the shampoo was frozen in its bottle; you couldn't wash or keep warm, the van wouldn't start half the time when we had gigs, and we all used to walk around with about thirty overcoats on, with Fish sitting in the middle of the floor on the phone hustling up the gigs. It was like a cross between a fairy tale and a nightmare – three or four gigs every week, which was great, then coming home to a bloody igloo in the snow.'

Despite the temporary privations of mounting overdrafts, the fierce cold, and the outstanding debts that were starting to pile up at about the same speed as the glowing press reviews the band were now starting to receive, Mark's affection for Marillion didn't stop growing.

'By the start of 1982 I think we all felt deep down that we had something good going on here, and that things could only keep getting better,' he says. 'I don't think anybody in the band was arrogant enough to know for sure that we would definitely make it. We all wanted to, of course, and we all believed enough in the band to think we could do it, but I don't think anybody would have predicted we would get as far as we have done now. It all seemed a bit far away sometimes, shivering around that bleeding paraffin heater!'

As the weeks melted away the snow and Marillion worked their way through a parade of small club gigs, including their first headlining show at the Marquee, the press started to roll in on big heavy waves and the radio rock shows took to mentioning their name and broadcasting their sessions. Momentarily, the band squirmed under the sudden spotlight. They knew the final test was coming soon and that from now on every movement they made would be scrutinised by the cool eye of the no longer disinterested media. It was time to bail out some of the passengers before the going got really hairy. Top of the list was Diz.

'When I first joined Marillion,' says Mark, 'the only really weak link in the band's music that I could hear was the bass playing. Jelliman always sounded all right to me, and I think it was more his general attitude than his playing which lost him the gig. Well, with Diz it was the other way around, really. He was a nice enough bloke, he just wasn't very good; quite awful some nights, in fact.

'But nobody in the band, up until then, had really discussed the matter. We all sort of knew he wasn't up to much, but no-one really said anything. The thing is, probably the most admirable thing about this band is that once we've discussed something we always go out and do something about it the next day, and I think perhaps one or two of us were a bit shy of saying anything in case it all snowballed and he did get the sack. No-one really wanted that responsibility.

'Then one night in February we had a gig in a college in Birmingham. Afterwards we were all spending the night sleeping in a dormitory room they had given us. That is, everybody except Diz: his girlfriend had driven up for the gig and when it was over he drove home with her. And, of course, the next morning driving back down to Aylesbury it finally came up – the dreaded subject! Diz's playing. *Nobody* had a good word for it, and everything escalated from there.'

The band's next gig was two nights later at the Starting Gate, in Milton Keynes. By then they had already decided that Diz was out of the group. All that was left was to tell him.

'To us it was a matter of honour that we at least tell him before he did the show with us, even if he refused to play and we were forced to blow out of the gig,' says Mark. 'I was supposed to be the one to tell him, because it was me that really opened my mouth about him in the first place, but Fish, who was Diz's closest friend in the group, came with me to see Diz when he arrived for the gig. And it was Fish that sat down with him and explained why we were sacking him, that it was nothing personal, just his playing. Diz was terribly upset, understandably, but it was just one of those things.'

Too upset to play his way through one last gig with them, Diz Minnitt fled back to Aylesbury. 'We did the gig anyway, in the end, with me playing the bass parts on the organ, and actually it was OK. Listening back to the tapes of that gig later we nearly persuaded ourselves that maybe we didn't need another bass player, maybe I could manage it all on the keyboards. But that idea went out the window pretty quickly the day Pete came down to play with us.'

Mark remembers the night Fish came home to the house in Aylesbury the two were now living in and sharing with Diz, and immediately started babbling about the new bass player he had just seen playing in another local Aylesbury band, the Metros.

'It was a bit embarrassing, to say the least, because we were still living in the same place as Diz and his girlfriend,' says Mark. 'But when Fish brought it up at a band meeting the next day we all sort of went, "Naw! Bollocks! Not someone from the bloody Metros!" The Metros were supposed to be our big local rivals, at that time, and we hated them – they were a real *pop band*, and nothing whatsoever to do with us,' he smiles, trying to fake the disdain he felt then.

'But Fish kept insisting that this guy was really good, could really play, and he said he'd already spoken to him and invited him down for an audition. In the end, we went along with it very grudgingly. But we had no choice, really, we needed a bass player and we had this massive tour of Scotland due to start any day, which Fish had booked for us, and so we said all right, bring him down.

'And then of course, Pete turned out to be just the man we'd been looking for – Fish was right again! We couldn't believe our luck, actually. Pete really was good, better than anybody else we'd seen, easily. And so we got him in the band straight away, rehearsed for a few days, then jumped in the back of Margaret – our old green Coma van – and took off for these mad dates in Scotland.'

Fish's parents owned a small property in North Berwick, on the East coast of Scotland; for four weeks between March and April of 1982, the band would use it as their temporary home base while they zig-zagged around the country on an endless round of small, often quirky engagements Fish had booked them into.

'There were a few dubious nights on that tour,' says Mark. 'And obviously some of the dates did turn out to be a bit like playing in someone's front room, but then we must be one of the only rock bands in the history of the world to ever complete a twenty-five date tour of Scotland! One place we played in we went down so well I think Fish talked the manager into letting us come back twice more on that tour. That's the sort of thing we were up to, and some of it was great fun!

'There were eight of us in all – the band, Privet, a new guy called Dave Walden, who'd sort of replaced Guy, but was along to give us some decent lights on-stage, nothing too expensive, obviously, but something to cheer up the set and add to the general effect, and Phil Bell, who'd written our first feature in *Sounds*, he was tagging around with us on most of those Scottish dates, too. It was a good little team; apart from Phil, obviously, and Mick Pointer, of course, it's one we've kept right up to the present day.'

On that tour, Marillion were pleased to pick up £50 a night, sometimes less. The biggest fee they were paid for any of those Scottish dates was the £80 plus free food, drink and board that the manager of a small establishment called the Kane Park Hotel, in Bathgate, paid them. 'His name was Robin Ingles and he was a really good mate to us while we were at his hotel,' says Mark. 'He didn't pay us the money because we'd drawn a lot of people, though – we hadn't! But I think Robin was just genuinely enthusiastic about the music and could see that we were completely broke, so he helped us out as much as he could . . . It was great, the money kept us going for days.'

Fish kept the gigs coming thick and furiously, no matter how low-key some of them seemed, and Mark was responsible for keeping the band's meagre gig-to-gig accounts. 'I think I allowed everybody £2 per day spending money,' he says, 'But of course, everybody kept asking me for subs so they could buy a drink or a bite to eat at the end of the night, and of course we all came back totally broke from the tour. It didn't matter though, we were very free and easy-going, and the gigs were fun.'

At one port of call, this time at a small hotel on the banks of Loch Lomond, the band took out some boats onto the dark and beautiful waters of the lake before the sound check.

'It was great,' says Mark. 'Not at all peaceful, though. We ended up having a huge great water fight and we all got completely soaked. I remember when we got back to the gig the landlady of the hotel threw all our clothes into her tumble-dryer and we did the sound check in our underwear!

'And then by the time we were ready to start the show only about five people had bothered to turn up! There were more people from the band than there were punters; we didn't care, though. At one point Fish actually left the stage and went up and started twiddling the knobs on the mixing board, while Privet came up on stage and did the vocal on "Forgotten Sons", the prayer section.'

It was also on the infamous Scottish tour that Pete Trewavas received his baptism of fire into the band. As a newcomer, Pete became the regular target of all the bad-minded, convoluted band humour and sarcastic pranks that any group of broke young men travelling around the country in the back of a seedy old van might be expected to come up with.

'Mick and Privet, though, could really give it to somebody *good*,' says Mark. 'I mean, we were all letting him have it in much the same way as we did amongst ourselves, only we could all handle it because we were much more used to it. But Mick and Privet, in particular, were *always* on Pete's back. In the end, it got so bad that Pete really did start taking it all to heart, and he got very, very upset.

'It happened at a gig we were doing at a place called the Cross Keys, in Kelso; I think Pete had had all he could take by then, and he actually broke down and started to cry. It was awful, I

177

felt so sorry for him. I mean, the poor guy leaves behind his job, his old band, and his girlfriend, to join us and come out on this tour and all we do is drive him half round the bend with snide comments and by making him the eternal butt of every stupid joke.

'Pete must have *hated* us for that. Thank God, when we all saw how upset he was everybody was suddenly really understanding about his feelings and we managed to patch things up. It would have been awful to lose him like that, really stupid on our part. He was such a nice bloke, after all, and we were being such a load of insensitive bastards!

'To make matters worse, that was also the night I dislocated my right shoulder for the first time, and we ended up having to blow out the gig.'

Over the years, Mark Kelly's shoulder has managed to slip its socket four times in all, the latest occasion being during the first week of recording the band's current album, *Clutching at Straws*, in February 1987. It's a recurring bad dream for him.

'It's the most painful thing to have happen to you,' he says, squirming in his seat. 'I looked down and I had one arm six inches longer than the other! And the pain was unbelievable! I started turning grey and pouring with sweat. Then I was bundled into the van and driven off to the nearest hospital.'

Mark had been horsing around with Fish at the sound check, 'Having a bit of a wrestle,' he says, 'and my arm just sort of shot out of the socket. Every time it's happened since then it's always been under similar circumstances, messing around with Paul Lewis, or Fish or somebody, pretending to fight, and the fucking thing has happened all over again!

'I got to the hospital, and they pumped me full of drugs, mighty great pain-killers which hit me like a ton of bricks, and I was so out of my tree I was offering to go back and do the gig anyway, arm or no arm! It was the best I'd felt in days,' he laughs.

Returning from Scotland at last, richer in fans but poorer financially than they had ever been, Mark Kelly and Marillion had to face the fact that it would be almost impossible to carry on without a fast injection of cash to keep them alive and back out on the road. At least until they got a record deal.

'We were flat broke,' says Mark. 'At that point I think Fish owed the Bank of Scotland about £1,500, which we thought we'd never be able to pay off, let alone go back and ask for more! It was a very lean period for us.

'But that's when we first went to Dave Stopps and more or less begged him to manage us . . . you know, *please!*'

Stopps eventually acquiesced, of course, after ceaseless petitioning from Fish, and Marillion had themselves a manager short on practical experience, but laden with enthusiasm for their music and, most immediately important, willing to put his hand in his pocket and temporarily bail out the band.

'We didn't even know what to expect a manager to do for us – apart from give us money,' says Mark. 'But we knew we needed one or would need one soon.

'The first thing that Dave did was give us some money to go out and buy ourselves some new stage clothes – the old sackcloth things were definitely on their last legs by then: torn, filthy, and the smell! I mean, those things were never washed. I wanted to *burn* mine! Just to make sure it didn't come back and haunt me,' he chuckles. 'Honestly, one wash in the machine and those things would have all fallen to pieces anyway.'

The six weeks or so that passed under Dave Stopps' brief reign as Marillion manager, Mark remembers as a positive, if not entirely productive, time.

'Dave was always very positive, and he was very generous with his money, and we thought he had exactly the right attitude and ideas to become a good manager,' he says. 'But the only thing he lacked was the one thing we needed most of all right then – *experience*. And Dave's no fool, so when we talked to him and told him we'd decided to go our own way, he was very decent about the whole thing, and just let us go . . . And, of course, we promised to pay him back the money he'd spent on us as soon as we got a deal. Which we did.'

By the middle of summer, 1982 Marillion were aware they needed a seasoned tactician on their team when the time came to wrestle the right kind of deal out of the right sized, square-talking major.

'We had two names we knew were interested in managing us – Peter Mensch and John Arnison – and we decided that we would talk to them both and pick whoever we felt was best for us,' says Mark. John Arnison got the job.

One of the first gigs John Arnison turned up to supervise was at a club in Liverpool called the Warehouse, a couple of weeks before the band's first appearance at the Reading Festival.

'Which also happened to be the night that John's regular tour manager, Paul Lewis, who we hadn't met yet, was having his stag-night. Paul comes from Liverpool anyway, and so after the gig John took us over to where he was having his party,' says Mark.

'In those days Paul used to have a very neatly coiffured beard and moustache that made him look a bit like d'Artagnan of the Three Musketeers. And when we got to this party everybody was walking around with these little d'Artagnan beards and moustaches drawn on their faces with felt-tip pens. We couldn't work out what was going on!' he laughs. 'But it was a great night. I don't think we actually got to meet Paul properly that night, but it was the first time we'd met Rage, a local Liverpool rock band that John was also looking after at the time. They were a great bunch of guys and we got on really well with them. Afterwards, when we'd done the deal with EMI, we used to see them all the time down the Marquee, and later on they supported us on the *Fugazi* tour of Britain.'

Mark says he remembers the weeks leading up to that first fateful appearance at the Reading Festival, and Fish's on-stage announcement that they'd at last done a deal with EMI, as both nerve-racking and exciting.

'We were terribly disappointed when the deal with Charisma fell through,' he says. 'But Strat's business manager spoiled Charisma's chances by not offering us a reasonable deal.'

However, by the end of August 1982, John Arnison had already laid the foundations on a serious deal with Hugh Stanley Clarke and EMI.

'Once all the fiddly details of the contract had been worked out, all that remained was to sort out exactly how much money we needed for the first year,' says Mark. 'I think it worked out that John got £20,000 straight away, to help us clear off all our outstanding debts, buy some new equipment, and put the band on wages. And then I think he got a budget of about £70,000 out of them to finance all the touring we would be doing that first year.

'Actually, one of my fondest memories of the day we actually signed with EMI was going to this little café with John afterwards, and we said, well John, when do we get any money? And he just pulled this cheque out from his pocket with £20,000 made out to us on it! It was like, wow! So record companies really *do* give bands money!'

With Reading Festival confirmed for Sunday 29 August, Fish decided it would be a great idea to warm the band up with a gig the day before.

'Jethro Tull were headlining at the Theakston's Festival on the same Saturday as Reading, and Fish just rang up Lord Theakston himself and asked him if we could play!' Mark laughs. 'And it turned out that he was already a bit of a fan of the band anyway, and he said yes, no problem! And then when we got there we made a complete pig's ear of everything . . . The start of our set was a *disaster*!'

Mark recalls with a scowl the failure of his keyboards and Steve's guitar amp at the start of the set, and describes the interval they were forced to endure before 25,000 or so impatient people while roadies scattered in all directions, desperately re-routing the wiring, as 'The longest ten minutes of my life! And of course we had Ian Anderson from Jethro Tull standing there watching us from the side of the stage, you know, brilliant! All anybody could hear on the first number was the drums and vocals . . . I remember we had a lot of arguments with each other while we were down at Theakston's, everything was going wrong and we kept blaming each other for mistakes. Honestly, when the time came for us to play Reading we didn't have any nerves *left*, we'd left them all behind us at Theakston's.'

Reading, of course, and as everybody was only too well aware, was to be the big one: certainly the biggest yet for Marillion. If the band made an impact at Reading, it could well be their most rewarding victory yet. Everybody approached the stage that day hoping for the best, but not quite knowing what to expect from the giant, and often merciless, Reading crowd.

'I remember walking on stage and looking out over this huge crowd of people – it was easily the biggest audience we had ever played to, there must have been over 35,000 people out there! Then right down the front I could see a big group of Marillion fans. They all had banners and flags that they'd made themselves with our names on them. I would guess there was probably about 2,000 of them, crowded right down the front for our set, and that immediately made us all feel brilliant! Just knowing that we had friends out there was really reassuring. It boosted our confidence straight away.

'Then as we started playing through the set you could see the wave start to roll right back through the crowd; more and more people were waving their arms in the air and applauding and getting into what Fish was saying about getting the deal with EMI. It was a great set, and we went down really well. And the reviews we picked up for that one gig were amazing! Suddenly the buzz about the band increased a thousand-fold . . . some of it was really quite out of proportion, though. I mean, for a band that came on, like, sixth on the bill, and who had never released a record in their lives, it all seemed a bit too much.

'It didn't stop us feeling well chuffed with ourselves, though,' he smiles, the ivory sparkling in those Irish eyes. 'We thought it was great, all the attention, and I think we let it go to our heads a little bit. Just for a short time. I mean, why not? We'd spent so long out in the cold dreaming of what it would be like to be recognised, and now it was happening! Suddenly, Marillion had become the flavour of the month – and about bloody time, too!' he laughs.

7

Toys in the Attic

By June 1984, Marillion's commercial horizons were slowly but surely beginning to expand beyond the hitherto almost exclusive domains of the British record-buying public. Their recent spate of European concerts had broken a lot of important ground for them on the continent, and with Ian Mosley now accepted into the band as a full-time member, the talk between John Arnison and the chief execs at EMI all centred around how to really capitalise on the band's increasing popularity in certain key overseas territories. In the absence of another ready-made hit single that could be pulled off the *Fugazi* album, corporate opinion decided that the only logical step to getting new product out on the streets that year was to hurriedly put together a live album. In time for the big Christmas sales, cheaply produced and quickly delivered, and backed by the band's longest and most concerted European tour yet, a live Marillion album might be just the thing to really fan the fires that already burned in a great many young European minds. EMI said it was a fool-proof plan.

'*Fugazi* had done so much better in Europe than *Script* . . . had done,' says Pete Trewavas, 'and we'd managed to get away the first year with actually doing very little in the way of really touring in Europe. But the things we had done – the festivals and the German radio thing, which got broadcast again and again in all sorts of places across Europe – had been high-profile enough for people to at least get to know our names.'

'And then when we started going there for four or five nights at a time in the spring, we were always headlining,' Mark Kelly takes up the story. 'But without more new product we could only afford to do so much. With a new record to promote, the European divisions of EMI would immediately see the advantage in backing us financially for a proper tour just as quickly as we could arrange it. And of course, in typical Marillion style, we wanted to strike while the iron was hot.'

'Places like Germany, France, Switzerland, and Holland were all suddenly showing a big interest in getting us over to play,' says Steve Rothery, 'but we couldn't possibly afford to go to all of these places the way we had been doing, you know, four days on and four days off, back and forth all the time. We needed to co-ordinate a proper European tour. So when EMI suggested we should release a live record of some sort we all thought about it and eventually said yes, all right we'll do it. But it would have to be a low-price budget-affair. We didn't think the band was anywhere near ready yet to release a proper double-live album. Originally, we saw the idea more as a live twelve-inch EP, something along those lines.'

'Also, I think what appealed to EMI a lot was the fact that Island Records had just done a similar thing with *Under A Blood Red Sky* by U2, which had proved phenomenally successful for them,' Fish points out, pragmatically. 'At the back of their minds I think EMI were hoping that a Marillion live compilation package would have the same results. Anyway, we'd have been the last to object if it *had* gone like that for us! I mean . . . yes, please!'

With the outline still suitably vague, but with the idea of a live Marillion release arranged for the autumn at least given full band approval, time was booked at the Marquee Studios for August where the live tapes would be mixed, and Marillion turned their attention to the next hot item on the new agenda John Arnison had been busy compiling for them: America! Again.

'John said, "What about another crack at the States then, boys?" and we told him to naff off,' says Steve Rothery. 'But then John told us what Capitol Records, our American record company, had been saying about the *Fugazi* album – how they said they liked it a lot more than our first, and how they thought "Assassing" would make a great single in America, and how, eventually of course, we should go back for a small tour to promote its release. We took a bit of convincing, though. After Rush, none of us was in a hurry for a repeat performance. If it was going to be like that again then as far as I was concerned we didn't need it. I was quite happy to stay and play to the people in Britain and Europe who had already proved that they were genuinely into the band's music.'

184

Despite Marillion's initial doubts as to the true viability of a return trip to America so soon after they had bombed so badly on their last visit nine months before, Capitol Records insisted that at the very least a short tour would be a useful PR exercise; they needed to be seen to be actively supporting the release in America of the new Marillion album and single. After all, Capitol quite reasonably argued, if the band didn't care how well their records sold in America, why should the record company? Without another US tour both *Fugazi* and 'Assassing' would die a commercial death anyway, advised Capitol. With some solid dates a little hoo-hah could at least be arranged and then everybody was in with a chance.

John Arnison and Marillion could only concur with the American record company's corporate logic and a short six-week North American tour was hastily arranged to run from the middle of June 1984 until the end of July. The band would begin with a string of dates in Canada, where they were already better known than in America and fast on their way to becoming a major concert attraction, then work their way down South across the Stateside border for a clutch of small club and college dates, again just on the East Coast, before rounding off the whole shy caboodle with Marillion's first major headline engagement in scary old New York, at an upmarket downtown 2,000-capacity venue called the Ritz.

'Canada at the start of that tour was great!' cries Fish. 'Really happening! It was starting to go the same way as Europe and Britain had gone for us,' he asserts, 'you can always tell when an audience starts singing all the words to something like *Script* . . . If they can manage that then we know we've got real fans in the audience, and that's what was starting to happen for us most nights in Canada.

'But as soon as we crossed over the border and moved down into America for our gigs, things started to change again pretty quickly. We still had a hell of a long way to go over there, that much was obvious from the first gig, and by the time we got to the Ritz in New York we were left in no doubt at all as to just how *lowly* we were regarded in America in 1984. I mean, there must have been all of about a dozen people there for our show at the Ritz! It was another complete waste of the band's time and money even playing there.'

Even on their best nights, Marillion were still only half-filling the clubs and college halls they had been booked into on that ponderous US tour. But that grisly fact in itself wasn't enough to deter the band's best efforts; after all, in Britain and Europe Marillion had always relished their past roles as underdogs. Their trick was always to play each show as though it were a sell-out. With just the right doses of charm and arrogance mixed together to make their smallest audiences stand up and stamp their feet.

What was pulling the American deal down around their ankles was the complete absence of the promised support from their American record company, Capitol. 'Assassing' bombed as a single in America; it was already dead when the band were still hiking their act around Canada. *Fugazi* didn't fare much better, and by the time Marillion arrived in New York for their last and possibly most prestigious date of the tour, at the Ritz, Capitol Records had washed their hands of all responsibility for the relative failure of the latest Marillion campaign in America.

'They said the band was too uncommercial for them to really do anything with at that stage,' said John Arnison. 'I said, well why didn't you tell us that *before* you tried persuading us to come back and tour? And it was like, oh, blah blah blah, we thought "Assassing" might open a few doors, but the radio people didn't like it, so why throw good money after bad, blah blah blah . . .'

'The Ritz wasn't as bad as those Radio City Hall shows with Rush,' says Steve Rothery, 'But it wasn't much better either . . . We didn't come on stage until about 3 a.m. by which time there were about ten people left, none of who gave a toss about the band playing on the stage. And John Arnison had gone out for a big meal with Capitol before the show, and they all got pissed together and never even made it back in time for the gig!

'But by then I almost couldn't blame them. Frankly, I didn't even understand what we were doing there. You know, I felt like, there are plenty of people who *would* like to see Marillion play, and we've got all the time in the world to worry about America, *so what the fuck are we doing here?*' he scowls.

Returning home to England at the end of July 1984, Marillion decided that there would be no more embarrassing, six-week experimental tours of America for them. Taking on the vast American public at their own game would always mean first convincing Capitol they had something the American markets would at least find palatable, and that was something the band would not stoop to do.

'We'd tried it once with 'Assassing', and that died a complete death as a single in America,' says Mark Kelly. 'Anyway, we all knew it would be the death of our originality if we started trying to graft an "American sound" – whatever that is! – onto our new material. If anything, all the bad experiences we'd had in America and all the wrong advice we'd been given made us even more determined not to bow and scrape our way into the American charts. We just went completely the opposite way around the problem and did our best to ignore whatever the American record company might want us to give them, and get on with what we did best. If that wasn't good enough for the States, then so what? That was *their* loss.'

Ensconced once more in the Marquee Studios in London, Marillion instructed John Arnison to place their US visas in temporary cold-storage, then set to work on what they had now decided would be a live, budget-priced, mini-album, already dubbed *Real to Reel*.

The band had three of their most recent, post-Mosley, shows on tape and ready to play around with in the mix: two at the Spectrum theatre in Montreal, Canada, recorded in June; and one dating back to the band's last UK tour in March, from the De Mont Ford Hall in Leicester. With Simon Hanhart again seated comfortably in the chair next to the band's as co-producer, work on mixing the *Real to Reel* tapes proceeded, in Mark Kelly's words, 'in a fast and fun fashion and was finished in time for the August Bank Holiday weekend.'

Vacating their dark and cramped quarters at the Marquee Studios, the band emerged blinking like vampires into the weak warm sunlight of another late summer Soho evening. With them they had six finished live tracks that were not so much the in-depth depiction of a live Marillion show, but the flickering highlights and fleeting vinyl echoes of what such a thing might be like to experience first hand. *Real to Reel* would be a glossary, a six-shot magazine, a timeless, shapeless, not unattractive bargain-priced Christmas stocking-filler.

Certainly the most *functional* of all the Marillion albums (with the exception of course of the American-only released *Brief Encounter* collection, which in August 1984 was still eighteen months away) EMI would ever be asked to release, *Real to Reel* would retail in the shops for just £2.99; and staying in line with the company's wishes to keep things cheap on this one, the band ditched the idea of asking Mark Wilkinson to come up with anything too extravagant for his sleeve illustrations this time and instead urged him to opt for a simple, non-gatefold design.

'Tasteful but cheap is what Mark Wilkinson was told to do for *Real to Reel*,' Pete Trewavas explains. 'And that's exactly how Mark kept things.'

'We made it known through the press at the time that *Real to Reel* was not intended to be promoted as The Next New Thing from Marillion,' says Fish. 'It wasn't our *new* album, nor was it our definitive statement in terms of what we would like a true live Marillion album to be; we were going out on tour again and *then* we would be writing and recording a new album, but in the meantime *Real to Reel* was like a postcard from the frontline, which is us, to the real Marillion fans. A flash and cheeky little artefact which you could buy cheap if you wanted to. No more no less.'

Side One, taken from the band's shows at the Spectrum in Canada, opens with 'Assassing' hissing from the speakers, the percussion slithering like an angry alligator, the cold reptilian eye of the assassin squinting in the shadows.

The sound is fatter, fuller around the shoulders and legs, on *Real to Reel* than on either of Marillion's two previous studio albums. Consequently, though their versions of 'Assassing', 'Incubus', and, say, 'Cinderella Search', which take up Side One, are far too faithful to their studio originals to be classed as invaluable, what we have here instead is the sound of Marillion captured in a way the sterile, self-obsessed production on *Fugazi* never could; in generous full swing and erupting before an audience.

Ian Mosley's drumming in particular is an innovation. Listening to *Real to Reel*, it's hard to find any trace of the ambitious and youthful wets blinded by stars that scampered into the Marquee Studios two years before to record their first album together. The arrival of Ian Mosley had changed everything. If it wasn't always so self-evident on some of the starker more introspective passages on *Fugazi*, then on *Real to Reel* Mosley really makes his presence felt where it counts, stoking up the boiler fit to burst through a flow of high-flying up-tempo exchanges that propel the rest of the band into lush musical vistas undreamed of back in the days of Mick Pointer. If Steve Rothery wanted to lean back and riff out awhile, that was fine by Ian, he could take his hi-hat, his bass-pedal, and his snares just as high up that fast-running slippery slope as the guitarist wanted to go; and if Mark Kelly suddenly wanted to make like a submarine and plunge into one of his deep, breath-held synthesised mists,

Mosley could shade the clouds in all the appropriate colours for him.

'Having Ian in the band is like knowing you carry heavy insurance,' says Pete Trewavas, 'you feel *safe*. You don't have to worry about anything except your own playing, and he allows you to get away with it and run away with a few ideas on stage without being terrified the whole thing is going to collapse around your ears.'

'Playing with Ian means really having to be on your toes,' says Mark Kelly. 'He's got a lot of imagination but he never hits a beat or a roll that shouldn't be there, he never wastes his moves, and his timing is impeccable. As a result, after Ian joined the band the rest of us improved as musicians virtually overnight! You can't play with someone like Ian for long periods of time without some of it rubbing off and having a positive effect.

'I mean,' Mark goes on, 'even though there's only one change in the line-up between the band that recorded *Script* . . . and the one that played on the *Real to Reel* album, if you listen to both records back-to-back it virtually sounds like two completely different bands . . . worlds apart, really.'

Side Two of *Real to Reel*, taken from the Leicester De Mont Ford Hall show on the *Fugazi* tour, is full of more up-tempo revelling.

'Forgotten Sons', the best number of the entire set of six, opens with a furious passion, Fish prefacing with it the words: '*This is dedicated to the people that fell on a pavement outside Harrods before Christmas . . . This is a song for peace . . .*' He was referring of course to the IRA bombing of London's most famous rich people's department store, in December 1983 . . . a dozen dead and three times as many brutally injured, thousands more shocked and appalled, the 'Forgotten Sons' lyrics a perfect echo of the crimes: '*. . . Death in the shadows he'll maim you, wound you, kill you/For a long forgotten cause, on not so foreign shores . . .*' The band cartwheeling through the bent nervous riff, guitars and keyboards ricocheting wildly off the walls of rapid-fire drums and percussion, striking sparks as they collide into the doleful and decorous finale.

'Garden Party', which follows, segues as-live into 'Market Square Heroes', both renditions faster-paced and forged more flamboyantly than their fey studio progenitors; Fish in great voice throughout, the falsetto cry edged and serrated, like the roar of a wounded lion in places, mean-eyed and vengeful; the band bristling with tense energy as they march towards a marvellously pompous climax.

Like the commercial precepts that inspired its release, the sleeve for *Real to Reel* is unexpectedly plain and straightforward. Marillion were keen that Mark Wilkinson's design should express the very downbeat nature of their releasing a budget-priced live mini-album, and this he had done . . .

A giant tape-reel smothers the front of the sleeve, each member of the band sashayed into equal individual compartments of the reel, live shots, natch, going in a clockwise direction: Mark, a painted Fish, Steve, Pete, Ian . . . And in the centre, the logo-fied figure of the Jester, characterless and miniaturised, fragmented into oblong strips of red, blue, green, yellow. The violin, of course, raised to his chin. . .

At the end of August 1984, with the *Real to Reel* package already on its way to the processing plant over at EMI, Marillion readied themselves for what should have been the crowning glory of all their achievements in Britain so far: their first much-vaunted headline appearance at that year's Reading Rock Festival.

However, it wasn't to be. Mere days before the three-day festival was due to start, on Friday 27 August, Reading Council revoked the promoter's license to hold a festival on the traditional Thames Mead site, which the authorities said they had now earmarked for sale and redevelopment. As a result, and in spite of the promoter's, NJF/Marquee, last-minute attempts to find a suitable replacement site in time for the Bank Holiday Weekend, Reading Festival, along with Marillion's chance to headline it, would have to be cancelled indefinitely.

'Losing Reading was a real shame,' says Fish. 'For us it was always one of those magic gigs, like the Marquee, like Friar's, or like the Edinburgh Playhouse. We knew if we did well there then we must still be doing something right,' he smiles. 'And not only that of course, but missing our chance to headline it then was a big disappointment to the whole band. I mean, if Reading was still going now in the same way as it was up until 1983, like *the* major British summer rock festival, I'm sure we'd still like to headline it and make sure we do well. But to have done it *then*, still not really knowing quite what we'd done to deserve to be there at the top of the bill, that would have been magic!'

Determined not to let the Bank Holiday weekend go

completely to waste, the band switched their attentions to another, smaller, festival also running that weekend, at Nostel Priory in Wakefield. Along with former Thin Lizzy mainman, Phil Lynott, and his new backing band, Grand Slam, who had also been a fixture on the aborted Reading '84 bill, Marillion put a late call through to the Nostel Priory organisers and asked if they could headline their own show on the last night of the Festival, Bank Holiday Monday.

'I don't think they took too much persuading,' smiles Ian Mosley. 'So we all piled in the van and drove up to Wakefield for the Monday night show. Phil Lynott's Grand Slam went on before us, and we headlined. It was a really good gig, as I recall, nice warm night, Fish and the rest of the boys going mental on stage, thousands of people in the audience singing and waving their arms – you can picture the scene.'

Indeed . . . the smell of dry trampled grass cooling as evening dies slowly and night falls . . . bodies littered in the darkness, sweating, cheering . . . distant sound of a jet-plane whistling by overhead . . . green and blue lights at the foot of the hill . . . sound of machines moaning, a rain of drums, a pinched guitar screaming . . . in a voice as dirty as money: '*I never say no, in chemical glow, we'll let our bodies meet . . .*' You can picture the scene.

While EMI busied themselves throughout September for a late October/early November 1984 release of the *Real to Reel* mini-album, Marillion retreated to a new set of rehearsal rooms John Arnison had hired for them, at Barwell Court in Chessington. For the next six weeks they would be tucked away writing outlines to the material that would eventually go to make up their next studio album: the one, though they didn't know it yet, that would hurtle them like a rocket nose-first into the 'satellite-infested heavens' of a new international success they wouldn't have dreamed possible in the summer of 1984; and the one that Fish had already long-ago christened *Misplaced Childhood*.

'I'd been tinkering around wth the idea of a concept based on the idea of a return to, and a kind of emotional reinvestigation of, a person's childhood experiences, those things that trap and shape our lives,' he says. 'As far back as when we were putting *Script* . . . together, the rest of the guys knew I had these lyrical ideas loosely based around a childhood, although I couldn't tell them much more than that, and I'd been making notes and jotting down ideas on bits of paper and in notebooks ever since.

'I'd deliberately taken my time before deciding I had enough material to write about to fill a whole album, though. The way I saw it, I wanted whatever came next to be our most radical statement yet, both musically and lyrically. And now that we'd lived through the struggles and disappointments of trying to make *Fugazi*, and now that Ian was a fully-fledged member of the band, I think we all felt it was the right time to push ourselves out on an artistic and commercial limb and really go for something *special* this time.

'And the most special piece of material I had, lyrically, was this whole *Misplaced Childhood* concept that I'd been working on. So we discussed it together, the band and I, and I explained to them that it wasn't just one song I was talking about, it was a whole series of links and ideas that dealt with different aspects of the character's experiences. And I think Mark, or Steve, or someone said "What, you mean like one long continuous piece of music?" And I said I didn't know, they were the musicians, what did they think? And so we talked about it some more and mucked around with a few ideas Mark and Steve had in the rehearsal studio, and suddenly, without really coming to any big decision, we just started writing stuff that interconnected. We'd never really done it before, even though we might have discussed the possibilities occasionally in the past, and the more we got into this thing called the *Misplaced Childhood*, the more everybody seemed really up for going the whole hog and making it a concept album; just one long, ever-changing piece of music with a true story connecting it all together.'

The first new number the band worked on at Barwell Court was based around a neat little guitar riff Steve Rothery had come up with that combined perfect melody with perfect rhythm in one brief flick of the wrist. Next to it Fish placed the first few scattered phrases of verses he had not yet finished writing, but that he had already entitled 'Kayleigh'.

' "Kayleigh" was the first number we wrote the music for at Barwell Court,' says Mark Kelly. 'In fact, the chorus we wrote for "Kayleigh" was originally part of an early version of "She Chameleon" which we ditched because it didn't really fit well enough there. It was just this rinky-dink guitar thing Steve had. So I said, why don't we take those chords and beef them up a bit and sort of repeat it a few times, and make that the chorus? Which is what we did.'

'Barwell Court was a particularly creative time for me,' says Steve Rothery. 'I was writing an awful lot of things, and the little riff that opens "Kayleigh" was actually just something that came about one day when I was mucking around on the guitar trying to show my girlfriend, Jo, something about the way the guitar combines melody and rhythm together, and suddenly there it was (humming) dum-dum-dum . . . dum-dum-dum . . . Simple, really. But it's the simplest things that are often the hardest to write well.'

'The only trouble with "Kayleigh", says Fish, 'once the music was written, was the title of the song. Kayleigh is the name of a real girl I used to be in love with, or at least thought I was in love with, who I'd broken up with around about the time we were recording the first album. In the context of the new album, it didn't matter really what name we gave to "Kayleigh", but because Kay is a real person some of the boys in the band didn't think it was a good idea to be so blatant about naming names, and originally asked me to try and think of another title. But I'd already conceived of the number as "Kayleigh", and really it was impossible for me to think of it in terms of being anything other than, well, "Kayleigh"!'

'With the exception of Ian, everybody in the band had known Kay personally, and I think at first we squirmed a bit when Fish walked through the door with a song named after her,' says Mark Kelly. 'I remember we definitely asked him if he couldn't change the title. But as time wore on, he never did, and by then we'd moved on to something else anyway. Besides, I don't expect "Deirdr-yyy" or "Cath-yyy" would have quite the same special ring to them,' he smiles.

The weeks at Barwell Court proved to be the most relaxed and productive time Marillion had spent working together on new ideas since they'd signed the deal with EMI two years ago.

'The material for *Script* . . . had almost all been written by the time Mark and I joined the band,' says Pete Trewavas, 'and most of the ideas and hard planning for the first album had already been worked out ages before we ever got into a recording studio. With the writing on *Fugazi*, I personally felt that we'd put too many restraints on the music and our ideas before we'd even started. EMI wanted the album to appeal more to the American market; "Punch And Judy" was already being touted as a big hit single; the whole are-they-or-aren't-they trying to copy Genesis thing was still hanging over us; and the one-hit-wonder thing . . . And I think we'd set our sights consciously too high and given ourselves too much to live up to. As a result, we missed the target with one or two things.

'At Barwell Court, writing *Misplaced Childhood*, we'd had enough of worrying about what everyone else expected from us and just let things happen as they happened. We never looked at anything in one particular way; we never once thought about writing hit singles, or what the Americans would make of it all. We just started writing, took things easy, and did our best to *enjoy* ourselves. And that way it really worked. Once we got started we had most of the first side of the new album written within about two weeks.'

With the band still writing and rehearsing their new material in Chessington, John Arnison busied himself from his snug managerial offices in Redcliffe Gardens making good his plans for Marillion's first proper large-scale headlining tour of Europe. It would be the band's biggest and most successful jaunt yet, John decided. He had made up his mind.

'Things had happened so fast for the band over the last two years at home in Britain we'd only had enough time, so far, to do a few well-selected European dates here and there, wherever it made sense and we could afford to go,' says John. 'In the meantime, we'd spent a fortune taking the band to America, where up until 1985 we got no encouragement at all. So we thought, right, sod America for the time being, we'll get out on the road in Britain and Europe and really build on our successes there.

'I mean, personally,' John goes on, 'I felt it was only a matter of time before the band became *huge* in Europe anyway, and with the *Real to Reel* tour I thought we were ready for our first serious crack at it.'

Scheduled to start at the beginning of November and ending seven weeks later, three days before Christmas, 1984, the *Real to Reel* tour John Arnison had devised for Marillion would consist of thirty-six dates – twenty-two in Europe sandwiched between fourteen in Britain. The British section of the tour, taken in two legs, would begin with shows at the Royal Court in Liverpool, on 3 November; the Poole Art Centre, on the 4th; the Gloucester Leisure Centre, on the 5th; Cardiff University, on the 6th; the Hanley Victoria Hall, on the 8th; and end with a night at the Surrey University in Guildford, on the 10th.

Forty-eight hours later, they would kick-off their most

ambitious campaign in Europe yet with their first of six concerts in France, at L'Auditorium in Nantes. According to John's plan, for the next four weeks Marillion would be zig-zagged around the continent, skipping the extra expense of staying in hotels whenever possible by sleeping in the back of a six-bunk tour bus, taking in brief and steamy one-nighters at different clubs and theatres in France, Holland, Sweden, Denmark, Belgium, Luxembourg, Switzerland, and West Germany. And after that they would return home for some more of their annual Christmas shows in Britain, starting with no less than three sold-out nights at the Hammersmith Odeon in London.

'It was a very well-thought-out tour,' says Steve Rothery, 'and we were all starting to get really excited about the prospect of going out on our first big tour of Europe. Having a new record out at the same time meant that all the EMI divisions in Europe got right behind us as well and spent loads of money promoting us over there, which meant that we could afford to put on the same-size show most nights as we do in Britain. And of course, the ace up our sleeve was that by now we'd also finished writing most of the first side of *Misplaced Childhood*, and what we thought we'd do is preview, like, fifteen minutes'-worth of the new material every night, just have Fish announce that it was new and go into it, do it straight and see what kind of reactions we got.'

However, in the midst of the build-up for the tour, Pete Trewavas took just enough time out from the band's hectic last-minute preparations to get himself down to a little church in Aylesbury where, on the afternoon of 7 October 1984, he finally married his long-standing and loving girlfriend, Fiona.

'It was great!' cries Pete. 'I mean, because the band were about to go out on the road again, we didn't have much time for a proper honeymoon or anything. We actually spent three nights in Guernsey and Jersey, and although that's hardly any time at all we still had a great time. And when we got back I went straight into rehearsals for the next tour with the band, and I couldn't wait to get cracking.'

Real to Reel was released simultaneously in Britain and Europe on Monday 5 November 1984.

The tour was already a week old when it happened, but unlike previous Marillion album releases, *Real to Reel* didn't quite throw itself immediately into the open arms of the UK Top 10.

Instead, it charted at twelve the first week and then began a steady climb to eight, where it languished for a fortnight at the beginning of December. In Britain, Marillion's budget-priced mini-album would go on to win for them their third round of gold and silver discs in just under a year; and in Europe, where by now the band were nightly dazzling their new and wall-eyed audiences with a series of spectacularly received performances, *Real to Reel* put Marillion in touch for the first time with the charts in over half a dozen different countries.

The tour itself had started at the Royal Court in Liverpool on 3 November. Keen to experiment with the existing live set and break completely with the pattern established on the *Fugazi* tour of eight months before, the set Marillion played for their first half-dozen shows in Britain featured a confused running order that began on an odd note with 'Forgotten Sons' opening the show; 'Assassing', the number they had been using to open with since Reading 1983, was now promoted to first encore; and 'Market Square Heroes', since its inception the traditional show closer, was displaced to somewhere in the middle of the set, where it sat incongruous and half-hearted.

'We were desperately seeking to alter everything about ourselves up till that point,' says Fish. 'Writing on the new album had been going really well, and we just felt like twice the band we ever were before. And on the *Real to Reel* tour I think we started off wanting to reinvent everything about the show around the new material we were previewing, but as usual we were in too much of a hurry probably, and looking back I have to admit we made a few mistakes messing around with the running order. I mean, it soon became obvious that "Market Square Heroes" can only ever come *last* in the set. And "Assassing" never works better than when it's used to open the show with. But we soon caught on to all of that though, steadied ourselves a bit, and by the time we got across to France for the first dates on the European leg of the tour we'd got the right set sorted out.'

The new still slowly-evolving Marillion set had reached perfect pitch by the time the band arrived in Stockholm, on the 19th, for their first-ever show in Sweden, at the Gote Lejon theatre. 'Assassing' was back in its rightful position at the start of the show: dry ice and glowing crystal stage-lights, shadows of the band criss-crossing the stage, a taped echo of cruel violins and Indian oboes lost in the dark rumble of drums.

And from there the band kept things suitably tight and up-tempo with howling walls-fall-down versions of first 'Garden Party', capriciously followed by 'Cinderella Search' and 'Punch And Judy'.

Their audience captured and already *'punch, punch, punch . . . and Judy!'* singing along, the band shifted mood, tip-toeing mournfully through 'Jigsaw'; then tumbling like a loose stone through the starry-eyed chambers of 'Chelsea Monday'; breaking the spell only to don the Harlequin's torn robes for 'Emerald Lies' . . . sex and death in a monologue of muttering accusations and stammering sleepless dreams . . . love on one knee, its eye to the keyhole.

A pause . . . then quietly, drink in hand, Fish walked up to the microphone and introduced the next number: 'This next number we're going to play tonight is brand new, and will make up Side One of our next studio album. This is called . . . *Misplaced Childhood.'*

Missing just 'Lavender' from the finished piece that would indeed go to make up the first side of *Misplaced Childhood*, Mark Kelly drew back the curtains just as he would four months later in a recording studio in Berlin, his darkly swirling synthesisers drilling the air with a distant sense of foreboding; a hollow screech, like a wailing ghost, the childhood *'spirit rising to speak its mind . . .'*

'Kayleigh', which followed, was note-perfectly the same as the recorded version that less than nine months later would storm singles charts all over the continent. That is, musically. Fish was still deliberately garbling a lot of the words on stage most nights. He explains: 'The truth is I had only finished writing the words to about seventy-five per cent of the new material we were previewing live. It was a good experiment though, it meant that I was practically writing the lyrics on stage some nights, making up bits and pieces as I went along and keeping the best bits stored for later.'

'Heart of Lothian', which ended the new piece, is more faithful to its later studio incarnation, and ended in Stockholm with the audience standing on their seats begging for more, the belly and eyes of the hall filled with a loud, heavy applause.

From there, Marillion wound the new show up with a bounty of more familiar live set-pieces: 'Script for a Jester's Tear', which again had the Swedes up on their seats and singing all the words; followed by a glowering and intense 'Incubus', the tall stark shadow of the singer creeping from under the narrow stage-

197

lights . . . And then the last number of the show, 'Forgotten Sons', which Fish reserved a special dedication for: 'This next number is dedicated to a word that seems to be missing from a lot of people's vocabularies these days . . . and this is especially dedicated to Northern Ireland, and not just there but El Salvador, Beirut, Iran, Iraq . . . Everywhere in the world where there is still conflict . . . This is a song dedicated to *peace*, and this is called . . .'

It was a spectacular exit, the band gunning the sound, Fish like a voice coming down from the mountain. One of their most emotionally turmoiled pieces, the grandiose theatricality of 'Forgotten Sons' brought the set to its knees in a shuddering climax; the sound of the band's monstrous lights being extinguished at the end followed by a shocked pause from the Stockholm crowd, then applause, like the roar of waves crashing against the stone face of a cliff.

The first encore, 'Fugazi', Fish dedicated, as he would every night of the tour, 'very respectfully to Mrs Gandhi . . . one of the poets, one of the prophets, one of the visionaries.' In keeping with his uncanny penchant for making the band's songs address directly the most up-to-date news, Fish had chosen the recent slaying of the Indian Prime Minister by her own Sikh body-guards as the most perfect and incriminating example in recent times of a world being driven totally foo-gah-zey.

'Market Square Heroes', restored to its former glory as the final encore of the night, spared nothing in its merciless battering of the senses: faster by now and more vicious, more titanic even than the version being peddled on *Real to Reel*, 'Market Square Heroes' brought everything to a blistering two-fisted *ba-boom!* finale that left the first-time Swedish buyers breathless in the aisles.

In the meantime, Marillion scooted back into their portable dens on their all-home-amenities-fitted tour bus and headed back out on the road. Next stop: Copenhagen, then on to Utrecht, Geneva, Hanover, Bonn. Just as John Arnison had predicted, Marillion's European tour was proving to be a tremendous success; the shows were starting to sell out; sales for *Real to Reel* on the continent alone were tipping six-figures; and for the first time the European media were splashing out on vast colour spreads in their most popular rock magazines like *Best* and *Metal Hammer*.

The British rock press wasn't far behind, either. Both *Sounds*, who again carried the story on the cover, and *Melody Maker* despatched scribes to document the shifting rise and rise of Marillion in Europe. *Kerrang!*, too, got in on the act and ran their own version of the story over a two-page colour spread in time for the band's spate of Christmas concerts in the UK. And the machine rolled on, better oiled and more trouble-free than at any time before.

'It was a great tour, probably the best and most enjoyable we'd done up until then,' says Pete Trewavas. 'I mean, it was brilliant to turn up in places we'd never been to before and find hundreds and thousands of people waiting to see the show! Sleeping on the tour bus could get a bit knackering sometimes, but it wasn't every night, we still ended up staying in quite a few hotels. And of course all the usual mischief went on!' he grins.

One popular activity the band indulged in on the *Real to Reel* tour, second only to the exploitation of fire-extinguishers, was taking part in something called the Upside Down Club.

Mark Kelly explains: 'One night Pete showed us a little trick he'd learned from his days as an apprentice TV engineer: he unscrewed the back of a TV set in one of the hotel rooms we were staying in, and made some tiny adjustment to the tubes, which didn't affect the quality of the sound or picture at all – except for one thing: now the picture was upside down! It was brilliant! Straight away *everybody* wanted one; Pete ended up spending half the night showing the rest of the band and the roadies how to do it. And it was dead simple to do and suddenly it really caught on . . . So we called it the Upside Down Club!'

'The thing is it became almost addictive after a while,' Mark laughs. 'As soon as we checked into a new hotel on that tour the first thing everybody did when they got to their rooms was immediately unscrew the back of the TV set and make the switch to the Upside Down Club! We just couldn't stop doing it . . . Looking at a normal, right-side-up TV screen just wasn't the same after that . . . and as we were virtually in a new country every day none of the programmes were in languages any of us could speak, so we couldn't understand a word coming out of the TV anyway . . . At least the Upside Down Club meant that people could now watch telly if they wanted to. It was fascinating!'

'The problem, as usual with Marillion, is that things started to get a bit out of hand!' smiles Pete Trewavas. 'Absolutely *everybody* was in the Upside Down Club . . . it got to the stage where if you walked in a room and there was a TV on with the picture the right way up someone would immediately insist on changing it . . . But of course, not everybody bothered to switch the picture *back* the right way up when we left a hotel. Consequently, we ended up getting chased half-way round Europe by irate hotel managers who couldn't figure out what we'd done to their TV sets! They thought they were all broken and wanted to charge the band for hundreds of brand new TVs they claimed they'd had to buy!'

Donning his headmaster's black cap, John Arnison despatched tour manager Paul Lewis with instructions for the band and crew to cancel their precious memberships to the Upside Down Club forthwith, on pain of heavy fines and, in the case of the crew, instant dismissal should his instructions not be instantly obeyed . . .

'I remember coming back up to John's room after just telling the band and crew the bad news about The Upside Down Club,' says Paul. 'I came through the door and there was John lying on the bed watching telly. I said, "OK, John, I've told everybody they've got to stop fucking around with hotel televisions." And he just sort of grunted at me . . . He obviously wasn't really listening to a word I said, he was too busy watching the telly.

'So I said, "What are you watching, John? Anything good?" And I sat down next to him and what was he fucking watching? The news, in bloody Dutch or something, with the picture turned upside down!' he laughs. 'I thought, what an old *fraud*!'

Returning to London for the start of the last leg of the tour, Marillion opened with three rapturously received sold-out nights at the Hammersmith Odeon, on 13, 14 and 15 December. After that, they made their way back home to Aylesbury via some splendidly staged one-off festive stints at the Manchester Apollo, the Nottingham Theatre Royal, two nights at the Barrowlands in Glasgow, and one at the Odeon in Birmingham, before settling back for a real last-night-of-the-tour Christmas knees-up on the stage of their beloved Friar's, the last Saturday night before Christmas 1984.

On the road again in Britain, Marillion found that the home fans still reserved their biggest cheers for the older, more classical Marillion numbers like 'Script . . .' or 'Garden Party'. The British fans listened patiently enough to the new twenty-minute *Misplaced Childhood* section of the show, entranced by the slow spell it cast on the night. But at the end of it all the shouts and cries for 'The Web' and, in particular, 'Grendel', would continue unabated throughout the rest of the set.

'I think there was an element of elitism creeping into the hearts of one or two of the older Marillion fans,' says Fish, thoughtfully. 'In Britain, where we'd had a steady following since the days long before we signed a deal with EMI, we were still attracting new fans all the time, and I think maybe calling out for the very oldest of our numbers was just a way of saying, hey, I've been coming to these Marillion gigs for a long time, what about some respect!

'Which is fair enough, in one way. But we hadn't played "Grendel" *once* since Ian had joined the band; I don't think Ian even knows to this day how the number actually goes. To be honest, it's just a song we've outgrown. And what we were trying to do with this *Misplaced Childhood* piece was far more important, far more interesting to us artistically than rehashing an ancient number from our past no-one in the band was really into anymore.

'As for "The Web", well we were only resting that one. There was no reason for the older fans to worry there, "The Web" would be back at some point in the future. For the time being, however, we were getting into something that we were starting to realise would make everything we'd ever done up until then seem like definite second division stuff. I, personally, felt that what we had in our hands with what we'd written so far of *Misplaced Childhood* was like a time bomb that would go off with an almighty *bang* the moment the album was released.

'It was either going to be a huge almighty success or a complete and utter *failure*, and the death of five fine young careers!' he laughs.

'We all felt pretty confident that *Misplaced Childhood* was going to be the best thing we had ever done,' says Steve Rothery. 'Which was doubly nice as it was also really the first album that this line-up of Marillion had actually sat down and worked on and written together right from start to finish. With the tour having gone so well for us too, all we wanted now was to get back in the rehearsal studio as fast as possible and finish off writing the new album.'

There was a celebration party held after the show every night the band played the Hammersmith Odeon. The first night the party had been held mostly in Ian's room back at the hotel; the second, EMI threw an official bash to which a host of media representatives were also invited; and the third, and best, night of all, John Arnison threw an eat-and-drink as much as you like banquet party for the Marillion road crew, which went on from midnight until nine o'clock the following morning, at a private suite of rooms in London John had hired especially for the occasion.

It was at this last party, to which I was also invited, that I encountered Fish in particularly eloquent mood. We were standing at the bar, he dressed in a long red hooded Santa Claus outfit, both of us a bit the worse for drink. The party was still only a few hours old.

We were talking about the new *Misplaced Childhood* idea. Fish was adamant that it should be publicised as a Concept Album. I argued that unless this Concept Album was a very big success the critics would have a field day tearing the whole thing apart, the old sad ghosts of Genesis *et al* rising to speak their minds.

He looked down and smiled at me. Shook his head. Some of the grease-paint still smudging the corners of his eyes.

'That's not what bothers me at all,' he said. 'I already *know* that this next album is going to be *mega*! There's no doubt in my mind; this is the one that's going to break the band *everywhere*! It'll be regarded by the record company as commercial suicide to call it a Concept Album and just have one long continuous piece of music, of course. And they'll drive themselves mental trying to edit-out singles from it somehow, I know. But it won't matter, because I also know that this next album is going to open people's eyes to us properly for the very first time. I feel like with *Misplaced Childhood* we've finally been given the keys that unlock the door to all the toys in the attic.'

'Well, then, if that's the case, you have nothing to worry about. Drink up!' I said, cheerfully.

'You still don't understand, do you?' he said, straightening his shoulders. 'Knowing that this next album is going to be huge isn't enough.'

'What do you mean?' I asked him.

'Well, what happens *next*?'

'Next?'

'Yeah . . . so the new album is huge, what then? What's the challenge *then*?'

'To do it all over again, of course.'

'Do it all over again?' I could see the words left a taste in his mouth.

'Of course! Anyway, you don't really know for sure yet what might happen to your next album.'

'Oh, *don't* I . . .? Come back and tell me that again in a year from now!'

Ho ho, Santa . . .

8

Daydream Believer
(*Profile – Pete Trewavas*)

'Being a child was probably one of the happiest periods of my life,' says Pete Trewavas. 'I used to wander around in a sort of cloud of permanent happiness. The way I remember it, anyway . . . I mean, I was always in a world of my own until I was about ten, always daydreaming and staring off into space. It used to get me into all sorts of trouble at school. Not just with teachers, either – other kids would be talking away to me and I wouldn't really be listening to a word they said. Then they'd suss that I wasn't really there, I was off somewhere daydreaming inside my head, and they'd get really pissed off at me and start having a go. It's a hard habit to kick, actually,' he smiles, 'daydreaming your life away.'

Born in Middlesborough, an average-sized typically non-descript city in the North East of England, on January 15, 1959, Pete Trewavas is the shortest member of Marillion with the longest laugh.

Always very amusing company, listening to Pete talk and hearing what he has to say is always to see life from the comic angle. Not Mr Life & Soul Of Every Party exactly, Pete is usually the wittiest voice commentating from the sidelines. And if there is a buried streak of bitterness or undue hardness tinting his character, then I've never seen it. Nor do I believe it exists. At heart, Pete Trewavas is still the daydream-believing kid who never quite grew up. For a start, he *looks* like an overgrown kid: long, brown, wavy hair that tumbles like a girl's down past his shoulders; puppy eyes that never sit still; pale, freckled face, and a mouth permanently turned up ever so slightly at the corners. And when he walks on stage with the band and picks up that big, heavy-looking bass he can make sing some nights, he doesn't so much walk one foot in front of the other as appear to *bounce* his way to the front of the stage. Pete is all child–like energy and enthusiasm. Just another little boy with a big happy face who wants to play.

His father, John, worked as a solicitor for the local borough council, and his mother, Elsa, worked for various local voluntary agencies like Meals on Wheels.

'I didn't exactly come from a poverty-stricken family, but we lived in a very poor industrial town,' says Pete Trewavas. 'My mum and dad owned a small semi–detached house in a fairly nice little area of Middlesborough, but most of the place was very poor, quite rough. The early sixties was supposed to be a boom-time in England, but I don't think it ever spread as far as the North East. I don't remember us having much money for new things.

There was one other child in the family; a girl, Patricia, born four years before Pete.

'My older sister was my best friend when I was little,' says Pete. 'Although she's only four years older than me, in those days that seemed like forever, you know. And like I say, Middlesborough was a pretty rough place to grow up in, and because I was short and a daydreamer and never paying attention to what was going on around me, I was always getting in trouble, but my big sister was always there to rescue me. It was amazing, really, she was so good to me, really took care of me.

'And it was through her that I started listening to pop music on the radio. I was really young at the time, about four or five years old, but I remember her getting my mum to buy certain records.

'The one I remember most from the earliest days of when I first started listening to the radio and watching TV shows like "Jukebox Jury" is probably "Twist & Shout" by the Beatles. I remember the day my mum brought that one home; it was an EP and even though I was only about five years old I really liked it! I thought they were great, the Beatles, they were my favourite band for years and years.'

Other, seminal Sixties rock figures like the Rolling Stones and The Who were never particular favourites in the Trewavas household.

'I used to think bands like that were a bit vulgar, a bit too noisy, and a bit too, well, sort of *rude!*' Pete laughs. 'And neither my mum nor my sister were into them – they were more into things like the Four Tops, and Gerry and the Pacemakers – so I never really got a chance to discover that heavier kind of rock music until I was already in my teens. I was too busy being a little Paul McCartney fan.'

When he was six, Pete's family made the move down to Aylesbury.

'That was a bit of an eye-opener after Middlesborough,' he says. 'Open air and hills and little countrified towns. But best of all it was where I met another boy about my age who went to the same school in Aylesbury as I started going to, and he became my best friend and we used to hang around together. The thing is he was learning to play the guitar – this was when I was about seven years old. And so straight away I started copying him and wanting to learn how to play guitar too.'

Pete was lucky enough to have an acoustic guitar on hand for him to practise on. His older sister had started guitar lessons earlier but abandoned them after a few weeks.

'I persuaded my mum to let me take lessons,' he says, 'and this guy used to come around once a week and charge her 50p an hour to give me guitar lessons. After about two or three months I really started to get the hang of it, and then me and my little mate, Robin, used to practise together and he'd teach me how to play songs like "Hard Day's Night" and "Help".'

Pete Trewavas' 'little mate Robin' was actually Robin Boult, an accomplished rock guitarist who would later lead his own path through a string of local Aylesbury outfits before ending up as John Otway's guitarist, the post he still holds today. Together, the two budding infant minstrels polished up a little act that won them several talent competitions at school.

'I loved all that – a pop star at eight!' he laughs. 'Actually, the thing I liked best of all about it was that it made me and Robin different from most of the other kids in school. Suddenly I wasn't bullied about my size any more, and girls started to take an interest. I remember we used to bang together a two-guitar-and-vocals set that consisted of whatever was popular in the charts at the time. By the time we got to twelve or so we were really getting good at it and we had a set made up of really good versions of Slade, the Monkees, and a few older numbers as well to keep the mums and dads happy, things like "Won't You

Come Home Bill Bailey". Oh, we had it all worked out!'

Outside of his burgeoning talents as a guitarist, Pete's chief interests during his school days centred around the sports-field. Outside of a passing interest in Maths and English, he hated lessons. But he liked football.

'I wasn't a very good footballer, I didn't have much talent for the game, but it kept me out of the classroom, and that was the main thing as far as I was concerned. Academically, I was having a pretty tough time at school.

'In fact, when my family first moved down from Middlesborough to Aylesbury I was having such a bad time of it at my new school that the headmaster wanted to send me to a special school for the educationally subnormal!

'Of course, my mum and dad freaked and told him he must be joking – you know, "He's a bright lad!" So I had to take all these I.Q. tests to determine how intelligent I really was. I did the tests and they found out that I was as bright as most kids my age, but that I needed glasses and that I was dyslexic as well.'

Being dyslexic meant that though Pete would be able to learn how to read and write, he would always have trouble with over-long words, and his spelling would be fifty per cent phonetic.

'It's actually no great drawback being dyslexic,' he says, 'it just meant that I always had an inbuilt reason for finding lessons boring.'

By the time he was thirteen and ready to put together a full band with his regular partner, Robin, Pete had already switched from guitar to bass after being forced to admit that he wasn't now or ever going to be as good a guitarist as Robin.

'For years the only criticism I had to take was that I wasn't as good on guitar as Robin,' he smiles. 'But I always used to use the excuse that he'd starting playing three months before I did. After about four years though it was obvious to me that I'd never catch up with him. So when I was about eleven I decided I'd really go the full Paul McCartney and become a bass player!'

The band Pete and Robin first formed – a basic two guitars, bass, and drums garage line-up – spent most of their time rehearsing, but still managed a handful of lunchtime gigs at school, playing for crisps and pop under the suitably exotic *nom-de-plume* of . . . Manantus!

'We used to play cover versions of things like Hawkwind; for instance we used to do a really, really *long* version of "7 by 7", which was the B side of "Silver Machine". And then we started writing a few very basic things of our own, which amounted to not much more than long runs down the frets, just thrashing away. Then one of the guitarists would take a solo; then the other guitarist would take one; then I'd take a solo; and then we'd all stop and let the drummer have a bash, you know, and then we'd start all over again.

'And we'd go on playing like that *forever*, like, no *let up*! Only it would all be going on in the drummer's garage and things never really got any further than that, so we only lasted about a year.'

The peak of Pete Trewavas' short-lived career with Manantus occurred when the band played for free to a packed classroom at the drama lesson in school, when he was fifteen.

'I remember the teachers wanted us to charge 2p entrance fee, in order to raise funds for the school minibus,' says Pete. 'But we were a very high-principled band,' he smiles, 'and we were very anti-capitalist and we wouldn't agree to do the gig unless they let us put it on for free. I remember they tried to get us to compromise and let them sell tickets for a penny, but we still said no, and eventually they let us do it for free.

'It was a great moment! I'd never seen so many little kids crammed into one room, and us going mental through our set of Hawkwind covers!'

By his mid-teens, Pete was slowly starting to lose his sweet tooth for the slick Sixties pop of the Beatles (though they were still his favourites. 'I cried when I heard they had split up,' he says, 'I mean, *Sergeant Pepper* was the first album I ever bought!') and other like-minded spin-offs like the Monkees, the Kinks and the Small Faces. Now he turned his attention to the less mellifluous, more determinedly esoteric endeavours of new contemporary giants like Yes, Caravan, and Genesis.

'The first album like that that I really got into was *Fragile* by Yes,' he says. 'It took me a bit of time to fully appreciate what was going on musically, but in the end it really grew on me.

'I wasn't completely sort of serious-minded though,' Pete points out, gleefully citing Alice Cooper's *Billion Dollar Babies* album as just as important an influence as *Fragile*, or anything else by Yes at that time.

'It was very different music but I liked it all the same,' he says, 'and then I bought the Genesis *Live* album, because I really liked the cover, and that was great, almost Yes and Alice Cooper all rolled into one! It had some long, complicated numbers that could send the tingles down your back the same way Yes could, but it also had the sound of a live band really going for it on stage; and judging by the pictures of the band on the album sleeve they looked easily as theatrical and imagey as Alice Cooper.

'It was listening to the Genesis *Live* album that really made me thirst to get back into a live band of my own.'

With Manantus still in a state of flux – 'we had a new member in the band every week,' says Pete, 'and we never really got anything going,' – Pete filled in the gaps by playing clarinet in the school orchestra. Or sometimes he would provide some guitar for occasional school productions of plays like *Joseph and his Amazing Technicolour Dreamcoat*.

'I actually studied playing the clarinet for three years,' says Pete. 'My dad, who played a bit of piano and saxophone, was a very, very keen jazz fan. And although I might have started off listening to someone like Acker Bilk and his "Stranger on the Shore" and all that stuff, I found out quickly enough what was good and what was bad. That's when I started listening seriously to people like Artie Shaw.

'It was weird though; me and Robin were still trying to get a band together and start writing some songs and doing some proper gigs, but that seemed to be taking forever and in the meantime I was quite into the clarinet, and some of the really great jazz masters that my dad was always playing at home. At the same time I was also building up my collection of rock albums by people like Yes, Alice Cooper, and Genesis, and a lot of other less well-known but similar sounding groups too, and starting to get out to a few real gigs for the first time as well.'

The first rock concert Pete Trewavas ever went to see was, appropriately enough, at the local Friar's in the market square, where Darryl Way's Wolf were headlining. It was 1975 and Pete was sixteen.

'Which was really weird!' he says, laughing. 'Because I found out years later that the drummer in Wolf that night was none other than *Ian Mosley*!

'We worked it out together one night, out on the road somewhere not long after Ian joined the band permanently. I think we were both a bit shocked to find that one out! But we had to laugh. I mean, what a coincidence!'

With the doubtfully named Manantus increasingly more like a dream neither Pete nor his guitar-wielding sidekick, Robin, really believed in any more, when the pair were asked if they would consider joining forces with another truly dreadfully named local Aylesbury outfit called Orthi, they both jumped at the chance.

'What attracted me to Orthi was that they seemed light years ahead of anything either Robin or I had ever attempted. They used to rehearse in a little church hall, and they used to play fairly regular gigs. And they had what I thought at the time was some pretty impressive equipment.

'Orthi was a garage band with *high* aspirations!' he chuckles. 'When I joined they already had a vox organ, and a Roland's synthesiser, and they had an electric violin, lots of keyboards, and a moog! I thought this is *it*! You know? Like, wow, now we're ready to *go* places!'

They were indeed. Mainly places like the backrooms in some of the small local pubs dotted around the Buckinghamshire area.

'We stuck at it, though,' says Pete. 'And before very long we had our own little following. Nothing world-shattering, of course, just a couple of hundred Orthi freaks from the Aylesbury area.'

Enough 'Orthi freaks' in fact to vote the band Best Local Band in the local Friar's annual poll three years running!

'We never meant a thing outside of Aylesbury, nobody had ever heard of us,' smiles Pete, 'but for a couple of years we were definitely local legends in our own lunchtime. We had a van and a couple of roadies, and a lot of dreams. More dreams than gigs probably but we were doing all right for what was essentially a part-time band.

'Actually, one of the guys that roadied for us in Orthi was Doug Irving, who later went on to form the first version of Marillion with Mick Pointer! That's another weird coincidence. I remember Doug was trying to learn how to play a bass when he was roadying for Orthi. It was only after we broke up that he got together with Mick.'

With a constantly fluctuating line-up that had, by the time Pete was eighteen, seen the electric violin, the synthesisers, and much of the percussion and keyboards all at one time or another walk out the church hall doors, Orthi evolved into a more rugged, blues-based outfit.

'Towards the end we were playing things like "Sweet Home Alabama" by Lynard Skynard,' Pete says. 'A couple of rough-and-ready up-tempo numbers like that, and some of our own original stuff that by then was sort of exclusively rhythm and blues. Lots of guitars and heavy drums.

'We were like the world's first progressive boogie band!' he laughs.

Encouraged by the steady following Orthi enjoyed in the area, Dave Stopps, who would figure again later in the Marillion story, booked the band for a solid string of supports at the prestigious Friar's hall.

'I remember we supported the British Lions, which was a mixture of old Mott the Hoople and Medicine Head members. And then another time we opened the show for Ian Gillan. It was all great experience for me, not only playing on the same stage as some of these real seen-it-all professionals, but getting to meet them and chat to them afterwards. I mean, someone like Ian Gillan was really, really nice. You know, I learned something just by chatting to him for a few minutes. And it all got put to good use later on.'

Joining Orthi around about the same time as he left school, at sixteen, Pete entered a local College of Further Education, where he spent the next two years struggling through a crash course in O and A level studies.

'I'd failed most of my O level exams at school – in fact, the only one I managed to get a pass in was music – so I ended up going to college for the next two years trying to get enough O levels to take some As. I ended up with about 20 O levels and no A levels. I was still playing in Orthi all through that and the band took up almost all of my spare time.'

Leaving college at eighteen, armed in fact with six O levels, Pete decided to make his career in the music business. If not immediately as a full-time working muso, then perhaps as a tape-op, or tea-boy apprentice, in a professional recording studio. He started writing off for job interviews.

'I'd have done *anything* – sweep the floors, make the tea, polish the mixing desk – just so long as it had something vaguely to do with music,' he says. 'In the end I went along to about three or four interviews with different recording studios, but none of them had anything going that I could really do. So that was that.'

Out of luck with his search to find a place that paid near to the music he loved so much, Pete took a job as an apprentice television engineer.

'It was a four-year, day-release course at college, and the next

211

best thing I could think of close to music. I thought that if I had a training in TV maintenance then maybe later I could worm my way into a recording studio with a detailed knowledge of electronic engineering. So I did that for four years – bored out of my mind!'

By 1978, Orthi had changed its line-up and musical direction so many times, Pete and Robin, by now the only two surviving members of the original set-up, decided it was time for a complete break with the past.

'It was time for a fresh start,' says Pete. 'And by now the punk thing was creeping into our musical perspective. So we changed the line-up again, changed the music to a more streamlined, new wave-ish sort of sound, and we changed our name: we called the band the Robins! We desperately wanted to be young and trendy, and we speeded everything up and tried dressing a bit sharper on stage too. We were like a mini-version of Eddie and the Hot Rods.'

Despite the contrived 'punk influence' that the Robins introduced into their music, Pete Trewavas still maintains that the whole punk rock deal was one he found very hard to swallow and keep down for long.

'Deep down inside, I really hated punk,' he says, unsmiling. 'It single-handedly destroyed lots of the sort of music I liked at that time. There were loads of good new bands around that were effectively killed off because suddenly they just weren't *fashionable* any more . . . Bands like Split Enz, Racing Cars, Band Called O, Sassafrass, Stackridge, *loads* of them were finished off in this country by punk!'

However dubious he might have been by the onset of the last great upheaval pop was to suffer in the Seventies, Pete Trewavas found he was still absorbing as much of the celebrated 'new wave' as he could.

'The first band that sort of turned me on to what some of the other, more influential punk bands were doing, was the Stranglers,' he admits. 'They sounded a lot more *musical* than most other punk bands making the news; they'd got that sort of Chris Squire bass sound, and all those keyboards. I thought, you know, now *this* is getting back to the sort of thing I like, but with a bit of *balls* to it!'

The Robins continued following the same narrow tracks Orthi had been ploughing for the last three years: pubs and small student halls in and around Aylesbury, occasionally managing to break out into one-off gigs in the Midlands, but never getting any closer to the prestigious London club circuit than a couple of small-time gigs in Luton.

However, picking up where Orthi left off, the Robins soon attracted a stronger local following. One of their biggest fans was the highly respected, Aylesbury based rock critic, Pete Frame. A former publisher and editor of *Zig Zag*, Frame had written for every important music paper in Britain, also contributing a long line of his famous Family Trees to a number of book, magazine and newspaper publications all over the world.

'Pete Frame was a good mate of ours,' says Pete Trewavas. 'I think he genuinely thought the Robins had something going for them. We even wrote a song together once! Pete had some lyrics to a song he had written called "Kim Fowley", and we went in and wrote some music to go with them. I think we even demoed it. Kim Fowley is this weird Hollywood record producer that Pete Frame had some great stories about. Fowley used to manage the Runaways, the ultimate jailbait band, and lots of other things Pete had managed to put down into a lyric. We thought it would be a great first single,' he laughs, 'but nothing really came of it. We used to play it live, though.'

The Robins continued running in ever-decreasing circles around the limited Aylesbury circuit of pub venues. By 1980 the gigs were starting to dry up as fast as the band's ideas. The Robins were driving themselves into the ground and had lost the inspiration to carry on under their present under-achieving guise. It was time for another name change and a policy rethink.

'Me and Robin knew that the band wasn't getting any better, and we certainly weren't getting any bigger, so what we did was we knocked it on the head as the Robins, kept the drummer though, then stole the singer from another local band, and changed our name to Heartbeat.'

Heartbeat was, by Pete's own admission, his and Robin Boult's 'first real stab at the avant-garde'.

The new singer, though according to Pete vocally much limited, nevertheless proved to be something of a revelation on stage.

'He didn't really have the talent vocally,' says Pete. 'But he wrote really weird lyrics and was a very unusual sort of person. He came over very well live. Mr Weird and Wonderful. Me and Robin thought he was all right.'

213

Determined not to fritter more years away chasing the same pub gigs they already knew only too well from their times with Orthi and the Robins, Pete Trewavas and Heartbeat decided to ditch the idea of playing live and instead rehearse five of their original songs really well and then record them cheaply. At the end they would have a five-track demo ready to hawk around the major and not-so-major record companies in London. At least, that was the idea.

'We went up to Norwich University, to the music college there, where our old electric violinist was still studying. He'd sort of conned one of his lecturers into letting him have access to one of their small recording studios; it all fell under Light Entertainment Studies or something, and so we went up to Norwich for a long weekend and recorded five songs.'

Unfortunately, their three days in East Anglia were to be the peak of the much-maligned Heartbeat's creative achievements. The demo-tape was duly mailed out to a host of entirely unresponsive record labels, and finally Pete and Robin had to admit that nobody really liked the tape. In fact, outside of the people actually involved in Heartbeat, nobody really much liked the band.

'We got the inevitable support gig at Friar's,' says Pete, 'and I remember playing away on stage and thinking this really *is* shit, isn't it? Us going out of our way to be deeply meaningless. We're not fooling anyone! The audience didn't like any of it and by the end of the night I had to admit I agreed with them. Me and Robin definitely must have had our heads buried in the sand for a long time over that one. We knocked it on the head a short time afterwards. I couldn't stand it any more; it was just pretentious twaddle!'

Still seeking the right vehicle to mould into their own adolescent self-image, Pete and Robin did the next best thing and joined somebody *else's* band: Tamberlane, originally formed by ex-members of Orthi, which Robin and Pete again quickly turned into a machine more in tune with their own new ultra-pop mode.

'Tamberlane were a soft-rock, big vocal harmonies, Eagles-type thing,' says Pete. 'But before long Robin and I had pretty much changed everything around to give the band a more flash pop edge. We made everybody get really short haircuts – I mean, my hair used to be really *long*, right down my back – and we changed the name of the band to the Cameras.'

It was as a member of the Cameras that Pete Trewavas played his first gig at the club that was later to make him and Marillion famous: the Marquee.

'By then we actually had a manager who worked for Chappell's, the music publishers, and he had a bit of sway, so we used to get gigs at quite a few different little spots in London,' he says. 'The Marquee, the Rock Garden, a placed called Annie's Wine Bar; mostly just supports, but at least we were getting to play in town.

'We hadn't got the metamorphosis completely right yet though, to becoming the New Beatles or anything,' he laughs. 'We'd taken it from the Eagles to a sort of speeded up, less polished, Dave Edmonds-sounding thing. So we started again, this time under the name of Red Stars!

'We all got into wearing jackets on stage and nice shirts, and the music was becoming more and more like pure pop music.'

However, before Red Stars' career got properly off the ground, the one thing Pete Trewavas never expected to happen *happened*: Robin Boult upped and quit the band!

'I must admit I was a bit surprised and a bit disappointed, at first, when Robin told me he was leaving the band,' says Pete. 'But he'd been offered a good gig as the guitarist with this guy called John Wilson; he was Mari Wilson's brother, and had his own band together doing regular gigs and making a bit of money, called Heartbeat, funnily enough. So the Red Stars sort of folded on the spot. We stayed together as a four-piece, but we spent the next few months locked away rehearsing new material together. Robin going affected everything in the group, we more or less had to start again.

When the band resurfaced in January 1981, they had yet another new monicker to flaunt. This time they were called the Metros. Drums, bass, two guitars and vocals, the Metros were a spunky little outfit raised on coca-cola rhythms and heavily sugared guitars; the drums running far too fast for their own good; the vocals a cheerful mish-mash of breathless chorus-girl vitality and about as much raunch as Cliff Richard with a heavy cold. They were ineffectual and entertaining, full of contrived good cheer, and occasionally some very nifty guitar riffs.

'The Metros was the most successful band I was in before I joined Marillion,' says Pete Trewavas. 'Not that we really did that well together. But we *did* manage to release an EP, and that was a first for me! And we did manage to get out and about a bit, everything considered.'

The Metros were nothing if not a live band. Always making sure that they looked suitably sharp and very 1981 at all their gigs – bright red jackets, shiney thin ties and pointed shoes bounding youthfully about the stage! – The Metros got people dancing to original self-penned material like 'Plastered in Paris' mingled in effortlessly with sure-fire after-midnight ravers like the Beatles' 'I Saw Her Standing There'.

For the record, the Metros consisted of Frank Walsh and Tony Duke, taking turns on guitars and lead vocals, drummer Gary Duke and, of course, Pete Trewavas on bass and backing vocals. Or rather, Pete *True*, as he liked to be known then.

'I changed my name to Pete True because I thought Trewavas was a bit of a mouthful for radio DJs to handle,' he admits, smiling. 'Which just sort of shows you where we were at in the Metros. I think we all thought we wanted to be the next Duran Duran!' he groans in mock agony.

The band recorded one self-financed twelve-inch EP, which they released on their own label in Britain in the summer of 1981, called *The First 33 & 1/3 EP – Driving Us Crazy*. Boasting six tracks, three on one side recorded live, three on the other recorded almost-live in the studio, the Metros' EP is an untidy, blustering, high-energy pop rant that buzzes with punchy guitars and knitting-needle drums; the quintessential garage band wigging out on the most slender of antiquated pop choruses.

'I haven't a clue where you could buy a copy now,' says Pete, 'but very occasionally I see one advertised in the music press going for a few quid – the ad usually says the Metros – featuring Pete Trewavas of Marillion, you know? Very unfair to both bands, but there you go.'

Of the six tracks on that first (and last) Metros EP, only 'Love Me Tomorrow', which Pete describes fairly accurately as a 'Hall & Oates type of thing' really sounds like anything special. The rest is mostly well-intentioned pop pap.

However, . . . *Driving Us Crazy* quickly sold out of its initial 1,000 copies pressing, and the band pressed another 1,000 copies and watched entranced as they too vanished into the hands of local fans who turned up regularly at all their gigs, and more impressively, they felt, via mail-order from kids in places they hadn't even heard of, let alone played in yet.

'We got very lucky with that record,' says Pete. 'The band

John Arnison, Paul Lewis and Pete Trewavas – the razzle dazzle trio

Fish at the Club Fugazi, San Francisco, 1986

Chris Kimsey, Hansa Studios, Berlin 1985

Memories of a Misplaced Childhood

"Misplaced Childhood"

MARILLION

4.11.85 Bonn	· Biskuithalle	18.11.85 Hamburg	· Musikhalle
5.11.85 Offenbach	· Stadthalle	21.11.85 Osnabrück	· Stadthalle
11.11.85 Stuttgart	· Liederhalle	22.11.85 Kassel	· Stadthalle
12.11.85 Karlsruhe	· Stadthalle	25.11.85 Aachen	· Eurogress
13.11.85 Ludwigshafen	· Eberthalle	26.11.85 Völklingen	· Sporthalle
14.11.85 München	· Circus Krone	27.11.85 Mainz	· Rheingoldhalle
16.11.85 Düsseldorf	· Philipshalle	28.11.85 Fürth	· Stadthalle
17.11.85 Hannover	· Rotation		

Eintrittskarten sind an allen bekannten Vorverkaufsstellen erhältlich.

Fish in Japan, 1985

Fish, 1987 (Russell Young)

Mark Kelly, 1987
(Russell Young)

Ian Mosley, 1987
(Russell Young)

Pete Trewavas, 1987
(Russell Young)

Steve Rothery, 1987
(Russell Young)

Marillion at the start of the *Clutching at Straws* tour, 1987 (Russell Young)

always used to thrive on playing gigs, and we used to play all the time because the managers of the pubs and clubs thought we were good at getting people up and dancing. So selling the records at gigs was easy really. We had a lot of fans locally. But somehow the word-of-mouth thing worked really well for us, which is something you can never predict or rely on, and we couldn't sell copies of the EP fast enough.'

With the proceeds, which had been reasonable, from the sales of their modestly-produced EP now tucked away in the bank, the band prepared to take their most dramatic step yet in their continuing search for greater commercial success – they decided to uproot and re-station their act in New York!

'We had this mad plan,' says Pete. 'Colin Medlocke, who was the chap managing us at the time, had been in contact with this very dubious character in America called Matt – that's all we knew of him, his first name, but he reckoned he could get us four weeks'-worth of gigs in the New York City area, so we thought why not? America, you know! None of us had ever been further than Devon to play a gig before and we were really up for it!

'The other thing,' he goes on, 'is that we always saw the Metros as having a much greater chance of really making it in America than we ever had in England. We were very commercial by now and thought we would appeal right across the board to all tastes, but we decided that the business was probably much better geared in America to something as straightforward as that.

'So the idea was to get across to New York for four or five weeks of gigs, make it big, and never come home!' he laughs.

Going across to America, even if the trip did last no more than a few weeks, was still a big step for Pete to take. It meant giving up his job as a TV repair-man, which meant goodbye to four years of training and a nice steady wage. And it meant goodbye to home, friends and lovers for a while too.

'I remember the one thing I was dreading most was having to go home and tell my parents that I was giving up my day-job and going into music full-time,' he says. 'What made matters worse was that my dad had just been made redundant from Aylesbury Borough Council, and times were very hard at home. My dad was pretty despondent about the whole thing. But anyway I said "Look, I've been given the chance to go across and try my luck with the band in America, and I really want to do

217

it!" And my mum turned around and asked me what I really thought of the idea, was it a proper opportunity or was I just kidding myself? And I was like, no, no, no, it's all above-board and carefully worked out, and I'll be back in a couple of months rich and famous!

'Then my dad said, "Well, no job's that safe any more these days", and that was that – I was going! After they'd sort of given me their blessing they stopped asking questions and really supported me. They were great about the whole thing and I was *so* relieved.'

Five one-way tickets from Heathrow to Kennedy airport later, Pete True and his Metros were on their way to New York City, where they would spend the next three months bouncing like a pinball, footloose and half-starved, from one weird gig to another; from the Village to Queens, out to Long Island and back, deep into the perfumed bowels of neon-tinted old Manhattan.

It was September 1981, the boys were strangers in town, and Matt knew all the places to go and was only too willing to put the band on first-name terms with all the dives his fevered imagination could buy or talk his way into on their behalf.

'When we first got to New York we still had enough money on us to make us feel like we were on holiday for the first couple of weeks. It was great! We were sharing this house with some friends of Matt's, which was out in Queens, actually in a district of Queens called Kew Gardens, would you believe? And it was a really nice little area. And that was our base for a while, waiting for the first gigs to start.'

As the temporarily resident English 'pop stars', the Metros got known pretty quickly in their neighbourhood for being nice, polite boys who only wanted to work hard and go far. And in America, why not? That was what The Dream was all about, was it not?

The Metros were on the American gravy train all right, but the wheels still turned stubbornly slowly for them. Gig followed gig, usually.

'We used to vary our live set wherever we played,' says Pete. 'If we were playing a regular rock club we turned in our usual set – some originals and some covers, stuff like "Fire Brigade" by the Move and "I Think Of You" by the Merseybeats. But then a couple of times we were booked into these poky little late-night drinking bars. So then we used to revert back to a lot of the old

Tamberlane material and chuck out stuff by Poco and the Eagles. It was all done in the spirit of good fun, and anyway we had no choice a lot of the time – you took one look at the faces of the audience and you knew immediately what set to play.'

At the peak of their activity in New York, Pete and the Metros played as many as one gig every three days. As the weeks turned into months though, the gigs were becoming more scarce and the band were starting to suspect they ahd outstayed their welcome.

'Looking back on it now, it must have been the longest twelve weeks of my life!' sighs Pete Trewavas. 'When you're broke and in a foreign country it's not really much fun. I mean, I think we all enjoyed every minute of our stay there, but towards the end, as we got nearer and nearer to a broke and lonely Christmas, I think we were on our last legs. We couldn't have survived for much longer. We were ready to *collapse.*'

As chance would have it, one of the very last gigs the Metros played in New York was supporting Duran Duran at a theatre in Westchester.

'It was their first tour of America and they needed somebody to open the show for them in this one town, and someone must have put a good word in for us because we got the gig!

'We actually went down quite well with their audience, which quite pleased us of course,' Pete smirks, 'but when they came on there was just no comparison! I mean, really, they were great at what they did! And it was around the time of their first album, which I've still got, and they were playing quite good stuff like "Girls on Film", stuff like that. I admit, I was *impressed.* Really, they were just doing what the Metros longed to do, only they did it so much *better* than us!'

By December 1981, Pete and the rest of the Metros were destitute. Worse, they were starting to run up heavy debts they had no hope of repaying. It was time to leave town and head for home.

'Even the friends we had made over there in New York were telling us it was the best thing to do,' says Pete. 'We'd had enough of sleeping on cold floors and not a penny between us to spare for anything. We still felt that if we could hang on for another six months or so things might drastically alter – there was some talk of getting us on a tour with Hall & Oates, or something, which never amounted to anything more than talk, but we were a very trusting band and let ideas like that go to our heads a little bit,' he smiles. 'But the closer it got to Christmas the more bleak things were starting to look for us, and in the end we all couldn't wait to come home.' Which they did, in time for Christmas 1981.

It had been an interesting year for the Metros all right, but a physically and mentally exhausting time which left Pete Trewavas feeling drained and vaguely depressed, he says, about the prospect of having to start all over again, in the New Year, with the same ideas in the same pubs and village halls he had now been running around in with one band or another for the last six years.

'When we first got back from New York I must admit we played it up a bit like The Return of the Vanquishing Heroes!' laughs Pete. 'Because obviously it *was* a bit of a talking point amongst our friends and family. I mean, straight away we forgot all about the nights we had nothing to eat or drink, five of us huddled up together on some complete stranger's living-room floor. All we could talk about was the night we played with Duran Duran, or how many times we headlined at Trax. We never thought to mention how the last couple of times we played some of these places we'd started off headlining in we actually ended up playing *supports*!

'And of course, the local press made a big fuss about Local Band Flies Home From Successful American Tour! You know, all the bollocks! And we had our photos taken and asked for quick interviews . . . It was a right old game,' he says, winking.

'But by the New Year, when all that had died down, the fact is I don't think we really knew what to do or where to go next. Plus, we were all still totally broke – worse than broke. I owed *everybody* money! We'd had to touch everyone we knew back home in England just to raise the air fares home. So the immediate future for the Metros looked pretty bleak as far as I was concerned.'

With just enough strength left to don one more disguise, the Metros metamorphosed for one night into East Goes West; with Robin Boult temporarily reinstated into the fold, the 'new' band managed just the one gig, at the Embassy Club in London, in January 1982, peddling a set Pete frankly admits was his and Robin's aborted attempt to emulate the then burgeoning New Romantics scene that was flowering like a poppy down in London, as evinced by the recent successes of plummy new pop stylists of the time like Spandau Ballet, Duran Duran, and Ultravox. 'That was the week we all went a bit Steve Strange!'

chortles Pete Trewavas. 'I even stopped using a plectrum to pick the strings with on my bass; I started *popping* and *slappin'*, and getting my hands caught up in the strings . . . We did that one gig and that was more or less the end for me. I'd had enough of playing at being a pop star. I wanted to get back to playing the sort of music I really liked, just for the sake of playing to the best of my ability, and not worrying about if I had the right haircut or not.'

Eventually, Pete Trewavas decided the time was right to strike out on his own, away from the stale Aylesbury scene, maybe into a band with a lot more going for them down in London, or perhaps somewhere further north, like Manchester and Liverpool, where so many of the most innovative new pop bands of the late Seventies and early Eighties had sprung form.

At any rate, somewhere outside of Aylesbury which, so far anyway, had brought him no real luck.

'I just more or less decided that I'd tried getting every possible permutation of band off the ground in Aylesbury, and that so far all it had got me was broke and back in Aylesbury. I definitely wanted out, and so did Robin, so we agreed to do one last farewell gig, as the Metros, and then that was gonna be it. I was off!'

The Metros' farewell performance was at a pub called the King's Head, in Aylesbury, at the end of February 1982. Whatever their relative failings as a band, the Metros still knew how to pack 'em in locally and that night for their final gig together the King's Head was jammed with wall-to-wall people. Amongst the crowded huddle of heads watching the band from the bar was a person Pete had only met once or twice before, but who was about to make the disenchanted bass player an offer he was fortunate enough not to refuse and that would eventually change his life irrevocably, for better or for worse, for richer or poorer . . . but mostly just richer.

His name was Fish and he was the singer in another local band.

'I'd met Fish once before the night we did that last gig as the Metros,' says Pete. 'About a year before that I'd been sitting in a pub one lunchtime, having a quiet bite to eat and a drink on my own, when this sort of amazingly tall Scotsman tapped me on the shoulder and introduced himself. He'd recognised me from the Metros, and he said, "Hi, I'm Fish, I'm the singer in Marillion!" as if everyone in the world had heard of Marillion, even though I think they'd probably only done a couple of gigs

221

at that stage. I mean *I* hadn't even heard of them! But within a few weeks I started seeing their name everywhere I went in Aylesbury. There were always hundreds of hand-made posters advertising their gigs nailed to trees and plastered on walls all over the place. And whenever I used to go and sign-on I'd see loads of posters all over the DHSS office walls advertising a string of Marillion dates. Because, of course, Fish was *ẅrking* at the DHSS at the time, so he was always putting them up. You know, new ones every week!

'And the weird thing is about meeting him that first time is that I think he wanted to pick my brains about where the Metros were playing outside of Aylesbury. And I don't think I was much help. We'd played a few places *lots* of times, sort of thing. Then lo and behold two weeks later I started making special trips to the DHSS just so that I could copy down the list of gigs Marillion were playing that month, and then go home and start ringing some of these places up ourselves. I mean, the Metros were supposed to be *the* big local band, but Marillion were the ones playing in places like Luton, Dunstable, Watford, Oxford, Banbury, Coventry, loads of places we didn't have the first idea how to get into.'

By the time the Metros were ready to sound the death-knell on their own doomed career as Local Boys Making Good, Marillion were already a regular headlining act at illustrious little London dives like the Marquee, and attracting big double-page spreads in big-wig music weeklies like *Sounds*, along with a host of live reviews that when they weren't crowing on about certain *influences* were mostly loaded with deafening literary applause.

Musically, Marillion couldn't have been more different from the trim pop antics of the Metros. Marillion were about long, complex musical statements; they shunned the pop aesthetic and wallowed in the shadow of their own gigantic artistic ego; anti-fashion, anti-bullshit, anti-haircuts, and anti-empty pop smiles, they were everything the Metros were not. Fish turning up like that for their last gig came as a surprise to all and sundry, most of all Pete.

'I was dead surprised when he came up to me and said hello before we went on stage,' says Pete, smiling. 'He was the *last* person I expected to come to the farewell Metros gig . . . Both bands attracted *very* different crowds!

'But we started talking and he told me that the band had just sacked their bass player and straight away I asked him if I could

222

audition. He sort of said, yeah, yeah . . . *maybe*. And then it was time for me to go on stage and play, so I left him there, watching the band.'

After the gig, which was the first time Fish had even seen the Metros play, Pete renewed his request for an audition with Fish and the rest of the Marillion boys, and this time the singer allowed his caution to drop and named a time and place for Pete to turn up for his audition. Could Pete come down *tomorrow*? Was he free for that? Because, if not, well.

'I hadn't really sussed it,' says Pete, 'because Fish can be very hard to read sometimes, but in actual fact the real reason he came down that night was to check me out. I mean, I didn't know it then, but it turned out that Marillion were pretty desperate to get a new bass player in a bit sharpish because they had a whole lot of Scottish dates arranged that they had agreed to play. But Fish being Fish, he had to play his cards a little bit closer to his chest, and we said no more really until I turned up for the audition.

'I didn't know what to expect once I got there; they didn't exactly seem like the friendliest bunch, not at first anyway. I think the fact that I used to be a member of the Metros – the White Shoe Brigade, as I later found out they used to call us – really put them off the idea of me actually joining their band, and I was *terrified* that I was going to blow it and they'd all laugh me out the door!'

Aware of the obvious differences in terms of both style and presentation between the band he had just left behind and the one he now hoped to join, Pete admits that he consciously dressed *down* for his audition with Marillion.

'I definitely made sure I wasn't wearing the white shoes *that* day!' he cries. 'Even so, when I turned up they still all looked at each other in horror because I looked so different from the rest of them! Even dressed down I couldn't get to look as scruffy as that lot did that day!

'But anyway, once I'd plugged in my bass and started tuning up I suddenly sensed the whole atmosphere of the room relax. I thought to myself, Blimey! Haven't they seen a bass player tuning up before? But I was still very nervous and so I kept tuning up, trying to look busy and like I knew what I was doing, and they all stood around sort of watching me out of the corners of their eyes, pretending to ignore me.'

And out of the corners of their eyes the offer was made, and accepted, by no more than the silent nods of heads. Suddenly, in early March 1982, Pete Trewavas was asked to hang up his white shoes for the last time and become the new bass player in Marillion, a band who in the final analysis would turn Pete into a bigger pop star than he could ever have dreamed of being back in the now dead days of the Robins, the Red Stars, the Cameras, and the ill-fated Metros.

'They said, "What are you doing for the next six weeks? We're doing a tour of Scotland, do you want to come along?" And I said, "Yeah, I've never been to Scotland." '

Pete Trewavas' introduction into the surly ranks of the young and upwardly hostile Marillion cavalcade on that long and rambling busman's holiday Fish had arranged for them up in Scotland throughout March and April of 1982 has been well documented elsewhere in these pages. Needless to say, Pete's memories of the early part of the mischievous tour are not altogether happy ones.

'Being the newest member of the band, obviously I expected to get my leg pulled a bit, maybe even a lot, to begin with,' says Pete. 'But they were *merciless*! I was the butt of every daft joke and prank for about the first three weeks we were away, and after a while it really did start to get me down. I mean, it was one thing to be expected to put up with everybody really getting on my case, but some of the remarks Mick Pointer was making were really unnecessarily nasty, I thought. And I didn't know how to handle Privet's humour *at all*.'

When everything finally came to a head, the night Mark Kelly dislodged his shoulder for the first time, and Pete broke down and started crying, it was, he says, more out of frustration than self-pity that he lost control of myself.

'I just felt really angry and pissed off,' he says. 'I'd come into the band determined to have a real go at things and make them work, and being the only one who didn't know anyone else I was probably over-friendly to begin with as well, which of course they took the piss out of mercilessly! I couldn't do a thing right for the first three weeks we were away together!

'I just wasn't enjoying it at all; playing with Marillion seemed like something special, but off-stage they were such a bunch of creeps I just couldn't handle it any more, and I got really upset and let it all come out and told them what I thought of them. And then after that, everything changed suddenly, everybody started to relax and be themselves, and I started getting on great with everybody, even Mick.'

Appalled at their own thoughtlessness and inane insensitivity, Marillion rallied round their new bass player and at last, properly and hospitably, welcomed him into their off-stage hearts.

'There are a lot of bastards in this world,' says Pete Trewavas enigmatically, 'but I'm not one of them, and though the band were right to want to protect themselves and not open up to a new face *too* quickly, once they realised that I was in it for exactly the same reasons they were the barriers all dropped, thank God, and I could get off being on the defensive all the time. After that we all got on really well together, and now they're all probably the best friends I'll ever have!'

Returning to Aylesbury in May 1982, with only more headline spots at the Marquee to look forward to, and their first headline appearance at Friar's in June announced and fast on its way to becoming a sell-out show, the question of Pete's long-term future with Marillion had now been firmly resolved in everybody's mind: Pete was in. Deep. And now he would have to help the band mount their search for the right manager to help lift them out of the margins of off-beat notoriety and into the heady realms of real success; the kind you could hold in your hand like a recording contract; like a tour itinerary with 100 dates on it; or like a soft round piece of black plastic, with enough copies to decorate their bedroom walls if they wanted to.

'It was an exciting time and I think we all felt that we were on the verge of something big,' says Pete, 'but we needed a manager, with lots of experience to go in with these record companies that were now calling to check up on us, and really negotiate a good deal for the band.'

Dave Stopps, who was given the job briefly over the summer of 1982 of managing the band, is remembered by Pete Trewavas as, 'a very nice bloke who went right out of his way to help Marillion.' His only problem, as Marillion manager, was his 'complete lack of experience. That's what it boiled down to . . . Dave was a great guy, and he's proved with Howard Jones, who he now manages, that he always did have it in him to really do the business for a band. But at that time he was still *learning* what being a rock manager was all about. And the trouble was we couldn't afford to wait for Dave while he was doing it, so we had to get rid of him.'

Whittled down to two main choices – the ubiquitous Peter Mensch, or the more outwardly roly-poly John Arnison – Pete Trewavas says he had no hesitation in making his own personal choice of who he thought should be the next manager of Marillion.

'I took to John immediately,' says Pete. 'He was very nice, very good-humoured, and he talked a lot of sense. He was very down to earth in his attitudes as a manager. He told us the last thing he was going to do was pump loads of money into the band upfront, that we would have to live within our means, and that if we did that he could definitely *make* plenty of money for us, get us a major deal sorted out with a label, and get us on our way in the direction we wanted to go in – which for us meant albums, long tours, and a long-term plan that didn't rely totally on hit singles and regular appearances on Top of the Pops for its success.'

With John Arnison installed as the new Marillion manager, Pete says he remembers the next few weeks leading up to signing the deal with EMI as a constant blur of fast adventures and a steady stream of solid good news.

'The first thing I remember John doing for us that won the band over to him immediately, was he came backstage after the first gig we ever played after he officially became our manager, and said: "Right boys, seeing how I'm now your manager I expect you want to know about how much money you made from the gig?" And we all said yeah, and John said well, the PA cost so much to hire, the cost of the petrol for the van came to so much, and against the fee we'd earned from the gig that left us with . . . about £35! That was, like, *each*! We couldn't believe it – we had never ended up with more than about £5 each from a gig before! So John was definitely in our good books from then on.'

The last few days leading up to Marillion's first fateful appearance, lowly though it must have seemed to some, at the twenty-second Reading Rock Festival, held over the Bank Holiday Weekend in August 1982, Pete remembers spending in a nervous state of tension he describes as being 'like a mixture between barely contained excitement and paralysing *fear*'. The band's appearance at the Theakston's Festival, which they used as a warm-up for the following day's intended showcase at Reading, Pete says was 'a sheer bloody nightmare!'

'Honestly, I think it took us until about half-way through the set to get everything sorted out . . . I don't think anybody could hear Fish for the first three numbers! It was a terrible scene . . . The audience sort of bored already, not knowing why we sounded so dreadful, us screaming at the roadies and tearing our hair out, and all the time Ian Anderson still standing there *watching* us screw up! It was like, thank you very much God!

'Yeah . . . it was a nightmare, the actual gig. Which was a shame, because the actual Lord Theakston and his family seemed like really nice people. They were in it just because they liked the music and wanted people to have a good time. Which is amazingly nice considering the destruction to their property and grounds the festival would have been responsible for. Even inadvertently, the fact of 20,000 or so people suddenly arriving for three days in your back garden is bound to leave someone a hell of a mess to clear up afterwards.'

Pete says he sometimes wonders though whether the nightmare of Theakston's was simply part of the price the band would have to pay for the daydream come true that the following afternoon's appearance at Reading would prove to be.

Backstage at the Reading Festival for the first time the following afternoon, Pete Trewavas says he remembers the place positively 'breathing of big business and bucks! Everybody was talking about making it and being in the right place at the right time, which is exactly what we felt we were.

'We all went on stage that day determined to be brilliant! We just *willed* it to happen for us! And the press we got as a result of that one apperance at Reading that year was unbelievable . . . Honestly, more people "discovered" Marillion that day than I can remember! Suddenly everybody seemed to want to be on our side . . . I thought, great! We could do with some rich friends,' he chortles.

A small Aylesbury home-coming dream was about to come true.

9

The Morning Mare Rides!

The Hervis Hotel in Berlin, West Germany, April 1985. It's five o'clock in the morning again. Outside, night falters and recedes beneath the first grey light of dawn. It looks like the beginnings of another cold spring day here in Berlin. Inside, in room 205, Fish pours himself another whiskey, punches the 'start' button on the portable tape-deck he's had installed in the room, then lies back on the bed listening, a hard smile cracking his face. '*Strung out, under a necklace of carnival lights/Cold moon, held on the crest of the night . . .*'

The music, ethereal and piquant, floats like smoke rings clouding the air. It's an unmixed passage from the finished *Misplaced Childhood* recording, the 'best and most important album we've ever done!' says Fish, the light dancing in his eyes.

For the last six weeks, Marillion have been recording at Hansa Studios, by the Wall. Now the hard work is almost over; only the final mix remains. To describe the band's mood at this point as 'confident' would be an act of gross understatement. Reclined on his bed, crooning along to the sound of his own voice wafting from the tiny portable speakers set up on his bedside table, Fish has the slightly indecent, distanced look of a man who has somehow been allowed a privileged glimpse into his own future and not found it wanting.

'I just can't wait to take this album out on the road,' he grins. 'It'll be a fucking monster of a show! Honestly, I don't think any of us have ever felt so excited about a new album. I mean, not only is this the best thing this band has ever done, but I think we'll have a hell of a time trying to top it. Believe me, this is the first really tall peak of our careers. If we all dropped dead tomorrow, this is what we'd be remembered for, I'm sure of it.

In the past, we'd have probably gone down in history as the weird band from Aylesbury that sounded a bit like Genesis and had a singer who used to paint his face – if that.

'But now, I promise you, that's all about to change!' the smile broadens. 'This new album is going to change everything.'

Still beating the night at its own funny games, Fish turns off the bedside lamp, lights another cigarette, tops up his glass, and goes back to lying on the bed, listening. *'A lonely stretch of headlight/Diamonds trapped in black ice/A mirror cracked along the white lines'*.

The grey Berlin dawn presses its long, empty face up against the window and looks in at him. Weak sunlight stings his eyes.

It's not late any more. It's early.

The first six weeks of 1985, Marillion had spent at Bray rehearsal studios in Surrey, finishing off the writing of the new material. Still buzzing from the excitement of their European and British tours, the work at Bray proceeded quickly and easily.

'We'd pretty much convinced ourselves that we weren't going to be talked out of making the new album conceptual,' says Mark Kelly. 'And, without really forcing things to go that way, we found working within the format of one continuous piece of music seemed to take its own logical course. We didn't force anything, it just sort of fitted together better like that.'

'We went with the flow,' says Steve Rothery, 'and we didn't hold back on ourselves like we might have done in the past. This time we didn't feel like we still had something to prove, and consequently what we were coming up with was just so much more striking than anything we'd done up until then.'

Rough demos of the new material were made, and by the end of February the search for a producer had begun. Nick Tauber would never work for the band again, that much had long ago been unanimously decided. Finding an available top-notch producer to replace him, though, proved to be more difficult than either the band or EMI had at first anticipated.

'There were quite a few names we bandied around before settling on Chris Kimsey,' says Pete Trewavas. 'There were a couple of American guys John Arnison and Hugh Stanley Clarke were in touch with, but as soon as they were told we were making a *concept* album, they all freaked out and wouldn't come near us!'

'I remember we came close to offering the job to Glyn Johns,' says Mark Kelly, 'but again, as soon as we told hm that we were deliberately going out of our way to make a concept album, that was it, he lost interest straight away. The same thing happened with Rupert Hymes, who we discussed working with for a while – the minute the words *concept album* were whispered in his ear he took off, never to be seen again!'

'Partly, these people thought we were being very boring bothering to try and make a credible concept album in 1985,' says Fish, 'but mostly, their main problem was that they couldn't see where the hit singles were going to sprout from to make the whole thing worthwhile to them. Very few of these guys turned us down on the basis that they didn't actually like what we'd written, they were just put off because they thought a concept album was too uncommercial. They weren't prepared to take a dive in at the deep end with us, and take a fucking *chance* for a change, risking everything on a gamble. What we were up to down at Bray wasn't *secure* enough for them.'

Nevertheless, Marillion stood firm. For a short time, still no closer to finding an experienced producer, the band even considered going it alone and co-producing the album with Simon Hanhart, as they had for *Real to Reel*. But the idea was soon rejected. This next album – concept or not – was too important a step to take without the steadying hand of a good heavy-weight producer to guide them through the recording.

Enter stage-right, clutching a cigar and a chilled bottle of Lanson Black Label champagne, Mr Chris Kimsey!

'Chris came down to see us while we were still working at Bray,' says Mark Kelly, 'and listened to a rough recording we'd made of what would eventually be Side One of the new album. He offered us some useful criticism and some ego-boosting praise – probably just the right amount of each. Which impressed us straight away; he was the first producer we'd seen who actually sat down with us and started talking about the music and nothing else. No reprimands for wanting to call it a concept album; no ear-ache about "Where's the hit singles?"; none of that stuff, just some solid comments about what we'd already written, enough to make us realise he wasn't bullshitting and that he was actually listening very carefully to what was going on.'

'Chris came as a real surprise to us,' says Fish. 'All we really knew about him before we met at Bray was that he'd produced a couple of albums for the Rolling Stones – one of which, *Tattoo You*, was the biggest selling album they'd released in about five years – and worked with a variety of different other people like Killing Joke, The Cult, and some of the less obscure reggae bands; he had a very diverse scope in different sorts of music. In truth, we'd had so much bad luck trying to find a new producer, I half expected Chris to come on really big time, and perhaps be a bit dismissive, as so many other people had been, about us wanting to do a concept album.

'But we sat down and started talking to him and he wasn't like that at all. He had a few interesting things to say about what we'd written so far, but he didn't push us on any points, he just said he'd be up for doing it, and left us to think about it and let him know.'

Marillion didn't have to think for long before deciding that Chris Kimsey was the man to produce their next album for them. There was, however, a slight snag involved in working with Chris: the album would have to be recorded in a studio outside of Britain. Following his highly lucrative work with the Rolling Stones, Kimsey was now obliged to live as a tax exile. Chris suggested using Hansa Studios in Berlin, by the Wall, where he had only recently been recording a new Killing Joke album.

'Apart from Fish, who really fancied the idea of working in Berlin, I think the rest of us had to think twice before agreeing to record the album abroad,' says Steve Rothery. 'It wasn't Hansa Studios we objected to so much, just the inconvenience of having to live abroad for a couple of months. We'd never worked that way on an album before. But, in the end, I think it probably worked to our advantage. We had no outside pressures at all while we were in the studio, and there just wasn't anything else to do or worry about while we were there, so all we had to think about was getting on and making the album. Being away from everybody and everything at home in England was actually quite a useful way of focusing our concentration. We got more done in less time, and with much better results, than we ever had before. It was good.'

With a new producer firmly secured and the arrangements already under way for the band to start work at Hansa Studios with Chris Kimsey at the beginning of March, EMI fixed the budget for the recording of *Misplaced Childhood* at £80,000 – five grand more than had been allowed originally for *Fugazi*, and Marillion relocated to the Hervis Hotel in Berlin, where they would remain for the next eight weeks.

'I remember when we agreed the budget with EMI they made it plain to me that they did *not* want a repeat of what happened with *Fugazi*, where we spent over twice the amount they'd originally let us have,' says John Arnison. 'But they needn't have worried. *Misplaced Childhood* turned out to be the first studio album the band had ever done that actually came in *under* budget! Not only that, but it was also the *cheapest* album they'd ever done!

'The whole thing came in at about £74,000 – six grand less than we were given by EMI, less than *Script . . .*', and half as much as *Fugazi*.

'It's ironic, really,' John smiles, 'when you stop to consider that the album that made us all the most money we'd ever seen in our lives actually cost less to make than anything we'd ever done before.'

From the beginning of March until the beginning of May, Marillion toiled away with Chris Kimsey in the studio. Most days they worked from lunchtime until late into the evening, concluding the night usually with a late dinner and, often, several drinks at any one of the number of late-night drinking clubs the producer was fond of introducing them to in Berlin.

'It was a hell of a time we were having, looking back,' says Fish. 'Working with Chris was such a pleasure. He's very together and methodical in the studio, and he never misses a trick. Unlike Nick Tauber, who would have mountains of these "great ideas" which never actually ever made it on to tape, Chris was in command of everything from the word go. There was no messing around searching for the missing guitar chord, it was just straight down to business.

'At the end of the night, though, when we were all ready to unwind, Chris really came into his own taking us around to all these glitzy drinking clubs and late-night restaurants and bars. He'd worked in Berlin before, of course, and so he enjoyed showing us around. And, of course, there was fuck all else to do back at the hotel room anyway, so he was never usually short of people in the band to go out razzling with.'

'Chris used to drive this little Honda Jazz, while we were in Berlin,' says Mark Kelly. 'And at the end of the night all six of us used to squeeze into it and go zooming off to another of these places that Chris knew. Then we'd all get totally plastered somewhere at one of these clubs. The recording engineer Chris was using, a guy called Thomas Steimler, used to come with us sometimes, too. He used to drive a clapped-out old Volvo, and I remember we were all coming out of this café one night, it must have been about four in the morning, after we'd all been drinking Tequila Gold for about the last four hours, completely pissed and raucous, and I said, "Let's do a bit of car-walking!" It was something I'd done as a kid, you know; it meant climbing up onto the roof of a car and hopping down the street from bonnet to bonnet – a quite horrendous thing to do to somebody's car, of course, but we were all so drunk I think we were game for anything by then.

'Anyway, all that happened was that me and Fish and Thomas ended up dancing up and down like lunatics on top of Thomas' poor old Volvo. And then the roof and bonnet started caving in! We were literally mangling the car to pieces, all mad drunk and raving, laughing our silly heads off, not realising what damage we were doing to Thomas' car.

'And then somebody started throwing eggs at us!' he laughs. 'So we finally got down off the car, and that's when we saw what we'd done.

'I don't think poor old Thomas knew whether to laugh or cry. He drove us back to the hotel in it, though.'

Berlin wasn't just all about drowning the small hours in a bath of Tequila Gold, of course. There were also the daylight hours to be seen to, as well.

'The thing about that period we spent recording *Misplaced* . . .,' says Fish, 'is that it was a bit like being in a space capsule. We used to eat, sleep, and breathe the album twenty-four hours a day. There was no respite from it. It wasn't like in the past where we could always knock off and go home if we wanted to, or see friends and relax on the days when you're not actually needed in the studio, stuff like that.

'In Berlin we were cocooned in the whole thing. There were absolutely *no* distractions . . . German TV is boring, nobody could read the newspapers, and it just felt like we were completely cut off from the rest of the world for about two months. And, of course, being the infamous walled-in city, living in Berlin produces its own kind of claustrophobic vibe anyway. That, and the heavy turns the music was starting to make, meant that we were living the album in every sense possible.

'By day we'd work until we were ready to drop in the studio; then at night we'd run like dogs to the nearest bar. How else do you expel all the tensions at two in the morning after another twelve hours in the studio? The album was starting to sound awesome, and there was no way you could go back to the hotel and sit quietly reading a book after another day of trying to get to grips with it in the studio. Everything was charged with adrenalin, and sometimes we needed to burn it off.'

As was customary by now, once the hard bulk of the recording had been accomplished, the first track Chris Kimsey mixed was to be the first single from the album, 'Kayleigh'. Although ostensibly produced as one, long continuous piece, the album could be broken down into as many as nineteen different 'parts', with at least six different discernible 'songs' featured throughout. Selecting 'Kayleigh' as a single presented neither Kimsey nor the band with any technical problems; the producer simply lifted it clean out of the mix, cut Steve Rothery's guitar break in the middle by about thirty seconds, and added plenty of post-production spit and polish.

'I don't think anyone had quite realised how commercial "Kayleigh" was beginning to sound until Chris played us the final mix before it went out as the first single,' says Ian Mosley. 'I mean, we knew we had a really good song on our hands there, but listening to it in the studio just after it had been mixed, I was really bowled over; it sounded great! Like something *really* special. Every time I listened to it I got a great big stupid grin on my face! It was just, well, really catchy! It got under your skin straight away; it was played really well, had great lyrics, and it sounded like a song anybody could cover, it really stood up on its own. I think we all felt very proud.'

The B side, of course, was 'Lady Nina'; named after another of the notorious Berlin night-spots Fish had attempted to lead various members of the band and their entourage astray in after another sweaty day and night in the studio.

' "Lady Nina" started out as our idea of a joke,' says Mark Kelly. 'We didn't want to lift something else off the album for the B side, we wanted to keep as much of the album a surprise as possible. But we hadn't actually got anything else written that we could use.

'And then Ian came up with this drum pattern on a little drum-machine in the studio one night and we all ended up trying to write a song around it. I don't think any of us really knew what we were doing. We just sort of cobbled it together as quickly as we could and got Chris to try and do something with it in the mix. It was amazing that it turned out as well as it did.'

So well did 'Lady Nina' turn out, in fact, that more than one voice at EMI casually suggested it might even make a better choice of single than 'Kayleigh'; and Capitol Records in America were also quick to point out the commercial potential of the number, even going so far as to suggest it might make an interesting additional track on the album.

'There was absolutely no way we were going to let that happen, though,' says Steve Rothery. '*Misplaced Childhood* was a completely separate entity, a law unto itself almost, and sticking "Lady Nina" on at the end just to please the American record company would have been a ludicrous thing to do. It would have ruined everything that we'd been working so hard to achieve.'

'It was a groovy little track, though,' smiles Fish. 'It's far too throw-away, of course, to be taken too seriously – a bit like Marillion doing their Euro-disco bit, but for all that it still has a certain swagger to it which gives the track bite.

'It was never a single in a million years though, not in my opinion,' he goes on, 'and not while we had a real flag-waver for the album like "Kayleigh" that we could put out. As far as me and the rest of the band were concerned, "Kayleigh" was the one that should be the single and to hell with what anyone else said!'

'Kayleigh' became the sixth Marillion single to be released by EMI, on Tuesday 7 May, 1985. The band were still in Berlin, engrossed in the final mix of the album, but everybody admits to being cautiously optimistic about the chances of their new single becoming a success.

'If you'd told me that we were about to have our first Top 10 single, though, I honestly don't think I would have believed you,' says Pete Trewavas. 'A successful single to us in those days meant sticking our nose into the UK Top 20 for a couple of weeks, then dropping down again. But I think we all secretly felt that if ever we *were* going to do better than that, then "Kayleigh" was probably the record to do it for us. I mean, if that wasn't a hit single, then nothing we ever did would be.'

Nobody in Marillion was prepared for what happened next. Within a week of release, 'Kayleigh' had shot straight into the UK charts at fifteen! The highest chart placing of any previous Marillion single had only been sixteen, where 'Garden Party' had resided for one week in the summer of 1983. The band were overjoyed.

'Of course, we were all still convinced that it would probably do like most of our singles and go down a couple of notches the following week,' says Steve Rothery, 'but the fact that it had gone in so high meant that we immediately felt vindicated for sticking to our guns about the album, and doing things just the way *we* wanted them done.'

The following week, however, 'Kayleigh' broke all the rules: not only did the record not go down, as expected, it actually climbed eight places higher in the chart to number seven! It was the first time a Marillion single had ever burst the bubble of the UK Top 10, and this time the band were astonished.

So, too, were EMI, who hurriedly arranged for a lunchtime reception to be held in the band's honour to celebrate the unexpected success of their new single, at Ronnie Scott's famous jazz club, in Frith Street, London. With the final mix of the rest of the new album now complete, the band flew in from Berlin, with the *Misplaced Childhood* master-tapes safely in tow, especially for the occasion.

There was much to celebrate. Only the day before they left Berlin for the very last time, the new UK singles chart had been announced. Despite already being informed by EMI that 'Kayleigh' was selling up to 25,000 copies *a day* in Britain alone, most days of the week, the majority of the band remained sceptical about their chances of the record getting any higher in the UK Top 10.

But 'Kayleigh' had jumped another three hurdles and shot up to number four!

'I remember we had the champagne all laid on, just in case "Kayleigh" surprised us all and actually did go a bit higher in the charts,' says Mark Kelly.

'And then, of course, as soon as we heard the news that it had gone up to number four, we all started jumping up and down and cheering and going completely over the top! Everybody was walking around and saying "I *told* you so!" and "Next stop number one!" We had an outrageous champagne binge to celebrate.'

'Kayleigh' hit the British charts like a bolt from out of the blue. It was a classic single that, like so many great records of its ilk, transcended critical analysis, striking like queer lightning into the quirky and unpredictable domains of mass public appeal.

'Kayleigh' was for Marillion what, say, 'Maggie May' had been for Rod Stewart; what 'Layla' was for Eric Clapton; even, in more recent times, what 'Roxanne' proved to be for the Police; or 'Sultans of Swing' for Dire Straits – a hit single so huge it became almost their theme tune, an international calling-card to fame and wealth.

Across Europe, too, 'Kayleigh' was already repeating its fabulous success, becoming a Top 10 hit in a dozen different countries: from the shabby beach-side discos of the Mediterranean to the suave, mirror-walled nightclubs of Paris, Munich, and Amsterdam, 'Kayleigh' assumed the status of the first big summer hit of 1985. You couldn't escape from it. In Britain, by the middle of June, it had become the most popular record played on national day-time radio, and TV companies not just in Britain but all over the continent suddenly started clamouring for the band to appear on their shows.

A video for 'Kayleigh' had been shot in Berlin, while the band were still ensconced at Hansa Studios. Directed by Clive Richardson – a new face in the Marillion camp – the 'Kayleigh' video is one of the more impressive examples of the band's work in this genre. At bottom, a straight performance piece shot 'live' in the studio, the video is cut-through with shots of Fish hovering mournfully around the drab grey streets of Berlin, singing his maudlin heart out.

However, there were two extra faces featured in the video that would figure again later, with varying degrees of significance, in the Marillion story. The first was that of a very young man called Robert Mead, whose face had first been seen adorning the sleeve of the 'Kayleigh' single, where Mark Wilkinson had captured him in warm oils, mid-act, drawing one of those *chalk hearts melting on a playground wall*' Fish sings about in the first line of the song.

The twelve-year-old son of a local publican, who ran the bar Mark liked to spend most of his spare evenings in, Robert Mead would also later crop up as the main portrait on the forthcoming *Misplaced Childhood* sleeve Mark was still working on. In the meantime, Robert opened the 'Kayleigh' video with a shot of him, large brown eyes darting back over his shoulder at the camera, again drawing a chalk heart, only this time the 'playground wall' imagery of the lyric is replaced by the more wanton symbolism of the Berlin Wall. And then, later into the video, Robert gets to trade lines with Fish as the camera juxtaposes each of them against the grey graffitied backdrops of a crumbling and malign cityscape.

'He was a great little kid,' says Fish. 'Mark Wilkinson had used him to model for all the *Misplaced Childhood* artwork he was producing. Robert's face had such a perfect expression of wide-eyed innocence, and he was at just the right half-man half-child stage in his physical development, that he was *perfect* for what Mark and the band had in mind for the album sleeve. And his sombre little face popping up all the time in the "Kayleigh" video was a beautiful touch. He was a natural in front of the camera.'

The other face in the video that was to make a lasting impression amongst the Marillion fans in general, and Fish in particular, belonged to a beautiful young German woman called Tamara Nowy – 'Tammy' to her friends.

Ironically, in the video it's Tammy's job to play the part of 'Kayleigh', staring cow-eyed up at Fish through the railings of a fence, across an empty wind-swept square, or just as a pretty face drifting in and out of focus under a veil of glycerine tears. I say ironic because Tammy was already on her way to becoming the new love in Fish's life. Here was the singer at his most pained and thoughtful, singing about the real-life girl who first broke his heart to the girl he would eventually marry.

However, in May 1985 in Berlin, their love affair was only a few evenings old and any irony that might be found now in the 'Kayleigh' video is, as Fish explains, purely accidental.

'Tammy used to work in one of those mega-expensive, ultra-hip nightclubs in Berlin that Chris Kimsey had taken us to,' he says. 'That's where I spotted her. She was blond and stunningly attractive. But she used to hang out with a very rich crowd, very monied people, and at first I found it difficult to get to know her. But the fact that she seemed to unattainable only spurred me on to keep trying.

'Eventually, though, I managed to break down her defences and we had a couple of dates together. What happened with the "Kayleigh" video was that originally the director had hired a professional model to do the shots in the street with me. Then at the last minute she got sick or something and couldn't make it. It was really short notice, and the director was panicking trying to find another girl, so I suggested using Tammy. Not because she was my girlfriend – we'd only just met a couple of weeks before – but because she had a model's good looks, she definitely looked right for the part we had in mind, and I knew I could get hold of her at short notice.

'It wasn't until much later that we started getting serious about each other. But so what, anyway? Life is always full of irony and coincidence and strange little harbingers of the future. If as a band we can reflect that in our music, then why not in our videos, occasionally? It's all good meat for the pot, isn't it?'

By the end of June, 'Kayleigh' was still overtaking everybody's expectations. From four in the UK charts, the record had continued unabated to the number three position, and then, finally, to the number two spot, where it lay for a fortnight, burning holes in the Top 10.

For a very short period, Marillion thought they might even be on for their first number one single, but that wasn't to be. The band could console themselves though with the knowledge that they hadn't been beaten to the very top by another musical act, but by a charity raising money for the families of the victims of the Bradford City football ground fire disaster.

'The club had put a special one-off single out, with all the guys in the team, plus a lot of more famous footballers from other clubs, all singing along. All the money raised by the record went straight to the people who were affected by the fire,' says Mark Kelly. 'So, really, if we were going to get beaten to the number one spot, it couldn't have been to a better record. Under the circumstances, I don't think we had any right to feel disappointed.'

'We'd done well enough out of "Kayleigh" 's success, anyway,' says Pete Trewavas. 'It may not have actually reached number one, but technically, we were still the top-selling band in the singles charts for two weeks, and the radio never stopped playing it. Number one, or number two, it didn't matter any more, by then it seemed like the whole world was going bonkers for "Kayleigh". We were just trying to keep up with everything.'

June 1985 was nothing but busy. With 'Kayleigh' still working its charms to such devastating effect on the charts, the band had fitted in TV appearances on Top of the Pops and Wogan with an increasingly hectic schedule of press and radio interviews, all of which they managed to sandwich in between some sporadic last-minute rehearsals for the first round of live dates that John Arnison had arranged for them in Europe.

Misplaced Childhood was due out any day now, and in the space of four weeks Marillion had picked up front-cover stories in *Kerrang!*, *Sounds*, *Record Mirror*, and the *Melody Maker*. EMI had pushed their publicity machine into overdrive for the coming Marillion album. And not just in Britain, but in Europe, too, where 'Kayleigh' was continuing to storm the charts.

'Suddenly, the world seemed to have gone mad for Marillion!' cries Fish. 'With the album about to come out what we would have liked to have been doing was getting ready for the next tour, trying to get a really good show together. But there was no time to pause and think about *anything* . . . It was all getting *extremely* hectic for us. John had already pencilled-in some dates for us in Europe, in June, but in the meantime we set off on this sort of mega-promotional tour of Europe, flying all over the place like lunatics doing TV appearances and radio and press interviews.'

'It was an amazingly busy time for us,' Mark Kelly confirms. 'Where normally we would have been focusing all our attention on the album coming out and getting ready to go on the road, with "Kayleigh" still happening in a big way in so many different places, we ended up bouncing like yo-yos around the continent. Honestly, it got to a ridiculous stage where we were taking three flights a day, trying to cram in as many of these media things as possible. We used to split up into pairs and all go off and do about a dozen interviews each.'

'We couldn't complain, though,' smiles Ian Mosley. 'I mean, it's always nice to be in demand, isn't it? Although, personally, I must admit it was a bit of a relief when we got back to playing a few gigs.'

From 5 June until 19 June, Marillion flitted from one gig to the next in Spain, Portugal, France, and Italy. The full show, featuring the *Misplaced Childhood* set-piece in its entirety, that the band would carry around the world with them for the next twelve months, evolved slowly over the space of those first dozen concerts.

At first, only Side One of the new album was premiered live, but as time wore on and their fans grew more familiar with the new material following the release of the album, the band grew more adventurous, discarding older favourites from the set like 'Assassing', 'Forgotten Sons', 'Punch And Judy', and 'He Knows You Know' to make way for the full uninterrupted performance of the album that would do so much to alter the course of all their lives.

One other important change to the steadily-growing Marillion show was that Fish had suddenly started appearing on stage *without* his make-up!

'Again, it was all part of a conscious need I had to want to break with the past totally,' he explains. 'So much had changed about the band, and in my personal life, since we'd recorded *Fugazi*, it was a different world we were inhabiting now. We'd grown about 100 times more confident, the band was playing better than at any time before, I thought I was singing better than I ever had before, and I just felt that we had moved on so much the make-up, and some of the props I'd been using, just felt like old hat suddenly.

'I remember we were in Madrid for one of the first gigs, I'd started putting on the make-up in front of a mirror, and I suddenly thought, "Why am I bothering to do this any more? This is boring the pants off me!" I was overwhelmed with a feeling of total lethargy, looking at this grotesquely painted face staring back at me in the mirror . . . It was *depressing*,' he shudders.

'So for the first couple of gigs I used to come on stage with the face make-up still intact, but when I went off stage to change before we went into *Misplaced Childhood* I used to wipe all the make-up off with a towel, then come back out on stage and do the rest of the show straight. By about the fourth or fifth gig, though, I didn't even bother to do that. I'd decided the time was right to finally unmask this jester and let the world have a good look at his face for a change. Or at least enough to let them know the true colour of his eyes,' he smiles, enigmatically.

Misplaced Childhood was released on Monday 17 June 1985. Accompanied by a fanfare of brilliant reviews, the album rocketed into the number one position on its first week of release!

'We had been told that on pre-order sales alone we stood a very good chance of *Misplaced* . . . going straight in at number one,' says Steve Rothery. 'So we were all pretty excited the day the charts were announced, waiting to hear how high we'd actually gone. But there's a world of difference between being told that you *might* have a number one album, and being told that you *have* got a number one album. When we heard we went mad! It was just such a dream come true! I think we were all walking on air for about the next three weeks.'

'It's funny, though,' says Fish, 'when you're still a kid you sit there and dream about what it must be like to be told your new album has just gone straight in at number one in the charts . . . *your* album . . . *number fucking one*! Then when it happened to me it just didn't seem real. I couldn't quite get to grips with what it

241

meant. I don't think I stopped drinking for a week, it was just one party after another that first week, but once we'd all calmed down a bit, I still couldn't quite figure out what it meant. One thing I *had* decided though; whatever the fuck it all meant, it *felt* great!'

'The most striking thing of all, for me, was the timing of the whole thing,' says Mark Kelly. 'So many bands have had tremendously successful albums which aren't necessarily the best they might have ever done. I mean, there always seems to be a sense of assimilation, of somehow blanding-out, when most bands have got to the stage where they're having really mega-successful albums. Whereas, with us, I don't think anyone could accuse us of blanding-out, or allowing our material to be assimilated into a more commercial format.'

And he is right, of course. Not only was *Misplaced Childhood* easily their most successful album to date, it was just as easily their most remarkable musical creation yet.

It had it all: drama, mystery, pathos, a stinging wit, and a musical verve and dynamic to surpass anything from their recent past, *Misplaced Childhood* brims over with an illicit confection of charms. In keeping with the spirit of the piece, it would be unfair, not to mention unwieldy, for me to attempt to break down the album into its multitude of movable parts. However, it is fair to say that *Misplaced Childhood* is an album absolutely *crammed* with highlights.

From the opening mists of Mark Kelly's synthesisers that come creeping like a ghost into the room at the start of 'Pseudo Silk Kimono', to the bent and breathless leg-kicking finale of 'White Feather', the guitars on fire, the percussion machine-gunning the horizon, Fish crying, '*I won't walk away no more!*' in a voice that echoes like a tomb, from A to Z and back again, Marillion blaze a compelling trail few other bands would have the imagination even to consider emulating. This was not the world of the three-minute pop song Marillion had brought their fans to on *Misplaced Childhood*, this was a maze booby-trapped by emotional minefields, full of uncertain origins, with all the escape doors concealed. Any hit singles to be found here are merely the precious stones studded in an otherwise war-torn and emotionally ravaged landscape.

Taken literally, the lyrics Fish has written could be described as almost too pointedly autobiographical; 'Kayleigh', 'Heart of Lothian', 'Lords of the Backstage', 'White Feather', the words to

242

all relate to intimate personal experiences Fish has had. Indeed, on the inside of the sleeve all lyrics are credited to Fish *and* Derek W. Dick.

But then, why not? His unique talents as a singer, writer, and performer do not make Fish any less of a human being. His problems, his visions, his dreams, are not that much different from our own. His ways of dealing with those things may not always be so conventional, and perhaps that is why he is such a charismatic figure to his followers, but in the main his lyrics here transform whatever lunacy may have scarred parts of his personal life into an artistic rite-of-passage; as accessible as any gutter, and lit by the rays of a glowering, idiot moon. *Misplaced Childhood* was a masterpiece of fact and fiction mangled in together, a collision of stars. Unravelling its clues was all part of the fun.

Musically, Marillion have never sounded more commanding. Steve Rothery's guitar playing is superbly lyrical throughout, shimmering like a cold blue light on the haunting 'Bitter Suite' section, or humming like a wire on the spine-tingling intro to 'Childhood's End?'. The entire band, in fact, play with a tireless inventiveness. At different moments they all take turns to reach out from the shadows with a blinding display of dexterity, passion, and panache.

At last, with *Misplaced Childhood* sitting pretty at number one in the charts, the odious questions of plagiarism could no longer be safely levelled at Marillion. The very idea that this was 'just another Genesis rip-off' became absurd. No longer could the critics accuse the band of stealing anything from anybody. The praise and recognition that one Marillion album had received put them way out ahead of the rest of the field.

Mark Wilkinson's sleeve illustration is a beautifully crafted, deceptively simple affair. Again, it's a gatefold sleeve that folds out to reveal another typically surreal Wilkinson painting. The front of the cover is devoted to the figure of Robert Mead in his role as Fish's 'half-man half-child', dressed in an ornately fastened red cavalry tunic with a small scarlet heart pinned to his breast.

The figure of the 'child' is juxtaposed against an impression-istic backdrop of swirling clouds gathering with a muted fury in the distance. On his right arm sits perched the first of two chattering magpies depicted in the scene; at his feet lies a discarded wedding ring, and, close by, a poppy. Behind him, from deep within the clouds, a giant rainbow arches its marvellous back, connecting the front of the cover to the rear. There we see, at last, the familiar figure of the Jester, clad in his rainbow-coloured glad-rags, taking a running leap through a window. A caged chameleon looks on, mouth agape, eyes blank; perched on top of the cage is a second magpie (one for sorrow, two for mirth . . .), a stolen key dangling from its beak. And in the foreground Mark has painted a vacuum, shaped like a jigsaw missing the last piece.

The symbolism isn't quite so literal as on either *Script . . .* or *Fugazi*, though the setting is less cluttered, more lavishly represented. Gone is the simple-minded innocent in the belled-cap we were introduced to on the first album; gone, too, is the decadent anti-life rock star with a head full of bad dreams we get to know on the second album. To be replaced with . . . what? A son? The bastard off-spring of a seed turned bad? A guilty secret from the unknown past unearthed to reveal the certain future?

It's your guess.

With the considerable success Marillion were now enjoying in the UK charts, the music press were no longer the only media pursuing the band for interviews: Fleet Street were suddenly interested.

'We'd always done reasonably well with getting the band into the daily newspapers,' says Brian Munns, head of press at EMI. 'But, of course, it wasn't until "Kayleigh" was such a massive hit that the Fleet Street papers really started fighting for an interview with them.'

The *Daily Mirror* was first into the chase, sending its top pop reporter, John Blake, out to Milan in June to catch the band live and secure an 'exclusive' interview with Fish.

The story appeared, as a double-page centre spread, in the *Daily Mirror*, 20 June 1985. Under a headline that read: 'FISH HOOKED – the True Story of a Dream Girl Who Inspired A Hit!'

'I must admit, I was extremely pleased with the story John Blake wrote,' says Brian Munns. 'But the band didn't like it at all! Their main objection was to the lack of emphasis on the band's music, and so much of the focus being turned on Fish's old love-affair with Kay. But that's just the way Fleet Stret works. They simply don't write about music *per se*. They leave all that to the music papers. But for Fleet Street, especially when you consider some of the sick stories they do try and carry about other pop stars, I thought the *Daily Mirror* piece on Marillion was really very good. And coming just three days after the album was released, the publicity it brought them couldn't have been better timed.'

'We should have known better, of course,' admits Fish, 'but I really thought the piece was cheap. The Story of a Dream Girl Who Inspired A Hit! God, it just made the whole thing seem so shabby. After that, whenever anyone asked me about who Kay was, or anything about her, I just used to clam up. I didn't want the real sentiment behind the song to be robbed of its dignity. I don't think I've talked to Fleet Street more than once or twice since then. And looking at the way some of the tabloids have treated people like Boy George, or Elton John, recently, I think that's been a wise move.'

In July, Marillion retreated into Abbey Road Studios in London, again with producer Chris Kimsey, and spent a week writing and recording a new track, 'Freaks', which the band had decided they needed to go out as the B side to the follow-up single to 'Kayleigh' EMI had urgently requested they prepare for a release at the end of August, ready to coincide with the next full-scale UK tour scheduled to start in September.

'Lavender' was the logical choice as the second track to be lifted from the new album as a single. With its big pop choruses, zinging guitars and soaring lead vocals, 'Lavender' was like Burt Bacharach meets the blues: commercial as hell, but with a kick like a mule.

' "Lavender" was actually one of the last tracks we decided to include on the album,' says Mark Kelly. 'We didn't really consider it strong enough at first. Then as we put a bit more work into it, it suddenly sounded really promising . . . very Beatle-ish in places, I suppose,' he smiles, 'all those ringing guitars and what have you, and so, after "Kayleigh", "Lavender" became the next most obvious choice as single.

'The B side, though, "Freaks", I didn't regard as one of our better numbers,' Mark goes on. 'It was just a bit too throw-away for me, like "Lady Nina". Although, if you ask Fish, he'll probably tell you he really likes that one, because the lyrics on it are good. For me, though, it was only half a number; a good B side, and not much more.'

As the band and EMI had hoped, 'Lavender' made for a

delightful late summer single. With some additional guitar added to extend the length of the song by an extra forty-five seconds, and packaged in another splendidly evocative Mark Wilkinson sleeve design, 'Lavender' was released on Tuesday 27 August 1985. It became a hit almost immediately, peaking at number five in the UK charts three weeks later. Before that, however, Marillion announced that they would be playing on the bill at that year's Castle Donington Rock Festival, on 17 August.

Held annually in the Midlands of England, next-door to the famous Donington race-track, the Castle Donington Festival had effectively replaced the old Reading Festival as the year's major outdoor rock event. Headlining the bill in 1985 were ZZ Top; second on the bill and publicised as Special Guests were Marillion. Sixty-five thousand people were expected to show up that day, and it would be the first time the band had appeared live in Britain since the current mad rush of success had begun three months before.

Marillion say they couldn't wait to get out there.

'It was a very big day for us,' says Steve Rothery. 'The moment we walked on stage the crowd just all got on their feet and started cheering. I'd never seen anything like it. Playing second on the bill at Reading two years before had been similar, but this time everybody really had an excuse to go mad and really enjoy themselves. A number two single and number one album had probably gone to the fans' heads much more than to our own, and everybody just started going *wild* the moment we came on . . . It was like the return of the conquering heroes!' he laughs.

As they had been doing during their brief jaunt around Europe promoting 'Kayleigh' in June, the band performed only Side One of the new album. The rest of the evening was lost in a celebratory romp through an array of good solid crowd pleasers . . . 'Script . . .', 'Assassing', 'Garden Party', 'Fugazi' . . . And, of course, as was now the rule, Fish wore no make-up: dressed in a simple black and white track-suit, a white sweat-band over his brow, and with just the beginnings of a beard starting to show around the mouth, the singer led the band through a tremendous performance that left the critics grasping for new superlatives.

'Goddamn, but they're sure going to be a hard act to follow!' one of the ZZ Top aides was overheard to comment.

And he was right. Goddamn, but they *were* a hard act to follow! As a result ZZ Top's set, though sprightly enough and generally well received, lacked passion and attack. And the spark had all but gone out of the Donington crowd. They'd given it all away to Marillion.

The full *Misplaced Childhood* British tour was due to kick off with two concerts in Dublin on 4 and 5 September. Initially, there were seventeen dates booked, including four consecutive nights at the Hammersmith Odeon in London, with the possibility of second nights in over half the venues left open as an option they were almost certain to pick up.

Every ticket had been sold weeks before Marillion had begun the tour, and with the success of 'Lavender' in the singles charts now forcing the band into a further round of TV, radio and press engagements, expectations for the success of the tour were running high. However, disaster was to strike on the eve of the Hammersmith Odeon dates, which opened the English leg of the tour, forcing Marillion to scrap the entire date-sheet.

Fish had lost his voice. Only temporarily, *this* time, said the doctor. But unless the singer wanted to continue having permanent problems with his singing voice, he would have to rest it completely for three weeks: meaning no *talking*, let alone singing; and certainly no cigarettes and alcohol.

'The problems started on the very first date in Dublin,' says Fish. 'My voice just cracked every time I tried to reach a high note, and by the end of the night I had a horrible sore throat. At first I thought I might be coming down with flu or something, but then in Belfast on the third night, it went completely in the middle of the set. I couldn't hit a note; the voice had gone, all that remained was this burnt-out croak.

'Why it went when it did, I put down to two reasons. The first and probably most important reason is that John Arnison and myself had spent the week before the British tour started out in Japan. The band had been invited over for our first tour of Japan in November; in the meantime they asked if I would go out there at the end of August and do some interviews and promotional work to publicise the release of the new album and the announcement of our first tour there.

'Naturally, I was really looking forward to it, never having been to Japan before. I thought it was going to be seven days of saki and geisha girls and trips to Hiroshima,' he chuckles, 'but all I did for ten hours a day every single day we were there was talk to journalists. I was still out of my mind with jet-lag for the first forty-eight hours; talking to hundreds of these Japanese journalists through the aid of an interpreter. Honestly, I'd be having these big three-way conversations, two thirds of which was in Japanese, and by the end of the week I was starting to get *brain damage*.

'Then, the moment it was over, me and John were back on a plane for another twenty-four hour flight straight to Dublin, where the rest of the band were already rehearsing, for the first gig of the tour! I was totally exhausted when I got there, and probably the last thing my voice needed was to be stretched through three shows on the trot.

'What didn't help at all, though,' Fish goes on, 'and the other big reason why I think my voice went that time, is that I should have been smart enough to pay attention to the tell-tale signs that my voice, my whole body, needed rest after I had so many problems at the first gig. Instead, I went out razzling with some of the guys from Spandau Ballet and Def Leppard, who were all living in Dublin in tax exile from Britain at the time. We used to hit the clubs together every night I was there. By the time we got to Belfast, I was ready to collapse. Something had to give, I suppose. And I ended up paying for my sins by losing the use of my voice for a month!'

However, despite the initial panic about having to blow out the British tour, all was not completely lost. John Arnison moved like lightning to get the entire tour re-scheduled for the beginning of the New Year; and as a precursor to the tour proper, the band announced that they would play seven special Christmas shows in Britain in December, including their first headline appearance at the vast 12,000-seater capacity NEC building in Birmingham.

And there was one last little surprise Marillion had in store for some of their disappointed fans; the night before the first Hammersmith Odeon concert, Marillion had planned to play a special one-off show for fan-club members only at the Marquee. Initially, following the results of Fish's visit to a Harley Street throat specialist, John Arnison had reluctantly advised the band to pull out of the gig.

'We only got the news about Fish's voice the afternoon we were supposed to be sound checking for the gig, though,' says Ian Mosley. 'And there were already hundreds of kids from the fan-club queuing outside the Marquee waiting to get in. We didn't know what to do. We didn't want to send them away again with nothing but an apology.

'Then John Arnison asked me if I could perform a drum clinic on-stage, just to keep people entertained for half an hour. I agreed, and then Pete said he might get up and have a jam about with me; and then Steve and Mark said they'd get up as well. And then Fish said, "Look, if everybody else is getting up on stage, *I* might as well get up there, too. I won't have to do any singing anyway, the kids can do it all." So we said, OK, great, and that's what we did.'

At 9.30, as planned, Marillion marched on stage at the Marquee for the first time since the foggy early days of 1982, when headlining there still meant everything.

'I have an announcement to make!' cried Fish, stifling the deafening roars of approval as the band shuffled into position on the tiny Marquee stage. Patiently, he explained about the cancellation of the British tour, and about his damaged voice.

He ended by saying, 'I'm not going to be doing any singing tonight, instead I want you all to help me out . . . Will ya do that?'

He didn't have to ask twice; the Marquee almost exploded!

'All right!' he said, 'we're gonna do four numbers and then we walk . . . this is the hit single . . .'

Steve Rothery hit the opening magic notes to 'Kayleigh', and 500 voices at the Marquee roared out the first verse in perfect time: *'Do you remember/Chalk hearts melting on a playground wall!'*

It was an unbelievable sound. The band played like hungry tigers, the Marquee sang its bottomless heart out, and Fish just stood there grinning and clapping his hands. 'Kayleigh', 'Lavender', 'Script for a Jester's Tear', 'Garden Party', even a wild thrash at David Bowie's 'The Jean Genie'. Marillion and the Marquee had the whole thing down pat.

They always had.

With September cancelled while Fish obeyed his doctors and rested his voice, the band consoled themselves with another appearance on Top of the Pops miming to 'Lavender', Fish holding up sheets of paper with the lyrics written on them so that, in echo of the recent Marquee date, the Top of the Pops audience could sing the words for themselves.

In America, 'Kayleigh' and *Misplaced Childhood*, which had both just been released to surprisingly good reactions from the media, had entered the Billboard Hot 100 with a bullet. And back home in England, John Arnison was plotting Marillion's most ambitious European tour yet, ready to begin as soon as Fish was, the first week in October 1985.

'September was *unbearably* quiet, almost *disturbingly* peaceful,' moans Fish. 'We were forced into total idleness while all over the world our records were starting to become big hits. I thought the days would never pass before my voice had mended and we could get back out there on the road.'

He didn't have to wait long. On Wednesday, 9 October, Marillion began a seven-week, fifty-date tour of Europe, at the Asker Hall in Oslo, Norway. For the next two months they would be performing nightly at some of the biggest halls on the continent, taking in eight different countries, in all of which both 'Kayleigh' and *Misplaced Childhood* had been monster hits.

'It was the most intense tour, and certainly the most successful we had done up to then,' says Fish. 'We started out in theatres that held about 4,000 or 5,000 people, which was amazing enough, but then, by the time we got into West Germany, where the singles and album had been *mega*, suddenly we were playing regularly in halls that held between 10 and 15,000 a night!

'It was an amazing period for us, and the confidence in the band was soaring. All the success had done was make us so supremely confident in what we were doing now that we ended up giving some of the best performances of our career. We were riding on the crest of a wave and it just felt like we were unstoppable!'

Oslo, Stockholm, Copenhagen, Lausanne, Rome, Milan, Strasbourg, Brussels, Paris, and ending with the seventeen dates that would sell enough tickets to make Marillion West Germany's top touring act of 1985, everywhere the band pitched their tent, people, mostly very young people, arrived in their tens of thousands to watch them do it.

'It was a bit like – they went out there nobodies, and came back STARS!' laughs Pete Trewavas. 'Honestly, it was ridiculous. We couldn't walk down the street in Germany because we'd get mobbed! It was weird. I don't think any of us had ever been mobbed before. And particularly Fish, of course, being the singer and the frontman, he couldn't show his face anywhere in Germany without starting a riot!'

So heavy was the attention that Fish and Marillion were receiving in places in Europe, Fish was persuaded for a time to hire a personal bodyguard.

'I did it for my own protection,' he says. 'Because of the way some of the kids interpret my lyrics, I started getting an awful lot of weirdos trying to get in contact with me. Mostly, they were just sincere people interested in what I thought about different things. But just occasionally, I got a vibe when I walked into a place, a bar or somewhere that I might like to go after the show some nights, and immediately my sixth sense would start sending me the danger signals. Some of it had to be just plain old paranoia, of course, I realise that. But you know what they say about paranoids.'

Marillion's last show in Europe, their fiftieth of the tour, was at the giant Stadhalle, in Furth, West Germany, on 28 November. In Britain, Marillion's third single from the *Misplaced Childhood* album, 'Heart of Lothian', was released the following day. Forty-eight hours later, the band were on a flight bound from Heathrow, London, to Tokyo, Japan, for their first-ever tour of the Orient.

'It was a very exciting time for us,' smiles Steve Rothery. 'The tour of Europe had gone better than any of us could have hoped, and now we were off for our first trip to Japan. The only fly in the ointment for me, personally, was when EMI insisted on releasing another single from the album. I just didn't think we *had* another hit single on there, so why kid ourselves? But a lot of people at EMI seemed convinced that "Heart of Lothian" would be a good single. I couldn't see it, but we let it happen because we didn't have the time to put up a proper argument against it.'

The band's lack of faith in the choice of 'Heart of Lothian' as a single was reflected by the record's poor chart placing, reaching only number twenty-nine, where it stayed for only one week before dropping like a stone out of the UK Top 40.

'We all knew it wasn't going to be a hit in a million years, I think,' says Mark Kelly. 'And we were in Japan for the first two weeks after it was released, so we never got a chance to promote it or anything. Our feeling was always that most people, if they were interested, would have got the album by then anyway, and "Heart of Lothian" just wasn't the type of song to appeal to most people who weren't Marillion fans already. It just wasn't a single; the fact that it wasn't much of a hit, either, says it all, really.'

Marillion arrived in Tokyo on 2 December, then travelled by bullet-train to Osaka for their first concert in Japan. After that, there would be four more shows: two in Nagoya, and two back in Tokyo.

'It was an amazing little tour,' says Pete Trewavas. 'It was like

251

nothing we'd ever experienced before. Unlike in Britain or Europe, where the shows would always start quite late, nine or ten o'clock, in Japan you have to be ready to go on stage at weird times like six or six-thirty; everybody comes into the hall looking like they've come straight from work, which of course they *have*, and there's strictly no alcohol allowed to be sold or drunk on the premises.'

'And while we were playing the audiences remained completely silent!' Mark Kelly takes up the story. 'At the end of every number for a couple of seconds it was so quiet you could hear a pin drop, and then they'd start clapping, but not *too* enthusiastically. At first, we all thought we must be going down really badly, but at the end of the set they all stood up and went *crazy*. I was shocked. And that was the pattern for all the gigs we did in Japan – everybody seated quietly throughout the whole performance and then at the end – bingo! They'd all go mad!'

'It was funny,' smiles Ian Mosley. 'Completely different from the way we view rock concerts in the West. Much more sedate. In Japan they seemed to treat going to a gig more like going to the theatre. I remember at one of the shows there was a guy who actually fell asleep while we were playing on stage! He was sitting in the front row as well, and we could all see him sitting there snoring his head off. He just looked like a bloke who'd had a hard day at the office and had just popped in to see a quick gig on his way home!' Ian laughs.

'In the end, I jumped off the stage and went over and woke him up,' says Fish. 'He looked horribly embarrassed, so I ended up handing him a drink, and then we all started handing out these drinks from the stage. I sent one of the roadies back to the dressing room and got him to bring out the bottle of Jack Daniels, and started handing out little paper cups of the stuff around amongst the audience. They loved it! We got into terrible trouble with the Japanese security afterwards but by the end of the gig the first three rows were drunk out of their minds, standing up and dancing along. It was the best night of the tour!'

Arriving back in London on 9 December, Marillion allowed themselves a day to get over the long flight home, then headed back down to the Marquee, where they would again take part in a special one-off show, this time to be filmed by the BBC and broadcast live on the Beeb's weekly TV show, *Whistle Test*.

It was an auspicious occasion. It had been six long months

since *Misplaced Childhood* had topped the British charts, and Marillion had only played live in England properly (not counting the five-song swinger at the Marquee in September) just once during all that time, at Castle Donington back in August. Now, their fans' patience had almost run out. The TV cameras were forced to the back of the club as the hordes of marauding Marillion fans waded into the Marquee and pushed their way to the front of the stage, the singing and the shouting already well underway.

It was also the first time the band played the whole of the *Misplaced Childhood* set-piece live in England, and they gave a wild and stunning performance of it. Fish, bearded and hard-eyed, was hypnotic that night, summoning up the ghosts of his past and having them dance like idiot children about the stage. The band played with a potent blend of subtlety and power, enough to crank out the sparks and send not just the people crammed into the Marquee, but the millions of home-viewers too, right over the edge, the BBC cameras kept on rolling, aiming for close-ups of the singer, capturing only the fit-ups, every TV eye agog.

Afterwards, drowned in applause and bathed in sweat and tears, most of Marillion, tired still from the journey back from Tokyo, and drained still further by the show, hopped into their cars and made their way home to Aylesbury. Not so Fish, who left the Marquee and took that old familiar walk across the street to the St Moritz Club, the scene of so much revelry from times past.

In the corner of the club, seated at a large round table, stewing over the inevitable Jack Daniels and Coke and a fresh pack of Bensons, Fish let his thoughts drift into a microphone.

'Tonight was a weird one for me,' he said. 'To come back and play the Marquee – scene of all our yesterdays – and play the whole album for the first time in this country live, and with all the cameras there to capture it as well, it became a very emotional occasion for me. I got very wrapped up in performing the album. And when I got to the "Mylo" section I swear I nearly broke down and cried . . . ('Mylo' was written about John Mylett, a good friend of the band's, and the drummer for a time in Rage, who John Arnison was also managing when he first hooked-up with Marillion. Mylett had been killed in a car crash on a holiday in Greece in June 1984. 'Mylo', apart from being the young drummer's nick-name, was written about the moment when Fish first heard of his death, by phone, while Marillion were on tour in Canada.)

'As I was singing the words I remembered all the times we'd played at the Marquee, dreaming of the days when we wouldn't have to any more but always knowing that we'd want to come back and do it anyway. And I remembered standing at the bar at the Marquee on so many nights, chatting to Mylo and the boys from Rage, and telling them that one day Marillion would be huge, huge, huge, and then feeling like a prat for talking like that and buying everybody a drink. A hundred different scenes were played out in my mind. It put me right back out on the edge.

'Sometimes the magic this band can work is just too strong. I find it very physically exhausting having to relive the *Misplaced Childhood* album on stage every night for months on end. Eventually, I've had to learn to be more artful and introduce more craft into my performances. I simply *couldn't* get through having to sing this stuff absolutely every night as though it were still happening to me for the first time. Only a certified madman would subject himself to that.'

Three nights later, on Friday 13 December (as luck would have it), Marillion played the first of their seven scheduled Christmas shows, at the Brixton Academy in South London. It was another climactic occasion, but not nearly so awesome as their first-ever appearance at the NEC in Birmingham a week later, on the penultimate night of the tour.

Over 11,000 fans gathered in the giant hall, the stage awash in the dense lurid colours of the spotlights, Marillion looking and sounding more commanding, more explosive, and more entertaining a spectacle than ever before on a British stage. Fish dedicated *Misplaced Childhood* to the memory of John Lennon, and by the time the band were cooking through an emotionaly piquant version of 'White Feather', all over the massive hall people everywhere were holding white feathers aloft.

'The NEC was probably the single best concert I think we'd ever performed in this country,' says Fish. 'It was a brilliant night. I don't think any of us has ever felt more nervous, more stage-struck, than just ten minutes before we went on. After such a year of so many incredible highs, it was fitting somehow that we should end it on such a brilliant note. That night, I almost didn't care if the voice went and never came back again. We just gave it our all.'

Christmas and the New Year passed by quietly and slowly

while the members of the band spent a fortnight recuperating from the strange excesses of the year behind them, before kicking off their rescheduled tour in earnest with three sold-out nights at the Hammersmith Odeon on 8, 9 and 10 January 1986.

Belated though it was, Marillion's UK tour, like the European tour that had preceded it, proved to be their most successful yet. Winning was a habit the band were slowly getting hooked on.

They followed their first three shows at the Hammersmith Odeon with fourteen concerts in eleven different cities in England, Scotland and Wales. And then they returned for *another* five nights back at the good old Hammy O, which by now had become almost as much of a home-from-home for Marillion as the Marquee had been in leaner times. For five nights in the first week of February Marillion pulled the house down to its knees. *Misplaced Childhood* Fish dedicated this time to Phil Lynott, who had tragically met his death over the Christmas holidays, collapsing at his home from heart-failure brought on by a combined case of septicaemia and hepatitis, and then the band did his memory proud by charging through a set of performances loaded with fire and emotion, their audiences left glass-eyed, breathless.

The eighth, and final, night at the Hammersmith Odeon was the seventeenth time in three years that Marillion had headlined there, and John Arnison says, if they'd wanted to, the band could have easily sold out a further seventeen nights there on this one tour alone, ticket demand had been so great.

'But that does start to veer into the realms of the absurd,' he reflects. 'When it gets to that stage, that's when the band have to start thinking seriously about taking on a string of shows at somewhere much bigger than the Hammy Odeon. Like Wembley Arena, and the NEC, those sort of sized places.'

The final night of the tour was to be a gala occasion for the band. It had been announced that all proceeds from their final show would be donated to Pete Townshend's Double 'O' Charity; a fund-raising organisation set up to aid people of all ages, sex and creed, suffering from any number of the so-called anti-social problems that beset the modern world: drug addiction, wife-beating, alcoholism, whatever the situaton, whatever the problem, but without moralising.

To make the occasion even more special, Marillion invited along a host of famous and not-so-famous names to help them out on stage. Setting the scene with a casual air of eccentricity

255

that was to characterise the rest of the evening, John Otway opened the show, no longer accompanied by his former guitar-strutting sidekick, 'Wild' Willy Barrett, but joined by none other than Robin Boult, former Metro, and life-long buddy of Pete Trewavas. The Odeon laughed and cheered through Otway's three-number four-handstands set.

Next on stage was Peter Hammill, whose doleful and prolonged twenty-minute set did not go down so well with the Hammersmith patrons. In fact, rather uncharitably given the occasion, Hammill was booed off the stage! 'Ah well, I guess Peter's used to it by now,' Fish chuckled. 'He always either goes down really well, or like a lead balloon.'

Then came Marillion. Strident, powerful, abandoned, wilfully gritty, playfully steamy, the band blasted their way out of the tour with a dazzling performance that cut like stone into ice.

They saved the biggest surprises for the encores, though.

Out from the wings skipped . . . guitarist Mike Oldfield, vocalist Roger Chapman, Oldfield's keyboardist Micky Simmons, GTR bassist Phil Spalding, and Oldfield's resident rhythm guitarist, Joel. All ten of them, including Marillion, spent a moment grinning at each other, then went into a rambling, skewwhiff, version of 'Shadow on the Wall', a track Mike Oldfield and Roger Chapman had written and recorded together on one of the guitarist's albums. Musically, it wasn't tight, but that wasn't the point. It was a lot of fun, and it didn't stop there.

With the applause still ringing in the air, another face stepped out from the side-stage shadows; a walking smile that plugged in a guitar, picked his spot near the lip of the stage, and started playing.

'Hammersmith, will you please welcome Mr Steve Hackett!' cried Fish, then stood back and listened while Hammersmith howled.

And then he started singing, '*It's one o'clock and time for lunch.*'

Out of the blue it came. 'I Know What I like (In Your Wardrobe)'. The old Genesis hit. The only one they ever really had while Peter Gabriel and Steve Hackett were still in the band. Still remembered, though, with a special fondness and nostalgia by certain old, old Genesis fans.

Every single word, right boys?

It was a weird, wonderful, wacky, winning moment: Marillion and their fans finally seeing all their chickens coming home to roost. Joined on stage by some of the very same people they used to pay money to see, in the days when Marillion were still having their photos taken self-consciously sprawled across a wooden bench back in the old Market Square in Aylesbury . . . and *then* cranking out an old Genesis crooner! It was rich and perverse.

'It was almost like being given the final blessing,' Mark Kelly reflects. 'A bit like being told we'd finally made the grade, or something.'

At the end of a dramatic night, Pete Townshend came out on stage in person and accepted a giant show-cheque from Fish. It was made out for £17,000, the whole night's takings.

'He's a big man with a great band!' cried Townshend into the mike.

Backstage, John Arnison was already talking about Marillion's next tour of America. After all, what else was there to think about, he said?

They'd been everywhere else.

10

With Bracelets of Smoke

(*Profile – Ian Mosley*)

Ian Mosley is the Consummate Professional in every sense, and a bit of a percussive genius on the quiet. His proper niche in Marillion, beyond his obvious role as resident rhythm-master, is not altogether easy to describe. He is part elder-statesman, part one-line delivery merchant, part virtuoso sticks artist, and part full-time outsider.

However, there is an important part of himself Ian Mosley likes to keep separate from others, including the band: a more private self that leaves the world and all its cares behind on the doorstep when he comes home from another tour, recording date, or rehearsal room.

'I have to have a certain amount of privacy otherwise I just can't function properly, and then I'm no good to anyone,' he says. 'But being in a band means spending most of the time you're not actually asleep in lots of other people's company – unless, of course, you're sharing a room with someone else in the band, then you don't get any time to yourself at all.

'Now, as a rule I don't mind all that. I mean, I must love it really otherwise I wouldn't have stuck at it all these years. Being out on the road with a band at its best *should* be all about sharing a certain camaraderie, all lads together and all of that.

'But when I come home at the end of a tour, for me, that's *it*! I switch off and do my best to completely forget about the band for a few weeks. I have to or I'd end up going mad, I think. And I don't want that! Not at my time of life,' he grins.

Born in North London, on 16 June 1953, the young Ian

Mosley, like Pete Trewavas, got his musical education in early. Ian's father, Raymond Mosley, was a professional musician; he played the violin and flitted between assignments as a classical soloist and fronting his own Westminster Symphony Orchestra, which specialised in providing the melodramatic soundtracks to a host of Hammer House of Horror movies.

As would be expected, Ian grew up in the family house in Highgate in an atmosphere where music counted for almost everything. It was, after all, the family's bread and butter and Mr Mosley Senior's abiding passion.

'I grew up with music all around me twenty-four hours of the day,' says Ian Mosley. 'It was always the most important thing going on at home. I remember when I was about four or five my dad put a violin in my hand and expected me to learn how to play it. I had to learn how to play things like "The Flight of the Bumble Bee", that sort of thing. I didn't like it, I sort of rebelled almost immediately. But my dad was quite insistent for a time; I remember he once spent about an hour getting my fingers just right on the strings, and the bow action all worked out properly, for a photograph he wanted to take of me playing the violin.

'I didn't mind all that much,' he says, 'I mean, I *was* getting a great musical education because of my dad. He used to play with the orchestra at different West End musicals which were on at the time, and he took me along to see as many as I wanted to. I remember going to see *Funny Girl* when it was on in London, with Barbra Streisand in the leading role. And of course, being as it was my dad's orchestra, I got to sit down in the pit with the band, right next to the drummer. He had a great kit, brilliant sound, and he was an inspiration to watch. Apart from the drums, he had to play about twelve other different percussion instruments at various points in the show; he was firing pop-guns, letting off sirens, rattling sheets of paper to make the sound of wind. Then in the middle of a number he'd nip off to the corner of the pit for a quick cigarette. He'd finish that, stub it out, then run back and keep perfect time with the rest of the band just as his next part came up. Honestly, he was my hero! I thought, yeah, now this is what it's all about! And that's what really gave me the buzz and excitement to want to be a drummer and a musician.'

The first time he actually climbed behind a proper drumkit, Ian Mosley was ten years old. It was a memorable experience, he says.

'Someone threw a shoe at me!' he laughs. 'The thing is, I'd been banging around tapping out rhythms with my hands since I was about six, and I'd always fancied having a go. Then when I was about ten there was this little band that used to rehearse sometimes at my school. They had a drummer who definitely fancied himself a bit, and I was standing around just watching them practise one afternoon when he turned around and asked me if I wanted to have a go on his drums? So I said, yeah . . . And then I remember getting up behind the kit and before I'd even got properly started someone threw a shoe at me! It hit me right in the back! I thought, well that's a promising way to start. It can only get better from here.'

Tantalised by the brief taste he'd had of what it was like to bludgeon seven shades of hell out of a well-sprung drumkit, Ian, now approaching his adolescence, saved up his pocket money until he had enough to purchase a snare drum, one cymbal, some brushes and some sticks.

'Obviously, I was too young to afford to buy myself a full kit,' he says, 'but to start off with the snare and the cymbal was all right. I used to try playing along to "I Can't Explain" by the Who, which was great practice for a budding young drummer, trying to keep up with what Keith Moon was doing! When I got bored with that, I used to try playing along to things like "Doo Wah Diddy . . ." by Manfred Mann, or things by the Beatles, Dusty Springfield . . . whatever I could get my hands on, which usually meant rifling through my older sister's record collection. I carried on like that, never bothering to get myself some proper drum lessons, until I was about thirteen.'

When he wasn't 'banging around on things with my hands', Ian remembers spending the remainder of his childhood harbouring a passing fondness for English and history lessons at school and getting himself involved in what he describes as a never-ending round of fights and battles with a gang of youths from a local council estate situated close by to where he and his family lived in Highgate.

'My mum and dad had a house in Hollylodge Estate, which was a quite posh, privately-owned part of Highgate,' says Ian. 'But we were right in the middle of a really tough area of the borough, between Parliament Hill Fields and the local grammar school. And all the really tough kids from the council estates used to come through Hollylodge Estate to go fishing on Hampstead Heath. And, of course, as they came through they'd invariably come across me, or me and some of my mates, and they'd pounce on us immediately! Because they all thought we were a bunch of posh wimps they'd attack us on sight,' he grumbles.

'I used to go home all the time with black eyes and a bloody nose! But in the end I got involved in so many fights that I got quite handy. By the time I left primary school and moved up to secondary school, when I was eleven, I knew how to take care of myself. Which is just as well, because the school I got sent to, Haverstock Hill, was *really* heavy . . . It was the kind of place where the kids didn't just fight each other, they would attack any teacher they thought was giving them too much lip!

'I only went there for the first year, and then the family moved to Ickenham, so I was spared having to spend the next five years there. But when I started at my new school, a place out near Ickenham called Abbotsfield, the first day I was there I ended up having about fifteen fights!

'Don't ask me why, I don't know. Maybe it was just because I was the new boy and they picked on me, or perhaps I'd forgotten how to communicate with other boys without hitting them first,' he chuckles.

Drumming, and finally settling down to some lessons, are what calmed the aggresively spirited teenage Ian Mosley down, he says.

'I definitely had a lot of pent-up feelings when I was a teenager, and they used to show themselves in very aggressive ways sometimes. But playing the drums took all of that out of me. If I wanted to get physical all I had to do was get behind a set of drums and let myself go. It was very therapeutic in a way, and the more I got into what I was doing on the drums, the more things started to make sense to me.'

Aside from still making the occasional excursion into town to see one of his father's theatre orchestras in action, the biggest inspiration Ian Mosley had as a teenager came – surprise! surprise! – from his music teacher at Abbotsfield.

'My second year there my regular form teacher, Mr Bean, was also the French and music teacher. When he first started taking my class I hated him! I had a bad attitude at school and if I didn't find lessons interesting immediately I never used to bother trying to learn anything about the subject at all, I would just give up straight away. And I could never see the point of learning French, so I never used to bother doing any work in his lessons. Because of that he used to give me a really hard time. We never used to get on at all!

'Then one day I was hanging around in the Music Room at school. There was this big old dusty set of drums piled up in the corner, so I went over and started having a bit of a bash around on them, a few rolls, a few funny beats. And Mr Bean walked in and just stood there listening to me for a while. When I stopped, he said, "I didn't know you were interested in the drums?" and I said, yeah. And we started talking about music. It turned out he was a really nice bloke, really into music. After that, we used to get on great together!

'He used to organise a school jazz orchestra, and although they already had a regular drummer, Mr Bean arranged things so that I could practise on their drumkit every lunchtime. That went on for a while, and then it got to the point where we would stay behind at school at four o'clock, after everybody else had gone home, and I'd practice on the drums and he'd play along with me on piano. Just the two of us in the Music Room, it was brilliant!

'He was a great guy, old Mr Bean. If anybody could be said to be truly responsible for getting me to play the drums, then it has to be him. He used to say to me, "It's obvious you're only interested in playing the drums, so you just concentrate on that, forget about everything else, and you'll find things will start to fall into place for you". It was great advice, and I've probably tried my best to stick to that way of thinking ever since.'

The enlightened attitudes of Ian's form teacher were to have a profound effect on the youngster. Fortified by the idea that it was OK to foresake the rigours of a more academic education in favour of a serious full-time study of the drums and music, Ian's growing enthusiasm for playing brought him many unexpected rewards. As his obsession for the drums began to blossom into a real and promising talent, the teenager's musical progress started to spill over into other important areas of his personal life.

'I stopped getting into so many fights, and I started paying more attention to my lessons in school,' says Ian. 'It sounds like such a cliché, I know, but learning to play the drums and getting involved in music and bands completely changed my life. I felt like I'd found something at last to believe in. You know, like, as long as I keep my drumming together, everything else will take care of itself. That's the simplified Mr Bean version, anyway. But it's definitely worked out like that for me.'

When he was fourteen, and their regular drummer had reached

school-leaving age, Mr Bean's student jazz orchestra invited Ian to join the band.

'I was thrilled,' he smiles, 'that meant I was definitely accepted as a real musician and a proper drummer!'

Mr Bean's jazz orchestra was a thoroughly well organised outfit. In keeping with the teacher's modern attitudes, the young musicians competing for their place in the orchestra were given Duke Ellington scores to rehearse and learn; and several concerts were arranged, and competitions entered. Above all, he inspired a superior sense of professionalism and pride in his school orchestra, and encouraged a bold sensitivity in his students towards the practice and furtherment of their febrile arts.

'I learned an awful lot by playing in that school orchestra,' says Ian. 'Everybody was really keen to play well, which meant that I picked things up about three times as fast as I would have just playing on my own, and we ended up winning a few competitions, doing a few gigs in England, and even doing one little tour of France. And with old Mr Bean always waving the flag for us and leading the way, we managed to do well for ourselves, have a good time, and learn quite a bit about music and playing as well. It was my first experience of the real thing, and I loved it!'

Leaving school at sixteen, Ian Mosley said his goodbyes to the school orchestra for the last time, but not to the hearty Mr Bean, who the drummer would stay in touch with on and off for a good many more years.

'When I left school I worked for a short while in a place called Drum City,' says Ian. 'Anything to do with drums, percussion instruments, or equipment, Drum City sold it, bought it, or repaired it. Then I managed to get myself into the Guildhall School of Music. So while I was there I supported myself by doing a milk-round and playing a few semi-pro gigs here and there.

'When I got accepted at the Guildhall I didn't need my old kit any more – I'd finally managed to get a full kit together for about 2p by the time I was fifteen – so in a moment of blind generosity I donated it to the school orchestra. The next thing is, Mr Bean wrote me this really nice letter thanking me for the drumkit and wishing me all the best for the future. And then we used to bump into each other occasionally and we'd have a cup of tea and a natter, and it was always "How's the drumming coming along?" and loads of encouragement, but no real advice except stick at it, don't worry about anything else, and everything will be all right.

'Then a couple of years after I'd left school he took off for Canada. I think he'd finally had enough of the cheapskate educational system in Britain, and gone off to try his hand in a country where he thought he might be able to get things done properly. For instance, in all the years I was at school he was forever fighting with the school authorities to let him have more money and resources for his music classes. He was always pointing out to them that in America kids were learning to play music on Ludwig drumkits and King saxophones, while in England all the kids had to help them was a recorder and a rusty triangle! He was always looking to America and Canada for his inspiration.

'Years after that, when I toured Canada with Steve Hackett, we bumped into each other again. He just turned up backstage one night at one of the gigs! I couldn't believe it . . . Mr Bean! He told me he'd started his own music school over there, and he seemed really happy and doing well for himself! It was great, a man who'd finally made his dream come true.

'Then he told me to stick at what I was doing again, and forget worrying about the rest, and then he left. That was the last time I ever saw him.'

Studying music at the Guildhall in his late teens, Ian Mosley says was, for him, a mixed blessing.

'By the time I got there I'd been playing the drums seriously for about four or five years; I already had masses of technique, and was used to improvising and being very percussive. But studying classical music at the Guildhall meant I didn't need to know anything about that sort of free-form playing. The first thing my tutor did was point out that I only needed a certain amount of technique and no improvisatory talents at all to be able to play the sort of stuff I would be learning at the Guildhall. The important thing for a drummer in a classical orchestra is to be able to *read* and keep perfect time,' says Ian.

'To be honest, I didn't think going to college there was altogether a good thing, really. What it meant was that almost all of the drummers that came out of there with a certificate couldn't actually play a thing unless they had their part written out and sitting right in front of them as they played. They couldn't absorb new ideas or improvise at all. In a way, because of my experiences with the school jazz orchestra, and then the

Guildhall, I think I came out at the end of it all with the best of both worlds: I could read well *and* I was heavily into improvisation. I was lucky.'

Not long after he had signed up for the course of studies at the Guildhall School of Music, Ian joined up with a small, locally-based jazz-rock outfit called Walrus. It was 1970 and he was seventeen years old.

'Walrus lasted about a year,' he says, 'but it was a good experience, playing in my first sort of rock band. We used to play tiny little gigs in places like the Chislehurst Caves in Kent, and lots of small pubs and clubs in the suburbs of London, mostly.

It was while the obliquely named Walrus was still out snuffling around for gigs that Ian Mosley also got involved with his first West End theatre orchestra. The production was *Hair*, and he got the job through a stroke of sheer luck.

'I was hanging around Drum City one day, which also served as a sort of occasional hang-out for drummers and their friends, and this guy called Peter Wolf walked in looking like death. He was the regular drummer in the orchestra for all the *Hair* performances, but he'd been doing it non-stop for something like eight years! Six nights a week, plus matinées! Can you imagine?

'And we were standing there chatting, and I said "You look terrible!" He said, "I know! I've got to get out of this for a while, I've got to have a break. Do you wanna do it?" I couldn't believe it! I mean, it was quite an outrageous suggestion to make. I was a kid who went to music college, played in a little jazz-rock band, and used to practise a lot. And he was asking me to take over and do his job in *Hair*? In those shows absolutely everything depends on the drummer keeping his act totally together. So I asked him if he was serious, and he said yes, perfectly. What did I reckon?

'Well, I went along with him to his next show, sat next to him throughout the whole show and followed his parts and watched what he was doing. At first it seemed like a bit of an awesome task, being asked to step into his shoes like that, even only temporarily. But when the show started and all these naked women came running on stage I thought, great! Yeah, I *like* this. I'll take the job!' he laughs. 'I was still quite naive then, you see.

'But I sat at home and studied all the parts and practised them for days and then I went back and got ready for my first show. Peter stayed by my side for that first show, but I was all right. To be honest, all I can remember is feeling terrified right up until the moment the curtain started to rise. Then the band started playing and all I remember next is the end! It all went by in a complete flash . . . It was brilliant!

'The second night was worse, though. In the theatre world a musician's second night in the orchestra is usually known as Sacking Night, because that's when you can really tell whether they're going to be any good over a long period of time. Generally speaking, you concentrate and try so hard on your first night that you can't hope to be as good as that twice in a row, and so the second night is the one the band leader and the other musicians really watch you. So my second show I really did feel the eyes on me, but luckily I didn't make any gigantic cock-ups so they kept me on while this bloke Peter Wolf went off and had a long holiday.

'The trouble is, though a lot of the other older musicians in the orchestra were really nice helpful guys, I was bored after about a week. Same old part every night *and* matinées. I soon found out how soul-destroying it can be playing exactly the same thing over and over, night in night out for weeks at a time. It's not fun. And there are guys, like Peter Wolf, and another drummer I met who played in the production of *Jesus Christ Superstar* for something like eight solid years, who get caught up in the West End theatre shows and don't know how to break out of them again. They get their £300 a week or whatever and stay with one show for ten years. Then the show closes, they don't know anybody any more because they haven't been out at night, except for Sundays, for the last ten years, and they're knackered! They end up auditioning for another show and then the whole vicious circle starts again.

'It's quite hellish, really, how the West End can smother a musician's career so completely. It's no place to be creative. But, like all new experiences, I really learned something from playing there.'

After a couple of months of *Hair* (plus matinées!), Ian turned down the offer of a short tour with the company and rejoined Walrus, albeit briefly.

'Walrus was pretty much all over by the time I'd finished doing *Hair*, though,' he says. 'It was pretty much impossible for me to hold down both gigs and go to college at the same time anyway, so I knocked Walrus on the head and started to look for occasional session work.'

With his good luck still holding, Ian thought he'd landed on his feet when word got to him that Manfred Mann's Earth Band – a very big noise indeed in the Seventies – were considering offering him the gig as their drummer for a forthcoming tour. However, there was one snag.

'Jeff Britten, the guy who was their regular drummer, had come down with glandular fever,' says Ian. 'And he rang me, because we knew each other fairly well at the time through meeting at gigs and places like Drum City, and told me that Manfred was going to contact me and offer me the gig. Jeff asked me if I would only accept on a temporary basis until he got well again. He said he desperately wanted to keep the gig if he could and would I do it as a favour to him?'

Ian agreed, but when Manfred Mann rang he was insistent that the post was for a *permanent* replacement for Jeff Britten.

'I didn't know what to do,' says Ian. 'I mean, I would have obviously loved to have had a chance of playing in a big band like that. It was exactly the sort of thing I was looking for. But I couldn't agree to do it. Not to Jeff . . . Besides, he *was* the current English karate champion at the time! Do you know what I mean?' he chuckles.

Politely and more than a little regretfully refusing the offer to join Manfred Mann's Earth Band, Ian did the gentlemanly thing: he gave Manfred John Lingwood's phone number. Lingwood was another unfortunate West End theatre victim currently at a complete loss after quitting his job as the drummer in *Jesus Christ Superstar*. He'd been there for eight years.

'John got the gig, too,' says Ian. 'Which meant that me and Jeff had talked each other out of a good gig. But there you go. You can't let your mates down in this business because you never know from one day to the next whose turn it is next to be the one asking the favours.'

By the time he was twenty years old, with his days at the Guildhall thankfully numbered, Ian Mosley continued to pick up odd, unexpected offers of work as a drummer. One of his earliest and most consistent benefactors was Richard Hartley, who, amongst his various claims to fame and notoriety, was also the man who wrote the music for the *Rocky Horror Show*.

'Richard wrote a lot of music for films and he used to ring me up and give me odd bits of session work,' says Ian. 'The most bizarre gig he ever hired me for though was the Alternative Miss World contest that they started holding every year in London in the Seventies . . . The year I played there, 1973 or 1974, I can't remember exactly, was one of the most horrific playing experiences of my life!

'Richard had rung me up and asked me down to play in the band he was organising for the show. He said, "You won't need much kit, just a bass drum, a snare, some cymbals, nothing too elaborate. It'll be a simple drums, piano, and bassoon line-up"! I thought that sounded a bit weird, you know . . . Drums, piano, and *bassoon*? I asked him what sort of show it was going to be and he said, "Oh, nothing too mad, just some *Rocky Horror Show* people and some theatrical types . . . people like that . . . *friends*"

'So I agreed to turn up. It was held in the top-floor of a warehouse in East India Docks. It was all very seedy. There was an obviously home-made stage set up, with a grand piano and some drums placed on it. In the middle of the stage they'd left a big hole which they'd lined in plastic and filled with water. I started setting up and getting ready and then the people started arriving . . . and that's when the fun really did begin!

'Honestly, it was like a scene from those weird Sixties movies . . . very Fellini, if you know what I mean. Most of the blokes were dressed in mini-skirts and stockings and suspenders. There were two girls who turned up in one dress; they both had one tit hanging out at the sides. Other girls were wearing monocles and had moustaches painted on their faces . . . And there were hundreds of these people crawling all over each other and getting drunk and completely wasted, climbing all over the drums while I was playing, and dancing on top of the piano.

'Then the actual contest started and everybody got up and started parading around the stage, then the two girls in the dress tripped over and fell into the pool they'd built into the stage. Everything started collapsing and the piano, the drums and me and everybody else on stage started to slide into the pool. And *that*'s when I started to lose my head.'

Worried that his drum kit would be destroyed and aware that he was out of his depth with the Satyricon-like scenes going on around him, Ian's nerve was starting to snap.

'I got so freaked out I started having all these morbid thoughts like, what happens if there's a fire? There's no way all these people are going to make it out of here alive!

'And that was it. I knew then I'd definitely had all I could take. So I packed up my drums as best I could, dived into my car and drove as fast as I could away from there. Looking back, Richard probably couldn't understand what was the matter with me. To him it was just another gig. To me it was a total nightmare.'

Making a detailed inventory of his battered kit at home the next morning, Ian discovered that the damage incurred wasn't as bad as he had feared.

'I rang Richard up and told him there was one broken drum-head and that I would forward the bill to him,' Ian grins. 'He said fair enough, and I calmed down a bit, and after that we did quite a few more funny little things together.'

After the Alternative Miss World show, the next most memorable thing Richard Hartley asked Ian Mosley to do for him was to put together a likely-looking group of guys to mime as a band in a small part in a movie Hartley was involved in producing.

'It was a film starring Michael Caine and Glenda Jackson, called *The Romantic Englishwoman*,' says Ian. 'Richard had asked me to get a few of my mates together to pose as the band, just as a background to one of the scenes they were shooting. It was being filmed in a big room at the Royal Gardens Hotel in Kensington. I went down there with some people I'd persuaded to help me, including a bloke called John Etheridge who was the guitarist in Soft Machine.

'They gave us these band-jackets to wear, then put us into a room with some seats and a bar and told us to wait until they called for us. Of course, we were there hours before anybody bothered us to do anything, getting completely pissed out of our heads on all this free booze they had laid on. Finally, they called us in for our scene.

'They had the room set up to look like a big restaurant with hundreds of extras all sitting at tables pretending to eat and chat and have a good time. Then there was a small stage in one corner where we had to go and pretend to be the band, and in front of that a dance floor with more extras dancing around. In the middle of the dance floor was where all the main action was taking place. Glenda Jackson and Michael Caine were going to do a scene, and the rest was just background that had to look convincing.

'So we started playing away, miming, and I thought, now this is a doddle. Then it came to the point where they'd panned around the whole room with the cameras and it was time for Glenda and Michael to do their bit. Well, suddenly everything started going really quiet. The taped music dwindled away to nothing and the noise of a crowded restaurant died away. They had to do that so that they could pick up the sound of the actors' voices. But it was really weird! I mean, everybody, including me and the band, had to carry on moving as though we were still making lots of noise, but without making a sound! It was surreal. All the extras were dancing together, or having dinner together, and laughing and chatting *but without making a sound*!

'And of course, me and the band are trying to do the same thing, only none of us could keep a straight face. Then suddenly Michael Caine's voice came booming out of all this weird silence. He yelled, "You keep your hands off her!" You know, in *that* voice! And that was it . . . the tears started rolling down my cheeks, I just started to crack up into a giggling fit. Once I'd started, of course, the rest of the band joined in, and John Etheridge collapsed over the piano laughing. Then it was CUT! DO IT AGAIN! Only each time we tried to do it, it just got worse. We just could not stop laughing! I thought, oh no, Richard's done it again.'

Still scratching around for gigs, by the start of 1973 Ian Mosley had already decided that one-off sessions and the occasional Richard Hartley-inspired forays into the showbiz underworld were fine as far as they went. Good bread and butter money and the reassuring feeling of being in demand. But what he really desired was to be in a working band, making monumental albums together and then taking them out on the road. After the disappointment of having to turn down the gig drumming in Manfred Mann's Earth Band, Ian was determined to grab the next chance he was offered with both hands.

'Like everybody else in Marillion, by my late teens and early twenties the dream I had was to get into a good regular line-up, and stick together and make a real go at having a successful career together,' says Ian. 'But the thing about drummers is that they very rarely form bands of their own. It's usually a guitarist, or a singer and guitarist who want to write their own material that go out looking for a drummer to form a band with. And, of course, it's virtually impossible for a drummer to sit at home by himself and write songs and then go out and look for a band to sing and play them for him. It just doesn't happen like that. So I was hoping to get asked to join somebody else's band, then perhaps to really become a part of the band, whoever it was. But what happened was that until I joined Marillion, which was still years away, every band I ended up playing with was always there to back one man, either the singer or the guitarist; the rest of the musicians were kept on strict wages. I was always in a No Royalties and No Say situation. Which again, was fine as far as it went, but never quite what I was really looking for.'

Via another good connection at Drum City, Ian Mosley finally got his first taste of what being in a bona fide touring and recording rock and roll band was all about. The band was called Darryl Way's Wolf, and at the start of 1973 they were looking for a good dependable drummer. Ian heard about the job, stormed the audition, and was promptly invited to join the band.

He stayed with them for just two years, during which time he helped them to record three rather unmemorable albums. Even so, Ian remembers his time with Darryl Way and the rest of the band as an excellent experience. It was the first small mark he had made in a professional rock band. He was still paying his dues but at least he had proved he could cut it on a pro-level.

'I thought I'd really made it when I got offered the gig with Darryl Way,' Ian smiles ruefully. 'The band's manager, a guy called Nigel Thomas, put me on £50 a week wages, and the band used to get picked up and ferried around in a Rolls Royce . . . you know, the whole bit! It went on like that for the first year and a half, and then suddenly it all stopped and I was brought right back down to earth.

'The trouble was that though we were a pretty good live band, the albums we recorded were pretty duff, really. Anyway, they weren't selling anything like the amount needed to justify the way we were living it up. Then the next thing I know, we're about to go on stage at the Marquee one night, and this bloke in a top hat comes up to me and says, "Mr Ian Mosley?" I said, "Yeah, what about it?" He said, "I have to issue you with this writ . . ." I thought, *what*?'

The writ was from Nigel Thomas, who had decided to sue the band in an attempt to regain the money he had persuaded the band's record company, Decca, to fork out in advances for Darryl Way's first two albums.

'I couldn't believe it . . . We ended up having to record the last album in order to pay back all the money Nigel reckoned we owed him and the record company. Which was a horrible situation to be in. But it shows you what it can be like in the music business – one day you're riding around in a big Rolls Royce thinking about the next gig, and the next you're having to sign on at the dole office. Worse, you get told you *owe* money.

'I must admit I was quite saddened by the whole thing. Because when I first joined the band I really, really thought that was it, I'd hit the big time. I mean, Darryl was quite a big star in those days. When he left Curved Air in 1972 it was front page news in the *Melody Maker* and big headlines everywhere. And there was a string of record companies all queuing up to sign whatever he did next. We'd got a good deal, been given lots of money, but of course not even Darryl saw a penny of that.

'When we decided we'd do this one last album to keep Nigel and the record company happy, it just delayed actually splitting up, which made everything so much worse. When it was all over it was a big relief. The whole thing really opened my eyes up to what can go on at the so-called top of this profession.'

At the start of 1975, with Darryl Way left behind to re-group with the ailing Curved Air line-up and the early glory days of Wolf now just a well-heeled memory, Ian Mosley began the year out of a gig and distinctly out of pocket. Work was thin on the ground.

With the unpaid bills starting to mount up on his mantelpiece, Ian was ready to take a shot at the first paying gig that came his way.

'I was ready to do anything,' says Ian. 'I really needed the money and wasn't about to be too choosy over the sort of work I'd take. Which is how I ended up being the drummer for Peter Gordino, probably one of the strangest gigs I think I've ever done,' he smiles.

Peter Gordino is a former chorus-line dancer in the West End who chanced his arm as a solo singer and performer and made it big momentarily at the turn of the Seventies. With an act that combined the smarmy gold-medallion nestled in the chest-hairs charm of a latter-day Englebert Humperdinck with the suggestive macho body movements of a fully wound-up and running Tom Jones, Peter Gordino's style was pure cabaret. He had supper-club eyes, wore pink frilly shirts opened to the navel, wide-lapelled tuxedos and sleek black flares, and he entertained his middle-aged audiences at prestigious night-spots like the Talk of the Town in London.

He was everyting, in fact, that Ian Mosley is not. However, the job paid £100 a week and Gordino's management were looking for a drummer to start work as soon as possible. Ian didn't have to think twice about taking it.

'I put my head on the chopping block with that one,' he chuckles. 'But it was better money than I was used to getting paid, and there was absolutely nothing else happening for me at the time so I thought, why not?'

Ian Mosley maintains that, like everything else he's ever done as a drummer, playing with Peter Gordino was still an experience he learned from.

'It's always a good thing, I think, as a creative person in any field of the arts to throw yourself in at the deep end occasionally. It can have really positive long-term results,' he says. 'Although, having said that, I couldn't stand playing all that cabaret stuff for long. After a while, I really had to get out of that scene before it drove me mad.

'When we played at the Talk of the Town, there was a big orchestra, a couple of girl dancers, and me. The rest of the guys in the orchestra were the really top sessionmen, all of them hardened by years of doing sessions playing similar sorts of stuff. And none of them liked me. Rock music was still very frowned upon, and *I* was very frowned upon because I had long hair and didn't wear the same colour shirt as them, and I played too loud, they said, and all that sort of thing. And, of course, they all used to sit there with their sheets of music all lined up nicely in front of them on the bandstand. I threw mine away after the first couple of nights because I'd learned all the parts off by heart. I mean, it wasn't difficult to do, but somehow they despised me for doing that. They thought I couldn't read music, and I said I can, I just don't want to! They were shocked.'

After the engagement at the Talk of the Town ended, Ian was invited along by Gordino for a small tour of the English provinces. Ian, however, had decided to hang up his frilly shirt and refused. He was still no nearer to joining his perfect band, but he certainly didn't intend making a career out of being a cabaret star. The money was good all right, but not *that* good!

'Gordino himself rang me up and offered three times what I had been getting at the Talk of the Town shows to stay on, because although neither of us ever liked each other, he was still desperate to keep me as a drummer because I played all his stuff well, kept my mouth shut and was no trouble,' says Ian. 'But I just couldn't do it. I'd had enough of wearing a frilly shirt on stage every night. I wanted to get back into a rock band, where I belonged.'

He didn't have to wait long. One night, shortly after quitting

273

his job with Peter Gordino, Ian received a phone call from Holland. On the line was a keyboard player by the name of Rick van der Linden. He fronted his own band; a trio of keyboards, bass and drums, called Trace, and he was looking for a drummer.

'Trace were the sort of Dutch equivalent of Emerson, Lake and Palmer,' says Ian. 'They had supported Curved Air on their reformation tour of Britain with Darryl Way after he'd split with Wolf, which is where I'd first come across them. But they'd had to cancel their shows half-way through the tour because their drummer had a big freak-out about something and had quit the band and gone back to Holland.

'I must admit, I'd never really heard of them before they'd supported Curved Air, but I wasn't doing anything except not answering the phone to Peter Gordino,' he smiles. 'So I thought, great! Holland here I come!'

Throughout most of Europe, with particular emphasis on Holland and West Germany, Trace were considerably better known than they were ever going to be in Britain. Van der Linden himself was and had been so successful on the continent, he was already said to be approaching millionaire status by the time Ian Mosley joined up with him.

'Of course, I had no idea how rich and successful this bloke van der Linden was,' smiles Ian. 'When I arrived in Amsterdam there was this Fleetwood Cadillac waiting to pick me up at the airport! I thought, 'allo, I've landed on my feet again.

'I got driven to this huge house in the middle of a forest, which I found out also served as a recording studio. I walked in and there were gold and silver albums hanging from the walls, and all the furnishings and fittings were really expensive and plush. I couldn't believe it! I thought, who *is* this guy van der Linden? I'd never even heard of him until a few weeks before I met him.

'It turned out that he'd made most of his money in a previous band called Acception, who apparently were *huge* in Europe in the early Seventies. And now Trace was like his personal baby. The bass player and I were both on wages, given some rooms to sleep in somewhere in one of the wings of the house, and we started work on the album almost straight away.'

In Ian Mosley's own words, the music of Trace, as directed by Rick van der Linden, was, 'a bit like James Last goes heavy, sort of jazzed-up Bach. Not as good as ELP, of course, and definitely a few years behind the times, but that sort of thing, lots of elongated keyboard extravaganzas with an atmosphere behind it. Old Rick was obviously doing well out of it though, even if no-one else was,' he chuckles.

After the Trace album was completed, Ian was kept on a weekly retainer to stay on as the band's new permanent drummer. There would be concerts to play in the near future, Rick promised. In the meantime, Ian was given a little house at the bottom of van der Linden's extensive gardens to live in, where he waited patiently for the keyboard player to emerge from his mansion.

'We did a few gigs together, playing in sports halls in places like Germany and Holland, usually with a whole string of other bands – Caravan, Golden Earring, that sort of scene,' says Ian. 'When the shows were over though, Rick would lock himself away again in his big mansion for weeks at a time. I'd be left to get on with it on my own in the little house at the bottom of his garden that he'd given me to live in, absolutely nothing to do. I used to get friends of mine over from England to stay with me, and we'd just sit around playing cards. It was pretty boring, mostly. But there was nothing waiting for me back home in England except a lot of unpaid bills and letters from the tax man asking why I hadn't declared any earnings for the last five years. So I stayed with Rick and Trace for about a year and a half in the end, but what a weird band it was.

'Because Rick was a millionaire he was the most eccentric person I'd ever had to work for. We would travel somewhere for a gig and when we got there Rick would find one of his keyboards wasn't working properly, or he didn't feel "right" that day or something, and he'd say, "OK, let's cancel the gig!"

'And Rick had all these flash cars, too. I remember driving home from a gig with him one night, it was about four o'clock in the morning. Suddenly, I could smell burning. I lifted up the back seat and everything was smoking and smouldering. Somebody had dropped a cigarette butt down there and the seat padding had caught alight. I said, "Rick, your car's on fire!" He said, "Oh? See if you can put it out" and just kept right on driving.

'I tried to put it out but it just got worse and worse. In the end I told him to stop the car. We got out and just as we did the whole car went up in flames! It was just like something you see in a film. A big explosion and suddenly no car! We were in the middle of nowhere, as well, freezing cold. And Rick just stood there looking at this burning wreck that used to be his car. He looked completely lost, like he couldn't understand what had happened. I thought, great, stuck in the middle of nowhere at four in the morning with an eccentric millionaire who doesn't even know what day it is from one week to the next. I wonder what *normal* people do for a living?'

Towards the end of 1976, Ian Mosley vacated his 'little house at the bottom of the garden', and resettled himself in Amsterdam.

'I was still drumming for Rick whenever he needed me,' says Ian. 'But that wasn't very often, so in the meantime I started getting into doing tons of session work in Amsterdam. I lived in this tiny flat in one of the really rough ghettos on the outskirts of the city, and played with a lot of really great local musicians. I worked for a while with a band called the Latin Explosion who were a great bunch of musicians and people, and I did lots of work playing on albums by obscure Dutch bands. I was really enjoying myself. I was still getting wages from Rick's manager, which gave me all the freedom I wanted to stay in Amsterdam and carry on playing with whoever I fancied.'

Ian's new found freedom only lasted a few short months, though. The extra-musical proclivities and strange, irritating quirks of character Rick van der Linden displayed finally provoked Ian into a terrible row with the other-worldly keyboard player.

'We had a huge argument because, as usual, Rick was behaving like a wally,' says Ian, 'and I went storming back to Amsterdam and went straight to Rick's manager and told him I'd had enough, I was quitting!

'Of course, that was the end of my wages, too . . . And although I was still doing as many sessions as I could get, I was suddenly really skint again. I mean, *really* skint. I lived on beanshoots for about ten weeks solid towards the end because that's all I could afford to buy.'

After nearly two years of living in Holland, the last few months minus the regular wages he had started off with, all Ian really had to look forward to was more rounds of guesting on nameless locally recorded albums, with still no sign of the 'proper band' he still yearned for. Every time he sat down to another plate of beanshoots, life as a Dutchman lost just a little bit more of its appeal for the young drummer. It was early 1977, and Ian was not fond of the sound of his belly rumbling in the night. It was time to quit Amsterdam and head back to London. See the sights.

'I knew I had to leave Holland soon or I would disappear completely,' he said. 'I had made a lot of good friends in Holland and most of the time I'd enjoyed myself living and working there. But after two years I didn't have any friends left in London. I mean, obviously I still had close personal friends, but I had lost touch with nearly all the people I had known in the music business. So as soon as I could afford the fare I hopped on a ferry home.'

Stopping off at his parents' house for a few weeks while he got his English bearings back, Ian Mosley eventually moved into a room in a flat in Rickmansworth, along with half a dozen other characters also on the hunt for a cheap pew with a view.

'It was a bit like a typical squat,' Ian smiles. 'Only it wasn't a real squat, we all had to pay rent. It only *looked* like one. It was a big flat above a fish-and-chip shop, and after six o'clock at night we didn't have any next-door-neighbours around to complain about the noise, which, of course, everybody took *full* advantage of.

'We had one room designated as the Music Room; we had a drum-kit permanently set-up in there and a Marshall stack amp, and anyone who fancied having a blow on an instrument would steam in there. It was really good fun. I was seen a bit as the Serious Musician though, who stayed a bit distant from the rest,' the smile grows broader at the memory, 'while the rest of the guys in the flat were more into smoking dope and not taking the idea of any sort of a career at anything too seriously. We all got on well together, though. But I was still trying to make it, still looking for a decent band. That's all that motivated me, and in that way I always seemed to be just on the edge of all the shenanigans that used to go on at the flat, which is probably just as well or I might *never* have gotten anything together.'

Returning to England and expecting to pick up regular session work in London wasn't easy, and to begin with Ian had to make do with whatever work was going.

'Applying my usual philosophy of Any Work pays more money than No Work, I did whatever came my way: I did a couple of pantomimes, some small one-off shows here and there, and just tried to pick up the threads again after two years away from the scene. After a few months I started getting bits of work here and there that was closer to what I wanted to do. I played drums on some sessions for Dave Greenslade. And then, in 1978, I was recommended by a bass player called John Perry for the job as drummer in the Gordon Giltrap band.'

Offered the gig on the basis of a quick fifteen-minute audition with the Giltrap band, Ian stayed as the drummer with Gordon Giltrap, on and off, for the next two and a half years.

'We toured a few times, did a bit of recording, and sort of plugged along gamely for a while,' says Ian. 'I had a lot of high hopes for the band at one point, but as time wore on Gordon was getting less and less work and I was back to scratching around for sessions to pull in some money.'

By 1981, Ian Mosley based the majority of his day-to-day activities around Roden Studios, where Giltrap had recorded some of his albums, and Ian had his kit permanently set up in a rehearsal booth.

'I used to practically live at Roden Studios in those days,' he says. 'If I wasn't actually working with Gordon down there, which was getting rarer by then anyway, or out doing a session for somebody, I would spend the rest of my time messing about on my kit, practising.

'By then I was nearly twenty-seven and still nowhere near being a real member of a real democratic band, and I was starting to think that that was never going to happen for me. I'd thought that Gordon's band might have been the one, at first, but Gordon wouldn't let go of the reins and he wouldn't take hold of them either. He took too much for granted with his career. He'd had one hit single, "Heart Song", but he hadn't built anything up from it. In the end, I got fed up waiting around for him to get it together. I rang him up and told him he'd got all his priorities wrong, and we ended up having a blazing argument which ended with me leaving the band.

'The shame of it is we never spoke to each other again for years after that. In fact, it's only in the last couple of years we've even seen each other again. Gordon phoned me up one night before Christmas one year and told me I'd been right. He said he regretted wasting so much time. But he's a good musician, he won't fade away.'

It was late one evening, after another day spent pottering around with his kit at Roden, that Ian Mosley discovered that Steve Hackett, former leading light and guitarist with Genesis, these days embarked on a highly lucrative career in America with his latest outfit, GTR, then a successful solo artist, had recently arrived to record his latest album in the recording studio at Roden.

'I walked past the studio door and I thought, "Wow! Steve Hackett!",' Ian laughs. 'Not that I was a big Genesis fan, or anything. I just knew of the band. I mean, bands like Genesis and Pink Floyd passed me by really; my heroes were always people like Chick Corea, Lenny White, Billy Cobham, those people. So I had no idea who actually played in Genesis or Pink Floyd, I never knew more than a couple of names in those days; I just knew that they were supposed to be *mega*!

'Anyway, through hanging around at Roden I got introduced to Steve Hackett a couple of times, and we got chatting. Funnily enough, he was in there recording an album using drum machines, no acoustic percussion at all. So I found all that very interesting, of course. And then one night Steve told me he needed to record some footsteps. He said, "Can you walk across the studio floor in time to this track?" So I said, yeah, and then he miked-up this big stairwell and I walked up and down that for him!'

Ian's acquaintance with Steve Hackett grew steadily during the course of the guitarist's stay at Roden. When, at the end of recording his new album, Hackett wanted to put together a live band for a tour, he didn't refuse the future Marillion drummer his shot at an audition.

'By then, of course, Steve knew all about me being a drummer,' says Ian. 'So when he started thinking about putting a band on the road we had a little jam together and he offered me the job!'

Landing the gig with Steve Hackett was to be a turning point in Ian Mosley's career. Over the next two years he would tour the major concert halls of Britain and Europe more than once with the Hackett band, and record one remarkable album, *Highly Strung*, released at the end of 1982.

Ian remembers his time with the guitarist as the first genuine high-point of his working life.

'He's an exceptionally nice bloke, Steve Hackett,' says Ian. 'He's got a great sense of humour as well, which always surprises people who meet him for the first time because of his so-called serious image. He was great fun to be on the road with, and about as gentlemanly as any boss of the band could be. It was a great time for me, and I learned ever such a lot as a musician through playing with Steve. I mean, he *is* very talented and in those days his solo stuff wasn't always in the *easiest* of time signatures for a drummer to follow and elaborate on. We never used to play any old stuff from his Genesis days, though. He was very keen to play down that part of his past. But of course, people were *always* asking about Genesis – what did Steve think of them now and would he ever get back together with them? He hated being asked all those sorts of questions.

'The only time, in fact, that we ever pulled an old Genesis number out of the bag on-stage was in Italy . . . We had to play "I Know What I Like", otherwise there would have been a riot.'

By the summer of 1983, Steve Hackett had decided to place the band on ice. His next solo album would feature a variety of different drummers and musicians, including Ian Mosley guesting on one track, but plans to record it were still twelve months away and in the interim Hackett would effectively be off the road and locked away at home writing new material.

'It was a shame when it came to an end,' remarks Ian, 'but everybody in the band sensed it was coming. He was very nice about it all, though. He didn't say goodbye so much as see you around, I'll be in touch. And even though we ended up playing in our own different bands, we did stay in touch and we're still good mates today. Every now and again he still calls me up and asks me to go down to a studio somewhere and have a blow with him on whatever new ideas he wants to try out that day.

'It's strange really how I ended up joining the very band that the press had spent ages saying sounded like Genesis, although I don't think Steve ever really saw the comparison. I remember on one of the last tours we did he started getting fans coming up to him and asking him what he thought of Marillion. He used to nod his head and say he thought they were very good, but he'd never even heard of them, I don't think, until people started asking him about them.'

Late summer 1983, Ian Mosley was back to doing sessions to keep up the mortgage payments on a house he had bought for himself during his high-salary days with Steve Hackett.

'I was doing radio jingles, some TV work, anything I could do that paid,' he says. 'By then I was convinced that I was never going to get myself out of the rut of jigging about from one temporary job to another. Then one day I opened a music paper

– I hadn't looked at one in ages; I didn't even know who half the people were they had in there! – and I saw this story with the headline: 'Marillion Look for New Drummer'. I thought, now that sounds interesting. Surely I must know someone that could introduce me to someone in the Marillion camp.'

Indeed he did. Steve Hackett's regular promoter in those days, and now the manager of Tears for Fears, a chap called Paul Crockford, told Ian that he knew Marillion's manager, John Arnison, and, at Ian's urgent request, agreed to write a letter of formal introduction to the Marillion office, recommending him for the vacant post as a drummer.

'It turned out that the boys in the band had already heard a bit about me because of my association with Steve Hackett,' says Ian. 'So John Arnison's secretary, Anne, rang me up as soon as they received Paul Crockford's letter about me and asked if I could make it down for an audition the very next day. The trouble was, I was actually out on the road at the time she asked, performing a drum clinic for Zildjan Cymbals. So I asked her if we couldn't arrange a date for the following week. But the answer was no, they needed someone as soon as possible.

'Unfortunately, there was really no way I could possibly have made it down the next day; at the time I was on my way from Manchester to Cardiff, or somewhere like that. But after a lot of hassling around and changing my arrangements I was able to phone Anne back a few hours later and tell her that I could probably make it the day after tomorrow. But she said, "I'm sorry, you're too late. They've already found somebody!" So that was that, or so I thought. Actually, I was a bit cheesed off with them that they wouldn't at least see me,' he laughs. 'Little did I know what would happen next.'

Less than a month later, with the drum clinic tour now over, Ian was sitting at home twiddling his thumbs when the phone rang. It was John Arnison.

'He said, "I've got a little problem, Ian. The boys are up in Monmouth writing and rehearsing material for the next album and they've sacked the drummer. Could you go up there and help them out for a while on a session basis?" So I said I would go along and have a blow with the band and see how we all got on together,' says Ian. 'I remember I asked him what Fish was like – I'd heard all these rumours that he was this sort of hard-drinking Scotsman who you didn't mess with – and John just laughed and said, "He's six-feet-five and Scottish! How soon can you be ready to leave for Monmouth?" I said, "I'm ready" . . . and that was how it started.'

Ian Mosley admits he didn't really know much about the band's music when he agreed to travel up to Monmouth to meet Marillion for the first time, in October 1983.

'Like a lot of other people in those days who hadn't really bothered to actually sit down and listen to one of their records, all I really knew about Marillion in 1983 was that they were supposed to be a Genesis rip-off,' he says, shaking his head. 'Then the first time I walked into the rehearsal room with them and they started playing me some of the new material they'd been working on, I couldn't actually see the Genesis connection at all. To me it didn't sound anything like Genesis. There were certain influences I could detect, but only one of them might have been pure Genesis. It was a great relief to discover that they were just into making their own music, and playing with them was really enjoyable, they were quite *musicianly* for a band so new to it all. I was really very impressed.'

The first project Ian worked on with Marillion, recording the farcically expensive and ill-starred *Fugazi* album, he still remembers as a long-winded and messy introduction into their ranks.

'On the one hand, I was really enjoying playing with the band,' he says. 'Doing those five or six gigs with them that Christmas was a real eye-opener for me; the atmosphere and the audiences, and the way the band was playing together and the way Fish performed on stage, it all made me feel really excited about being involved with them.

'But on the other hand, the experience of recording *Fugazi* with Nick Tauber was a bit horrendous, quite honestly. Because Nick was so untogether, and because, at first, the band allowed him to get away with being slap-dash and unpredictable, things took far too long to get done, which meant that towards the end everything was being done in a real rush. My main memories of recording *Fugazi* are of everybody in the band going bonkers trying to get the album finished in time for the tour, and loads of the boys' ideas having to be ditched because there just wasn't enough time left for us to carry on. We ended up getting thrown out of half the studios in London,' he sighs.

'The best part of all, working on *Fugazi*, was watching how quickly the boys in the band grew up over the space of recording that one album. I mean, they started out a bit like wide-eyed novices, I thought, and ended up working like hardened pros in the space of about three months. But then that's the whole Marillion story, really – everything seems to happen really quickly for them. I mean, by the time I became a fully-fledged member of the band, in early 1984, they'd only released two albums and already they were starting to have the kind of success most bands would only expect, if they were lucky, after about four or five albums together.'

Ian Mosley became the fifth official member of Marillion, as of January 1984. Apart from his dazzling prowess as a drummer, the most immediate contribution Ian was able to make to the band when he finally became a full-time member was to get everybody's wages put up.

Ian chuckles at the memory: 'I'd been getting paid session rates for the album which meant that, even though I'd taken a cut in wages because I really wanted to work for the band, I was still getting paid about twice as much as anybody else! Then when John and I discussed the details of me becoming a full-time member of the band, I told him that I was prepared to take a big cut in wages to make them parry with what everybody else was earning, which was about £75 a week at the time, but that I had to have a guarantee of so much money by the end of the year just so that I could keep up the mortgage payments on my house.

'John said that was fair enough and immediately put everybody's wages up to £150 a week! John must have had to scrimp around for the extra money, I know, but he did it because the band was really starting to come up with the goods now live, and as a result I became the most popular member of Marillion for about the next three weeks!

'The rest, as they say, is history,' smiles Ian Mosley. 'Or at least *will* be, one day . . .'

11

The Last Straw

When Marillion returned home from America in May 1986, they did so in style. Hiring the entire roof-top observation deck in the first-class compartment of a Virgin Airways jumbo jet, the band, John Arnison, Paul Lewis, and the rest of the small six-man crew enjoyed a champagne and cocktails party that lasted from the time the plane took off from L.A.X., in Los Angeles, until it landed, ten hours later, at Heathrow in London.

'It was brilliant!' cries Pete Trewavas. 'I think John organized it as a way of sort of allowing everybody to sit back at last and really congratulate themselves on having got through our first really good American tour. It was a great way to celebrate the end of the tour . . . and I tell you, after coming back from every previous tour we'd done there with nothing but long faces, I think we felt we deserved a bit of a party . . .

'I mean, we were still a long way from being *mega* over there,' he grins, 'but at least this time we knew we'd done well enough to really set us on our way. Besides, by that time we'd been on the road for the best part of a year solid, and I think we were all starting to look forward to getting home and putting our feet up for a while.'

Indeed, the unprecedented success of *Misplaced Childhood* had kept Marillion on the road for a longer stretch of time, and at a greater pitch of high-profile intensity than any of the band members had ever experienced before. While they were still taking their first tentative steps out on the road in America with Rush, John Arnison had been asked to consider taking the band out for their first small tour of Australia, where 'Kayleigh' had again been working her manifest charms. But the band were divided over whether or not to accept the invitation.

'We were asked if we would consider the possibility of making a flying visit to Australia for a handful of gigs, some TV and radio promotion, some press interviews, and so on,' explains Steve Rothery. 'It all sounded fine on the surface. But I, for one, was dead against it. It seemed like a long way to go at the end of a very long tour for us, just to play a couple of gigs more on a prayer than a promise. We'd been on the road nearly a year, but more than that it was now something like eighteen months since we'd last had enough time to sit down and write something new together. I wanted us to start thinking about the new album. It was time. If Australia was really interested in us going over there for a full tour, my feeling was they could wait until we had recorded a new album and do things properly . . .'

While Marillion continued to discuss the pros and cons of a last-minute departure for the antipodes, they received a much more attractive offer that put paid to any vague ideas anybody might have had of spending a few quiet days lazing away the hung-over afternoons on Bondi beach: Queen, one of the most enduringly successful British rock bands of the last fifteen years, led by the camply heroic figure of singer Freddy Mercury, had invited Marillion to appear as second-on-the-bill special guests at a series of huge outdoor festival dates in Europe which they had planned for the summer. Four shows in all, throughout June and July, playing to shared audiences with Queen of between 85,000 and 100,000 people a night!

The band had already announced their intention to headline their own special outdoor festival at the Milton Keynes Bowl in England on 28 June, and the added feather in the cap of the Queen shows in Europe would round off the last of the band's extended live work nicely, they felt. Then they could retreat once more into the rehearsal studio and begin to piece together the material that would provide them with the next Marillion album.

'It seemed like the perfect way to round off the year that we'd spent on the road since *Misplaced Childhood* had been released,' says Mark Kelly. 'It was only a few big outdoor festival dates dotted here and there around Britain and Europe, so it wouldn't be anywhere near as strenuous as taking on another full-scale tour . . . Plus, well there are quite a few old Queen fans littered amongst the Marillion band and crew – myself included – so we thought it would be good fun to do. We were right.'

However, the news that Marillion were on their way back to

Europe, where by 1986 the band was recognized as one of the continent's biggest-selling rock acts, brought an array of renewed offers of work from several European promoters. Eventually, nine concerts in Europe were arranged. Four with Queen: starting at the Hippodrome de Vincennes in Paris on 14 June, then on to West Germany for festival dates in Manheim on 21 June, Berlin on 26 June, and Cologne on 19 July. And five dates out on their own: Gothenburg Tivoli on 11 June, Stockholm Tivoli on 12 June, the Munich Festival on 15 June; the Stadthalle in Vienna on 17 June, and the Ahoy in Rotterdam on 19 June. Between the penultimate and last night of their dates with Queen, Marillion would headline their own outdoor festival in Britain, at the Milton Keynes Bowl, on Saturday 28 June, along with a bill of specially invited guests including Jethro Tull, Gary Moore, and Magnum.

'Ultimately,' says Fish, 'the idea behind the festival dates was nothing new for us. We'd always done summer festivals, and done well at them. The only real difference this time was the size of the crowds we were playing to – 85,000 people in Manheim with Queen, another 80,000-odd in Cologne. We'd never played to crowds that size before, and it was brilliant! Just brilliant! And then drawing 40,000 people to our own outdoor show in Milton Keynes – it topped off everything we'd managed to achieve in that mad year that followed the release of *Misplaced Childhood*. The shows we were doing on our own in Europe all sold out, as did the shows we appeared at with Queen. Manheim, in particular, where we had easily as many fans as Queen, was a very special occasion.'

Status, prestige, an ever-widening popularity amongst Europe's rock fan fraternity, and always with the unblinking eye of the media now upon them, Marillion marched like conquering soldiers through their fistful of high-profile summer concerts. With or without Queen, everywhere they went they were met with hysteria. Their fans in Europe, as in Britain all along, and now America, could no longer be counted in tens of thousands. By June 1986, they were starting to buy tickets for their gigs in *hundreds* of thousands! And, finally, along with all the high-profile publicity generated by this fact, came the money that's supposed to go with it.

In manager John Arnison's own words, 'The money the boys made from those nine shows in Europe and that one show in

Milton Keynes came to more than they'd earned in their first five years put together!'

'We did earn a lot of money from those dates in Europe and at Milton Keynes, particularly the ones with Queen, of course. But it was the first time we'd ever earned what you would call *serious* money since we'd been together,' says Fish. 'I tell you, I was fucking glad to get it! I didn't want to be an artist starving in an attic somewhere for the rest of my life. Who does, really? Anyway, I'd done all that. We all had. We'd paid our dues, whatever that means. It was great to finally see some kind of major return for all the work we'd put into the band all these years . . .'

'With the money we got from those shows at Milton Keynes and with Queen, we were all able to buy decent houses for ourselves, and a new car, maybe. But most of all, the money just bought us a bit of breathing space,' says Pete Trewavas. 'We did ten shows in all, over a period of about four weeks. When we weren't playing we just took it easy; it *was* summer, after all. And when we were playing, it was to bigger and more enthusiastic audiences than we'd ever known before, and because of that we ended up playing some of the best shows I think we've ever done. It was a very happy time for us, every gig was like a celebration.'

At Manheim, sharing the bill with Queen, Marillion careered through their ninety-minute set with all the energetic style and aplomb that had characterised their meteoric rise to international fame and notoriety twelve months before. Opening their late-afternoon set with a glammy, punched-out and wired version of – appropriately enough – 'Garden Party', the 85,000-strong Manheim crowd screamed and roared louder than anyone in Marillion had ever heard before. The band in turn strode furiously through the number . . . Rothery cranking out the chords mercilessly, Mosley thumping home the rhythm, Trewavas making it dance like dice, Kelly, his fingers dipped in treacly clouds, running amok on the keyboards, and Fish spinning like a dervish from one side of the giant stage to another, the thick dark beard he had worn since discarding the face make-up now no longer in evidence, screwing up his eyes, the mike pressed to his lips, reaching low from inside to pick at the words like old scabs . . . '*Angie chalks another blue/Mother smiles, she did it too . . .*'

From there Marillion swaggered confidently through gritty

versions of 'Freaks', and a revived 'Assassing', the vast Manheim crowd following the band's every move with wide, staring eyes. Then, as the band again unveiled the *magnum opus* of their set, the *Misplaced Childhood* saga, just as the light was dying in the sky, huge sections of the already volatile crowd seemed to fall into a deep swoon, and then the screams and the shrieking and the violent shouts erupted once more . . . *'Huddled in the safety of a pseudo silk kimono/A morning mare rides . . .'*

It was to become a famous performance, immortalised in part on West German TV and radio, who both broadcast the event, and in a myriad of press reviews which relied on more breathless adjectives and the pseudo silk prose of a banner headline to convey the magic of the occasion. Both Freddy Mercury and Brian May of Queen stood at the side of the stage and watched as Marillion tore into the extravagant climax of *Misplaced Childhood*, Fish ranting in English and German through the chanted improvised finale of 'White Feather', all the manic, screaming Manheim children going right with him . . .

As always, in the heat of the moment, Fish cooled the applause long enough to give the first encore its full introduction: 'This next song was originally about Northern Ireland, but this time it's dedicated to the people who are dying in El Salvador, to the people who are dying in Beirut, to the children who died in Tripoli, and to the people that died in Italian airports, and Frankfurt airport . . . This is a song for peace. This song is a prayer; and this is called "Forgotten Sons" . . .'

The rhythm pulsing like the beat of a racing heart, Marillion roared menacingly through the number, unrestrained and powerful at the death, Fish taunting the heavens with a heavy arsenal of strafing lyricism and immaculately timed word bombs . . . *'You're just another coffin on its way down the emerald aisle/Where the children's stony glances mourn your death in a terrorist's smile . . .'*

'Market Square Heroes' closed the show; the band taking off half-way through the extended middle-eight into first 'She Loves You' by the Beatles, and then, for kicks, another weird stab at Chubby Checker's 'Let's Twist Again (Like We Did Last Summer)'.

'They were a hard act to follow, no doubt about it,' said Roger Taylor, the drummer with Queen, afterwards. 'I think we were a bit taken aback at first at just how popular Marillion were in Europe. It definitely bucked us up, going on after them, and I think, together, we put on some really stunning shows . . .'

The pattern was repeated seven days later at Milton Keynes Bowl. Billed as Marillion's 'Welcome to the Garden Party' summer festival, the rest of the bill featured, in ascending order, Mama's Boys, Magnum, Jethro Tull, and Gary Moore. It was one of those gloriously hot, increasingly rare English summer days. Forty-eight hours earlier, Marillion had wowed the Queen fans at the Berlin Festival. Now they whiled away the afternoon before the Milton Keynes bash lazing by the pool at the Blakemore Hotel, where the band, accompanied by an entourage of music journalists and photographers, were holed up for the weekend. With only one more show with Queen left to do in three weeks' time, the band could afford to let the reins loosen a little at last and everybody had brought along their wives or girlfriends to help them pass the slow, sweltering hours leading up to the show.

'We definitely wanted to make a day of it for ourselves as much as for the fans,' says Fish, smiling. 'It was a very significant day for us in many ways. It was our first time to headline a major rock festival in Britain. It was exactly a year ago that week that *Misplaced Childhood* had gone straight in at number one in the British charts. And, as a few of the fans had already guessed, it was probably the last time we would perform the whole of *Misplaced Childhood* live in Britain for some time to come. It was the last time Marillion would be seen playing in this country before we went in to write the new album, so next time we went out it was safe to assume, or so we hoped, that there would be an influx of new material in the set.

'In the meantime, we wanted to go out at Milton Keynes, at the end of what had been the most successful year of our lives, with a real bang. Turn everything we did that day into a *party* . . .'

As Marillion took to the stage in the twilight of the muggy June evening, the 40,000 crowd, spread wide across the shallow hills that faced the stage, got to its feet and moved closer to the spot in the distance where the light was seeping from, bodies coiled like a snake around the neck of the stage. With the same set as the one the band had devised for their European festival dates, the band opened with 'Garden Party', knifed through 'Freaks' and 'Assassing', then bulldozed their way enigmatically through *Misplaced Childhood*, the air dry with heat, ringing with voices . . . *'Lavender's blue, dilly dilly, lavender's green/When I am King, dilly dilly, you will be Queen . . .'*

289

Later, after the show, back at the Blakemore, the hotel management had agreed to keep the swimming-pool area open and allow Marillion to celebrate in the style they were growing accustomed to with a party that would go on, for some, right through the night, past dawn, and on into the languorous Sunday lunchtime 'eye-opener' session organized by the posse of hacks that had travelled up from London to see the show.

Fish made sure enough people got ceremoniously tossed into the pool, and the hotel staff kept the bar open for as long as there were people from EMI, or the band, or the press still crazy enough to keep buying drinks. It was to be a fourteen-hour shift at the bar, where everybody stayed good and thirsty. It had been another one of those days, and now it was going to be one of those nights . . .

One last date awaited them, in Cologne, again with Queen, on 19 July, and then Marillion could finally bid adieu to the road and all its weird bends for the first time in more than a year. During that time, world-wide sales for Marillion albums had topped the four million mark, and at the end of it all, though the band were still a long way from becoming full-time millionaires, the individual members were now richer, and certainly more famous, than any of them will ever admit they dreamed possible.

With the exception of Fish, who was still hunting for the right property, everybody in Marillion spent a chunk of the profits they had made since the release of *Misplaced Childhood* on purchasing large and spacious houses. By mid-summer, Steve Rothery was already installed in a new house in Wendover, a smaller, much prettier town than Aylesbury and located a few miles closer to London. Mark Kelly also bought an impressive new property in Wendover, a five-minute car ride away from Steve's. Ian Mosley, who had never lived in Aylesbury, already owned a modestly sized house in Gerrards Cross, where he lived with his wife, Wanda. Now he treated himself to something bigger, grander, but again in Gerrards Cross. In time, Fish would also make a new home for himself outside of Aylesbury, taking the plunge before the end of the year and buying his own substantial property in Gerrards Cross, just around the corner from Ian, in fact. Pete Trewavas, though he too splashed out on a new house, is the only member of Marillion who stayed in Aylesbury. The reason, though, is practical rather than senti-mental. 'My wife, Fiona, still works as a nurse at Stoke Mandeville Hospital, so we didn't want to move too far away from there,' Pete explains, adding, 'but we're bound to make the move out sometime. I still like Aylesbury, but I've lived there most of my life, and there are plenty of other places I'd like to go.'

As a result of the frantic house-buying, and the new prosperity under which they could now comfortably labour, following their last festival date with Queen, the members of Marillion did something throughout the rest of the summer of 1986 nobody in the band could ever afford to do before: they stayed indoors and relaxed . . .

On Friday, 1 August, Steve Rothery interrupted the quiet by getting married to his long-standing girlfriend, Joanne, Jo to her friends. Dressed formally in a grey morning suit and top hat, and supported by the band, of whom Pete Trewavas acted as best man, Steve married Jo and never looked back.

It was an overcast afternoon at Our Lady's church in Aspinall, not far from Jo's family home in Bolton, Lancashire. But despite the dull weather it was a gay occasion. The evening reception, held at nearby Haigh Hall, began like most weddings with the families of bride and groom getting to know each other better while vying for the drinks and buffet tables, and ended with the whole of Marillion, plus the dynamic backing duo of John Arnison and Steve's 'party loving' uncle George, joining the band booked for the later hours of the night, Slice Bread – a rock and boogie outfit formed by ex-Rage singer, Dave Lloyd – for an impromptu romp an' roll through a loud and thoroughly raucous version of The Who's 'My Generation'. Not the most romantic send-off for the happy couple perhaps, but delivered straight from the heart . . . or at least from the bottom of everybody's beer glass.

The following day, Steve and Jo set off for a honeymoon on the tropical island of St Lucia, in the Caribbean. The same afternoon, the band's set and lighting designer, Robert 'Chops' Flury, was competing in the European Grand Prix of the International Hydroplane Championships, held in Nottingham. A little like speedboat racing, a hydroplane is a small, light craft, measuring only fourteen by six foot in total dimensions, but able to power its pilot across a body of water at speeds of up to a hundred miles per hour.

'The world-record speed for a hydroplane is actually 107 mph,' Chops explains. 'It rides on the air, never really touching the water, and it goes like a rocket!'

Sponsored by the band, Chops' hydroplane is christened *The Marillion*, and it has the band's logo painted down its sides. Having already done both himself and the band proud that year by coming first in the British Sprint Championship and second in the Driver's Championship, Chops went on to take a very distinguished third place at the European Grand Prix.

Everybody, with the exception of Steve of course, had said they would try and put in an appearance in Nottingham to cheer Chops and *The Marillion* on, but it *was* the day after the night of the party to celebrate Steve's wedding, and . . . well, let's just say everybody was too busy nursing a hydro-hangover to make it out of bed in time for the drive down to Nottingham.

The day after that, Sunday, 3 August, Marillion made a surprise appearance on stage at the Roland exhibition at Olympia, in London. Ostensibly a private function for business colleagues connected with the Roland manufacturers, the band insisted on opening the doors and allowing in a couple of hundred hard-core Marillion fans, who had somehow discovered that the band would be putting in a brief appearance on the Sunday afternoon and turned up on the off chance of gaining entry. They were not disappointed.

Steve Rothery, of course, was off on his honeymoon. In his place, the band had invited John Otway's guitarist, and old friend of Pete Trewavas, Robin Boult, to step in as Steve's temporary replacement. The band waltzed gamely through a shortened, for fun only, twenty-five minute set, including the obligatory snatch of the 'Kayleigh' – 'Lavender' – 'Heart of Lothian' section of *Misplaced Childhood*, and a familiar array of older underground hits. Fish relaxed enough to allow the Marillion fans present in the hall to sing as many words for him as they liked, and the rest of the band grinned and tore into the set with a jaunty, confident cool not even the momentary distraction of playing with the wrong guitarist could dent.

'It was just a fun one-off afternoon gig,' says Fish, 'nothing too heavy, just played for laughs, really. It was great.'

It was also the last time any of Marillion would appear on a stage together for the next five months . . .

From September to December 1986, Marillion hung the 'Do Not Disturb' sign on the door and took up temporary residence at Stanbridge Rehearsal Studios in Sussex, where they worked steadily on writing the first batch of new material. To begin with, the work was slow and uncharacteristically laboured. Days would be lost constructing ambitious new arrangements which would later be discarded as the band searched long and hard for the inspiration to better their impossibly near-perfect last album.

'*Misplaced Childhood* was like a big shadow hanging over us when we first started writing the new album,' admits Fish. 'At first we just didn't know quite what direction we should be taking. We decided it would be a real cop-out to go in and write another forty-five minute epic, and yet we felt we would be cheating ourselves by deliberately avoiding our natural inclination to write longer, interconnecting themes. We were very worried about falling prey to parody, though. It took us a long time to get things moving and off the ground . . .'

'The other thing to point out, though,' says Pete Trewavas, 'is that John Arnison more or less encouraged us to take our time a bit. Which, ultimately, was a very good thing for us, I think. After all, this next album was going to be our most important release yet and we didn't want to slip up by rushing into a recording studio or, worst of all, trying to write another 'Kayleigh' and repeating the pattern of *Misplaced Childhood*. Plus, it *had* been two years since we'd last written anything substantial, and to be honest, I think we all found the prospect of finally getting down to tackling the problem of how to follow *Misplaced Childhood* a bit daunting. At least, at first . . .'

As the English winter took hold, and the days began shrinking, the band's confidence and touch returned and slowly but surely the new material began taking shape. By the beginning of December, they had a dozen new titles just needing the rough edges knocked off them before they would be ready to be included on the next Marillion album. The band had already decided to christen it *Clutching At Straws*. Three new numbers in particular – 'White Russian', 'Warm Wet Circles', and 'Incommunicado' – were already well enough formed for Marillion to consider previewing them live.

With Christmas just a fortnight away, the band announced that they would play five of their now famous festive-season concerts. They would kick off with two shows at Friar's in Aylesbury on 27 and 28 December, all the proceeds from which would be donated to the building of a new Aylesbury Hospice currently in construction, then play two shows at the Royal Court in Liverpool on 29 and 30 December, finishing off with a special early evening performance at the Barrowlands Club in

Glasgow, Scotland. No London show was scheduled, no press were invited to review any of the shows, the whole thing was kept strictly low-key.

'We just wanted to get out and do what we've always done at Christmas,' says Fish. 'We didn't look at it like a tour, more just a quick jaunt through a couple of spots we never got to on the last British tour. And, of course, it gave us the perfect opportunity to break in some of the new material live and see what the fans thought of it.'

Before that though, in November, Charisma Records released an oddly timed single called 'Short Cut to Somewhere'. Its authors were Fish and – wait for it – Tony Banks, the keyboard player in Genesis! Fish explains this strange coupling thus: ' "Short Cut to Somewhere" is a track me and Tony Banks recorded together as part of the soundtrack to a film called *Quicksilver*. He had the music written and I supplied the words. I went up to the Genesis farm in England one weekend when we had a break for a couple of days on the European leg of the '85 *Misplaced Childhood* tour, and we just threw it together. Although I think we were both initially attracted by the curiosity factor in working together, the sessions turned out better than either of us probably thought they would, and I had a lot of fun working with him.

'The thing is though, I don't think either of us took what we were doing *too* seriously. But for what it was, I thought we came out with a decent enough track. I had been reading the John Belushi biography, *Wired*, around that time, and I wrote the lyrics with Belushi's story in mind. What neither of us had originally intended though, was that it should be released as a single. All that only really came as an afterthought . . .'

'Quite honestly, I didn't know much about Marillion, apart from the "Kayleigh" single, which I liked,' Tony Banks was quoted as saying in an issue of *Kerrang!* dating from that time. 'I liked Fish's voice, which *has* got an uncanny resemblance to Peter Gabriel's, and so (when I was asked to contribute to the soundtrack of *Quicksilver*) I contacted him, we got together, and the finished product is good.'

Indeed, 'Short Cut to Somewhere' is a good track, but not, however, an especially great one. The words are all there, and the voice, but the backing of muted synthesized horns is too lacklustre a setting to show them off to their best effect. The melody is unambitious, and were it not for Fish's contribution, the number would have little to distinguish it from any other averagely imaginative contemporary pop vignette.

Encouraged, though, by the obvious commercial possibilities of having one Marillion and one Genesis member together on the same track, Charisma released 'Short Cut to Somewhere' as a Fish/Tony Banks single in both seven-inch and twelve-inch formats, accompanied by a rather too obvious colour pic on the sleeve of both men grinning at each other, Fish sporting a Genesis T-shirt, Banks a Marillion T-shirt.

However, with Banks away with Genesis on their latest world tour at the time, and with Fish still writing furiously for the new Marillion album, the single received next to no personal promotion. Significantly, the record was not a hit, barely scraping the trouser legs of the UK Top 75. Fish admits he was disappointed.

'Like I say, we had never intended to make a single together, it was just a track Tony was working on for the soundtrack to *Quicksilver*,' he says. 'But if it *was* going to be released in its own right, then obviously it was a matter of pride that I would have liked to see it do better than it did. Ultimately though, what could I do about it? I certainly had no intention of promoting it as some kind of major solo outing, so it was all left in the hands of other people to try and make it work . . .'

On 23 December, Marillion abandoned their posts at Stanbridge Studios and headed home in time for the Christmas holidays. Not that they would have much time off: three days, in fact, is all they allowed themselves before setting out on their, by now, already sold-out UK Christmas dates.

The first two nights at Friar's, in Aylesbury, on the 27 and 28 December, the band, if understandably a little rusty after their five-month lay-off from touring, still managed to evoke all the atmosphere befitting the occasions. The very first night, though, Fish really set the scene and surprised everybody by walking on stage decked out in the full face-paint regalia he'd abandoned somewhere on the road in Europe eighteen months before! It was hard, though, to say who was the most shocked by the reappearance of the spectral jester's mask: the audience, or the rest of the band . . .

'As soon as I walked out on stage with the make-up on, I suddenly knew I'd made a mistake,' says Fish. 'I'd been wondering what it would be like to get into using some of the luminous face and body paint that I'd started experimenting with just before I knocked the whole thing on the head at the start of the *Misplaced Childhood* tour. What I had been considering was maybe the possibility of having a professional make-up artist out on the road with me for the next proper tour we did. But then on the night of the first show at Friar's, my curiosity just got the better of me and I started putting some of the make-up back on again. The thing is, I think I went off a bit half-cocked; I didn't really give myself time to think what I wanted to actually see. I just did it sort of half-jokingly, Christmas and all that, and why not, you know, for fun?

'But the minute I walked out on that stage, it felt like I'd suddenly taken one step forward and two steps back . . . Luckily, because it was the first of our Christmas gigs, I was able to get away with it as some kind of party-piece, or something. But it didn't feel good to me.'

The second night, Fish went back to playing it straight, leaving his make-up box unopened in a corner of the dressing-room, and the band, their muscles loosened by their exertions the night before, turned in a much better set. Speakers sizzling with ominous booms and hisses, the stage lights beginning to glow in the unnatural darkness of the stage, Ian Mosley steadily introduces the dark, bristling percussion that is the signal for the rest of the band to go crashing full-throttle into 'Assassing'; guitar and keyboard touches flash like strobes over the heads of the stomping Friar's crowd, Pete Trewavas skips to the edge of the stage, Fish, tall and imposing, crowding the mike, shoulders hunched, mouth distorted . . . *'Listen as the syllables of slaughter cut with calm precision/Patterned frosty phrases rape your ears and sow the ice incision/Apocalyptic alphabet casting spell the creed of tempered diction/Adjectives of annihilation bury the point beyond redemption . . .'*

'Freaks' was next, Mark Kelly's hat-tipped-back keyboard melody belying the desperate sense of paranoia the lyrics immediately hint at . . . *'Have you ever woken up sweating in the middle of the night/You search the darkness and you're scrambling for the light . . .'*

Between songs, Fish rapped to his audience, passing out drinks to the outstretched hands that fanned the footlights, always saving just one for himself . . . 'Fugazi' followed, timed unexpectedly to go off like a bomb right at the start of the set, the full weight of the blow compacted when, at the end, before the audience reaction has really built, Steve Rothery begins picking out the chiming needle-sharp intro to 'He Knows You Know'. Like everything else plucked from their first album, it receives some of the longest applause of the night. 'He Knows You Know' is, after all, one of the few Marillion numbers to have survived the years that have passed since the band took their first scary, tentative steps as a musical force to be reckoned with out on this very same stage, before some of these very same people. It was a grand moment. Never had the number sounded so bold, or so cutting: Ian Mosley's subtly timed strikes propelling the beat, shunting the band along to an edge they never quite reached on the original recording; Mark's keyboards and Steve's guitar taking it in turns to boss the sound, hoisting the musical backdrop that surrounds Fish's nightmarish verbal excesses . . . *'You've got venom in your stomach, you've got poison in your head/When your conscience whispered, the vein lines stiffened, you were walking with the dead . . .'*

A small pause followed, Fish groping in the darkness for a cigarette and a new drink. Then, striding purposefully up to the microphone, spotlight on, patiently ignoring the inevitable cries here and there for 'Grendel' or 'The Web', the singer introduced the next number . . . 'This next number is a brand new number,' he says, silencing all requests and stopping the regular Friar's crowd dead in their tracks. 'As a band we get to travel around a lot and see a lot of things first-hand that we wouldn't normally see . . . Well, we were travelling through Austria earlier this year and we saw some things going down there, in Vienna, that we found profoundly disturbing . . .

'I don't know if any of you are aware of what's been going down since this guy Kurt Waldheim got voted in as the new Austrian president, but this guy is a well-known fascist who's now got power in that part of the world. As a direct result, if you go down now to the Jewish Quarter in places like Vienna you can see armed police guarding the corners of all the streets, and you can see big red swastikas freshly painted on the walls of buildings . . . And, as a result of that, some of the same terrible things that happened in cities like Berlin fifty years ago are now starting to happen again in Austria . . .'

The momentarily silenced Aylesbury crowd listen harder as Fish ends his preamble with the words: 'This is a song about what's going on right now in Austria, and about the whole disgusting anti-semitic thing . . . It's also going to be a track on our next studio album, and this is called "White Russian"!'

297

The number begins slowly, just the lone cry of the guitar echoing across a grey horizon of muttering keyboards, Fish crooning in the foreground, '*Where do we go from here . . .*' His voice steadily rising . . . '*WHERE do we GO from HERE!*' Then the drums hit and the band pound into a mean, staccato rhythm, Fish switching gear, stabbing home the words . . . '*They're burning down the synagogues/Uzis on a street corner/The heralds of a holocaust/Uzis on a street corner/The silence never louder than now/How quickly we forgot our vows . . .*'

Still so new Fish had yet to complete a final draft of the finished lyrics, it is clear immediately that 'White Russian' is another classical Marillion *tour de force*, very much in the mould of earlier mind-benders like the haunted and hellbent 'Forgotten Sons', or the paranoiac and cynically layered 'Fugazi'; very much a statement, politically, emotionally, above all passionately expressed, then hurled around the stage by its feet and thrown into the lion's mouth of the audience, where it is consumed by the hungry pack.

Throughout the number, heads nod vigorously amongst the audience, bodies sway like drunks to the lilting, schizophrenic rhythms, big moon-eyes fixed hard on the stage. The rapturous applause that breaks out as 'White Russian' tumbles to its shaking conclusion is again stymied as Fish mumbles the words, 'I think this was a hit . . .' and Steve Rothery dips into his bag of tricks and teases out the shivering opening chords to 'Kayleigh' . . . Instant pandemonium! Faces everywhere shining with sweat, hoarse voices crowing out the choruses . . . '*Kayleigh!/I'm still trying to write that love song/Kayleigh!/It's more important to me now you're gone/Maybe it'll prove that we were right/Or it'll prove that I was wrong . . .*'

From there it was a straight run through the remainder of Side One of *Misplaced Childhood*, up to the football-terrace finale of 'Heart of Lothian', Marillion pumping it out and Aylesbury taking it on the chin like the world really was still new . . .

'Script for a Jester's Tear' followed, like 'He Knows You Know' and 'Kayleigh' providing the signal for one of the biggest crowd ovations of the night; the audience tense and concentrated as they recite the words *en masse*, the band loose and skilful on the build-up, then burning fiercely through the endless death of the climax . . . '*As you grow up and leave the playground/Where you kissed your prince and found your frog/Remember the jester that showed you tears . . .*'

'Cinderella Search' lightened the mood somewhat, the band trilling through the number, the stage dancing with pale beams of light . . . And then there was another long pause as Fish introduced the second new number Marillion were to preview that night, 'Warm Wet Circles'.

It began gently, Steve's guitar lines billing and cooing in the distance, Ian's drums bubbling pleasantly in the background, Fish almost whispering his sad opening asides . . . *'On promenades where drunks propose to lonely arcade mannequins/Where ceremonies pause at the jeweller's shop display . . .'*

The mood doesn't stay gentle for long, the guitars leading the rest of the band into a series of slowly wrought crescendos, skeletal funk patterns breaking out like a rash, then subsiding, a drifting tide revealing the rocks that lie just beneath the surface . . . *'I saw teenage girls like gaudy moths, a classroom's shabby butterflies/ Flirt in a glow of stranded telephone boxes/Planning white lace weddings from smeared hearts and token proclamations/Rolled from stolen lipsticks across the razored webs of glass . . .'*

Just as the pulse of the number threatens to finally give out, extinguished like the last flame of a dying fire, without any warning whatsoever the band begin pummelling out the riff to the third, and last, new number of the night, 'Incommunicado'. Destined to be Marillion's next single some five months later, 'Incommunicado' is Marillion at their most overtly rock and roll. Unlike previous attempts at integrating a little bit of old-style guitar ramalama into their own distinctive style, 'Incommunicado' really did dance and shake when it moved. On a first-impression basis, it definitely had more to do with a band like The Who at their most innovative, than it did more perennial Marillion influences like Genesis or Pink Floyd. Ultimately, though, this was Marillion showing off their new powers, their vast new confidence, in a display of out-and-out party-spirited charm; raving it up in a feast of bitchy guitars, sprinting keyboards, the drums and bass nailing down the beat, Fish, all leg-kicks and sharp, jutting elbows, his eyes screwed up into a wicked smile, plastering the walls and balconies with his defiant prose kisses . . . *'I'm a Marquee veteran, a multi-media bona-fide celebrity/I've got an allergy to Perrier, daylight, and responsibility/I'm a rootin'-tootin' cowboy, a Peter Pan with street credibility/Always making the point with the dawn patrol fraternity . . .'*

A rough sea of furiously bobbing heads, bodies jack-knifing into the air, the Friar's crowd went wild for it, as 'Incommunicado' flew maniacally like an out-of-control rocket to its final destination . . .

The applause still bombarding the stage, Steve Rothery tickled out the first breathless lines to 'Childhood's End?'. The band rattled proudly through that; then 'White Feather', guitars a-go-go, voices like hard rain, balloons and streamers and crazy-foam and custard-pies and another tray of those drinks Fish had been passing out to the crowd all night, an absolute cert for the encores . . .

'Incubus' was first; the rhythm snaking from the stage, Ian's percussion like tiny lethal hammers raining down on your skull in perfect time, Fish moving in slow motion, keyboards glittering like a red light in the doorway. The familiar 'Garden Party'/'Market Square Heroes' medley was next, roadies flying everywhere about the stage, planting enormous shaving-cream and paper-plate pies in the band's faces, fans hoisting themselves up on the stage to join in the merriment, the bedazzled musicians somehow keeping it all together long enough to blast out the last few rabble choruses . . . *I'm a market square hero/Gathering the storms to troop/I'm a market square hero/Speeding the beat of the street pulse/Are you following me?/Are you following me?/Suffer my fallen angels and follow me . . .*

With hardly a pause for breath, Ian Mosley struck up a marching tartan beat, and out from stage-left pranced Bruce Dickinson, lead singer with Iron Maiden and self-confessed Marillion fanatic. He joined Fish and the band on stage for a ramshackle and ribald crack at 'Margaret'; guitars like bagpipes, the drums hoofing it up the hill like a gaggle of kilted highwaymen, heels clicking, keyboards choked with cigarette smoke, Fish and Bruce's combined out-of-sync vocal duet pouring forth like spilt Drambuie.

The party resumed over the following two nights, at the Royal Court in Liverpool. The second night, some of the Marillion road crew dressed up in 'Silly Jock' costumes, which Paul Lewis had hired from a local carnival shop especially for the occasion. A long line of floppy Tam O'Shanters, shaggy stick-on beards, sporrans, and kilts came dancing out of the wings during 'Margaret', followed by the members of Pendragon, who had been the support act for Marillion's Liverpool dates, and last – but not least! – a leggy female 'professional dancer' the crew had also thoughtfully hired for the night, came on to loud wolf-whistles from the male section of the raucous Liverpool crowd, clad only in black stockings, bra, high-heels, and suspenders, and brandishing a twelve-foot-long bullwhip which she immediately put to unrestrained effect, lashing out at anything that moved, including most of Marillion, all of Pendragon, and a list of injured Tam O'Shanter-bearing roadies . . .

The last of their five dates, at the Barrowlands in Glasgow on New Year's Eve, picked up where the Liverpool shenanigans left off, starting early and lashing the 2,000 Glaswegian fans assembled there into just the right mood for the heeby-jeeby Hogmanay celebrations that would begin in earnest once the haunted midnight hour had struck.

After the show, back at the Holiday Inn where the band were staying, a large private room had been reserved for Marillion to celebrate and see in the New Year, 1987, properly. It was a skittish gathering of people, most of them far from the home they would normally celebrate the turn of the year in: all of Marillion, of course, along with their respective wives and girlfriends; John Arnison and Paul Lewis, again accompanied by their wives; the Marillion crew, along with their respective partners; and a smaller gaggle of friends and acquaintances who had all made it up to Glasgow for the last show of the year. Champagne was consumed quite diligently by all, and taped rock music blared from giant speakers stationed in the corners of the dance floor. With minutes to go before the casual entrance through the doors of another first-footin' New Year, the party was in full swing. The champagne was doing its work, and the music wasn't lagging far behind. For the first sixty seconds of 1987 everybody stood in a big, ungainly circle in front of the bar and sang, in voices fit to crack, all the verses they could remember to 'Auld Lang Syne', Fish, quite naturally, leading the way.

So here they were once more . . . at that cross in the road that connects the death of one year with the birth of the next. Only this time richer, certainly, more famous, without a doubt, and closer to fulfilling their long-imagined destinies than ever before. All that remained was for Marillion to show their class and do it, maybe even bigger and better this time, all over again . . . Not as easy as it sounds, of course. But well within their grasp. They'd never taken a tumble before, and on the evidence of the three new songs the band premièred every night of the Christmas tour, there was no reason to assume that Marillion weren't nearer to painting their next masterpiece than even they would admit to at the time. And there were still three weeks left to polish up the new material in time for the start of recording in London at the end of January '87, again with producer Chris Kimsey.

The signs were all encouraging, but the real graft was yet to be put in. It would be another five months before any of the band would again be seen in public. Whatever path Marillion took next would be decided, quite rightly and unequivocally, in the recording studio. The success of the next eighteen months, come or go as it pleased, would begin and end right there.

That was the score, and everybody knew it.

Epilogue

Happy Ending

Well, it's five months later. While Marillion have been keeping their heads down, feverishly recording the new *Clutching at Straws* album at Westside Studios in London, I've been working down the road from them lashing the wine-stained pages of this manuscript together. It's been neck and neck who would finish first. Eventually, they finished recording the album a week ahead of my finishing this book. However, losing that particular race has at least afforded me a tantalising glimpse into what the immediate future now holds in store for this unique and remarkable band.

Marillion's first single from the album, 'Incommunicado', was released on Monday, 11 May 1987. The day it was released, the EMI sales force reported seeing queues of Marillion fans lined up at record-shop counters all over Britain, waiting to purchase what is, after all, the band's first genuinely new piece of plastic for almost two years.

Within twenty-four hours of its release, 'Incommunicado' had already sold 68,000 copies! By the end of the week, sales figures were being counted in sixes, and advance orders alone for the album, scheduled for release on 22 June, had topped the 150,000 mark. The current number one album in the UK charts, Curiosity Killed The Cat's *Keep Your Distance*, has, to date, sold a little over half that amount. That *Clutching at Straws* will enter the UK charts this summer, during some of the longest warmest days of the year here in Britain, and go straight to the number one position is almost a foregone conclusion. The question now seems to be – for just how long will it stay there?

My guess is, *Clutching at Straws* is going to take its time about holding on to that number one slot. I'd even go so far as to say I think it will still be kicking around the Top 30 when the band are back out on the road in Britain, at the end of this year, rolling out the red carpet for another clutch of those magic Christmas gigs they like to do so much.

As I write, 'Incommunicado' has this day entered the UK singles chart at number six! Straight into the Top 10! First week of release! Like a bloody arrow. Twenty-four hours ago the band returned from a five-night promotional stopover in Milan, where they spent the nights toasting their good luck with fine wines and too much pasta, and the days being interviewed by Italian press and radio corps, and appearing in a long line of Italian TV pop shows, miming to their new single. Tomorrow night, they film an appearance for this week's *Top Of The Pops* show here in London . . . I might try and make that one: Fish playing it for hoots, the band bopping along fearlessly behind him . . . And then the day after that . . . Well, and then . . . and then . . .

Well.

'I know I said this to you the last time we were just about to release a new album, but honestly this next album is going to be fucking mega!' cries Fish. We were sitting on leather couches in the lounge, looking out through the French windows over a forest of trees that line the edge of the garden over at his new 'mini-mansion' in Gerrards Cross. It was just a few days ago, the night before he left for Milan, and we were drinking 'rusty nails', a typical Fish-type cocktail consisting of half Malt whiskey, half Drambuie.

'I shouldn't really be drinking one of these,' he says. 'They're very *fattening* . . .' Fish has been trying to lose some weight and get himself into shape for what already threatens to be the best part of another year out on the road. The weeks leading up to the release of 'Incommunicado' have seen him getting into the routine of making daily visits to a private gym and health club in London. For the time being, he's cut out all greasy or starchy foods, and he has almost completely cut down on his excessive drinking. Almost.

'I always put on a lot of weight when we're off the road or in the studio,' he says. 'But this has been the longest we've ever spent putting a new album together, and it will be nearly a year since we last toured extensively by the time we begin again in June, and I've allowed myself to get really out of shape. I thought it was about time I tried to reverse the process. I'm quite into it, too. I'm going to try keeping up the fitness regimen even once the world tour begins. I don't think anybody actually believes me yet, but I'm really going to try and stay *healthy* on this next tour. It'll make an interesting change!' he laughed.

Earlier in the evening, Fish had played me a tape of the finished *Clutching at Straws* album. Perched on the edge of my seat, holding a tight rein on my 'rusty nail', I sat and marvelled at it all and when it was over I didn't know what to say. I was speechless. I had only heard it once and already I knew it was a masterpiece. I wanted to ask him to play it again, but that would have been too much, and besides, by then my 'rusty nail' needed fixing . . .

'This next album of yours is going to be . . . mega!' I blurted.

'I fucking *told* you so,' he grinned.

Since then I have procured my own taped copy of *Clutching at Straws*. The editors at *Kerrang!* won't let me review it for the magazine because they say by now I am too prejudiced in Marillion's favour. They may have a point. Besides, by the time you come to read these last words you will have had far more time than I to decide what place this startling new collection should eventually take in the broader Marillion scheme of things. Myself, I've already said I think it's a masterpiece. Let me add that it is, in my not so humble opinion, the best thing Marillion have ever done.

Ten tracks in all, some of which connect and weave into a readable impressionistic pattern, others which stand resolutely alone, like ice thrones erected at the feet of a live volcano. Material like 'Torch Song', 'Sugar Mice', or 'The Last Straw', puts everything Marillion have ever recorded before into the shade. Next to it, even *Misplaced Childhood* starts to sound dated in places. It really is that good, that formidable, what they have managed to do here.

'The other side of the coin to all the success we had had with *Misplaced Childhood* was that now we were cornered into absolutely *having* to come up with something not just as good again, but something everybody would agree was actually *better* . . . The spotlight was on us to prove that having got a bit of success, we wouldn't just disappear and start churning out the same old stuff, that we *were* still capable of doing better than that,' says Mark Kelly. 'To begin with I think we almost felt it was a bit do-or-die, and we ended up taking *ages* to put the

305

whole thing together. Once we started working at Westside with Chris Kimsey though, everything started to pick up and we just got on with it. But we were still very careful all the time to make sure we weren't kidding ourselves about different parts of the songs. We really went over everything with a fine-toothed comb, knowing we had to come up with probably the best thing we'd ever done.'

'By the time we'd got into the studio with Chris and got our teeth into recording all the new material, we were already starting to feel that we were going to make it, that the new songs really *were* a definite step on from anything we'd done before,' says Fish. 'But being under that special kind of pressure to somehow measure up to our past and consciously attempt to better it was still a new thing for us. For a while we kept looking to see what the catch was . . .'

Musically, *Clutching at Straws* is advanced stuff. Awarded their largest overall budget so far by EMI – £135,000, to be precise – and utilising for the first time a lot of the new technology that has become available on the market in the two years since they last set foot in a recording studio, Marillion have produced a musical artefact for which they, and their vast legion of fans, can justifiably feel proud. Every individual performance is stunning; Steve Rothery has never sounded so in command of his guitar, so splendidly brash, or so breathtaking . . . the solo on 'Sugar Mice' alone is worth the price of admission; Ian Mosley, of course, is masterful throughout, creating a heady maelstrom of implacable percussive undertones that run like blood through the veins of every limb the rest of the band choose to stretch out on; chasing him through every turn in the road, Pete Trewavas' bass playing has never sounded more effective, adding dark, wooded textures to everything, humming like a wire; and Mark Kelly, in turn, has never recorded a more fluid or imaginative performance. His 'widdly-widdly' fetishes have evolved into a full-blown alphabet of poetic keyboard phrases, whether he is pounding it out on an acoustic piano or making rain clouds with his synthesizers and computers.

And Fish . . . well, what we seem to be witnessing here is the continued growth in maturity of a writer who is still only beginning to scratch the surface of the talent he seems to naturally possess for curling words around his tongue and letting them roll around in his mouth and throat like cheap whiskey . . . *'Hotel hobbies, padding dawn's hollow corridors'*, he sings at the start

306

of Side One . . . '*Bellboys checking out the hookers in the bar/Slug-like fingers trace the star-spangled clouds of cocaine on the mirror/The short straw takes its bow . . . !*' And from there nothing escapes the dreadful flames . . .

Other than saying that *Clutching at Straws* will do everything and more to the world's charts that *Misplaced Childhood* did during the time it took pride of place in my heart, I will make one more prediction before promising to shut my mouth and let somebody else have their say on the subject: 'Sugar Mice', already the band's choice as their next single from the album, will go on to become Marillion's first 'multi-media bona fide celebrity' number one hit single in the UK! I'm taking all the bets I can on that, and besides, like Marillion, I like to tempt fate as often as possible just to see how far it will get me.

But I digress . . . A brief last word about the 'Incommuni-cado' video, and the new Mark Wilkinson *Clutching at Straws* artwork. The video is directed by Julian Caidan, shot in the streets of Soho, with added live footage taken from a specially staged run-through performance before members of The Web late one night at the Marquee, and is their best yet.

Capturing the obvious humour of the song expertly, the 'Incommunicado' video is eye-catching and high-tech enough to amuse and entertain a TV audience on several levels. If anything, the band have never been so accurately depicted before. Gone are the dour faces that crowd the screen on 'He Knows You Know', 'Assassing', 'Kayleigh', and 'Lavender'. Back is some of the irreverent charm of the 'Garden Party' video, and odd moments in 'Heart of Lothian'. But most of all there is now a charismatic energy and confidence on display that perhaps they simply never all shared with the cameras before. Whatever the trick, it's a good one and I have a feeling this video is going to open a lot of important doors for Marillion over the coming months of 1987. Are you taking all this down, you people at MTV?

The *Clutching at Straws* sleeve, which by now you will be far more familiar with than I can hope to be at this time of writing, only having glimpsed Mark Wilkinson's finished artwork up at the EMI office one afternoon late last week, is, it seems to me, another quite outstanding piece of work. No jester in evidence this time; instead Mark has introduced a new and strangely garbed figure into the story – Torch – replete with traces of faded face make-up, cold staring eyes, and a face like stone. The setting is a bar, darkly lit, some high stools at the counter, at the back some tables, on the far left a pool table, around which, making their first appearance in a Mark Wilkinson painting, Marillion are anonymously positioned. More noticeable, though, are the faces of a further half-dozen characters also there making the scene . . . I'm sure I spotted Truman Capote, Dylan Thomas, Lenny Bruce, Robert Burns, John Lennon, James Dean, and – the single figure probably more enduringly inspirational to Fish *and* the younger Derek Dick than ten Peter Gabriel albums and a lifetime of Pink Floyd albums – Beat writer Jack Kerouac; as the lyrics to 'Torch Song' from the new album explain . . . '*Read some Kerouac and it put me on the tracks/To burn a little brighter now/It was something about Roman Candles fizzin' out/Shine a little light on me now . . .*'

The last track listed on the *Clutching at Straws* sleeve-notes is a track called 'Happy Ending'. In fact, all it consists of is Fish yelling out the word '*No!*', before dissolving into a long, dirty laugh.

'I've only ever had to write one happy ending,' he told me, 'and that was for the climax of the *Misplaced Childhood* album, and then it took me days and days to come up with anything I felt I would be able to live with later on.

'The truth is, I don't believe in nice, tidy happy endings; they belong tacked on to the end of those crappy third-rate American cop shows on TV. I look around at the world we all live in and I don't see any fucking happy endings at all . . . Not yet, not where it would count. So the last track on *Clutching at Straws* is a bit of a joke. If you can't end with a good word, at least end with a good joke . . .'

But what about the story of Marillion? Does that have a happy ending? Major American success would now seem to be inevitable for them before the decade is out, providing nothing shamefully untoward occurs within the ranks of the band to send each individual member scattering off in five completely different directions, strangers to each other suddenly, and, I would suspect, to their fans.

But that doesn't seem likely, not at this stage of the game. At the moment, the stakes are too frighteningly high. Another image from the new album sleeve is a picture of a cocktail glass with a miniature-sized Earth skewered like an olive, floating around on the surface of the drink. It might be a prophetic image of the band's burgeoning career in the international market-place over the next ten years, as world tour after world tour becomes the swivel stick to their happy hour dreams.

Then again, it might not. More than once over the last two years, Steve Rothery has mentioned the possibility of one day recording a solo project of some kind, distinct from the music of Marillion. 'Being asked to provide a soundtrack for a film, maybe, would be something I think I could really get my teeth into.'

And Fish has made no secret of his desire to explore the possibilities of taking on a small acting role, possibly in the style of such left-centre movie classics as Nic Roeg's *The Man Who Fell To Earth*, which starred David Bowie in his first major screen role in 1975, and is a particular favourite of Fish's; and publishing a slim volume of his prose and poetry. Also, following his collaboration with Tony Banks, it is hardly beyond the realms of reasoning that Fish will, at some stage in the future, experiment in further one-off collaborations. Though I doubt if he will be ready to consider a 'solo' album at any time in the foreseeable future.

'I'd get a much bigger kick out of being able to put the words 'The End' on the last page of a novel, or a book of my poetry, than I would ever get out of recording a solo album,' he once told me, and I have no reason to believe he has changed his mind since. Not yet.

Ian Mosley has always maintained his links with the friends and musicians he knew, or has played with at some time or another before joining Marillion. As the next few years start to creep by, it would be foolish to imagine that the Mosley monicker won't be cropping up here and there again on record sleeves which bear no mention of the name Marillion. As for Pete Trewavas and Mark Kelly, I don't imagine that either of them would baulk at the idea of playing the occasional session outside the band.

'A change is as good as a rest, they say,' Ian Mosley points out pragmatically. 'And if anything, doing the odd little project here and there away from Marillion can only be a good thing for all of us. I'd hate to think that any of us would allow the band to break up out of sheer musical frustration, just because one of us wanted to step outside of things for a little while and try their hand at something new . . .'

'The important thing is that whatever happens next, Marillion should stay as the most important thing any of us do with whatever time we have left,' says Fish, pointedly. 'Marillion is going to endure for years to come, we are going to make sure of it. And we won't allow ourselves to bland out and sell ourselves down the river like so many of the bands we've been compared to have done in the past. That is a promise, and Marillion always keep their promises. The day we go back on everything we've said and believed in about ourselves is the day it will all be over as far as this band is concerned, And believe me, that's not yet . . .'

In June 1987, Marillion kick off their next world tour with a series of dates in Poland, a country, one of many on the new itinerary John Arnison has been piecing together for them over these last few months, that the band will be visiting for the first time. In August, Marillion return for their second extensive tour of America. How well it will go, only time will tell, but you know where my money is on that one.

And then after that, they return for the second leg of their massive European tour, taking in, as far as is planned at the moment, seven UK dates: two nights at the Wembley Arena in London on 3 and 4 November; three nights at the Edinburgh Playhouse on 17, 18, and 19 December; and two nights at the NEC in Birmingham on 21 and 22 December. However, by the time Marillion have reached that stage of their world tour, Fish assures me that as many as five Wembley appearances might eventually be made, plus a third extra night at the NEC!

I think those limousines are going to have to sit there in the rain, waiting to pick the band up and ferry them to the next hotel, for quite a while longer . . .

Marillion Discography

VIDEO CASSETTES	*Release Date*
Recital of the Script	10.10.83
Video EP ('Grendel' and 'The Web')	12.3.84
1982–1986 The Videos	16.6.86

ALBUMS/CASSETTES
★ Script for a Jester's Tear	14.3.83
★ Fugazi	12.3.84
Real to Reel (*Live album*)	05.11.84
★ Misplaced Childhood	17.6.85
★ Clutching At Straws	22.6.87

SINGLES

'Market Square Heroes/'Three Boats Down From the Candy' (12″ version features 'Grendel')	25.10.82
'He Knows You Know'/'Charting the Single'	31.1.83
'Garden Party'/'Margaret' (12″ version features live recording of 'Charting The Single')	06.6.83
'Punch And Judy'/'Market Square Heroes'/ 'Three Boats Down From the Candy' (*re-recorded version*)	30.1.84
'Assassing'/'Cinderella Search'	30.4.84
'Kayleigh'/'Lady Nina'	07.5.85
'Lavender'/'Freaks'	27.8.85
'Heart of Lothian'/'Chelsea Monday' (*live version*)	18.11.85
★ 'Incommunicado'/'Going Under'	11.5.87
'Sugar Mice'/'Tux On'	13.7.87

★ *Also available on compact disc.*